EXTENSIVE READING

题源报刊精品阅读 100篇（泛读）

主编 朱伟

北京理工大学出版社
BEIJING INSTITUTE OF TECHNOLOGY PRESS

版权专有　侵权必究

图书在版编目(CIP)数据

题源报刊精品阅读100篇：泛读 / 朱伟主编. — 北京：北京理工大学出版社，2020.1 (2021.8重印)

ISBN 978-7-5682-8088-4

Ⅰ. ①题… Ⅱ. ①朱… Ⅲ. ①英语－阅读教学－研究生－入学考试－自学参考资料 Ⅳ. ① H319.37

中国版本图书馆 CIP 数据核字(2020)第 009590 号

出版发行 / 北京理工大学出版社有限责任公司
社　　址 / 北京市海淀区中关村南大街 5 号
邮　　编 / 100081
电　　话 / (010)68914775(总编室)
　　　　　 (010)82562903(教材售后服务热线)
　　　　　 (010)68944723(其他图书服务热线)
网　　址 / http://www.bitpress.com.cn
经　　销 / 全国各地新华书店
印　　刷 / 天津市新科印刷有限公司
开　　本 / 787 毫米×1092 毫米　1/16
印　　张 / 22.75　　　　　　　　　　　　　　　　　责任编辑 / 武丽娟
字　　数 / 568 千字　　　　　　　　　　　　　　　文案编辑 / 武丽娟
版　　次 / 2020 年 1 月第 1 版　2021 年 8 月第 2 次印刷　责任校对 / 周瑞红
定　　价 / 60.00 元　　　　　　　　　　　　　　　　责任印制 / 李志强

图书出现印装质量问题，请拨打售后服务热线，本社负责调换

主编的话
EDITOR'S WORDS

无论参加何种英文考试,在基本功的夯实阶段,大家只需做两件事:记单词和大量阅读相关真题题源文章。这是我从录制"恋练有词"课程一开始就坚持的理念。很多人会迫不及待地去做真题,但是,我要告诉大家,请不要受他人复习节奏的影响,做真题无须过早开始。你要相信,学习英语和学习武术是一个道理,师父总是让你先老老实实扎一年马步,然后才教你各种招式。所以,各位同学,一开始就做真题,效果并不会太理想,必须先从结合文章记单词开始。

那么,单词应该怎么记呢?比如,参加研究生招生考试的同学,在看到单词 value 时会觉得该词过于简单,甚至会认为,一本考研词汇书里出现这么简单的词是在骗钱。但是,考试当中会考查到它的形近词,例如,devalue 表示"低估",overvalue 表示"高估",这些你都知道吗?关于这两个单词,考研英语中主要考查其前缀 de-和 over-。其次,知道它的名词含义还不够,与其有关的短语,如 place a high value on sth.表示什么意思呢?一旦考试中出现对其动词含义进行考查的题目时,很多同学就会不知其义。例如,"Yet, being friendly is a virtue that many Americans value highly and expect from both neighbors and strangers."这句话中的 value 和 expect 是两个并列的动词,很多考生根本没有接触过 value sth. highly 这样的用法,更不用说把它活学活用到写作中去了。可见,只记忆单词 value 的名词含义是无法获得语感的。与学习汉语、日语等其他语言一样,学习英文也是有规律可循的。英语并不难学,考生不要心存畏惧,只要遵循正确的学习方法,就能慢慢培养出语感,找到适合自己的学习方法和途径。

大量阅读题源文章和记单词同样重要,首先给大家推荐一个免费的泛读素材 App,即 FT中文网,这是英国《金融时报》的中文版网站。其中很多文章可以进行中英文切换,是比较稀缺的优质资源。伟哥对大家的要求是:坚持每天阅读里面的一到两篇文章,至于读什么无所谓,可以根据你个人的喜好选择。当然,有些同学会质疑:"我参加的考试很少考到FT里的文章啊。"对于这一问题,我的回答是:多一些真诚,少一些功利主义的追求,多一些不为什么的坚持(Less interests, more interest),这样你会有意想不到的收获。是的,FT确实不是考研真题的主要来源,根据统计分析,考研英语阅读部分的文章主要会从《经济学人》《卫报》《美国新闻与世界报道》《时代周刊》《新闻周刊》等报纸、杂志,以及《大西洋月刊》《新科学家》《科学》《哈佛商业评论》等专业性极强的出版物中选取,但遗憾的是,这些报纸、杂志在国内并没有官方实时更新的中英文双语素材库。

为了增强同学们对英文文章的整体泛读和精读能力,我们从近十年最为流行的11种考研英语阅读题源英文素材中选取了近1 000篇文章,又从中精选出了100篇符合考研学生阅读水平和要求的优质文章,组织编写了《题源报刊精品阅读100篇(泛读)》;同时,精选出了30篇符合考研英语阅读理解命题规律和大纲要求的优质文章,组织编写了《题源报刊精品阅读30篇(精读)》。这两本书遴选出的130篇文章,涵盖环境、生物、经济、文学、医学、语言、家庭、传媒、教育、交通、人才、农业、历史、健康、法律、能源、体育、心理、信息、气候等数十个话题,是一套内容相当丰富的原版题源报刊阅读书。《题源报刊精品阅读100篇(泛读)》旨在帮助考生训练快速阅读的技巧,提高考生的阅读速度,培养考生迅速抓住文章主旨的能力;而《题源报刊精品阅读30篇(精读)》除了帮助考生进行快速阅读训练之外,还根据每篇文章的特点,为每篇文章设置了5道符合考研英语命题规律和特点的试题,并配以答案和设题思路讲解,这不仅能锻炼考生从宏观上梳理文章的能力,还能完善考生细节速记的技巧。

考生可在备考的第一阶段先做泛读,再做精读,好好地把这两本书吃透,以应对将来考试中可能出现的各种体裁和话题的文章。

最后,大家通过经常阅读考研英语的题源文章,也会慢慢熟悉西方人的行文结构及逻辑论述的展开方式,这对于今后从事英文文案工作的考生而言有着巨大的实际意义。

优秀没有偶然,请大家从现在开始,破除对人世间最欺骗人的两个字——"捷径"的幻想,脚踏实地,亲身体会自己实实在在的进步。伟哥也将与编写团队一起,专门开设基于这一系列图书内容的在线直播课,带着大家好好梳理知识点,共同学习。各位读者朋友,让我们一起加油!

主编　朱伟

本书文章主要来源

1. *The Guardian*《卫报》

《卫报》创办于1821年,是英国的全国性综合内容日报,与《泰晤士报》《每日电讯报》并称为英国三大报。设立之初,由于总部设于曼彻斯特而命名为《曼彻斯特卫报》,1959年改为现名,并且总部于1964年迁至首都伦敦。该报注重报道国际新闻,擅长发表评论和分析性专题文章。一般公众视《卫报》的政治观点为中间偏左,对国际问题持"独立"观点。该报的主要读者为政界人士、白领和知识分子。

2. *The Economist*《经济学人》

《经济学人》创办于1843年,是一份由伦敦经济学人报纸有限公司出版的杂志。杂志的大多数文章写得机智、幽默、有力度,严肃又不失诙谐,并且注重如何在最小的篇幅内告诉读者最多的信息。杂志主要关注政治和商业方面的新闻,但是每期也有一两篇针对科技和艺术的报道,以及一些书评。杂志中所有文章都不署名,并且往往带有鲜明的立场,但又处处用事实说话。

3. *Time*《时代周刊》

《时代周刊》又称《时代》,创办于1923年,是美国三大时事性周刊之一。《时代周刊》内容广泛,对国际问题发表主张和对国际重大事件进行跟踪报道,是半个多世纪以前最先出现的新闻周刊之一。《时代周刊》有美国主版、国际版,以及欧洲版、亚洲版和拉丁美洲版等,为日益增长的国际读者群开设了一个了解全球新闻的窗口。欧洲版(*Time Europe*,旧称 *Time Atlantic*)出版于伦敦,也涵盖了中东、非洲和拉丁美洲的事件;亚洲版(*Time Asia*)出版于中国香港;南太平洋版(*Time South Pacific*)出版于悉尼,涵盖了澳大利亚、新西兰、太平洋群岛的事件。

4. *Newsweek*《新闻周刊》

《新闻周刊》创办于1933年,是美国时政杂志中因评论优秀而获得荣誉最多的周刊,与《时代周刊》《美国新闻与世界报道》并称为美国三大新闻周刊。它是一份在纽约出版,在美国和加拿大发行的新闻类周刊。在美国,它是仅次于《时代周刊》的周刊,但是,有时,它的广告收入会略胜一筹。在这三份期刊中,《新闻周刊》通常被认为观点比《时代周刊》自由、比《美国新闻与世界报道》保守。

5. *The New York Times*《纽约时报》

《纽约时报》创办于1851年,是美国高级报纸、严肃刊物的代表,长期以来拥有良好的公信力和权威性。其成立之初的名字为《纽约每日时报》,后于1857年更名为《纽约时报》。由于风格古典严肃,它有时也被戏称为"灰色女士"(The Gray Lady)。在新闻报道方面,《纽约时报》将自己视为一份"报纸记录",报道的可靠性非常高,因此往往被世界上其他报纸和新闻社直接作为新闻来源。

6. The Washington Post《华盛顿邮报》

《华盛顿邮报》创办于1877年,是美国华盛顿最大、最老的报纸。报纸尤其擅长报道美国国内政治动态,而且通过在20世纪70年代初揭露水门事件,迫使理查德·尼克松总统退职,获得了国际威望。2004年,《华盛顿邮报》获得18项普利策奖,使该报成为最有影响力的媒体之一。

7. USA Today《今日美国》

《今日美国》创办于1982年,是美国唯一的彩色全国性英文对开日报,属美国最大的甘尼特报团。它以彩色版面、消息集中、多用图表、重视体育报道、便于读者迅速获得所需信息等特点吸引读者,有"报纸中的电视"的称号,拥有国内版和国际版。其最重要的新闻编辑原则就是:尽量简化信息使用手段,尽量迎合读者通过形象的方法获取信息的习惯,追求信息利用便捷,所以谓之"快餐化"。稿件简短是此报最突出的特点之一。

8. New Scientist《新科学家》

《新科学家》创办于1956年,是一个自由的国际化科学杂志,内容主要涉及科技发展近态。其网站于1996年开始运营,登载关于科技界的新闻。该杂志并非一个经同行评议的科学杂志,但在科学家和非科学家人群中被广泛传阅。杂志还经常刊登一些评论,比如对气候变化等环境问题的评论,通常被认为是与《科学美国人》(Scientific American)齐名的大众化、高水平的学术期刊。

9. Science《科学》

《科学》创办于1880年,由爱迪生投资1万美元创办,1894年成为美国最大的科学团体"美国科学促进会"(American Association for the Advancement of Science, AAAS)的官方刊物,为全世界最权威的学术期刊之一。《科学》是发表最权威的原始研究论文,以及综述和分析当前研究和科学政策的同行评议的期刊之一,全年共51期,为周刊,全球发行量超过150万份。

10. U.S. News & World Report《美国新闻与世界报道》

《美国新闻与世界报道》创办于1933年,成立之初名为《美国新闻》,1948年和《世界报道》合并后改为现名,是仅次于《时代周刊》《新闻周刊》的美国第三大新闻杂志。它以专题报道美国国内外问题及美国官方人物访问为特色,着重报道国际、国内新闻,内容侧重政治、经济和军事述评,栏目较少,内容较严肃,有关军事力量和战略动态的报道和分析颇有分量,广受各方重视。每期当中约有五分之二的内容是针对世界某一地区专门问题的报道。

11. The Atlantic《大西洋月刊》

《大西洋月刊》创办于1857年,是美国最受尊敬的杂志之一,内容主要涉及文学、政治、科学与艺术。在20世纪晚期和21世纪早期,《大西洋月刊》由保守党控制,是一个在政治上能与自由党的《纽约客》相提并论的杂志。近年来,在经历了财务困难和一系列的所有权变动后,《大西洋月刊》变成了一份普通的社论杂志,把目光集中在外交、政治、经济等文化趋势方面,以"思想领导者"为受众目标。

考研阅读题源分析

历年考研英语阅读理解的文章大多改编自以下几个英美权威报刊中的文章:《新闻周刊》(*Newsweek*)、《纽约时报》(*The New York Times*)、《卫报》(*The Guardian*)、《华盛顿邮报》(*The Washington Post*)、《经济学人》(*The Economist*)、《基督教科学箴言报》(*The Christian Science Monitor*)等。

随着社会的快速发展,考研英语阅读理解部分的取材也逐渐变得具有很强的时效性,大多选取近一两年甚至是当年的文章。以2016年的考研英语为例,考研英语(一)阅读理解Part A节的四篇文章中只有Text 2是出自2014年11月5日在《卫报》上登载的一篇文章,其余三篇分别出自2015年4月5日的《基督教科学箴言报》、2015年6月27日的《经济学人》和2015年3月26日的《大西洋月刊》。因此,考生在备考过程中,应多阅读上述英美报纸杂志上的最新发表的文章,尤其是涉及人文科学、社会科学和自然科学这三大领域的议论文、评论、新闻报道和说明文等。考生在阅读说明文时应重点弄清楚文章的说明对象、事实和数据;而在阅读议论文时,重点应放在掌握作者的观点态度、论点和论据方面。

考生在阅读英美报刊时,可以带着做题的心理去审视这些文章,并自行归类总结,如列出阅读文章的类型、题材、要素(what, when, where, why, who)等,这对培养考生英语语感、掌握西方行文逻辑、了解世界最新热点及话题都有很大帮助。

根据大纲的变化趋势,考研英语阅读理解Part A节的选材难度也经过了阶段性的重大调整,我们可将其归纳为四个主要阶段:

第一阶段(2002年之前):共提供5篇文章,每篇4小题,虽然在出题类型上和之后的年份差别不大,但由于文章在长度、段落数量方面的差异较大,使阅读难度、阅读方法和之后的年份略有不同。

第二阶段(2003—2009年):这几年考研英语阅读理解Part A节的出题风格保持稳定,分别从词汇、句意理解、例子功能、态度、主旨等多角度考查考生对单点细节、上下句关系、特定人物观点和段落主旨的理解能力。同时,虽然文章题材多样,但文章本身的难度处于可控范围之内,这意味着考生通过一定量的文章精读和训练后是可以适应的。

第三阶段(2010—2013年):这四年的考研英语阅读理解Part A节真题的选材难度有所提高(如2010年Text 2的"专利问题"、2011年Text 4的"生育问题"、2012年Text 3的"科学发现问题"和2013年Text 4的"美国人权问题"都是当年给考生造成极大阅读难度的文章)。考生需要具备单段内重点考点的发掘能力,并配合对较强长难句的正确理解,才能够取得相对理想的成绩。

第四阶段(2014年至今):这几年考研英语阅读理解Part A节的选材难度又呈现了下降的趋势,命题人在这几年的试卷中,重点考查考生利用题干信息进行定位的能力。在定位准确的前提下,定位点前后的原文内容相对于2010—2013年的真题而言更加容易理解。

为了让考生对考研英语真题中的阅读理解部分有一个较为直观的把握,本书整理了2010—2021年考研英语阅读理解Part A部分的文章来源和文章主题,以及出题较为集中的题源,详见表1和表2:

表1 2010—2021年考研英语阅读理解题源汇总

题 材	主题	题源	真题
社会生活	火车票价上涨	*The Telegraph*	2021英语一 Text 1
	维多利亚时期的人拍照时不笑	*BBC History*	2021英语一 Text 3
	支持还是反对网络中立?	*Los Angeles Times*	2021英语一 Text 4
	英国"文化之镇"的奖项提案	*The Guardian*	2020英语一 Text 1
	企业性别配额助长特权	*The Boston Globe*	2020英语一 Text 3
	首席执行官的高薪酬	*Time*	2020英语二 Text 2
	美国的Z一代	*Newsweek*	2020英语二 Text 4
	最高法院裁定电商需交销售税	*U.S. News & World Report*	2019英语一 Text 4
	有内疚感可能是好事	*The Atlantic*	2019英语二 Text 1
	网络分享中的审辨式思维	*The Christian Science Monitor*	2018英语二 Text 2
	管理自己的精力	*BBC*	2018英语二 Text 4
	美国机场安检耗时太久	*The Washington Post*	2017英语一 Text 1
	莫纳克亚山上的望远镜纷争	*Scientific American*	2017英语一 Text 2
	贪污受贿和正常接见之间的界限	*The Christian Science Monitor*	2017英语一 Text 4
	伦敦奥运遗产走向失败	*The Guardian*	2017英语二 Text 1
	美国社会看待森林大火的态度	*The Christian Science Monitor*	2017英语二 Text 4
	对时尚界身材标准的挑战	*The Christian Science Monitor*	2016英语一 Text 1
	英国乡村的规划	*The Guardian*	2016英语一 Text 2
	企业的社会责任	*The Economist*	2016英语一 Text 3
	美国年轻一代的成功之路	*The Atlantic*	2016英语二 Text 4
	欧洲皇室的存废	*The Guardian*	2015英语一 Text 1
	男女在家庭和工作中压力的异同	*Time*	2015英语二 Text 1
	英国财政大臣的失业改革计划	*The Guardian*	2014英语一 Text 1
	美国法律服务价格昂贵的原因	*The Economist*	2014英语一 Text 2
	如何聪明地花钱	*The Economist*	2014英语二 Text 1
	人们对自己评价过高的原因	*The Guardian*	2014英语二 Text 2
	英国住房危机	*The Guardian*	2014英语二 Text 4
	对快速时尚业的批判	*Business Week*	2013英语一 Text 1
	最高法院对亚利桑那州移民法的最后判决	*The Wall Street Journal*	2013英语一 Text 4
	改变对美国移民的分类方式	*The Washington Post*	2013英语二 Text 2
	欧洲性别歧视问题	*Project Syndicate*	2013英语二 Text 4
	同辈压力能否起到积极作用	*Time*	2012英语一 Text 1
	工会阻碍公共部门改革	*The Economist*	2012英语一 Text 4
	基因专利的法律纠纷	*The Economist*	2012英语二 Text 3
	明星父母对普通人生育观的影响	*Newsweek*	2011英语一 Text 4
	社会潮流的形成	*Harvard Business Review*	2010英语一 Text 3
	男女交谈为何如此艰难?	*The Washington Post*	2010英语二 Text 2
	美国陪审团制度的发展	——	2010英语二 Text 4

2

续表

题材	主题	题源	真题
经济贸易	是时候进行再培训改革了吗？	*The Globe and Mail*	2021 英语二 Text 1
	大型科技公司的"买断"策略	*Financial Times*	2021 英语二 Text 3
	数字服务税	*The New York Times*	2020 英语一 Text 4
	耐心是企业美德	*The Christian Science Monitor*	2019 英语一 Text 1
	如果没有外籍劳工，美国农场将失去竞争力	*Bloomberg Businessweek*	2019 英语二 Text 3
	美国邮局的转型之路	*The Washington Post*	2018 英语一 Text 4
	GDP 不等于国民幸福感	*The Independent*	2017 英语一 Text 3
	纸版印刷的未来	*The Atlantic*	2016 英语一 Text 4
	美国的就业问题	*The Huffington Post*	2015 英语二 Text 4
	安吉特公司违背承诺及其后果	*Boston.com*	2012 英语一 Text 2
	色彩效应与营销手段	*The Guardian*	2012 英语二 Text 2
	经济大萧条的利与弊	*The Atlantic*	2012 英语二 Text 4
	高级经理裸辞现象	*Business Week*	2011 英语一 Text 2
	新媒体为营销带来的机遇和挑战	*Mckinsey Quarterly*	2011 英语一 Text 3
	公司所聘请的外部董事	*The Economist*	2011 英语二 Text 1
	美国报业：一息尚存	*The Economist*	2011 英语二 Text 2
	欧洲的未来：凝视深渊	*The Economist*	2011 英语二 Text 4
	商业方法专利的数量将被缩减	*Business Week*	2010 英语一 Text 2
	会计准则制定者面临改变准则的压力	*The Economist*	2010 英语一 Text 4
	企业引导消费习惯	*The New York Times*	2010 英语二 Text 3
文化教育	学术出版：灾难性的资本主义	*The Guardian*	2020 英语二 Text 2
	大学成绩宽松政策	*The Atlantic*	2019 英语一 Text 2
	实践教育观	*The Christian Science Monitor*	2018 英语二 Text 1
	数字产品对孩子成长的影响	*The Independent*	2017 英语二 Text 2
	间隔年就学	*The Huffington Post*	2017 英语二 Text 3
	有效阅读	*The Guardian*	2016 英语二 Text 3
	新闻从业人员的道德准则缺失	*The Guardian*	2015 英语一 Text 4
	第一代大学生的问题	*Inside Higher Education*	2015 英语二 Text 2
	新交际用语的变化	*The Atlantic*	2015 英语二 Text 3
	美国人文教育的缺陷	*The Wall Street Journal Online*	2014 英语一 Text 4
	家庭作业新政策的弊端	*Los Angeles Times*	2012 英语二 Text 1
	古典音乐现场演出的危机	*Commentary*	2011 英语一 Text 1
	简约即美的建筑设计风格	*The New York Times*	2011 英语二 Text 3
	报纸文艺评论辉煌不再	*Commentary*	2010 英语一 Text 1
	世界艺术品市场的不景气	*The Economist*	2010 英语二 Text 1

续表

题材	主题	题源	真题
科学技术	老鼠可以与机器鼠交朋友	*New Scientist*	2020 英语二 Text 1
	AI的价值观与伦理问题	*The Christian Science Monitor*	2019 英语一 Text 3
	机器人与中产阶级	*Bloomberg*	2018 英语一 Text 1
	医疗领域的数字霸权问题	*The Guardian*	2018 英语一 Text 3
	科技巨头对用户数据的攫取	*The Guardian*	2018 英语二 Text 3
	大学生早接触计算机科学课	*The Atlantic*	2016 英语二 Text 1
	个人信息安全	*The Washington Post*	2015 英语一 Text 2
	学术杂志对论文数据的审核	*Nature*	2015 英语一 Text 3
	作者对自然科学界新科研奖项的分析与评价	*Nature*	2014 英语一 Text 3
	"人机矛盾"引发的工作问题	*Big Think*	2014 英语二 Text 3
	行为广告和互联网隐私	*The Economist*	2013 英语一 Text 2
	人类的未来充满光明	*New Scientist*	2013 英语一 Text 3
	科技变革对社会的影响	*The New York Times*	2013 英语二 Text 1
	科学发现的取信过程	*The Scientist*	2012 英语一 Text 3
能源环境	扶贫项目和保护森林	*Science News*	2021 英语一 Text 2
	英国脱欧后的粮食自给自足	*New Scientist*	2021 英语二 Text 2
	欧洲城市处理污染空气	*The Guardian*	2020 英语二 Text 3
	利用森林应对气候变化	*Bloomberg*	2019 英语二 Text 2
	别再说停用吸管会解决环境污染	*The Huffington Post*	2019 英语二 Text 4
	可再生能源已达临界点	*The Christian Science Monitor*	2018 英语二 Text 2
	美国对小草原榛鸡的保护	*Science*	2016 英语二 Text 2
医疗健康	关于直觉的8个真理	*Psychology Today*	2021 英语二 Text 4
	大脑的快速反应	*The New York Times*	2013 英语二 Text 3

表2 2010—2021年考研英语阅读理解重点题源分析

题源	选材篇数	对应真题
The Economist	共11篇	2016 年考研英语一 Text 3;2014 年考研英语一 Text 2 2014 年考研英语二 Text 1;2013 年考研英语一 Text 2 2012 年考研英语一 Text 4;2012 年考研英语二 Text 3 2011 年考研英语二 Text 1;2011 年考研英语二 Text 2 2011 年考研英语二 Text 4;2010 年考研英语一 Text 4 2010 年考研英语二 Text 1

题源	选材篇数	对应真题
The Guardian	共14篇	2020年考研英语一 Text 1;2020年考研英语一 Text 2 2020年考研英语二 Text 3;2018年考研英语一 Text 3 2018年考研英语二 Text 3;2017年考研英语二 Text 1 2016年考研英语一 Text 2;2016年考研英语二 Text 3 2015年考研英语一 Text 1;2015年考研英语一 Text 4 2014年考研英语一 Text 1;2014年考研英语二 Text 2 2014年考研英语二 Text 4;2012年考研英语二 Text 2
The Christian Science Monitor	共8篇	2019年考研英语一 Text 1;2019年考研英语一 Text 3 2018年考研英语一 Text 1;2018年考研英语二 Text 1 2018年考研英语二 Text 2;2017年考研英语一 Text 4 2017年考研英语二 Text 4;2016年考研英语一 Text 1
The Atlantic	共7篇	2019年考研英语一 Text 2;2019年考研英语二 Text 1 2016年考研英语一 Text 4;2016年考研英语二 Text 1 2016年考研英语二 Text 4;2015年考研英语二 Text 3 2012年考研英语二 Text 4
The Washington Post	共5篇	2018年考研英语一 Text 4;2017年考研英语一 Text 1 2015年考研英语二 Text 2;2013年考研英语二 Text 2 2010年考研英语二 Text 2
The New York Times	共5篇	2020年考研英语一 Text 4;2013年考研英语二 Text 1; 2013年考研英语二 Text 3;2011年考研英语二 Text 3; 2010年考研英语二 Text 3
Time	共2篇	2015年考研英语二 Text 1;2012年考研英语一 Text 1
Nature	共2篇	2015年考研英语一 Text 3;2014年考研英语一 Text 3
Newsweek	共2篇	2020年考研英语二 Text 4;2011年考研英语一 Text 4

根据表1、表2汇总的信息,结合近几年的题源走向,本书整理汇编了从《经济学人》《卫报》《大西洋月刊》《纽约时报》等高频题源中选取的近10年来发表的100篇文章。

本书所选文章主题涉及多个领域,包括社会生活、经济贸易、文化教育、科学技术、能源环境和医疗健康,与考研英语阅读真题文章所涉主题十分契合(见表1),并以社会科学类和科普类文章为主。每篇文章还设有参考译文、词语积累、长难句解析三个版块,适合考生备考期间的日常练习及知识扩展需要。阅读本书有助于考生在适应并熟悉英美国家报刊文章的行文风格和语言特点的基础上增强语感、扩大词汇量,最终提高英语阅读能力,顺利通过考试。

目 录 CONTENTS

第一部分 社会生活类

Text 1　Tracing the Roots of Human Morality in Animals
　　　　从动物窥探人类道德的根源 ………………………………………… (2)

Text 2　U.S. Birthrates Are Plummeting. Increasing Legal Immigration Can Help
　　　　美国出生率正在急剧下降,增加合法移民有所帮助 ………………… (5)

Text 3　Oregon Becomes Eighth State to Expand Background Checks on All Gun Sales
　　　　俄勒冈州成为第八个将背景调查扩大到全枪支销售的州 …………… (9)

Text 4　Children Divorcing Their Parents 孩子们正与其父母分离 ………… (12)

Text 5　India Will Be Most Populous Country Sooner than Thought, U.N. Says
　　　　联合国:印度即将成为人口数量最多的国家,速度比预想的更快 …… (16)

Text 6　Modern Love 现代爱情 ………………………………………………… (19)

Text 7　*The Guardian* View on Social Care and Disability: A Cruel Policy Vacuum
　　　　《卫报》对社会关怀和残疾的看法:一个残酷的政策真空 …………… (22)

Text 8　*The Guardian* View on Food Cultures: Sharing, Not Snatching
　　　　《卫报》对饮食文化的看法:分享,而不是抢夺 ……………………… (25)

Text 9　Gun Control 枪支管制 ……………………………………………… (28)

Text 10　U-Shaped Pandemic Jobs Crisis Hits Older and Younger Workers
　　　　 年老和年轻的工作者被"U型疫情就业危机"袭击 ………………… (31)

Text 11　Are Hospitals Intentionally Hiding Prices?
　　　　 医院在故意隐瞒价格吗? ……………………………………………… (33)

Text 12　Footage Showing a Farmworker Hammering Pigs to Death Provides Further Evidence of the Serious Failings in Britain's Animal Welfare System
　　　　 镜头中农夫捶打猪仔致死:进一步证明英国动物福利系统正在严重衰败 …… (36)

Text 13	Are We Losing the Art of Telephone Conversation?
	我们正在失去电话交谈的艺术吗？ ··· (39)
Text 14	Car Trips Are Bad Trips 开车旅行是糟糕的经历 ························ (42)
Text 15	*The Guardian* View on the Future of Work: Share Out the Benefits
	《卫报》对工作前景的看法：利益分享 ··· (46)
Text 16	Employers Can't Retrain the U.S. Workforce by Themselves
	雇主不能单独完成对美国劳动力的再培训 ···································· (48)
Text 17	Men Who Advocate for Others in the Workplace Face Backlash
	在工作场合为他人辩护的男性会遭到反对 ···································· (51)

第二部分 经济贸易类

Text 1	India Undermines Its Own Economy 印度削弱自身经济 ················ (56)
Text 2	Banking Is for the 1% 银行是为了1%的人服务 ··························· (59)
Text 3	The Euro Zone: Take One for the Team
	欧元区：为了集体利益，牺牲个人利益 ·· (62)
Text 4	America's Economy 美国经济 ··· (66)
Text 5	*The Guardian* View on Apple's Valuation: A Digital Milestone
	《卫报》对苹果公司的价值的看法：一个数字里程碑 ······················ (70)
Text 6	UK Losing Millions in VAT from Non-EU Sellers on Amazon and eBay
	英国在亚马逊和eBay的非欧盟卖家中损失了数百万的增值税 ·········· (73)
Text 7	Google Is fined €4.3 bn in the Biggest-ever Antitrust Penalty
	谷歌被罚款43亿欧元——有史以来最大的反垄断罚款 ···················· (76)
Text 8	Google and Facebook Can't Count on Consumers Saving Them
	谷歌和脸书不能指望消费者来拯救 ·· (80)
Text 9	A Strong U.S. Consumer Is a Lagging Indicator
	强大的美国消费者是一个滞后标志 ·· (83)
Text 10	Everywhere in (Supply) Chains 遍布供应链 ······························ (85)
Text 11	Why African Firms Create So Few Jobs?
	为何非洲的公司创造的就业机会如此之少？ ································ (89)
Text 12	G7 Tax Accord Is a Game-Changing Opportunity
	七国集团税改协议是一次改变游戏规则的机会 ····························· (93)

Text 13　Finding the Perfect Pace for Product Launches 为产品发布找准节奏 …… (96)

Text 14　Facebook's ＄5 Billion Penalty Misses the Point
　　　　　脸书的 50 亿美元罚款错失了重点 ………………………………………… (100)

第三部分　文化教育类

Text 1　Grad School, a Leg Up—in Debt 研究生院,债务占了上风 ……………… (105)

Text 2　A Turning Point for a Polish Ballet Company 波兰芭蕾舞公司的转机…… (108)

Text 3　A New Language for Pakistan's Deaf 巴基斯坦聋哑人的新语言 ………… (113)

Text 4　It's a Boy Thing (Or Is It?) 这是男孩的问题(是吗?) ……………………… (116)

Text 5　The Diplomatic Power of Art 文化外交力量 ……………………………… (121)

Text 6　*Maps to the Stars* Shows an Oscar Winner's Untamed Side
　　　　　《星图》展现了奥斯卡得主野性的一面 ……………………………………… (124)

Text 7　*The Guardian* View on Librarians: Guides to Life, Not Just to Books
　　　　　《卫报》对图书管理员的看法:人生向导,而不仅仅是图书向导 ………… (126)

Text 8　The Favre Connection 法佛尔情结 ……………………………………… (129)

Text 9　Does Birth Order Affect Personality?
　　　　　出生顺序会影响人格吗? ……………………………………………………… (132)

Text 10　Snow Flower and the Not-So-Secret Metaphor 雪花和并不隐秘的隐喻…… (135)

Text 11　Universities: Pile Them High 大学:多多益善 ……………………………… (138)

Text 12　Flipping the Floppers 轻惩假摔 ……………………………………………… (142)

Text 13　Why So Little Chinese in English? 英语中的汉语借用词为何如此之少? …… (145)

Text 14　A Grim Half-Century 糟糕的半个世纪 …………………………………… (148)

Text 15　The ＄1-a-Week School 每周一美金的学校 ……………………………… (151)

Text 16　Schools Get Permission to Skip Standardized Tests
　　　　　学校获得准许跳过标准化考试 ……………………………………………… (155)

Text 17　Thanks but No Thanks 心领了,但不用了 ………………………………… (158)

Text 18　*The Guardian* View on Creative Workers: Britain Needs Them
　　　　　《卫报》对创造性工作者的看法:英国需要他们 …………………………… (162)

第四部分　科学技术类

Text 1　Advances in Neuroscience Raise Medical Hopes, Social Questions

　　　　　　神经科学的进步燃起了医学希望,也引发了社会问题 ……………………（166）

Text 2　The Newly Discovered, Very Important Ice Mountains of Pluto
　　　　　　最新重要发现:冥王星上存在冰山 ………………………………………（169）

Text 3　The Internet of Everything Holiday Shopping Guide
　　　　　　万物联网——假日购物指南 ……………………………………………（173）

Text 4　The Call of Mars 来自火星的呼唤 …………………………………………（176）

Text 5　Apple's Privacy Rules Force Marketers to Find New Ways to Target Ads
　　　　　　苹果的隐私条例迫使营销商另寻新径精准投放广告 ………………（180）

Text 6　Time to Build a More Secure Internet
　　　　　　是时候建立一个更安全的网络环境了 …………………………………（183）

Text 7　Google Car's Computer Got Smarter in 2015
　　　　　　谷歌车载电脑在 2015 年变得更智能 …………………………………（186）

Text 8　The Social Network's Shares Recover as It Fixes Its Search Problem
　　　　　　修复自身搜索问题,该社交网络股价回升 ……………………………（190）

Text 9　Technology Brought Us All Together. That's Part of What's Holding Us Back
　　　　　　技术使世界互通互联,但也是阻碍我们进步的部分原因 ……………（193）

Text 10　When a New Study Debunks Science, don't Ignore It
　　　　　　当一项新的研究揭露科学的真相时,不要忽视它 ……………………（196）

Text 11　Mirrors Could Replace Air Conditioning by Beaming Heat into Space
　　　　　　镜面可将热量传送至太空,有望取代空调 ……………………………（199）

Text 12　Admit It, Older People—You Are Addicted to Your Phones, Too
　　　　　　承认吧,老年人们,你们也对手机上瘾了 ……………………………（202）

Text 13　Ichthyosaurs and the Bends 鱼龙与减压病 ……………………………（205）

Text 14　Thigh Bone Points to Unexpectedly Long Survival of Ancient Human Ancestors
　　　　　　股骨化石表明古人类祖先长期存在 ……………………………………（207）

Text 15　Wake Up, Humanity! A Hi-Tech Dystopian Future Is Not Inevitable
　　　　　　醒醒,人类！高科技反乌托邦的未来是可避免的 ……………………（210）

Text 16　Chips off the Old Block 机器人也能像监护人一样（照顾孩子） …………（213）

Text 17　A Better Way to Use Satellite Images to Save Lives After Tremors
　　　　　　震后利用卫星图像救生的更有效的方法 ………………………………（218）

第五部分　能源环境类

Text 1　Cleaning Up Plastic Pollution in Africa
　　清理非洲的塑料污染 ·· (223)

Text 2　Is Texas the Greenest State? By One Measure, Maybe
　　得州是最"绿色"的州？在某种标准下，可能如此 ················ (225)

Text 3　Numerous States Prepare Lawsuits Against Obama's Climate Policy
　　多个州准备通过法律途径阻止奥巴马的气候政策 ················ (228)

Text 4　Climate Change Forces New Pentagon Plan 气候变化敦促五角大楼新计划 ··· (233)

Text 5　Build That Pipeline! 建那条管道！ ·································· (237)

Text 6　EPA Tells BP to Use Less-Toxic Chemicals
　　美环保署要求英国石油公司使用低毒化学物质 ···················· (240)

Text 7　Japan's Hydra-Headed Disaster 日本灾难重重 ······················ (243)

Text 8　Blooming Horrible 可怕的富营养化 ································· (247)

Text 9　Japan May Have Lost Race to Save Nuclear Reactor
　　日本或许未来得及挽救核反应堆 ······································ (251)

Text 10　Carbon Targets, Renewables and Atomic Risks
　　碳目标、可再生能源与原子能风险 ·································· (254)

Text 11　Plastic Fishing in the Southern Ocean 在南太平洋打捞塑料 ········· (260)

Text 12　Fossil Fuel Divestment Campaign's Victory in Australia Will Be a Moral One
　　澳大利亚矿物燃料撤资活动的道德胜利 ···························· (264)

Text 13　Australia Needs U.S.-Style Green Card Deal for Climate-Threatened
　　Pacific Islanders
　　为了受气候威胁的太平洋岛民，澳大利亚需要美国式绿卡 ········ (268)

Text 14　Great Barrier Reef Is Becoming a "Theme Park" with Underwater
　　Hotels and Attractions as Its Beauty Fades, Tour Operator Warns
　　旅游运营商警告：随着大堡礁美丽的褪色，水下酒店和旅游景点
　　使其成了一个"主题公园" ·· (272)

Text 15　How Natural Resources Can Save Africa
　　自然资源如何能拯救非洲 ·· (275)

Text 16　Let the Sun Shine 让阳光闪耀 ······································ (278)

第六部分　医疗健康类

Text 1　Low-Fiber Diets Cause Waves of Extinction in the Gut
　　　　低纤维饮食习惯引起肠道微生物一波接一波的灭绝 ·················· (284)

Text 2　For Toilets, Money Matters 对于厕所来说,钱比较重要 ·················· (288)

Text 3　Warning to New Yorkers: There's a Lot of Salt in That
　　　　给纽约人敲响警钟:这些食物里盐过多 ····························· (292)

Text 4　American Red Cross Offering Amazon Gift Card in Exchange for Critically
　　　　Needed Blood Donations 美国红十字会急需献血,用亚马逊礼品卡作交换 ··· (296)

Text 5　The Booster in Your Future : The Pandemic Will Challenge All to Behave
　　　　Differently
　　　　未来的"加强剂":疫情逼迫所有人采取不同行动 ····················· (298)

Text 6　Better Health, Not Just Better Health Care 更健康,而不只是更好的医疗服务 ··· (301)

Text 7　Wireless Health Care 移动卫生保健 ·································· (305)

Text 8　A New York State of Mind 纽约人的心境 ······························ (308)

Text 9　Special Report: Stretching the Safety Net 特殊报告:延长安全网 ·········· (311)

Text 10　The Nobel Prize: Good Eggs 诺贝尔奖:有用的卵子 ···················· (314)

Text 11　To Improve Health Care, Governments Need to Use the Right Data
　　　　改善医疗,政府应采用合理数据 ··································· (317)

Text 12　Threat to Mental Health Programme That Aims to Get Patients Back to Work
　　　　帮助患者重回岗位的心理健康项目因经费缩减而受威胁 ·············· (320)

Text 13　5G Is Coming: How Worried Should We Be About the Health Risks?
　　　　5G即将到来:我们应该对健康风险有多担心? ······················· (324)

Text 14　Computer Test Could Spot Children at Risk of Developing Depression
　　　　电脑能检测出有患抑郁症风险的儿童 ······························ (327)

Text 15　Scheme Sees Police Work with Mental Health Staff to Manage Crisis Call-Outs
　　　　分类方案见证警察与心理健康从业人员协作应对出警危机 ··········· (330)

Text 16　Swaddling Babies Can Cause Them Hip Problems, Doctors Warn
　　　　医生警告:用襁褓包裹婴儿会导致其髋关节出现问题 ················ (334)

Text 17　Creation: The Origin of Life; The Future of Life
　　　　创造:生命之源;生命未来 ······································· (337)

Text 18　*The Guardian* View on Genetics: Diversity Is Destiny
　　　　《卫报》对于遗传学的看法:多样性是注定的 ······················· (341)

第一部分 社会生活类
SECTION ONE

Text 1 Tracing the Roots of Human Morality in Animals
从动物窥探人类道德的根源

The Bonobo and the Atheist and *How Animals Grieve* show that we must be careful when studying animals to learn about the origins of human traits and behaviours.

Where does morality come from? Throughout the history of Western civilisation, thinkers have usually answered either that it comes from God, or else through the application of reason.

But in *The Bonobo and the Atheist*, primatologist Frans de Waal argues that there's another answer that fits the data better: morality comes from our evolutionary past as a social primate. Like our closest relatives the apes, humans evolved in small, tightly knit, cooperative groups. As a result, again like the apes, we are exquisitely sensitive to one another's moods, needs and intentions.

This well-developed empathy provided the trellis on which morality later flowered. De Waal, who is based at Emory University in Atlanta, Georgia, has been making this case eloquently for many years and over several books, notably in *Good Natured* back in 1997, and in *Primates and Philosophers*, 12 years later.

In his new work, he bolsters the argument by drawing on a lot of new research, carefully footnoted for those who want to dig deeper. De Waal distinguishes two degrees of morality. ①The first he calls "one-on-one morality", which governs how an individual can expect to be treated, and the second "community concern," a larger, more abstract concept that extends to the harmony of the group as a whole.

《倭黑猩猩和无神论者》和《动物如何悲伤》两本书向我们揭示：在通过研究动物来探究人类特性和行为起源时，我们必须要谨慎。

道德到底是从何而来？纵观西方文明史，思想家常有两种回答：道德来自上帝或来自理智的运用。

但是在《倭黑猩猩和无神论者》一书中，灵长类动物学家弗兰斯·德瓦尔辩称更能解读数据的答案在于：道德来自人类的不断进化。就像我们的近亲类人猿一样，人类生活在一个小而又紧密合作的群体中。因此，也像类人猿一样，我们对彼此的情绪变化、需求、目的很敏感。

这种充分的同理心提供了道德生长的环境。佐治亚州亚特兰大埃默里大学的德瓦尔多年以来一直进行相关研究，并出版了许多著作，尤其是1997年的《生来温顺》，以及12年后出版的《灵长类与哲学家》。

在他的新书里，他从许多新研究中得出结论，从而进一步证明了该观点，他在脚注中详细说明了这些新研究，以方便其他人进行更深入的研究。德瓦尔把道德程度分为两种。①第一种被他称为"个人道德"，即决定着一个人希望自己如何被对待；第二种是"集体关心"，是一种能够延伸到集体和谐的更大、更抽象的概念。

---

bonobo *n.* 倭黑猩猩　　atheist *n.* 无神论者　　primatologist *n.* 灵长类动物学家
social primate 社会灵长类　　exquisitely *adv.* 剧烈地　　eloquently *adv.* 富有表现力地

Chimps and bonobos certainly have the former—they respect ownership, for example, and expect to be treated according to their place in the hierarchy. But de Waal presents several examples such as a chimp stepping in to stop a fight between two others—that suggest that they also have a rudimentary form of the latter.

The book's title, incidentally, draws on bonobos because they are more likely than chimps to behave morally, to have concern for each other, to value harmony and so on. This, imagines, de Waal, is something morally inclined atheists would want to emulate.

If humans inherited morality from our ancestors, though, what are we to make of religion? Here de Waal moves into territory he has not explored before. Clearly, religion must do something important, since every human culture has it. But instead of religion giving us morality, de Waal turns the tables. Morality, he argues, probably gave us religion as a way of reinforcing the pre-existing community concern.

If he's right, then there may be no absolute code of right and wrong out there to be discovered. Instead, each individual's evolved sense of empathy and concern for the group may help shape the group's consensus on what kind of behaviour is appropriate. In short, says de Waal, morality may be something we all have to work out together. It's a persuasive argument, and de Waal's cautious and evidence-based approach is one that many *New Scientist* readers are sure to find congenial.

"Individual empathy and concern for the group may shape consensus on what behaviour is appropriate."

That careful approach is less evident in another book covering some of the same ground. In *How Animals Grieve*, anthropologist Barbara King sets out to explore the question of whether non-human animals grieve for their dead. ②It's an intriguing question, but unfortunately King's book is largely a succession of anecdotes: the cat who roams the house, crying, in search of its dead litter mate; the dog who waits

---

chimp *n.* 黑猩猩
emulate *vi.* 模仿
intriguing *adj.* 复杂的
hierarchy *n.* 等级制度
congenial *adj.* 意气相投的
rudimentary *adj.* 基本的
set out to do sth. 开始做……

daily at the train station for its dead master; a dolphin trying to keep her dead calf afloat for days.

Some of these stories make a persuasive case for some animals especially apes, elephants and cetaceans sometimes grieving. No surprises there: I suspect most readers would have conceded that ground right from the start.

But King makes little effort to dig any deeper by exploring, for example, the neural machinery and cognitive skills an animal needs in order to be capable of grief. After all, solitary species such as cats have less need for empathy and its corollary, grief than social animals, and small-brained creatures such as turtles may simply lack the brainpower or not form lasting pair bonds.

(*New Scientist*, 2013.5)

找死去的小伙伴；一只小狗每天在车站默默等待它去世主人的归来；海豚妈妈一连几天试图让它死去的幼崽再次漂上海面。

动物有时确实会为死者哀鸣，尤其是猿、大象和鲸类动物，以上的例子增强了此观点的说服力。但这毫不出奇，因为据我猜测，大部分的读者打一开始就相信这一观点。

但是金并没有进一步去探索，比如说，动物产生悲伤这种情感需要的神经组织和认知能力。毕竟，像猫这类独居动物，其同情心以及其衍生物——悲伤，要比群居动物低；而像乌龟这类脑容量小的生物也许仅仅缺少智力或者无法形成持久的配对链。

长难句解析

① 本句为主从复合句。主句为倒装结构，还原正常语序后主干为 he calls the first...and the second...，句中包含两个并列的复合宾语，由 and 连接。and 前的复合宾语中，which 引导的非限制性定语从句修饰 morality，该从句中嵌套了一个 how 引导的宾语从句，作 governs 的宾语；and 后的复合宾语中，a larger, more abstract concept 是 community concern 的同位语，that 引导的定语从句修饰同位语中的 concept。

The first he calls "one-on-one morality", which governs how an individual can expect to be
宾语1 主语 谓语 宾语补足语1　　非限制性定语从句　　　宾语从句
treated, and the second "community concern", a larger, more abstract concept that extends to
宾语2　　　　宾语补足语2　　　　同位语　　　　　　定语从句
the harmony of the group as a whole.

② 本句为 but 连接的并列复合句。两个句子均为主系表结构。冒号后的内容是解释说明 anecdotes 的三个并列结构，可看作 anecdotes 的同位语。同位语1中 who 引导的定语从句修饰 the cat；同位语2中 who 引导的定语从句修饰 the dog；同位语3中动名词结构 trying to...作后置定语修饰 a dolphin。

It's an intriguing question, but unfortunately King's book is largely a succession of anecdotes:
主系　　　表语　　　　状语1　　　　主语　系动词 状语2　　　表语
the cat who roams the house, crying, in search of its dead litter mate; the dog who waits daily
同位语1　　　　定语从句1　　　　　　　　　　　　　　　　同位语2 定语从句2
at the train station for its dead master; a dolphin trying to keep her dead calf afloat for days.
　　　　　　　　　　　　　　　同位语3　　　后置定语

---

calf *n.* 幼崽　　　cetacean *n.* 鲸类动物　　　corollary *n.* 必然的结果

Text 2

U. S. Birthrates Are Plummeting. Increasing Legal Immigration Can Help

美国出生率正在急剧下降,增加合法移民有所帮助

The decades-long decline in the U.S. birthrate accelerated in 2020, as the average number of babies born to American women over the course of their lifetimes fell to its lowest level since government record-keeping began nearly a century ago. ①After a decade in which the population grew at the most sluggish pace since the 1930s, last year's slowdown in births, which intensified as the pandemic took hold, suggests a new demographic normal—one that poses daunting economic and geopolitical challenges.

In a country where fertility is now well below the replacement rate required to compensate for deaths, an obvious question arises: As the United States ages, how will a dwindling cohort of younger, working-age Americans sustain the expensive social services that their parents and grandparents are counting on in retirement?

②The rational answer is a robust immigration system, one that affords the nation a ready supply of scrappy, striving employees in jobs for which there are insufficient numbers of native-born Americans, as well as a steady stream of well-educated professionals to fill engineering, scientific, technology and medical jobs, among others. Immigrants are twice as likely to start new businesses

2020年,美国数十年保持下降的人口出生率加速下降,美国女性一生中所生婴儿的平均数量下降到近一个世纪前政府有记录以来的最低水平。①在经历了自20世纪30年代以来人口增长速度最缓慢的十年之后,去年出生率的下降随着疫情暴发而加剧,这表明了一种新的人口统计常态——带来了严峻的经济和地缘政治挑战。

在一个生育率远远低于补偿死亡所需的更替率的国家,一个明显的问题出现了:随着美国人口老龄化,越来越少的处于劳动年龄的年轻美国人将如何维持他们父母和祖父母在退休时所指望的昂贵的社会服务?

②合理的解决办法是建立一个健全的移民体系,这个体系能为美国提供充足的、奋发有为的雇员,他们从事着本土出生的美国人数量不足的工作,同时还能源源不断地提供受过良好教育的专业人才,以填补工程、科学、技术和医疗等领域的工作岗位。移民创办新企业的可能性是本

---

sluggish *adj.* 萧条的;迟钝的
geopolitical *adj.* 地理政治学的
compensate *vi.* 补偿,赔偿;抵消
cohort *n.* (有共同特点或举止类同的)一群人,一批人
ready *adj.* 准备好的;现成的

daunting *adj.* 使人畏缩的;使人气馁的
fertility *n.* [生]能生育性;繁殖力
dwindle *vi.* 减少;变小

scrappy *adj.* 生气勃勃的;好斗的

as native-born Americans and buttress economic growth—think of Tesla, Google and PayPal, all started by entrepreneurs born elsewhere.

Yet as the 2020 Census demonstrated, immigration flattened out following the Great Recession in 2008, was actively impeded by the Trump administration and fell once the coronavirus tightened its grip. That reversed a trend toward rising numbers of immigrants since the 1960s, when a half-century boom in foreign-born arrivals, the vast majority of them legal, helped fuel economic growth.

Granted, no celestial mandate dictates that the United States must grow at a faster clip than other developed countries, as it has for most of its history. But population stagnation may mean a very different future, and probably a less vital one, than many Americans might imagine. In the short run, it might mean jobs that go begging for workers as caretakers for the elderly, truck drivers, computer programmers and other occupations. In the long run, it could impede the country's ability to maintain its status as a superpower, project influence and compete with China.

Among the many theories to explain the falling birthrate are women's increasing labor-force participation; the daunting cost of living, particularly housing, in job-rich urban areas; a dramatic drop-off in teen pregnancy; and a social media-distracted younger generation that may be having less sex. ③ Whatever combination of factors is driving the baby

---

buttress *vt.* 支持
grip *n.* 紧握；控制力
celestial *adj.* 天国的；神圣的
stagnation *n.* 停滞；滞止
project *vt.* 突出；促进；投射

flatten out 下降或升高后变平
fuel *vt.* 刺激；给……提供燃料
mandate *n.* 授权；命令，指令
occupation *n.* 职业

bust, what's clear is that there will be no easy answer to reversing it, though family-friendly government and corporate policies could help.

By contrast, increasing the level of legal immigration is a policy choice that comes with a direct positive impact. ④Making that choice would entail forging a political consensus on a uniquely divisive issue that President Donald Trump, among others, has helped turn into a question of tribal identity after years in which it was a matter of bipartisan consensus. But not making it is likely tantamount to acquiescing to an era of demographic stagnation and, over time, diminished national stature.

(*The Washington Post*, 2021.6)

生育低谷,显而易见的是,要扭转这一趋势并不容易,尽管有利于家庭的政府和企业政策可能会有所帮助。

相比之下,提高合法移民水平是一种具有直接积极影响的政策选择。④做出这样的选择需要在一个独特的引起分歧的问题上达成政治共识,多年来,这个问题一直是两党共识的问题,而唐纳德·特朗普总统和其他人一样,已经把这个问题变成了一个部落身份问题。但不这样做可能等于默许了一个人口停滞和随着时间的推移国家地位下降的时代。

长难句解析

①本句为主从复合句。主句的主干为 last year's slowdown in births suggests a new demographic normal。句首 After a decade…为主句的时间状语,其中包含 in which 引导的定语从句1修饰 a decade,since the 1930s 作定语从句1的时间状语;which 引导非限制性定语从句修饰主语;破折号后面的 one 为宾语的同位语,that 引导定语从句2修饰 one。

> After a decade in which the population grew at the most sluggish pace since the 1930s,
> 时间状语　　　　　　　定语从句1　　　　　　　　时间状语
> last year's slowdown in births, which intensified as the pandemic took hold, suggests
> 　　　主语　　　　　　　　非限制性定语从句　　　　　　　谓语
> a new demographic normal—one　that poses daunting economic and geopolitical challenges.
> 　　宾语　　　　　同位语　　　　　　定语从句2

②本句为主从复合句。主句的主干为 The rational answer is a robust immigration system。one 是主句表语的同位语,that 引导的定语从句1修饰 one;for which 引导定语从句2;as well as…professionals 与 a ready supply of scrappy, striving employees 构成并列;不定式 to fill engineering, scientific, technology and medical jobs 作目的状语,among others 是介宾短语作补充性状语。

---

bust *n.* (经济)萧条;没价值的事物　　entail *vt.* 使成为必需;使成为必然
forge *vt.* 锻造;缔造　　　　　　　　consensus *n.* 一致;舆论
bipartisan *adj.* 两党联立的;代表两党的　　tantamount *adj.* 同等的;相当于……的
acquiesce *vi.* 默许;勉强同意　　　　　stature *n.* (精神、道德等的)高度;名望

The rational answer is a robust immigration system, one that affords the nation a ready
　　主语　　系动词　　　　表语　　　　　　同位语　　　　定语从句1
supply of scrappy, striving employees in jobs for which there are insufficient numbers
　　　　　定语从句　　　　　　　　　　　　　　定语从句2
of native-born Americans, as well as a steady stream of well-educated professionals
　　　　　　　　　　　　　　　　　　并列结构
to fill engineering, scientific, technology and medical jobs, among others.
　　　　　目的状语　　　　　　　　　　　　　　　　　　　补充性状语

③本句为主从复合句。主句为主系表结构。句首为 Whatever 引导的让步状语从句1，从句为主谓宾结构；主句主语为 what 引导的主语从句；that 引导一个表语从句作主句的表语；最后为 though 引导的让步状语从句2。

Whatever combination of factors is driving the baby bust, what's clear　　　is
　　　　　　让步状语从句1　　　　　　　　　　主语（主语从句）　系动词
that there will be no easy answer to reversing it, though family-friendly government
　　　　　表语（表语从句）　　　　　　　　　　　让步状语从句2
and corporate policies could help.

④本句为主从复合句。主句的主干为 Making that choice would entail forging a political consensus。介词短语 on a uniquely divisive issue 作后置定语修饰 a political consensus；issue 后面为 that 引导的定语从句1，修饰 issue；after years 为时间状语，其后为 in which 引导的定语从句2，修饰 years。

Making that choice would entail forging a political consensus on a uniquely divisive issue
　　　主语　　　　谓语　　　　　　　宾语　　　　　　　　　　　后置定语
that President Donald Trump, among others, has helped turn into a question of tribal
　　　　　　　　　　　　　　定语从句1
identity after years in which it was a matter of bipartisan consensus.
　　　　　时间状语　　　　　　定语从句2

Text 3

Oregon Becomes Eighth State to Expand Background Checks on All Gun Sales

俄勒冈州成为第八个将背景调查扩大到全枪支销售的州

Oregon on Monday became the eighth state to expand criminal background checks to include all private gun sales, even transactions on the Internet, when Democratic Governor Kate Brown signed the bill into law.

A federal law, commonly known as the Brady Law, requires licensed firearms dealers to perform background checks on prospective purchasers and to maintain records of the sales. ①But unlicensed private sellers at gun shows and online are not required by federal law to observe the same policies, which allows people to buy and transfer firearms without first passing a background check.

Forty percent of guns sold in the U.S. are done so without a background check, according to a 2014 report by the Brady Campaign to Prevent Gun Violence.

②Since the Brady Law was enacted in 1994, background checks have stopped more than 2 million gun purchases by people who may pose a risk to public safety, such as felons and domestic abusers, according to the Brady Campaign.

In 2000, Oregon passed legislation requiring background checks at gun shows. Monday's expansion of the law closes a preexisting loophole to include all private transactions, including online sales. The measure, which took effect immediately, also will require background checks on all transfers, with some exceptions, in 90 days. There are exemptions for family members and people who lend guns for hunting reasons.

Brown's signing of the law is a big win for gun-reform groups after gun activists, including the

本周一，民主党州长凯特·布朗签署了管控枪支的法案，俄勒冈州成为第八个将犯罪背景调查扩大到所有私人枪支销售的州，甚至包括网上枪支交易。

一项俗称为《布雷迪法案》的联邦法律，要求特许枪支经销商对潜在的购买者进行背景调查并做好销售记录。①但是联邦法律对未经授权的枪支展销会以及网上销售的私人枪支卖家并没有约束力，这使得人们不需要首先通过背景调查即可购买和转让枪支。

根据2014年的防止枪支暴力的布雷迪运动所做出的一份报告显示，在美国有40%的枪支交易都是在没有背景调查的情况下进行的。

②根据布雷迪运动显示，自1994年《布雷迪法案》颁布以来，背景调查有效地遏制了超过200万支枪的订单，这些买家包括重罪犯和家暴者等可能对社会安全构成威胁的人。

2000年，俄勒冈州通过立法要求对枪支展销会进行背景调查。周一，新增的法律补上了一个先前存在于私人交易（包括网上销售行为）上的法律漏洞。这项立即生效的措施还要求对90天内所有的转让进行背景调查，也有些情况例外。如一般家庭成员和借枪狩猎情况除外。

在包括全国步枪协会在内的枪支激进主义者多年来对先前试图收

---

transaction n. 交易　　　domestic abuser 家庭暴力的施虐者　　　loophole n. 漏洞
exemption n. 解除

National Rifle Association (NRA), for years successfully blocked previous attempts to tighten firearms laws.

Oregon is the sixth state in the past two years to apply background checks to all gun sales, in the wake of the December 2012 shooting at Sandy Hook Elementary School in Newtown, Connecticut, where 20 first-grade students and six educators were killed by 20-year-old Adam Lanza.

In the aftermath of the Sandy Hook massacre, President Barack Obama's efforts to enact stricter gun laws failed in Congress when lawmakers didn't approve a background checks bill in April 2013. Gun rights groups like the NRA argued against the bill, warning lawmakers that the legislation would factor into the group's congressional scorecard. The gun organization gives grades and endorsements to politicians who defend the Second Amendment on the local, state and federal levels. As a result, many of the Democrats who were up for reelection in 2014 voted against the bill and joined almost the entire Republican opposition. Only four Republicans voted in favor of the bill.

Since the tragedy at Sandy Hook, five other states besides Oregon—Colorado, Connecticut, New York, Delaware and Washington—have expanded background checks to include all firearms sales, an illustration of how legislators are working at the state level to prevent gun violence. Six months ago, Washington became the seventh state after residents passed Initiative 594 during the November midterm elections. California and Rhode Island implemented background checks on all gun sales before the Sandy Hook shooting.

A total of 18 states now require background checks for some—but not all—gun purchases.

The NRA and Republicans have argued that background checks won't prevent mass shootings like the one in Newtown because individuals will

---

in the wake of 作为……的结果　　　massacre *n*. 残杀　　　scorecard *n*. 记分卡

find ways to obtain a weapon. Lanza's mother, Nancy, whom he fatally shot before driving to the school on the morning of December 14, 2012, legally purchased the guns earlier. The Lanza home in Newtown contained more than 1,600 rounds of ammunition for multiple weapons, including the rifle and handgun the gunman used to carry out the massacre, according to a 2013 report published by the Office of the State's Attorney for the Judicial District of Danbury. The report also concluded that Lanza had significant mental health problems that affected his ability to live a normal life and interact with other people.

Critics have said the legislation in Oregon will fail to keep guns out of the hands of criminals and people who are mentally ill. Republican leaders called the law "deeply flawed" and "unenforceable" because they believe law-abiding residents are being targeted without increasing mental health services. The signing of the bill "represents another milestone in what is already becoming the most partisan and misguided session in recent memory," Oregon House Republican Leader Mike McLane wrote Monday in a statement.

States with expanded background checks see 46 percent fewer women murdered with guns by intimate partners, 48 percent fewer law enforcement officers killed by guns and 48 percent fewer gun-related suicides, according to a recent report by Everytown for Gun Safety, a group created in 2014 that works for passage of laws at all levels to reduce gun violence.

(*Newsweek*, 2015.5)

找到方法来获得武器。兰扎的母亲南希早先合法购买了这些枪支,兰扎在 2012 年 12 月 14 日上午开车前往学校前残忍地枪杀了其母亲。根据 2013 年丹伯里地区法院州律师办公室发布的报告称,在兰扎位于纽顿的家中有超过 1 600 发为多个枪支配备的子弹,包括用来进行大屠杀的步枪和手枪。报告还推断,兰扎有明显的心理健康问题,这对他的正常生活和社交能力产生了很大影响。

批评人士说,俄勒冈州的该法律将无法保证枪支不会落入罪犯和精神病人的手中。共和党领导人称其"漏洞百出"和"无法执行",他们相信守法居民仍会成为受害者,因为法案中没有新增精神卫生服务条款。签署该法案"代表了另一个里程碑——刷新了近年来最偏袒和误导的立法",俄勒冈州众议院共和党领袖麦克凯伦在周一的一份声明中写道。

在实施扩展背景调查的州中,被亲密伴侣用枪支谋杀的女性减少了 46%,被枪支杀害的执法人员减少了 48%,与枪支相关的自杀事件也减少了 48%,该消息源自"全城枪支安全组织"最近的一份报告,该组织创建于 2014 年,且一直致力于通过各级法律减少枪支暴力。

长难句解析

① 本句为主从复合句。主句的主干结构为 unlicensed private sellers are not required to…。句中 at gun shows and online 作 sellers 的后置定语;which 引导的非限制性定语从句修饰 policies。

---

fatally *adv.* 致命地 ammunition *n.* 弹药 flawed *adj.* 有缺陷的
law-abiding *adj.* 遵纪守法的 session *n.* 会话

But unlicensed private sellers　at gun shows and online　are not required by federal law
　　　主语　　　　　　　　　　　　后置定语　　　　　　　　　谓语　　　　　　　　状语
to observe the same policies, which allows people to buy and transfer firearms without first
　　　宾语　　　　　　　　　　　　　　　非限制性定语从句
passing a background check.

② 本句为主从复合句。主句的主干结构为 background checks have stopped gun purchases。who 引导的定语从句修饰 people，such as…举例说明。

Since the Brady Law was enacted in 1994, background checks have stopped more than 2
　　　　时间状语从句　　　　　　　　　　　　　　主语　　　　　　　谓语
million gun purchases by people　who may pose a risk to public safety, such as felons and
　　宾语　　　　　　状语　　　　　　　　　　　　　　定语从句
domestic abusers,　according to the Brady Campaign.
　　　　　　　　　　　　　　状语

Text 4 — Children Divorcing Their Parents
孩子们正与其父母分离

Unhappily married for many years, Peter waited until his children were grown up before he divorced their mother. He hoped this would make the experience less upsetting for them. Yet in the six years since, he has not seen either of his two sons. He speaks to the younger one, who is in his 20s, once or twice a year; the eldest, in his 30s, has cut off all contact. His middle child, a daughter, has at times tried to act as go-between, an experience she has found distressing. "For me it has been completely devastating," he says. "I get on with my life, but I get teary when I think about them." Losing contact with children is like bereavement, he says, but with the painful tug of

不幸的婚姻维持了多年，彼得一直等到孩子们长大才和他们的母亲离婚。他希望这能让他们不那么难过。然而，在那之后的六年里，他再也没有见过他的两个儿子。他和20多岁的小儿子一年联系一两次；和30多岁的大儿子已经断了所有联系。他的第二个孩子，是个女儿，有时试图扮演一个中间人的角色，她觉得这让她很痛苦。"对我来说，这完全是毁灭性的，"他说，"我继续过着自己的生活，但一想到他们，我就会泪流满面。"他说，失去与孩子的联系就像丧亲之痛，尽管十分痛苦，但他仍然

---

upsetting adj. 令人心烦意乱的，令人苦恼的
go-between n. 媒人；中间人；媒介者
teary adj. 哭泣的，悲伤的；易流泪的
tug n. 一股强烈的感情

cut off 切断；中断
distressing adj. 使痛苦的；悲伤的；使烦恼的
bereavement n. 丧友，丧亲

hope that they might one day be reconciled.

Though people tend not to talk about it much, familial estrangement seems to be widespread in America. ①The first largescale nationwide survey, recently conducted by Cornell University, found that 27% of adult Americans are estranged from a close family member. ②Karl Pillemer, a professor of sociology who led the research and wrote a book about its findings called "Fault Lines", says that because people often feel shame, the real figure is likely to be higher. The relationship most commonly severed is that between parent and adult child, and in most cases it is the child who wields the knife.

Because family estrangement has been a subject of research only for the past decade, there are no data to show whether it is becoming more common. But many sociologists and psychologists think it is. In one way this seems surprising. Divorce heightens the risk of other family fractures. ③Joshua Coleman, a psychologist and the author of "Rules of Estrangement", found in a recent survey of 1,600 estranged parents that more than 70% had divorced their child's other parent. In recent years America's divorce rate has fallen. Yet Dr Coleman reckons other trends are making parent-child estrangements likelier than ever. Other therapists, who do not specialize in family rifts, concur.

A rise in individualism that emphasizes personal happiness is the biggest factor. People are increasingly likely to reject relatives who obstruct feelings of

---

reconcile *vt.* 使和解；使接受
largescale *adj.* 大型的；大规模的
sever *vt.* 割断，断绝；分开；使分离
in one way 在某种程度上
fracture *n.* 破裂，断裂
specialize in 专门研究……
concur *vi.* 同意；一致

estrangement *n.* 疏远；失和
estrange *vt.* 使疏远；离间
wield *vt.* 使用；行使；挥舞
heighten *vt.* 提高；增加
therapist *n.* 治疗学家
rift *n.* 裂缝；不和
obstruct *vt.* 妨碍；阻塞

well-being in some way, by holding clashing beliefs or failing to embrace those of others. Personal fulfillment has increasingly come to displace filial duty, says Dr Coleman. Whereas families have always fought and relatives fallen out, he says, the idea of cutting oneself off from a relative as a path to one's own happiness seems to be new. In some ways it is a positive development: people find it easier to separate from parents who have been abusive. But it can also carry heavy costs.

Those who decide to break off contact with their parents find support in a growing body of books, as well as online. ④ Threads on internet forums for people who want to break ties with their parents reveal strangers labelling people they have never met as narcissistic or toxic and advising an immediate cessation of contact. This may make it easier to shelve feelings of guilt.

Raising awareness about the issue in this way is likely to be important, and not only because some broken bonds may be fixable. Parent-child estrangement has negative effects beyond the heartbreak it causes. Research suggests that the habit of cutting off relatives is likely to spread in families. But most immediately, it is likely to exacerbate loneliness in old age.

(*The Economist*, 2021.5)

---

displace *vt.* 取代;置换;转移
fall out 失和;争吵
cut oneself off from 某人自己与……断绝关系
abusive *adj.* 辱骂的;虐待的
a growing body of 越来越多的……
thread *n.* (互联网留言板上帖子的)系列相关信息;思路
narcissistic *adj.* 自恋的;自我陶醉的
shelve *vt.* 将某事放到一旁不予考虑
have negative effects beyond… 除了……还有其他消极影响
exacerbate *vt.* 使加剧;使恶化

filial *adj.* 孝顺的;子女的

break off contact with 与……断绝联系

cessation *n.* 停止;中止;中断
fixable *adj.* 可固定的;可修复的

长难句解析

①本句为主从复合句。主句的主干为主谓宾结构，recently conducted by Cornell University 作后置定语修饰 survey，found 后为 that 引导的宾语从句，作 found 的宾语。

The first largescale nationwide survey, recently conducted by Cornell University, found
　　　　主语　　　　　　　　　　　后置定语　　　　　　　　　谓语
that 27% of adult Americans are estranged from a close family member.
　　　　　　　　　　　宾语从句

②本句为主从复合句。主句的主干为主谓宾结构。a professor of sociology 是主语 Karl Pillemer 的同位语；who 引导定语从句修饰 a professor of sociology，called "Fault Lines" 作后置定语修饰 a book；that 引导宾语从句作 says 的宾语。

Karl Pillemer, a professor of sociology who led the research and wrote a book about
　主语　　　　　同位语　　　　　　　　　定语从句
its findings called "Fault Lines", says that because people often feel shame, the real
　　　　后置定语　　　　　　　谓语　　　　　　　宾语从句
figure is likely to be higher.

③本句为主从复合句。主句的主干为主谓宾结构。a psychologist and the author of "Rules of Estrangement" 为主语 Joshua Coleman 的同位语，对主语做进一步解释说明；谓语 found 后的 in a recent survey 作状语，介词短语 of 1,600 estranged parents 作后置定语修饰 survey；that 引导宾语从句作 found 的宾语。

Joshua Coleman, a psychologist and the author of "Rules of Estrangement", found in
　主语　　　　　　　　　　　同位语　　　　　　　　　　　　谓语
a recent survey of 1,600 estranged parents that more than 70% had divorced their child's
　状语　　　　　后置定语　　　　　　　　　　宾语从句
other parent.

④本句为主从复合句。主句的主干为主谓宾结构。介词短语 on internet forums 作状语；who 引导的定语从句修饰 people；strangers 是宾语，labelling people… contact 是后置定语修饰 strangers，其中包含一个省略引导词 that 的定语从句 they have never met，修饰 people。

Threads on internet forums for people who want to break ties with their parents reveal
　主语　　　状语　　　　后置定语　　　　　　定语从句　　　　　　　谓语
strangers labelling people they have never met as narcissistic or toxic and advising an
　宾语　　　　　　　　　　　　　后置定语
immediate cessation of contact.

Text 5

India Will Be Most Populous Country Sooner than Thought, U.N. Says

联合国：印度即将成为人口数量最多的国家，速度比预想的更快

Demographers have known for some time that the number of people in India would surpass the number in China, the two most populous countries in the world. But they did not anticipate that the change would happen so quickly.

The United Nations reported on Wednesday that India's population will probably surpass China's by 2022, not 2028, as the organization had forecast just two years ago.

In its 2015 revision report, the population division of the United Nations Department of Economic and Social Affairs said China's population was now 1.38 billion, compared with 1.31 billion in India. But in seven years, the populations of both are expected to reach 1.4 billion.

①Thereafter, the report said, India's population will grow for decades, to 1.5 billion in 2030 and 1.7 billion in 2050, while China's is expected to remain fairly constant until the 2030s, when it is expected to slightly decrease.

Over all, the report said, the world's current population of 7.3 billion is expected to reach 9.7 billion by 2050, slightly more than the 9.6 billion forecast two years ago. The number could reach 11.2 billion by the end of the century.

Much of the overall increase between now and 2050 is expected in high-fertility countries, mainly in Africa, or in countries with large populations, the report said.

Half the growth is expected to be concentrated in just nine countries: India, Nigeria, Pakistan, the Democratic Republic of Congo, Ethiopia, Tanzania, the United States, Indonesia and Uganda.

人口统计学家早已有预测，作为世界上人口最密集的两大国家，印度人口数量将会超过中国。然而，他们没有料到，变化会如此之快。

联合国本周三发布的报告称，印度人口数量很可能将在2022年超越中国，而非该机构两年前预测的2028年。

联合国经济和社会理事会人口司在2015年的修订报告中指出，中国现有人口数量为13.8亿，印度为13.1亿。预计在未来7年内，两国人口数量都将达到14亿。

①报告称，今后几十年里，印度人口数量将持续增长，预计在2030年达到15亿，在2050年达到17亿，而中国人口数量则有望保持平稳，并且从21世纪30年代开始有望有小幅下降。

报告称，总体看来，目前世界人口数量为73亿，2050年有望达到97亿，略高于两年前估计的96亿。到21世纪末，世界人口总数预计达到112亿。

报告还称，截止到2050年，预计人口增长主要集中在出生率高的国家——主要是非洲或者人口基数大的国家。

据估计，人口增长半数会集中在九个国家：印度、尼日利亚、巴基斯坦、刚果共和国、埃塞俄比亚、坦桑尼亚、美国、印度尼西亚和乌干达。

---

revision *n.* 修订，校订　　　　　　high-fertility *n.* 高出生率

By contrast, the populations of 48 countries are expected to decline in that period, mainly in Europe, because of a slowdown in fertility rates that started decades ago. The report said several countries faced a population decline of more than 15 percent by 2050, including Bosnia and Herzegovina, Bulgaria, Croatia, Hungary, Japan, Latvia, Lithuania, Moldova, Romania, Serbia and Ukraine.

Among the 10 largest countries by population, one is in Africa (Nigeria), five are in Asia (Bangladesh, China, India, Indonesia and Pakistan), two are in Latin America (Brazil and Mexico), one is in North America (the United States), and one is in Europe (Russia). ②Among these, Nigeria's population, currently ranked seventh largest, is growing the fastest, and it is expected to surpass the population of the United States by 2050, which would make it the world's third most populous country.

The population revision report also included some notable findings on aging. The number of people 80 or older is projected to more than triple by 2050 and increase more than sevenfold by 2100, the report said. In 2015, 28 percent of all people 80 and older lived in Europe, but that share is expected to decline to 16 percent in 2050 and to 9 percent by 2100, as the populations of other areas increase in size and grow older.

The revision report confirmed that substantial improvements in life expectancy have been made in recent years.

Globally, life expectancy has risen to 68 years for men and 73 years for women in 2010—15, from 65 years for men and 69 years for women in 2000—05.

The highest levels of life expectancy in 2010—15 are in Hong Kong of China, followed by Japan, Italy, Switzerland, Singapore, Iceland, Spain, Australia and Israel.

相反，由于出生率数十年来的持续下降，到 2050 年，以欧洲国家为主的 48 个国家的人口数量可能会下滑。报告称，到 2050 年，部分国家将面临 15% 以上的人口跌幅，其中包括波斯尼亚和黑塞哥维那、保加利亚、克罗地亚、匈牙利、日本、拉脱维亚、立陶宛、摩尔多瓦、罗马尼亚、塞尔维亚和乌克兰。

全球人口最多的十个国家中，一个在非洲（尼日利亚），五个在亚洲（孟加拉国、中国、印度、印度尼西亚和巴基斯坦），两个位于拉丁美洲（巴西和墨西哥），一个在北美洲（美国），还有一个在欧洲（俄罗斯）。②在这些人口大国中，尼日利亚当前排第七位，是增长最快的国家。尼日利亚有望在 2050 年超过美国，成为世界第三人口大国。

该人口修订报告中关于人口老龄化的发现也值得关注。预计到 2050 年，80 岁及以上的人口数量将增长三倍以上，到 2100 年将增长七倍以上。2015 年，80 岁及以上的人群中有 28% 居住在欧洲，但随着其他地区人口数量的增长及老龄化的加重，预计到 2050 年和 2100 年，居住在欧洲的 80 岁及以上的人群占比将分别下降至 16% 和 9%。

修订报告证实，近年来人类的平均寿命有显著的延长。

从 2010 年到 2015 年，全球男性平均寿命延长至 68 岁，女性延长至 73 岁。而在 2000 年到 2005 年间，男性平均寿命是 65 岁，女性是 69 岁。

2010—2015 年间，中国香港是人类平均寿命最长的地区，紧随其后的是日本、意大利、瑞士、新加坡、冰岛、西班牙、澳大利亚和以色列。

---

be projected to 预测

Globally, the report said, life expectancy is projected to rise to 77 years in 2045−50 and 83 years in 2095−2100, from 70 years in 2010−15.

The population estimates and projections from the United Nations are an important benchmark for global trends, as well as for helping provide demographic data to calculate many other important indicators, including health data, around the world.

(*The New York Times*, 2015.7)

长难句解析

① 本句为"the report said+间接引语"结构。间接引语是由 while 连接的并列复合句;其中,while 前的句子中的 and 连接了两个并列的状语,表示在2030年和2050年人口分别增长到多少。while 后的句子中,宾语3为不定式结构;when 引导的非限制性定语从句修饰先行词 the 2030s;while 在句中表对比。

Thereafter,	the report said,	India's population	will grow	for decades,	to 1.5 billion
状语	主语1 谓语1	主语2	谓语2	时间状语	结果状语

in 2030 and 1.7 billion in 2050, while　China's　is expected　to remain fairly
　　　　　　　　　　　　　　　　　　　主语3　　谓语3　　　宾语3

constant until the 2030s, when it is expected to slightly decrease.
　　　时间状语　　　　　　非限制性定语从句

② 本句为 and 连接的并列复合句。and 前的句子中,currently ranked seventh largest 作后置定语修饰主语 Nigeria's population;and 后的句子中,it 为形式主语,真正主语为后边的 to surpass...不定式结构;which 引导的非限制性定语从句中的 which 指代前面 it is....by 2050 整个句子。

Among these, Nigeria's population, currently ranked seventh largest, is growing
　状语　　　　主语　　　　　　　　　后置定语　　　　　　　　　谓语1

the fastest, and　it　　　is expected　to surpass the population of the United States
　状语　　　　形式主语　　谓语2　　　　　　真正主语

by 2050, which would make it the world's third most populous country.
状语　　　　　　非限制性定语从句

---

benchmark *n.* 标准　　　　demographic *adj.* 人口方面的

Text 6 Modern Love 现代爱情

The internet has transformed the way people work and communicate. It has upended industries, from entertainment to retailing. But its most profound effect may well be on the biggest decision that most people make—choosing a mate.

In the early 1990s the notion of meeting a partner online seemed freakish, and not a little pathetic. Today, in many places, it is normal. Globally, at least 200m people use digital dating services every month. In America more than a third of marriages now start with an online match-up. The internet is the second-most-popular way for Americans to meet people of the opposite sex, and is fast catching up with real-world "friend of a friend" introductions. Digital dating is a massive social experiment, conducted on one of humanity's most intimate and vital processes. Its effects are only just starting to become visible.

Meeting a mate over the internet is fundamentally different from meeting one offline. In the physical world, partners are found in family networks or among circles of friends and colleagues. Meeting a friend of a friend is the norm. People who meet online are overwhelmingly likely to be strangers. As a result, dating digitally offers much greater choice. A bar, choir or office might have a few tens of potential partners for any one person. Online there are tens of thousands.

This greater choice—plus the fact that digital connections are made only with mutual consent—makes the digital dating market far more efficient than the offline kind. For some, that is bad news.

互联网改变了人们工作和交流的方式。它颠覆了各行各业,从娱乐业到零售业。但其最深远的影响可能在于大多数人做出的最大的决定——选择配偶上。

20世纪90年代初,在网上认识伴侣的想法似乎很怪异,而且相当可悲。如今,这在许多地方被认为是正常的。在全球范围内,每月至少有2亿人使用数字约会服务。现在,美国三分之一以上的婚姻始于网上相亲。互联网是美国人认识异性的第二大流行方式,并且正在迅速赶上现实世界中"朋友的朋友"的介绍方式。数字约会是一个大规模的社会实验,针对人类最亲密、最重要的进程之一展开,其影响才刚刚开始显现。

通过互联网结识配偶与在现实中结识配偶完全不同。在现实世界中,人们通常在家庭或在朋友和同事圈子中寻找伴侣。与朋友的朋友见面是很正常的。在网上见面的人绝大多数都是陌生人。因此,数字约会提供了更多的选择。任何一个人,在酒吧、合唱团或办公室可能有几十个潜在的伴侣。而在网上则有成千上万个。

更多的选择——加上数字联系只有在双方同意的情况下才能实现——使得数字约会市场比线下约会更有效率。对一些人来说,这是个

---

upend *vt.* 倒放,颠倒;竖立　　notion *n.* 看法　　freakish *adj.* 怪异的
pathetic *adj.* 可悲的　　intimate *adj.* 亲密的　　mate *n.* 配偶
overwhelmingly *adv.* 压倒性地　　choir *n.* 合唱团

Because of the gulf in pickiness between the sexes, a few straight men are doomed never to get any matches at all. On Tantan, a Chinese app, men express interest in 60% of women they see, but women are interested in just 6% of men; this dynamic means that 5% of men never receive a match. In offline dating, with a much smaller pool of men to fish from, straight women are more likely to couple up with men who would not get a look-in online.

For most people, however, digital dating offers better outcomes. ①Research has found that marriages in America between people who meet online are likely to last longer; such couples profess to be happier than those who met offline. The whiff of moral panic surrounding dating apps is vastly overblown. Precious little evidence exists to show that opportunities online are encouraging infidelity. In America, divorce rates climbed until just before the advent of the internet, and have fallen since.

Online dating is a particular boon for those with very particular requirements. Jdate allows daters to filter out matches who would not consider converting to Judaism, for instance. A vastly bigger market has had dramatic results for same-sex daters in particular. In America, 70% of gay people meet their partners online. This searchable spectrum of sexual diversity is a boon: more people can find the intimacy they seek.

There are problems with the modern way of love, however. Negative emotions about body image existed before the internet, but they are amplified when strangers can issue snap judgments on attractiveness. Digital dating has been linked to depression. The same problems that afflict other digital platforms recur in this realm, from scams

---

gulf *n.* 鸿沟, 差距
overblown *adj.* 夸张的
Judaism *n.* 犹太教
snap *adj.* 仓促的
scam *n.* 诈骗

doomed *adj.* 命中注定的
infidelity *n.* 不忠行为
spectrum *n.* 范围
afflict *vt.* 使苦恼

profess *vt.* 表示
boon *n.* 福利
intimacy *n.* 亲密
recur *vi.* 重现

whiff *n.* 轻微的迹象
filter out 滤除
amplify *vt.* 放大
realm *n.* 领域

to fake accounts: 10% of all newly created dating profiles do not belong to real people.

This new world of romance may also have unintended consequences for society. ② The fact that online daters have so much more choice can break down barriers: evidence suggests that the internet is boosting interracial marriages by bypassing homogenous social groups. But daters are also more able to choose partners like themselves. Assortative mating, the process whereby people with similar education levels and incomes pair up, already shoulders some of the blame for income inequality. Online dating may make the effect more pronounced: education levels are displayed prominently on dating profiles in a way they would never be offline. It is not hard to imagine dating services of the future matching people by preferred traits, as determined by uploaded genomes.

(*The Economist*, 2018.8)

虚假账户:新创建的约会资料中有10%是虚假信息。

这种浪漫的新世界也可能使社会产生意想不到的后果。②网上约会者有更多的选择这一事实可以打破障碍:有证据表明,互联网通过避开同族社会群体,促进了跨种族婚姻。但约会对象也更能选择与自己类似的伴侣。"门当户对"的婚姻,即教育水平和收入水平相近的人结成伴侣,是造成收入不平等的部分原因。在线约会可能会使这种影响更加明显:教育水平在约会资料中以一种永远不会离线的方式显著地显示出来。不难想象,未来的约会服务会根据人们的偏好特征来配对,这是由上传的基因组决定的。

长难句解析

① 本句为主从复合句。句子的主干结构为 Research has found that…。that 引导宾语从句,其中包含 who 引导的定语从句修饰 people。

| Research has found | that marriages in America between people | who meet online | are |
| 主语　谓语 | 宾语从句 | 定语从句 | |
| likely to last longer; such couples profess to be happier than those who met offline. |
| 宾语从句 | | | |

② 本句为主从复合句。句子的主干结构为 The fact can break down barriers。第一个 that 引导同位语从句修饰主语 fact;第二个 that 引导宾语从句。

The fact	that online daters have so much more choice	can break down	barriers:	evidence
主语	同位语从句	谓语	宾语	主语
suggests	that the internet is boosting interracial marriages by bypassing homogenous social
谓语	宾语从句			
groups.				

---

unintended *adj.* 非计划的　　　　　　interracial *adj.* 种族间的
bypass *vt.* 避开　　　　　　　　　　homogenous *adj.* 同种类的
assortative *adj.* 相配的　　　　　　　shoulder some of the blame 承担部分责任
pronounced *adj.* 明显的　　　　　　　prominently *adv.* 显著地

Text 7

The Guardian View on Social Care and Disability: A Cruel Policy Vacuum
《卫报》对社会关怀和残疾的看法：一个残酷的政策真空

There cannot be many adults in the UK who are unaware of the importance of social care. ① Whether they have encountered the issue through personal experience of supporting friends or relatives, or on the news, most will also recognise that meeting the needs of the growing number of people who cannot take care of themselves is a serious challenge. ② What fewer may notice is that the most common framing of the care issue, as primarily linked to ageing, longer life expectancy and rising numbers of people with dementia, is partly misleading.

In 2018-2019, almost 300,000 people aged between 18 and 64 received council-funded social care in England (arrangements in Scotland, Wales and Northern Ireland are somewhat different). Most of this care went to people in their homes, and around 70% of those who qualified did so due to learning difficulties. This group made up around a third of the total and accounted for around half of public spending on social care. The social care crisis, as it is often called, is thus as much about disability as ageing.

It is also a crisis about children. In 2018-19, public spending on adult social care in England totalled £18bn. The children's social care bill is a further £10bn, and represents a distinct though linked problem. Its distinctness lies in the nature of

在英国，没有多少成年人不知道社会关怀的重要性。①无论他们是通过亲朋好友的亲身经历，还是在新闻中遇到这个问题，大多数人都会认识到，满足越来越多无法照顾自己的人的需求是一项严峻的挑战。②很少有人注意到的是，护理问题最常见的框架——主要与老龄化、预期寿命延长和痴呆症患者数量的增加有关——在一定程度上是有误导性的。

2018—2019年，英格兰有近30万年龄在18至64岁的人获得了议会资助的社会护理服务（苏格兰、威尔士和北爱尔兰的安排略有不同）。这些护理大部分是在患者家中进行，大约70%符合条件的患者是因学习困难才受到护理。这一群体约占总数的三分之一，消费约占社会福利公共支出的一半。因此，正如人们常说的那样，社会关怀危机既与老龄化有关，也与残障有关。

这也是一场关于儿童的危机。2018—2019年，英格兰用于成人社会关怀的公共支出总额为180亿英镑。儿童社会关怀支出也高达100亿英镑，这是一个虽然相互关联但截然不

---

encounter *vt.* 遭遇；邂逅；遇到
dementia *n.* [内科] 痴呆
qualify *vi.* 取得资格，有资格
account for （比例）占
distinctness *n.* 不同；明显；有特殊性

expectancy *n.* （将来拥有的）可能性，预期
misleading *adj.* 误导的；引入歧途的
due to 因为，由于
total *vt.* 总数达

the spending: there is no equivalent in adult services, for example, to the £1.7bn spent on foster carers, or the budget for special needs education. The links include the impact of disability. Just as adults with physical or mental impairments need support with living, so do children. Another link is poverty. Although disabilities affect people in all income brackets, there is a close connection between poor health and lack of money.

A review of children's social care is under way. It has already been criticised for terms of reference that ignore "the harm of poverty". ③Challenged on this last week, Caroline Dinenage, who was care minister until February, could only say that it is a "very, very complex issue" that ministers will return to when the pandemic is on a "more even keel".

The dysfunctional market for social care, and the lack of funds to pay for it, are not the only injustices faced by disabled people. Benefit cuts have also caused serious harm, including death. The mortality rate among disabled people during the pandemic far exceeded that of the general population. The number with learning difficulties or autism in inpatient wards remains unacceptably high, while the use of physical restraint is rising rather than falling. Earlier this month, the Equality and Human Rights Commission (EHRC) recommended that disabled people's right to live independently should be strengthened by placing new obligations on councils, including in relation to housing.

---

foster *adj.* 代养的,寄养的
bracket *n.* (年龄、收入等的) 等级段,档次
on an even keel 平平稳稳;保持着水平位置
mortality *n.* 死亡人数;死亡率
ward *n.* 病房;保卫

impairment *n.* 损伤,削弱
under way 进行中;在行进
dysfunctional *adj.* 机能失调的,功能障碍的
autism *n.* 孤独症,自闭症;臆想
obligation *n.* 义务;职责;债务

That intervention was timely. Many disabled people say that they were better off when they had their own watchdog, but the EHRC has at least put some proposals on the table. ④After a year in which people with disabilities have suffered particular hardships, including prolonged separations from loved ones due to care home regulations, and with the NHS facing continued uncertainty and pressure on resources, ministers must stop the endless deferrals. Deficiencies in social care provision could affect any of us in time. Right now, they are hurting some of the most vulnerable in our society.

(*The Guardian*, 2021.6)

这种干预是及时的。许多残疾人士说，当他们有自己的监督机构时，他们会过得更好，但EHRC至少提出了一些建议。④在过去的一年中，残疾人士遭受了特别的困难，包括由于护理之家的规定而与所爱的人长时间分离，随着国家医疗服务体系（NHS）面临持续的不确定性和资源压力，部长们必须停止无休止的拖延。社会关怀方面的不足迟早会影响到我们中的任何一个人。现在，它们正在伤害我们社会中一些最脆弱的人。

长难句解析

①本句为主从复合句。主句的主干为主谓宾结构。句首为Whether引导的让步状语从句，介词短语through personal experience of...作让步状语从句里的方式状语；主句谓语recognise后为that引导的宾语从句，该从句的主干是meeting the needs is a serious challenge，为主系表结构，同时该从句还包含一个who引导的定语从句，修饰people。

> Whether they have encountered the issue through personal experience of supporting friends
> 让步状语从句　　　　　　　　　　　　方式状语
> or relatives, or on the news, most will also recognise that meeting the needs of the growing
> 　　　　　　　　　　　　　主语　　　谓语　　　　　　　　宾语从句
> number of people who cannot take care of themselves is a serious challenge.

②本句为主从复合句。主句的主干为What fewer may notice is that...，是主系表结构，主句主语为What引导的主语从句；表语为that引导的表语从句，其主干是the most common framing of the care issue is partly misleading，为主系表结构；两个逗号中间的as primarily...people with dementia为插入语，进一步解释说明the most common framing of the care issue。

> What fewer may notice is that the most common framing of the care issue, as primarily
> 　主语(主语从句)　系动词　　　　　　表语(表语从句)
> linked to ageing, longer life expectancy and rising numbers of people with dementia, is
> 　　　　　　　　　　　　　　　插入语
> partly misleading.
> 表语(表语从句)

---

intervention *n.* 介入；调停；妨碍
prolonged *adj.* 延长的；持续很久的
deficiency *n.* 缺陷；缺乏

better off 有较多钱的，较宽裕的；更好的
deferral *n.* 延期；迟延
vulnerable *adj.* 易受攻击的；易受伤害的

③本句为主从复合句。主句的主干是 Caroline Dinenage could only say that...，为主谓宾结构。句首的 Challenged on this last week 作状语；who 引导一个非限制性定语从句修饰主语 Caroline Dinenage；that 引导宾语从句作 say 的宾语，该从句中包含一个 that 引导的定语从句，修饰 issue；when 引导一个时间状语从句。

> Challenged on this last week, Caroline Dinenage, who was care minister until February,
> 　　状语　　　　　　　　　　主语　　　　　　非限制性定语从句
> could only say that it is a "very, very complex issue" that ministers will return to
> 　谓语　　　　　宾语从句　　　　　　　　　　　　定语从句
> when the pandemic is on a "more even keel".
> 　　时间状语从句

④本句为主从复合句。主句的主干是 ministers must stop the endless deferrals，为主谓宾结构；句首为时间状语，其中包含 in which 引导的定语从句，修饰 year；including... care home regulations 为插入语，对 particular hardships 做进一步解释说明，其中 due to care home regulations 表示原因；介词短语 with the NHS... on resources 作伴随状语。

> After a year in which people with disabilities have suffered particular hardships, including
> 　　　　　　　　　　时间状语
> prolonged separations from loved ones due to care home regulations, and with the NHS
> 　　　　　　　　　　　插入语
> facing continued uncertainty and pressure on resources, ministers must stop the endless deferrals.
> 　　　　　　伴随状语　　　　　　　　　　　　主语　　谓语　　　　宾语

Text 8

The Guardian View on Food Cultures: Sharing, Not Snatching
《卫报》对饮食文化的看法：分享，而不是抢夺

Much of the joy of food lies in sharing: the passing of dishes across the table; the adoption of new ingredients and techniques. Curries and pasta have become staple parts of the British diet, while Malaysian hawkers use an Australian malted chocolate drink to make "roti Milo." Even if some adaptations have niche appeal— durian pizza, anyone? —exchange enriches us all.

饮食的乐趣大部分在于分享：在桌子上传菜；采用新的食材和烹饪技术。咖喱菜肴和意大利面食已经成为英国人日常饮食的主要组成部分，而马来西亚的小贩则用澳大利亚的麦乳精巧克力饮料来制作"美禄"。甚至有些创新的饮食也有市场吸引力——榴莲披萨，有人知道吗？——交流丰富了我们的生活。

---

curry n. 咖喱菜肴　　　　　staple adj. 主要的　　　　　hawker n. 沿街叫卖者；小贩
malted adj. 麦芽的　　　　niche n. 商机（针对特定消费者群体的市场需求）
durian n. 榴莲

This is why some are worried by suggestions of "cultural appropriation" when it comes to cooking. In Britain, the issue has boiled over after the discovery of a string of offensive posts and videos from a white chef who makes Thai food. He exchanged the letters L and R to mock Asian accents, made vile remarks about Thai people and others, and told people to "go down to the jungle and ask the monkey for a coconut" over a still of Brixton market. He has since been fired by the restaurant Som Saa, and its co-founder (who had praised one of the videos) has also apologised.

It is true that the primary issue here is one of plain racism. But the other one is that this man made his living from the accumulated work and knowledge of people he treated with contempt. In doing so he highlighted broader issues about who owns, profits from and takes the credit for food cultures. ① The American writer Ruth Tam has written powerfully about the bittersweet knowledge that "the same dishes hyped as 'authentic' on trendy menus were scorned when cooked in the homes of the immigrants who brought them here."

These issues are particularly raw, so to speak, given other recent controversies. Activists in the US have targeted the Chicago-based Aloha Poke Co chain (none of its owners understood to be native Hawaiians) for sending legal letters telling restaurants, including those run by Hawaiians, to stop using "aloha" or "aloha poke" in their names; both the word aloha and the dish poke (diced raw fish) originate in Hawaii. The firm says it is only trying to stop misuse of its trademark "Aloha Poke" in connection with restaurants.

There's nothing wrong with experimentation; an obsessive veneration of "authenticity" can be a kind of exoticisation in itself. ②The problem comes

---

appropriation *n.* 占用　　　　boil over 爆发　　　　mock *vt.* 嘲弄　　　vile *adj.* 卑鄙的
coconut *n.* 椰子　　　contempt *n.* 轻视，蔑视；耻辱　　take the credit 居功；认为是……的功劳
hype *vt.* 大肆宣传　　　　　　　　scorn *vt.* 轻蔑；藐视　　　　　raw *adj.* 真实的
dice *vt.* 把(食物)切成小方块　　　　veneration *n.* 崇拜　　　　　authenticity *n.* 真实性

when making a food more fashionable, or an easier fit for western tastes, is equated with making it "better."

Equally, no one is suggesting it is wrong to cook food from another culture. Mexico gave the Englishwoman Diana Kennedy its highest honour for her remarkable knowledge of its cuisine. Some of those querying the Gordon Ramsay show suggested the late Anthony Bourdain, who showed such genuine curiosity and enthusiasm in approaching different cultures, as a model for how it should be done.

The issue, as the food writer Sejal Sukhadwala observed, is cooking another's food without understanding or respect, and then profiting from it. The recipe for happy exchange demands one essential ingredient: humility. Enjoy the feast, but do not insult your host or hog the dishes. Sharing is delightful. Snatching is not.

(*The Guardian*, 2018.8)

合西方人的口味就等同于让它变得"更好"时,问题就来了。

同样,没有人认为烹饪来自另一种文化的食物是错误的。墨西哥授予英国女性黛安娜·肯尼迪最高荣誉,以表彰她对墨西哥食物有着非凡的烹饪知识。一些质疑戈登·拉姆齐节目的人认为,已故的安东尼·波登在这方面做出了榜样,他在接触不同的文化时表现出了如此真诚的好奇心和热情。

正如美食作家塞贾尔·苏哈德瓦拉所言,问题在于,在不理解或不尊重他人的情况下烹饪别人的食物,并从中获利。快乐交流的秘诀需要一个基本要素:谦逊。享受盛宴,但不要侮辱主人或狼吞虎咽。分享是令人愉快的,抢夺却不是。

长难句解析

① 本句为主从复合句。主句的主干结构为 Ruth Tam has written about the bittersweet knowledge。that 引导同位语从句,解释说明 knowledge,该从句中又包含一个 when 引导的时间状语从句和 who 引导的定语从句。

The American writer Ruth Tam	has written powerfully about	the bittersweet knowledge
主语	谓语	宾语

that "the same dishes hyped as 'authentic' on trendy menus were scorned when cooked in
　　　　　　　　　　同位语从句

the homes of the immigrants who brought them here."
　　时间状语从句　　　　　　定语从句

② 本句为主从复合句。主句的主干结构为 The problem comes。when 引导时间状语从句修饰主句。

The problem	comes	when making a food more fashionable, or an easier fit for western
主语	谓语	时间状语从句

tastes, is equated with making it "better."

---

late *adj.* 已故的　　　insult *vt.* 侮辱　　　hog the dish 狼吞虎咽

Text 9　Gun Control
枪支管制

Grace Mcdonnell's parents gave one of her paintings to Barack Obama. The seven-year-old, who dreamed of being a painter, was shot dead in her classroom last month. The picture now hangs in the president's study as a reminder to act. Even in a country as accustomed to gun violence as America, the murder of 26 people, including 20 children, in a Newtown, Connecticut school last month was especially shocking. On that day a tearful Mr. Obama said serious action was needed to prevent any more tragedies. ①On January 16th Mr. Obama, along with Vice-President Joe Biden, who headed the president's gun task-force, unveiled the most sweeping gun-control proposals Washington, DC, has seen for two decades. Whether they will be implemented or make much difference is another matter.

The president's plan was inspired not just by the children killed in Newtown, but by the more than 30,000 deaths caused by guns every year. Mr. Obama announced 23 executive orders, which do not need congressional approval. These include strengthening the system of background checks (which is notoriously ineffective) and providing more support to law-enforcement agencies. Another order seeks to make schools safer by ensuring that each one has an emergency management plan (most of them, including the Newton one, already do).

But Mr. Obama will need congressional backing for the main part of his plan: a proposal to renew an assault-weapons ban that went into effect in 1994 but expired ten years later. The ban would include, as it did back in 1994, a ban on

---

congressional *adj.* 国会的　　notoriously *adv.* 声名狼藉地　　assault-weapon *n.* 攻击性武器

high-capacity ammunition magazines, containing more than ten rounds. The trouble is that ban, especially the magazine part of it, proved impossible to enforce.

States, meanwhile, have jumped the gun. Andrew Cuomo, New York's governor and a gun-owner, signed the NY Safe Act on January 15th. ②<u>The state, which already had strong gun laws, has now banned military-style assault weapons, and has mandated universal background checks, including on buyers of ammunition.</u> Martin O'Malley, Maryland's governor, is about to introduce a sweeping gun-control package which echoes many of New York's measures. Colorado's governor has called for background checks for private gun sales, which are currently exempt. Deval Patrick, the governor of Massachusetts, wants to limit gun sales to one a month. Of course, one can do quite a lot of damage with one gun a month.

Cities, too, are taking a stand. Since the Newtown shooting, more than 100 more mayors have joined Mayors Against Illegal Guns, the 800-strong coalition founded by Michael Bloomberg, New York's mayor.

Welcome as these state and city actions are, without federal backup they are not much use. They may also be vulnerable to recision by the Supreme Court. Would-be killers need only cross state lines to places with weak gun laws to get access to weapons. Nor is it clear whether the president's plan would have prevented the Newtown massacre. There, the shooter did not have a background check; he used his mother's guns.

Mr. Obama faces steep opposition, and not just from congressional opponents: even his fellow Democrat, Harry Reid, the majority leader of the Senate, has indicated that the assault-weapons ban will be a hard sell. While states like New York and California are moving to strengthen gun laws, other

---

take a stand 表态　　recision *n.* 废除　　steep *adj.* 险峻的

states are doing the opposite. Lawmakers in Arizona and Texas, for instance, intend to introduce bills that would loosen gun restrictions. A Kentucky sheriff has said he will not enforce any new gun laws that he deems unconstitutional.

Most shockingly, gun sales have soared in recent weeks. In the month since the Newtown shooting 250,000 more people have joined the National Rifle Association, which has vowed to oppose the ban. The group is getting so cocky that it launched a free shooting app this week. For an extra 99 cents, players can use a MK-11 sniper rifle to shoot coffin-shaped targets.

(*The Economist*, 2013.1)

忙于加强枪支法令时,其他各州却背道而驰。如亚利桑那州和得克萨斯州的立法者正引入法案放宽枪支限制。一位肯塔基州的治安官表示,他将不会执行任何"违宪的"新枪支管制法律。

最令人震惊的是,枪支销售量在近几周扶摇直上。纽顿枪击事件之后的一个月内,已有超过25万人新加入了美国全国步枪协会。该协会立誓反对枪支禁令,甚至狂妄到在本周发布了一个免费的射击应用程序。玩家只要支付额外的99美分就能用MK11式狙击步枪射击棺材形状的靶子。

长难句解析

① 本句为主从复合句。句中定语从句1为非限制性定语从句,修饰先行词 Vice-President Joe Biden;定语从句2省略了连接词,修饰先行词 proposals。

On January 16th Mr. Obama, along with Vice-President Joe Biden, who headed the president's gun task-force, unveiled the most sweeping gun-control proposals Washington, DC has seen for two decades.

② 本句为主从复合句。句中包含 and 连接的两个谓语,其主语都是 The state。which 引导的非限制性定语从句修饰先行词 The state。

The state, which already had strong gun laws, has now banned military-style assault weapons, and has mandated universal background checks, including on buyers of ammunition.

---

cocky *adj.* 自大的   sniper rifle 狙击步枪   coffin-shaped *adj.* 棺材形状的

Text 10

U-Shaped Pandemic Jobs Crisis Hits Older and Younger Workers
年老和年轻的工作者被"U型疫情就业危机"袭击

Older workers suffered the biggest annual fall in employment since the 1980s after the pandemic led to a spike in redundancies, according to research by the Resolution Foundation.

The think tank said that the virus had created a "U-shaped crisis" with younger and older workers the worst affected.

The fall in employment among the over-50s was twice as big as that experienced by workers aged 25 to 49. "Becoming unemployed during the pandemic can potentially have a big impact on older workers' retirement plans," it said. "Either forcing them to retire earlier than they would have planned to, thereby reducing their income in retirement, or forcing them to work longer to make up for lost earnings."

It called on the government to provide retraining opportunities for older workers and to ensure that its support was tailored to their needs as well as to those of younger workers. This included support with job searches and greater rights to flexible working.

The report also noted that after losing work older workers took longer to return to employment. It found that six months after becoming unemployed nearly three quarters of 16 to 29-year-olds and 30 to 49-year-olds had returned to employment, compared with fewer than two thirds of those over 50.

根据决议基金会(the Resolution Foundation)的调查，这次疫情导致裁员人数急剧上涨，较年老的工作者的年度就业率出现了自20世纪80年代以来最大幅度的下降。

该智库说，新冠病毒已经造成了一场"U型危机"，即年轻和较年老的工作者受到的影响最严重。

50岁以上群体的就业下降率是25~49岁群体的两倍。"在这次疫情期间失业，可能会严重影响老年人的退休计划，"报告称，"要么迫使他们比原计划提前退休，由此减少他们的退休收入，要么迫使他们延长工作时间以弥补收入损失。"

该报告呼吁政府为年长工作者提供再培训机会，以及确保政府支持能够迎合年长和年轻工作者的需要，比如支持求职和让其拥有更多灵活工作的权利。

报告还指出，失业后，年长的工作者需要更长的时间才能重新就业。调查发现，失业半年后，16~29岁和30~49岁的群体已有四分之三重新就业，然而50岁以上的群体只有不到三分之二重新就业。

---

redundancy n. (因劳动力过剩而造成的)裁员，解雇
potentially adv. 潜在地；可能地
make up for 弥补；补偿
tailor vt. 专门制作
unemployed adj. 失业的；待业的；下岗的
thereby adv. 因此；由此
call on 要求；呼吁；号召
note vt. 指出；特别提到

① "Furthermore, when older workers return to work following a period of unemployment they face the highest income hit of all age groups, with typical hourly earnings falling by 9.5 percent, compared to their pre-unemployment earnings," the report said.

The jobs market has defied the broader downturn in the economy thanks to extensive government job support programmes. Although the economy contracted by almost 10 percent last year, the unemployment rate has barely edged above 5 per cent and is still close to record lows. The burden of job losses has not, however, been felt evenly. ② Younger groups have been the hardest hit, with employment in the 16 to 24-year-old category dropping by 3.9 percentage points as vacancies shrank and jobs in the hospitality and retail industries disappeared.

Workers aged 50 to 69 suffered a 1.4 percent decline, the biggest annual fall in employment in this age group since the 1980s, when the country was going through a painful period of deindustrialisation. The report said that 25 to 49 year olds had weathered the storm relatively well, registering a 0.7 percent drop in employment.

The new figures come after decades of extraordinary jobs growth for older workers. Men over 50 experienced only a relatively small drop in employment after the financial crisis and employment rates among women aged 50 to 64 rose from 46 per cent in 1990 to a record high of 68 per cent on the eve of the pandemic.

(*The Times*, 2021.4)

①报告称:"而且,当年长的员工失业一段时间重返工作岗位时,他们在所有年龄组中会面临最大的薪酬打击——一般的小时薪酬相比失业前下降了9.5%。"

多亏政府实施了广泛的就业支持计划,劳动力市场经受住了较大规模的经济衰退。尽管去年经济收缩了近10%,但失业率几乎没有高于5%,仍很接近历史低点。然而,失业压力并没有被平均分担。②年轻群体受到的冲击最大,因为职位空缺缩减,服务业和零售业的工作岗位甚至消失不见,16~24岁群体的就业率下降了3.9%。

50~69岁员工的就业率下降了1.4%,这是自20世纪80年代以来该年龄段面临的最大幅度的失业率,那时国家正经历着痛苦的去工业化时期。报告说,25~49岁的年轻人相对平安地渡过了这场风暴,他们的就业率下降了0.7%。

这些新数据是在较年长员工的就业岗位非同寻常地增长数十年后问世的。金融危机后,50岁以上男性就业率的下降幅度相对较小;1990年50~64岁女性的就业率为46%,本次疫情暴发前夕,这项数据已创历史新高,上升至68%。

---

defy *vt.* 经受住;顶住;抗住
contract *vi.* 收缩,缩小
edge *vi.* 略为增加(或减少)
vacancy *n.* (职位的)空缺;空职;空额
register *vt.* 显示(读数);记录

downturn *n.* (商业经济的)衰退,下降,衰退期
barely *adv.* 几乎不;几乎没有
evenly *adv.* 平均地;均等地
hospitality *n.* 服务;款待

长难句解析

①本句为"直接引语+主谓"结构。直接引语部分的主干是 they face the highest income hit，为主谓宾结构；when old workers... unemployment 为时间状语从句，with... by 9.5 percent 为 with 引导的独立主格结构作状语，compared to... 为比较状语。

"Furthermore, when older workers return to work following a period of unemployment they face the highest income hit of all age groups, with typical hourly earnings falling by 9.5 percent, compared to their pre-unemployment earnings," the report said.

②本句为主从复合句。主句的主干为 Younger groups have been the hardest hit；with... 3.9 percentage points 为独立主格结构作状语；as 引导原因状语从句。

Younger groups have been the hardest hit, with employment in the 16 to 24-year-old category dropping by 3.9 percentage points as vacancies shrank and jobs in the hospitality and retail industries disappeared.

Text 11 Are Hospitals Intentionally Hiding Prices?
医院在故意隐瞒价格吗？

In an unprecedented move, the Centers for Medicare & Medicaid Services recently proposed that hospitals must disclose their negotiated rates with insurers for certain services. ① The rule comes on the heels of a Trump administration executive order that proposes hospitals post their standard list of charges online and provide patients with estimates of their out-of-pocket costs prior to scheduling a procedure.

②Aside from the fact that no other service industry is required to reveal their contractual business negotiations—indeed, it is currently illegal for hospi-

美国医疗保险和医疗补助服务中心最近提出，医院必须向承保人公开其对特定服务的协商费率，该举动是前所未有的。①该规定是继特朗普政府的一项行政命令之后发布的，该命令建议医院在线公布其标准收费清单，并在安排手续之前向患者提供其自付费用的估算值。

②除了没有其他服务业被要求公开其合同商务谈判这一事实外——实际上，医院向其他医院披露

on the heels of 紧跟在后面；接踵而来；紧接着
out-of-pocket （需）现款支付的；不列入预算的

tals to disclose to other hospitals their negotiated rates with insurers—the requirement to give preservice cost estimates to patients is meant to give timely, practical insight into the cost of care.

So why haven't more hospitals provided this information to date? Given the above policy proposals, it would be easy to assume that hospitals deliberately complicate pricing in order to grossly inflate the cost of care. Yet if we take a moment to examine what is behind the heightened calls for price transparency, a different perspective comes into focus.

The reality is that for hospitals, communicating with patients about payment—especially up-front collections—is a relatively new development. Previously, payment discussions occurred mostly with the insurance companies who paid for the vast bulk of care. As such, hospitals designed most of their staff training and payment infrastructure around communicating directly with insurers about reimbursement.

In recent years, however, the cost burden has significantly shifted to patients through health plans with exorbitant deductibles and coinsurance. According to the Centers for Disease Control and Prevention, by 2017 about 43 percent of privately insured Americans under 65 were in high-deductible health plans.

Calls for more price transparency have escalated in parallel with the advent of these plans—along with warnings that the plans are having an adverse impact on both patient and hospital finances. In a survey of hospital leaders, a majority of respondents—59 percent—asserted that high-deductible, high-coinsurance plans are driving bad patient debt. As for collecting on this debt, 50 percent of respondents stated they expected to collect on less than 10 percent of it.

---

to date 至今;到现在为止
up-front *adj.* 预付的;在前面的
development *n.* 新事实;新情况
exorbitant *adj.* 过分的,离谱的,荒唐的
in parallel with 与……平行,与……同时,与……并联

grossly *adv.* 严重地;十足地
collection *n.* 收款,征收
reimbursement *n.* 赔偿;退款
deductible *n.* 免赔额

These aren't **unwarranted** concerns. A widely cited joint study by the Kaiser Family Foundation and the *New York Times* made this startling revelation: "62 percent of those who had medical bill problems say the bills were incurred by someone who had health coverage at the time (most often through an employer)." To **reiterate**, these people are struggling to pay medical bills despite being insured.

Not every hospital's response to this sharp change in reimbursement has been admirable. Some have reacted by going after recovering patients with aggressive litigation, while others likely have overpriced certain services to make up the difference. ③ But while it's hard to defend such tactics, it is equally difficult to predict what any of us would resort to if our main sources of income suddenly changed to a new, not very reliable source.

However, more hospitals than not strive to make payment assistance options available. And a growing number are catching up with the shift to patient-as-payer. These hospitals are retraining staff to have conversations with patients about their cost of care, while implementing systems and processes that facilitate patient payments prior to service, with options for payment assistance.

(*Scientific American*, 2019.9)

这些都不是无根据的担忧。凯撒家庭基金会和《纽约时报》开展的一项被人们广泛引用的联合研究得出了这一惊人的事实:"在有医疗账单问题的人中,有62%的人说这些账单是由当时有健康保险的人(通常是雇主)支付的。"重申一下,尽管这些人投保了,但仍在勉强支付医疗费用。

并非每家医院对赔偿金急剧变化的应对方式都值得赞扬。一些医院的回应是用激进的方式起诉病愈的患者,而另一些可能会抬高某些服务的价格以弥补差异。③虽然很难为这种策略辩护,但是,如果我们的主要收入来源突然变成不是非常可靠的新来源,届时我们会采取什么措施将同样难以预测。

但是,更多的医院在努力提供支付援助。而且越来越多的人正加入患者付款这一转变。这些医院正在对员工进行再培训,以便与患者沟通医疗费用,同时执行在服务前便于患者支付费用的系统和流程,并提供支付援助。

长难句解析

① 本句为主从复合句。主句的主谓结构为 The rule comes。介词短语 on the heels of...作状语;that 引导的是定语从句,修饰 a Trump administration executive order。

> The rule comes on the heels of a Trump administration executive order that proposes hospitals post their standard list of charges online and provide patients with estimates of their out-of-pocket costs prior to scheduling a procedure.
> 主语　谓语　　　　　状语　　　　　　　　　　　　　　　　　　　　
> 　　　　　　　　　　　　定语从句
> 　　　　　　　　　　　　　　　　状语

② 本句单独成段,句子很长。句子的主干部分为 the requirement is meant to give...。句首的介词短语作状语,短语中包含一个 that 引导的同位语从句;破折号中间为插入语,进一步解释说明句首的状语,该插入语中的 it 为形式主语,真正的主语是 to disclose to other...;

---

unwarranted *adj.* 没有根据的,无正当理由的　　　　reiterate *vt.* 重申

to give preservice cost…是主语 requirement 的后置定语；be meant to give 为复合谓语。

Aside from the fact that no other service industry is required to reveal their contractual business negotiations—indeed, it is currently illegal for hospitals to disclose to other hospitals their negotiated rates with insurers—the requirement to give preservice cost estimates to patients is meant to give timely, practical insight into the cost of care.

状语：Aside from the fact
同位语从句：that no other service industry is required to reveal their contractual business negotiations
插入语：it is currently illegal for hospitals to disclose to other hospitals their negotiated rates with insurers
主语：the requirement
后置定语：to give preservice cost estimates to patients
谓语：is meant to give
宾语：timely, practical insight into the cost of care

③ 本句为主从复合句。主句的主干为 it is equally difficult to…。while 引导的是让步状语从句；主句中的 it 为形式主语，真正的主语是动词不定式 to predict…；predict 后为 what 引导的宾语从句；if 引导的是条件状语从句。

But while it's hard to defend such tactics, it is equally difficult to predict what any of us would resort to if our main sources of income suddenly changed to a new, not very reliable source.

让步状语从句：while it's hard to defend such tactics
主系表：it is equally difficult
真正的主语：to predict
宾语从句：what any of us would resort to
条件状语从句：if our main sources of income suddenly changed to a new, not very reliable source

Text 12

Footage Showing a Farmworker Hammering Pigs to Death Provides Further Evidence of the Serious Failings in Britain's Animal Welfare System

镜头中农夫捶打猪仔致死：进一步证明英国动物福利系统正在严重衰败

Britain prides itself on being a nation of animal lovers. Pubs take their names from every creature under the sun. Meerkats sell us car insurance. Every morning, the prime minister is photographed running in the park with his dog. Britons spend fortunes feeding, grooming and treating their pets. In 2019 animal welfare charities received 26 percent of all charitable donations, more than any other cause. So why then do we still treat farm

英国一直以"自己是热爱动物的国度"为傲。英国的酒吧用全世界的动物命名。海猫公司卖给我们汽车保险。首相每天早晨都被拍到和他的爱犬在公园里跑步。英国人斥巨资喂养、打扮和照顾宠物。2019年，动物福利慈善机构收到的捐款占所有慈善捐款的26%，超过其他任何慈善捐款。那么，为什么我们仍要如此

---

meerkat *n.* 海猫
groom *vt.* (给动物) 梳毛，刷洗

fortune *n.* 大笔的钱；巨款

animals with such cruelty?

①We report today that a farmer has resigned as chairman of the pigs standard setting committee of Quality Meat Scotland (QMS) after undercover footage allegedly shot at his farm in Aberdeenshire purported to show a worker hammering pigs to death. Sadly, reports like this are all too frequent. Earlier this month, another undercover investigation found calves at a dairy farm in Shrewsbury being beaten and deprived of water.

Nor are reports such as these an aberration, reflecting the rogue actions of a handful of barbarous farmhands, transgressing within an otherwise humane and justifiable system. Britain is fond of trumpeting its own animal welfare standards, and it is true that the UK has historically led the way in promoting animal rights. But for some years now those standards have been slipping.

Moreover Britain is now rapidly falling behind its European counterparts on animal welfare standards, despite claims that Brexit would allow Britain to strengthen its rules. ② Farrowing crates, which hold pregnant sows for the whole 16 weeks of their pregnancy and prevent them from moving or even turning around, are still legal despite having been banned in Sweden and Germany, the largest pork producer in Europe.

Worse, it is clear that the bodies responsible for ensuring livestock are looked after correctly are not doing their jobs properly. Nearly always it is welfare charities and local activists who uncover acts of

①我们今天报道的是，一位农场主辞去了苏格兰优质猪肉（QMS）标准制定委员会的主席一职。此前据说在他的阿伯丁郡农场拍摄的秘密录像显示，他的一名员工捶打猪仔致死。可悲的是，这样的报道层出不穷。本月早些时候，另一项秘密调查发现，什鲁斯伯里郡一家奶牛场的小牛犊遭到殴打，小牛还被禁水。

类似这样的报道也不是偶发事件，这反映了少数残忍农场工人的暴戾行径，另外也违反了人道和正当的制度。英国喜欢宣扬自己的动物福利标准，确实，从历史角度来说，英国在促进动物权利方面处于领先地位。但最近几年来，这些标准一直在下滑。

而且，目前英国在动物福利标准方面正迅速落后于欧洲其他国家，尽管有人声称脱欧可能使英国加强相关管理。②产仔箱可容纳孕期母猪整整16周，并防止母猪移动甚至转身。欧洲最大的猪肉生产国瑞典和德国已经禁止使用产仔箱，但这在英国仍然是合法的。

更糟糕的是，负责确保牲畜得到正确照料的机构显然没有做好本职工作。揭发这些残忍行为的几乎都是福利慈善机构和当地的积极分子，

---

resign *vi.* 辞职；辞去（某职务）
undercover *adj.* 秘密工作的；暗中做的；私下进行的
allegedly *adv.* 据说，声称　　　　　　　purport *vt.* 自称；标榜；声称
aberration *n.* 偶发事件；非典型行为　　　rogue *adj.* 行为失常的；暴戾的
barbarous *adj.* 残酷的；骇人听闻的　　　transgress *vi.* 违背道德（或行为）准则
justifiable *adj.* 有理由的；可证明是正当的　　trumpet *vt.* 宣扬；鼓吹；吹嘘
slip *vi.* 下降；退步；变差
counterpart *n.* 职位（或作用）相当的人；对应的事物
strengthen *vt.* 加强；增强；巩固
crate *n.* 板条箱，大木箱　　　farrow *vt.* 产（小猪）
　　　　　　　　　　　　　　sow *n.* 母猪　　　uncover *vt.* 发现；揭露

cruelty, rather than bodies such as QMS in Scotland or Red Tractor in England, who are supposed to be responsible for monitoring standards. *The Times* has previously found that only one in 1,000 farms certified by Red Tractor received unannounced inspections in 2018.

Clearly Britain's system of animal husbandry is in urgent need of reform. Emotion in animals remains a topic of debate among scientists. Nevertheless, our understanding has advanced a long way from previous centuries when animals were seen as little more than unfeeling machines.

Meanwhile, the western world is at a turning point where it is rethinking its relationship with the animal kingdom, most notably seen in the rise of veganism. What may have been acceptable in the past, the public will no longer tolerate today.

Boris Johnson has frequently pledged to improve animal welfare, yet so far no action has been taken. That needs to change. Ministers need to strengthen the existing rules and ensure that they are properly enforced. Farmers will of course worry about the cost but they should have little to fear from high standards. Consumers too should be prepared to pay more. Britons spend an average of just 8 percent of their total expenditure on food, less than any other country in the world except the US and Singapore. This country professes a great fondness for animals. It's time to show it.

(*The Times*, 2021.4)

而不是像苏格兰的质量管理体系或英格兰的红拖拉机这样负责监管标准的机构。《泰晤士报》之前发现，在2018年，每1 000个获得红拖拉机认证的农场中，只有一个接受了突击检查。

显然，英国的畜牧业体系急需改革。科学家们仍然在争论动物的情感这一话题。尽管如此，相比于前几个世纪，我们的理解已经进步很多了，那时动物只被看作是无情的机器。

在此期间，西方世界正处在一个转折点，它正在重新思考与动物王国的关系，最显著的是素食主义的兴起。过去可能被接受的事情，公众现如今不会再容忍。

鲍里斯·约翰逊经常承诺要改善动物福利，但迄今为止仍未采取任何行动。这需要做出改变。部长们需要加强现有规则，并确保能够真正执行这些规则。当然，农民将会担心成本，但他们应该不会担心高标准。消费者也应该做好消费上涨的准备。英国人的食品支出平均占总支出的8%，仅高于美国和新加坡。英国声称非常喜爱动物，是时候展示一下了。

长难句解析

①本句为主从复合句。主句的主干是 We report that…，为主谓宾结构，宾语为 that 引导的宾语从句；宾语从句的主干是 a farmer has resigned, of the pigs… Quality Meat Scotland (QMS) 作后置定语修饰 chairman；after undercover… death 为时间状语从句，该从句的主干为 undercover footage purported to show…，为主谓宾结构，allegedly shot… Aberdeenshire 为

---

certify *vt.* 证实；保证
inspection *n.* 检查；查看；审视
advance *vi.* 发展；进步
acceptable *adj.* 可接受的；认可的
enforce *vt.* 强制执行，强行实施（法律或规定）

unannounced *adj.* 未通知的；未打招呼的
husbandry *n.*（尤指精心经营的）农牧业
veganism *n.* 素食主义
pledge *vt.* 保证；正式承诺

过去分词短语作后置定语修饰 footage。

We report today that a farmer has resigned as chairman of the pigs standard setting committee of Quality Meat Scotland (QMS) after undercover footage allegedly shot at his farm in Aberdeenshire purported to show a worker hammering pigs to death.

② 本句为主从复合句。句子的主干是 Farrowing crates... are still legal，为主系表结构；which 引导一个非限制性定语从句修饰 crates，从句中 and 连接两个动词短语；despite having been... 为介词短语作让步状语，the largest pork producer in Europe 为 Sweden and Germany 的同位语。

Farrowing crates, which hold pregnant sows for the whole 16 weeks of their pregnancy and prevent them from moving or even turning around, are still legal despite having been banned in Sweden and Germany, the largest pork producer in Europe.

Text 13 Are We Losing the Art of Telephone Conversation?
我们正在失去电话交谈的艺术吗？

Statistics illustrating our addiction to our smartphones come out quite frequently and receive a lot of attention for information so unsurprising; it will come as no shock to anyone that the average Briton checks her phone every 12 minutes. Indeed, I'd like to pick a fight with the blandness of the questions asked in Ofcom's latest telecommunications report. I wish they'd included: "Have you ever picked up your phone to Google where your phone is?" Or: "Have you ever smashed or otherwise been suddenly deprived of your phone, and wanted to stand

显示我们沉迷于智能手机的数据层出不穷，并且这些数据也得到了大量的关注，这并不让人意外；英国人平均每12分钟会查看一下手机，这不会让任何人感到震惊。事实上，我想挑衅 Ofcom 最新的电话交流报告中乏味的问题。我希望这些问题包括："你是否曾经用谷歌搜索你的手机？"或"你的手机是否曾经被摔碎或突然被抢，而你想站在街上像狼一样哀嚎？"

---

pick a fight with 挑衅　　　　blandness n. 平淡无奇　　　　smash vt. 粉碎

in the street howling like a wolf?"

The report belongs in the news category "things we already knew, but are worried about, so will continue to pick at like a scab." Yet there is one new element to our behaviour: we've stopped using telephones for talking to one another. The number of calls made dropped for the first time in 2017. It's not a huge drop—1.7%—and the figure may be misleading since calls made on WhatsApp and Facebook weren't counted. Three-quarters of people still believe that voice calls are important. But that's not as many—92%—as the number who value their phones mainly for internet access.

Etiquette is underdeveloped in the world of the smartphone: there are people to whom sending six questions in six separate texts is itself rude and you will call instead to solve the whole lot in a conversation; there are other people to whom this is horrible manners, since you should always stick to the medium via which you were contacted, unless explicitly invited to move to a different one. This tribalism has to be resolved, so we all know where we are. I once swapped media and personnel, replying to an email I had from one half of a couple with a phone call to the other. This was agreed to be the rudest thing that had ever happened.

It is commonly assumed that extroverts like phone calls and introverts like texting, but this isn't necessarily the case: introverts tend to develop techniques for phone calls—a special voice, pacing about—which act like armour and allow all the communicative benefits of conversation without actually having to meet. Extroverts often prefer a face-to-face because they find it energising. There are people who genuinely love talking for hours over the phone—siblings, my plumber —but the true chat

---

howl *vi.* 咆哮
misleading *adj.* 令人误解的
swap *vt.* 交换
armour *n.* 盔甲
pick at 触及(问题)的表面
etiquette *n.* 礼节
extrovert *n.* 性格外向者
plumber *n.* 水管工
scab *n.* 痂
tribalism *n.* 部落文化
introvert *n.* 性格内向的人

constituency was always adolescents, trying to escape their families by diving into the company of the intimates they'd chosen.

Digital natives probably wouldn't understand a phone call of the olden days; meandering, one-on-one, hours long. The classic familial row of the 1980s—how much it had just cost for you to talk about nothing to a person you'd spent all day at school with—would be completely alien, with phone calls almost free and conversations seeming curiously thin unless there are six people in them. The slightly older native, say a millennial, seems a bit chary of the voice call: they text in advance to schedule them, or if they ring unannounced, start by apologising. The phonee in this scenario (as in, the person receiving the call; not the phoney) is the person whose liberty has been encroached upon.

①Contrast that with the older phone user, the over-65, who will run to pick up a call regardless of what they're doing, as if whatever random person who has got in touch them is automatically more important than whoever's in front of them, by dint of … well, who knows what this dint is? Nobody understands it. Perhaps one of them would like to explain.

It is always easier to have a tricky conversation by text or email, or you think it is: what you've forgotten is how quickly, once discord has been established, it will escalate when using the written word. ②It is far more difficult to be a jerk in person, even from a distance, which is why phone calls can seem harder but are in fact easier.

(*The Guardian*, 2018.8)

---

dive into 投入
one-on-one *adj.* 一对一的
scenario *n.* 方案
by dint of 凭借
jerk *n.* 傻瓜，笨蛋

digital native 数字原住民
familial *adj.* 家族的
phoney *n.* 骗子
dint *n.* 作为……的结果，凭借
distance *n.* 疏远

meander *vi.* 漫步
chary *adj.* 谨慎的
encroach *vi.* 蚕食

长难句解析

① 主句的主干结构为一个无主语的祈使句，即 Contrast that with the older phone user, the over-65 作同位语, who 引导的定语从句修饰这个同位语, 其中包含一个 regardless of 引导的让步状语从句; as if 引导方式状语从句, 其中包含一个 who 引导的定语从句修饰 whatever random person; 同时 than 又引导了比较状语从句。

> Contrast that with the older phone user, the over-65, who will run to pick up a call
> 谓语 宾语   状语   同位语   定语从句
> regardless of what they're doing, as if whatever random person who has got in touch
>   让步状语从句   方式状语从句   定语从句
> them is automatically more important than whoever's in front of them.
>   比较状语从句

② 本句中 It 为形式主语, 真正的主语是后面的 to be a jerk in person; which 引导非限制性定语从句修饰整个主句, 其中还包含了 why 引导的表语从句。

> It   is   far more difficult to be a jerk in person, even from a distance, which
> 形式主语 系动词   表语   真正的主语   状语
>   is   why phone calls can seem harder but are in fact easier.
> 非限制性定语从句   表语从句

Text 14 Car Trips Are Bad Trips 开车旅行是糟糕的经历

Henry Ford's instrument of democratic liberation has become an oppressive tyrant, imprisoning us.

As a child, my perceptions were formed in the back of a car. The world was viewed through Triplex toughened glass at 35mph. Notions of luxury and wellbeing were permanently influenced by the slippery leather chairs of a Humber or the curious ultraviolet light illuminating a Jaguar's walnut-veneered dashboard. Here I was psychologically secure, my regular companions a bag of

亨利·福特的民主解放工具已经成为一个压迫的暴君, 一直在囚禁着我们。

孩童时, 我的世界观就是在车后座形成的。在35英里时速的车上, 隔着三层钢化玻璃, 我就是这样感知着这个世界的。亨伯汽车内光滑的皮质座椅, 捷豹核桃木面板仪表盘上闪耀的令人好奇的紫外线光, 这些都永久性地影响了我们对奢侈品和幸福的理解。当我们优雅地驶入过去曾是乡野的地方, 往

---

slippery *adj.* 滑的
walnut-veneered *adj.* 核桃木的

ultraviolet *adj.* 紫外线的
dashboard *n.* 仪表板

crisps and a Penguin book as we motored stylishly into the "country", wherever that used to be.

I come from the last generation to know the extraordinary institution of a recreational drive. My father, nattily dressed and mustachioed, would on certain fine days suggest an outing in the car that had no purpose other than to be an outing in the car, such was the pleasure involved for all participants. There was no destination, just a circular journey: a notion as deliciously paradoxical and absurdist as a play by Samuel Beckett. And just as historic.

The psychological aspects of driving today are altogether less comforting, as a new survey of 2,000 motorists commissioned by Shell makes clear. One-third of drivers never drive for pleasure, and the rest do so only occasionally. Suffocating legislation and predatory local authorities threaten to criminalise even the saintliest individual suddenly possessed by the anti-social chutzpah required to drive a car. The only rational response to confiscatory tickets and invasive speed cameras is either intense spasmodic psychomotor agitation or harrowing paranoia.

The only rational response to traffic conditions is hysteria. ①Last night I met a successful businesswoman (my wife) who had been moved to hopeless tears of frustration by the barbaric tussle of driving a mere three miles in central London: a grim cast of purple-faced and cruelly determined black-cab drivers, psychotic rubble-trucks, crawling buses, lost souls and no respite from the Inferno because there is never, ever, anywhere to park. There are days, I suspect coming soon, when it will actually not be possible to complete a simple

---

nattily *adv.* 整洁地 mustachioed *adj.* 有大鬈曲八字胡的
suffocating *adj.* 令人窒息的 criminalise *vt.* 使非法
saintly *adj.* 圣洁的 chutzpah *n.* 胆识
confiscatory *adj.* 没收的 spasmodic *adj.* 一阵阵的
psychomotor agitation 神经运动性激动 harrowing *adj.* 悲惨的
paranoia *n.* (心理)偏执狂 tussle *n.* 争斗
grim *adj.* 冷漠的   psychotic *adj.* 精神病的   Inferno *n.* 地狱

car journey.

As a result, my children regard cars as unneces-sary and expensive encumbrances, not the status symbol or romantic attribute they remain for me. Recent U.S. research showed that very few people under 30 considered any automobile manufacturer a "cool" brand. ②And those who owned cars would much prefer to keep their smartphone, if required to make a competitive choice between wheeled transport and the electronic type of connectedness.

But there is poetry as well as pain here. Henry Ford created his gasoline buggy to escape from the deadening tedium of life on a midwest farm. Against all the contrary evidence, cars retain this magical potential to transport the spirit as well as the body. Harley Earl, Detroit's coruscating wizard of kitsch with his repertoire of chrome and pleated Naugahyde, rightly understood that even the meanest car journey should have the intoxicating suggestion of an exotic vacation. It is curious to consider how an instrument of democratic liberation has become an oppressive tyrant, imprisoning us.

Roads too have lost their glamour. Movies and rock music glorified some of the world's great roads: Route 66, the Grande Corniche and the Pacific coast highway are part of our collective dreamscape. The delightful journey deluded fiction of roads as romance. It is difficult, surely, to experience anything other than terrible bathos on the M25 or the East Lancashire Road.

So why do people still drive? One answer is

---

encumbrance *n.* 累赘
buggy *n.* 双轮单座轻马车
coruscating *adj.* 闪光的
kitsch *n.* 迎合低级趣味的作品
chrome *n.* 铬
Naugahyde *n.* 瑙加海德革(乙烯基树脂表层的织物)
exotic *adj.* 异国情调的

connectedness *n.* 连通性
tedium *n.* 单调乏味
wizard *n.* 奇才
repertoire *n.* (某个领域的)所有组成部分
pleated *adj.* 起褶的
glamour *n.* 美丽

that using a car is, literally, enjoying intercourse with a machine, thus allowing the driver total engagement with high-modernist wish-fulfilment, even on a modest journey to the superstore. Then there is the design aspect. For many people, possession of a brand-new car provides, no matter how briefly, access to perfection that is unique in a troubled world. Or put it this way: the meanest Korean hatchback has an interior finer than the majority of homes (with better ventilation and sound).

When I first went to New York, in the 1970s, I found myself at a swanky party at which the hostess took me aside to point out some other more distinguished guests. "There's a Pulitzer prize-winning novelist! He's a judge! That woman's on the board of MoMA!" And then she asked darkly: "Do you know what they are all thinking about?" I confessed I did not. She said: "Parking." A generation later we have caught up with Manhattan's pioneering motoring anxieties. To adapt the demotic of that age: a road trip has become a bad trip. Cars, Roland Barthes said, are our cathedrals. Best, perhaps, to enjoy your cathedral when it's parked.

(*The Guardian*, 2014.6)

长难句解析

① 本句为复合句。主句的主干为 I met a businesswoman。括号里的 my wife 为 a successful businesswoman 的同位语；who 引导的定语从句修饰先行词 businesswoman；冒号后的内容为同位语，解释说明 frustration；because 引导原因状语从句。

Last night I met a successful businesswoman (my wife) who had been moved to
时间状语 主语 谓语 宾语 同位语 定语从句
hopeless tears of frustration by the barbaric tussle of driving a mere three miles in central
London: a grim cast of purple-faced and cruelly determined black-cab drivers, psychotic
　　　　　　　　　　　　　　　　　同位语
rubble-trucks, crawling buses, lost souls and no respite from the Inferno because there is
　　　　　　　　　　　　　　　　　　　　　　　　　　　　　　　　　　　　　　原因状语从句
never, ever, anywhere to park.

---

hatchback *n.* 有仓门式后背的汽车　　　　swanky *adj.* 时髦且豪华的
cathedral *n.* 教堂

② 本句为主从复合句。主句的主干结构为 those would prefer to…。句中 who 引导的定语从句修饰 those；if 引导的条件状语从句承前省略了主语和系动词，完整结构应为 if they are required…。

And those who owned cars would much prefer to keep their smartphone, if required to make a competitive choice between wheeled transport and the electronic type of connectedness.
- 主语 | 定语从句 | 谓语 | 宾语
- 条件状语从句

Text 15 The Guardian View on the Future of Work: Share Out the Benefits
《卫报》对工作前景的看法：利益分享

California is one of the few economies large enough to set the rules in a globalised world. The state's initiatives on car safety and emissions have in the past set an example that was followed by car manufacturers everywhere. ① In a less beneficial way, California was also the birthplace of the gig economy and the widespread use of webs of casual labour tied together by algorithms to subvert labour laws and other regulations in all sorts of fields, ranging from taxi firms to B&Bs. So it's an important development that the state's senate has now turned decisively against the exploitation of casual workers. This week it passed a law that would reclassify many of the so-called independent contractors who work in the gig economy as employees, entitled to a minimum wage, paid parental leave and unemployment insurance.

The ride-sharing companies Uber and Lyft have reacted with a mixture of defiance and obfuscation, which makes it clear just how central it is to their business model to deny workers these benefits. ② Both claim they are happy to give their workers benefits, so that the law is not really needed,

加利福尼亚州是少数几个足以在全球化世界中制定规则的经济体之一。过去，该州的汽车安全和排放倡议树立了一个榜样，引得各地汽车制造商纷纷效仿。①就算以一种不太有利的方式，加利福尼亚州也是零工经济的发源地，其最先广泛使用由算法连接的临时工网络，来推翻从出租车公司到带早餐的旅馆等各种领域的劳动法和其他法规。因此，该州参议院目前坚决地反对剥削临时工，这是一个重要的发展。本周，它通过了一项法律，该法律会将许多所谓的独立承包商重新分类，这些承包商在零工经济领域工作，有权享有最低工资、带薪育儿假和失业保险。

乘车共享公司优步(Uber)和来福车(Lyft)的反应中有反对也有困惑，这清楚地说明了在他们的商业模式中，剥夺工人这些福利有多重要。②他们都声称很乐意给予他们的工人福利，因此法律并不是必须

---

gig economy 零工经济　　　　　　　　　casual labour 临时工；散工
subvert vt. 推翻；颠覆；破坏　　　　　　entitle vt. 使……有权利
defiance n. 反抗；蔑视；挑战　　　　　　obfuscation n. 困惑；昏迷

but that it is at the same time a terrible threat to their businesses—neither of which has ever made a profit, despite their astronomical valuations. Uber has said the law will have no effect on it when it comes into operation. The two companies, along with a food delivery business, have also pledged $90m towards a referendum campaign aimed at repealing the measure. This has the potential to be one of those struggles that determines how and for whose benefit the third industrial revolution will continue.

The economist Roger Bootle has just published a book in which he predicts, as many have done before him, that the rise of artificial intelligence technologies will lead to the creation of new jobs to replace some of those which it will undoubtedly destroy, and that these jobs will be better, or less time consuming, than those we have at present. This is not entirely impossible. There is no call for absolute pessimism. But the rise of the gig economy companies shows that the future of work that economists and others have worried about has already arrived, and it is not what the optimists promised.

We were promised that robots would take away much of the drudge work in which people are presently employed, and that artificial intelligence would solve problems that mere humans cannot. Yet there are many problems that AI cannot even simulate understanding, and many things that robots cannot manipulate with the subtlety and dexterity of human fingers. Although some futurists talk about the possibilities of embedding silicon chips into human bodies to enhance their capabilities, what has actually happened is almost the opposite.

The Californian laws—and similar attempts to rein in the gig economy companies in this country—show that none of these developments were inevitable. And none are irresistible, either. It is half true that these companies are, as their

---

astronomical *adj.* 庞大的；天文的
repeal *vt.* 废除；撤销
dexterity *n.* 灵巧；敏捷；机敏

referendum *n.* 公民投票权；外交官请示书
drudge *n.* 苦工；做繁重无聊工作的人；繁重的劳动
embed *vt.* 使嵌入，使插入；栽种；使深留脑中

boosters boast, disruptive, but they also reinforce age-old tendencies towards exploitation and inequality. It is up to us as citizens and legislators to disrupt this great disruption and make it work for everyone.

(*The Guardian*, 2019.9)

破坏性,但它们也加强了由来已久的剥削和不平等趋势,这种说法只对了一半。作为公民和立法者,我们需要终止这种巨大的破坏并使其造福于每个人。

长难句解析

① 本句主干为 California was also the birthplace。of the gig economy 和 the widespread use 作 birthplace 的定语; of webs of... by algorithms 为 widespread use 的后置定语; to subvert labour laws and other regulations 为目的状语; in all sorts of fields...为状语。

In a less beneficial way, California was also the birthplace of the gig economy,
方式状语　　　　　　　主语　系动词　　表语　　后置定语1
and the widespread use of webs of casual labour tied together by algorithms to subvert
　　　后置定语2　　　　　　　后置定语3
labour laws and other regulations in all sorts of fields, ranging from taxi firms to B&Bs.
　　目的状语　　　　　　　　　　　　状语

② 本句为主从复合句,主句的主干为 Both claim they are...。they are happy to...为省略了引导词 that 的宾语从句; so that...为结果状语从句; but 后面为 that 引导的宾语从句,作 claim 的宾语;破折号后面是 which 引导的非限制性定语从句,修饰主语 both。

Both claim they are happy to give their workers benefits, so that the law is not really
主语 谓语　　　　宾语从句1　　　　　　　　　结果状语从句
needed, but that it is at the same time a terrible threat to their businesses—neither of
　　　　　　　　　宾语从句2
which has ever made a profit, despite their astronomical valuations.
　非限制性定语从句　　　　　　　状语

Text 16　Employers Can't Retrain the U.S. Workforce by Themselves
雇主不能单独完成对美国劳动力的再培训

Regardless of industry, today's workers are bound by a common anxiety: their jobs will one day be performed by robots. While the threat is more

无论哪个行业,如今的劳动者都为同一件事而焦虑:他们的工作有一天将由机器人来完成。虽然某些人

---

booster *n.* 支持者　　　　　　　　　　　disruptive *adj.* 破坏的;破坏性的
reinforce *vt.* 加强,加固;强化

imminent for some than for others, nearly everyone will need new skills in order to succeed. Businesses should help workers prepare for the challenges posed by automation—but they can't shoulder the task on their own.

In the U.S., more than 7 million job openings remain unfilled. A shortage of workers is to be expected in a tight labor market, but that's only part of the explanation. More than one in five employers say applicants lack skills necessary for the jobs on offer—not just competency in digital technologies, but also soft skills like communication and problem-solving.

As more workplace tasks become automated, this deficit threatens to leave millions of less-educated workers behind. According to a McKinsey report, low and middle-wage workers are at greatest risk of seeing their jobs become obsolete by 2030. Nearly two-thirds of the U.S. labor force will require additional training just to hold on to the jobs they currently have. High-wage jobs are expected to grow as a share of overall employment, but the country's education system isn't producing candidates with the skills required.

Last month, Amazon.com Inc. announced a $700 million investment to help workers learn new skills and advance their careers. The "Upskilling 2025" program is better than nothing, but still only a limited response to the problem. The company plans to create a software-engineering school to teach non-technical workers how to code. Warehouse staffers will receive paid time to study for credentials to work as IT support technicians. Amazon has also pledged to cover 95% of tuition costs for employees who pursue certificates and degrees in occupations outside of Amazon's core businesses, such as aircraft mechanics, web design and nursing. Spread over six years, however, the company's planned spending per worker each year will still be lower than the current national average.

To upgrade the skills of Americans at greatest

---

imminent *adj.* 迫近的;即将来临的
opening *n.* (职位的) 空缺
hold on to 保住;守住
shoulder *vt.* 负起责任;担任工作
obsolete *adj.* 过时的;淘汰的
credential *n.* 资格证明书

risk from automation, a more comprehensive approach is required—one that's backed by government. To start, states and the federal government should boost tax credits to encourage small and medium-sized businesses to invest more in retraining low-skilled workers. ① States should bolster workforce development boards that help community colleges and technical schools customize course offerings to meet the needs of local industries.

The government should also do more to promote apprenticeships, which allow workers, including mid-career professionals, to earn a salary while they learn new trades. ②The Trump administration has approved modest increases in federal grants to apprenticeship programs, but the U.S.'s investment remains paltry compared to that of countries, like Germany, with well-developed apprenticeship systems.

Workers themselves need to embrace the idea of retraining as a lifelong endeavor. Policy makers can assist by making short-term certificate programs eligible for federal student aid, as the bipartisan JII Act aims to do. Subsidized individual training accounts, like those offered by Singapore's government, would encourage more adult learners to complete unfinished degrees or seek additional credentials. And Congress should revive the previous administration's proposal to extend wage insurance to displaced workers who take new jobs at lower salaries. That would give middle-class workers the financial cushion to pursue more education while continuing to work.

Creating an educational and training system suited for the future of work will require government, educational institutions and industry leaders to collaborate. Success is possible, but it won't come cheap. There are some things big business—even Amazon—can't deliver.

(*Bloomberg*, 2019.8)

---

tax credit 税收抵免
customize *vt.* 定制,定做
paltry *adj.* 微不足道的;无价值的
displaced *adj.* 被免职的;被解雇的
deliver *vi.* 履行;实现

bolster *vt.* 支持,鼓励(某人)
apprenticeship *n.* 学徒身份,学徒资格
embrace *vt.* 欣然接受提议;利用机会
cushion *n.* 起缓冲作用的事物;减轻不利作用的事物

长难句解析

① 本句为主从复合句。主句的主干为 States should bolster workforce development boards。that 引导定语从句修饰主句的宾语,不定式作目的状语,修饰主句。

States should bolster workforce development boards that help community colleges
主语　　谓语　　　　　宾语　　　　　　　　　　　定语从句
and technical schools customize course offerings　to meet the needs of local industries.
　　　　　　　　　　　　　　　　　　　　　　　　　　目的状语

② 本句是由转折连词 but 连接的两个并列句构成。分句 1 的主干为 The Trump administration has approved modest increases。in federal grants 作后置定语修饰 modest increases;to apprenticeship programs 为后置定语修饰 federal grants。分句 2 的主干为 the U.S.'s investment remains paltry。compared to that of countries…作状语,其中 that 指代的是 investment;like Germany 为插入语,表示举例说明;with 介词短语为 countries 的后置定语。

The Trump administration　has approved　modest increases　in federal grants　to
　　　主语 1　　　　　　　　　谓语　　　　　　宾语　　　　　　后置定语 1
apprenticeship programs, but　the U.S.'s investment　remains　paltry　compared to
　　　后置定语 2　　　　　　　　　　主语 2　　　　　系动词　表语　　状语
that of countries,　like Germany,　with well-developed apprenticeship systems.
　　　　　　　　　　　插入语　　　　　　　　后置定语 3

Text 17　Men Who Advocate for Others in the Workplace Face Backlash
在工作场合为他人辩护的男性会遭到反对

Back in March, a group of Hollywood elites signed an open letter asking men to take more responsibility for creating workplaces that are free of sexism. ①The letter was in response to the #MeToo movement that spurred people across the world to use social media to bring attention to the prevalence of sexual harassment and abuse. The letter signers pledged to act as advocates for victims and to speak out openly against sexism, thereby launching #AskMoreofHim, a movement that highlights the role that men play in preventing gender-based violence.

早在今年三月,一群好莱坞精英就签署了一封公开信,要求男性担负起更多责任,来创造没有性别歧视的办公环境。①这封信是在回应#MeToo运动,该运动激励世界各地的人们使用社交媒体来关注性骚扰和性虐待这一普遍现象。公开信的签名者承诺将作为受害者的拥护者公开反对性别歧视,从而发起了一场#AskMoreofHim运动,该运动强调了男性在防止基于性别的暴力行为中所扮演的角色。

---

elite n. 精英　　　　sexism n. 性别歧视　　　spur vt. 激励　　　　prevalence n. 普遍
harassment n. 骚扰　　abuse n. 虐待　　　　　pledge to 许诺　　　advocate n. 拥护者

It seems reasonable to assume that men, especially those occupying positions of power, are in a unique position to act as advocates and allies for victims of sexism and sexual abuse. However, recent research suggests that men may face a backlash for speaking out on behalf of others. Janine Bosak at Dublin City University and three of her colleagues published a study suggesting that men who take on an advocacy role in the workplace may suffer penalties for going against how we typically expect men to behave. ②While the study did not look at men who speak out against sexism per se, it strongly suggests that men who advocate for others in general may be seen as less competent.

Common stereotypes about men hold that they show ambition at work and focus most of their energy on promoting themselves and their own accomplishments. In contrast, stereotypes about women involve emphasizing other people's feelings and welfare above their own. Social scientists have shown that people who act contrary to these stereotypes tend to elicit "backlash" from both men and women. This backlash may take the form of being seen as less likeable, less competent, and less suitable for certain jobs.

The researchers recruited 149 working professionals to participate in an online study that was ostensibly about "perceptions and decision-making." The participants were evenly divided by gender and although they held a variety of jobs, the majority worked in human resources. Each participant was presented with written application materials from either a man or woman job candidate. The candidate was described as someone who either tends to advocate primarily for themselves or for their team.

After reviewing the application materials, participants filled out a survey asking them about their impressions of the candidate. Specifically, they rated the candidate's likability, competence, and how

---

backlash n. 反对　　　penalty n. 惩罚　　　per se adv. 本身　　　elicit vt. 引起
likeable adj. 讨人喜欢的　　　　　ostensibly adv. 表面上　　　perception n. 感知

much they would recommend that the person be let go if the company were to downsize. Overall, the findings supported the idea that men who advocated for others were seen less positively. Both men and women rated the other-advocating man as less competent, and they were more likely to recommend that he be laid off in the event of downsizing. Participants also liked the other-advocating man less than they liked the other-advocating woman.

Surprisingly, participants in the study did not display the same kind of backlash towards the woman applicant who was described as being highly self-advocating. Previous research has demonstrated that people penalize women who behave in highly self-promoting ways, however, this study did not find that to be true. The researchers offer two possibilities for this unexpected finding: previous studies had participants watch videos of job candidates which may elicit stronger reactions than just reading written materials; and, many of the study participants were trained human resource professionals who may have been more attuned to biases against women.

Backlash against atypical men poses a serious dilemma for those who believe that men are vital to helping battle workplace inequality. We know that men, and in particular White men, are more likely to hold leadership positions in a variety of industries. Movements like #Askmoreofhim rest on the assumption that men will be motivated to advocate for others if they are sufficiently convinced to do so. However, the present research suggests that men may shy away from advocacy in order to avoid being perceived negatively by others. Although we may laud the integrity or compassion of men who speak out on others' behalf, we may simultaneously question their competence compared to men who do not advocate for others. Therefore, when it comes to fighting sexism and gender-based

---

downsize *vi.* 裁员
atypical *adj.* 非典型的；不合规则的
simultaneously *adv.* 同时地
penalize *vt.* 处罚
shy away from 避免
attuned *adj.* 适应的
laud *vt.* 赞扬

violence, we might want to start by examining how our own stereotypes may be contributing to the problem. By loosening up our expectations for people of all genders, we can help ensure that people feel free to act in ways that promote equality in the workplace for all.

(*Scientific American*, 2018.8)

下我们自己的传统观念是如何促成这一问题的。通过放松对人们的期望不论其性别，我们可以帮助确保人们能够自由地采取行动，为所有人促进职场平等。

长难句解析

① 本句为主从复合句。主句的主干结构为 The letter was in response to the #MeToo movement。that 引导定语从句修饰#MeToo movement。

The letter	was	in response to the	#MeToo movement	that spurred people across the world
主语	系动词	表语		定语从句

to use social media to bring attention to the prevalence of sexual harassment and abuse.

② 本句为主从复合句。主句的主干结构为 it strongly suggests that...。While 引导让步状语从句，其中包含一个 who 引导的定语从句修饰 men；that 引导宾语从句，其中包含一个 who 引导的定语从句修饰 men。

While the study did not look at men	who speak out against sexism per se	, it strongly
让步状语从句	定语从句	主语

suggests	that men	who advocate for others in general	may be seen as less competent.
谓语	宾语从句	定语从句	宾语从句

第二部分 经济贸易类
SECTION TWO

Text 1 India Undermines Its Own Economy
印度削弱自身经济

When Indian Prime Minister Manmohan Singh last visited the White House in 2009, he heralded "a moment of great opportunity" for the two countries, calling on both sides to work together to "harness the immense potential of our talented and enterprising people and support each other's growth and prosperity." Yet, as Singh prepares for his visit to Washington this week, India's trade and investment policies threaten to undermine, rather than harness, this potential.

With the United States still recovering from a recession and the continued slowdown in India's economic growth, the potential value of a deepening partnership has only increased. ①From my personal experience in India over the last two decades, I have witnessed firsthand the progress that has been made to solidify the relationship between India and the U.S. Between 2000 and 2011, revenue from U.S. exports to India increased seven fold, and India's exports to the U.S. more than tripled as the trade and investment relationship gathered momentum.

Yet, four years after Singh's initial visit, the potential of the relationship still remains largely unfulfilled. Surprisingly, India remains only the 13th largest trading partner of the United States, even though it may soon become the world's third largest economy. The United States trades more with Korea than with India, despite its being only a tiny fraction of India's size.

Recent actions taken by the Indian government have only impeded further progress in the relationship.

当印度总理曼莫汉·辛格在2009年访问白宫时,他预言这对两国来说是"一个绝佳的时机",呼吁双方共同努力,来"发挥两国才能出众、积极进取的人们的巨大潜能,支持彼此的发展和繁荣"。然而,就在辛格准备本周访问华盛顿的同时,印度的贸易和投资政策威胁要削弱而非发挥这种人才潜力的优势。

在美国经济复苏、印度经济持续放缓的环境下,加深伙伴关系的潜在价值有增无减。①根据我个人过去二十年里在印度的经验来说,我亲眼见证了进步——印度和美国之间的关系得到了巩固。2000—2011年之间,美国对印度的出口收入增加了7倍,印度对美国的出口增长了3倍多,贸易和投资关系越发密切,势头正强。

然而,辛格首次访问四年后,在很大程度上,贸易和投资的潜力仍没有得到充分发挥。令人惊讶的是,尽管印度可能很快就会成为世界第三大经济体,但在美国的贸易伙伴中,印度仍只排到第13位。美国与印度的贸易比它与韩国的贸易还要少,尽管韩国国土面积只相当于印度一角。

印度政府最近采取的行动只会阻碍两国关系的进一步发展。印度

---

herald *vt.* 预示……的来临
gather momentum 方兴未艾
seven-fold *n.* 七倍
impede *vt.* 阻碍

India has resorted to "compulsory licensing" to appropriate foreign firms' intellectual property in violation of international trade norms. It has overridden, revoked or infringed upon approximately a dozen pharmaceutical patents held by foreign firms since 2012 alone. And its industrial policy expressly calls for such measures in other sectors as well. These actions create an atmosphere of distrust that will only discourage new investment in India.

India has also mandated local content requirements, charged exorbitant tariffs at the border in certain sectors and maintained onerous market entry barriers and foreign equity caps. One headline aptly captured India's ambivalence towards easing market access: "The License Raj is Dead. Long Live the License Raj." These barriers hinder investment in banking, financial services, insurance, retail, telecommunications and many other sectors.

This year, India will experience only 5 percent growth—the lowest in a decade. Foreign investment has fallen by nearly two-thirds in the past year, and the rupee has plummeted. ② Although short-term protectionism may appeal to domestic constituencies as the campaign begins for next year's elections in India, history has proven that such policies are inconsistent with a dynamic economy that generates wealth over the long-term. And given the state of its economy, this is hardly the time for India to alienate foreign investors.

Certainly the U.S. can do its part, too, by implementing sorely needed reforms to our immigration policy and ensuring that highly-skilled workers can continue to learn from and contribute to

已经采取"强制许可"办法来侵占违反国际贸易规范的外国公司的知识产权。仅 2012 年一年，印度就推翻、撤销或侵犯了十几个外国公司持有的制药专利。其产业政策也在其他领域明确要求采取此类措施。这些举措制造了一种猜疑氛围，这将只会阻碍印度新投资的引进。

印度还实行当地含量要求，在某些行业设置高额的关税，维持市场准入的重重壁垒和设立外国股权上限。一个报道的标题恰如其分地表现出印度政府在市场准入宽松政策上的举棋不定："许可证统治与世长辞。许可证永垂不朽。"这些壁垒阻碍着银行、金融服务、保险、零售、电信等许多领域的投资。

今年，印度将经历十年来经济增长的最低点，预计仅有 5% 的增长。外国投资在过去的一年中已经下降了将近三分之二，与此同时卢比暴跌。②随着印度明年大选的竞选活动拉开序幕，短期贸易保护主义可能受国内选民青睐，但是历史已经证明，这些政策与有活力的经济相悖，不能为国家带来长期的经济繁荣。鉴于其经济状况不佳，目前并非印度疏远外国投资者的时机。

当然美国也能采取措施——通过 H-1B 签证项目，实行急需的移民政策改革，确保高技能工人可以继续学习，为经济做贡献。但坦白地说，

---

compulsory licensing 强制许可，是指不经专利权人同意，直接允许其他单位或个人实施其发明创造的一种许可方式，又称非自愿许可

in violation of 违反　　　　　　　　override vt. 推翻　　　　　　　　infringe vt. 侵犯
pharmaceutical adj. 制药学的　　　　exorbitant tariff 高额关税　　　　onerous adj. 繁重的；麻烦的
barrier n. 贸易壁垒　　　　　　　　equity cap 持股上限　　　　　　　ambivalence n. 举棋不定
rupee n. (货币)卢比　　　　　　　　plummet vi. 暴跌

our economy through the H-1B visa program. But frankly there is far more to be done on the Indian side to ensure fairness in our economic relationship. Respecting intellectual property rights and beginning to remove restrictive barriers to trade and investment will be essential first steps along this path.

  President Obama should use Prime Minister Singh's upcoming visit to raise concern that the relationship's "immense potential" that was heralded four years ago remains unfulfilled. While important progress has been made on the strategic front, India's recent economic policies are hurting the relationship. Mr. Singh's visit represents a new moment of opportunity—we can only hope that the opportunity is seized more effectively than four years ago.

(*U.S. News & World Report*, 2013.9)

印度一方需要做更多来确保两国经济关系的公平，尊重知识产权、移除贸易和投资壁垒将会是这条道路上至关重要的第一步。

  辛格总理即将到访，奥巴马总统应借此机会引导人们对四年前就已被预示了的美印两国关系的"巨大潜力"予以关注，因为这个潜力还没有得到实现。尽管在战略力量方面已经取得了重要进展，但是印度最近的经济政策仍在伤害两国间的关系。辛格先生的来访代表了充满机遇的新时刻的到来——我们只希望，能比四年前更有效地利用这次机会。

长难句解析

① 本句为主从复合句。句中 that 引导的定语从句修饰 the progress。

> From my personal experience in India over the last two decades (状语), I (主语) have witnessed (谓语) firsthand (状语) the progress (宾语) that has been made to solidify the relationship between India and the U.S. (定语从句)

② 本句为主从复合句。句中 although 引导的让步状语从句中嵌套了一个 as 引导的时间状语从句；主句谓语 has proven 后为 that 引导的宾语从句；句末 that 引导的定语从句修饰 economy。

> Although short-term protectionism may appeal to domestic constituencies (让步状语从句) as the campaign begins for next year's elections in India (时间状语从句), history (主语) has proven (谓语) that such policies are inconsistent with a dynamic economy (宾语从句) that generates wealth over the long-term. (定语从句)

H-1B visa 美国签证的一种，即特殊专业人员/临时工作签证（Specialty Occupations/Temporary Worker Visas）

Text 2

Banking Is for the 1%
银行是为了1%的人服务

The rich are different, as F. Scott Fitzgerald famously wrote and so are their banking services. ①While most of us struggle to keep our balances high enough to avoid a slew of extra fees for everything from writing checks to making ATM withdrawals, wealthy individuals enjoy the special extras provided by banks, which increasingly seem more like high-end concierges than financial institutions. If you are rich, your bank will happily arrange everything from Broadway tickets to spa trips.

Oh, and you'll have an easier time getting a loan too. ②A recent report by the Goldman Sachs Global Markets Institute, the public-policy unit of the finance giant, found that while the rich have ample access to credit and banking services six years on from the financial crisis, low- and medium-income consumers do not. Instead, they pay more for everything from mortgages to credit cards, and generally, the majority of consumers have worse access to credit than they did before the crisis. As the Goldman report puts it, "For a near-minimum-wage worker who has maintained some access to bank credit (and it is important to note that many have not in the wake of the financial crisis), the added annual interest expenses associated with a typical level of debt would be roughly equivalent to one week's wages." Small and midsize businesses, meanwhile, have seen interest rates on their loans go up 1.75% relative to those for larger companies. This is a major problem because it damps economic growth and slows creation.

It's ironic(and admirable) that the report comes from Goldman Sachs, which like several other big

F.斯科特·菲茨杰拉德写过一句名言:有钱人是不一样的。他们的银行服务也是不一样的。①当大部分人努力维持着较高的账户余额,只是为了免掉办理业务的较多的手续费时,比如开支票或者在ATM上取款,有钱人却很享受银行的收费服务。银行更像是一个高端的私人管家,而非金融机构。只要你有钱,无论是百老汇的入场券还是温泉旅行,它都乐意为你安排得妥妥帖帖。

当然,贷款也会容易得多。②财经巨头高盛下属的公共政策部门全球市场研究中心近期发布了一项报告。报告显示,在经济危机爆发后的六年里,有钱人可以选择的信贷和银行服务有很多,而中低收入人群却甚少。相反,中低收入人群无论是房贷还是信用卡的支付金额都更高,而且通常情况下,与经济危机前相比,大众消费者获取贷款的难度更大。高盛报告指出,"对于最低收入标准的银行贷款客户来说(值得一提的是,经济危机爆发后,他们中有很多人无法维系贷款),普通水平的债务年利息大概相当于他一周的工资。"与此同时,与大企业相比,中小企业的贷款利率上调了1.75%。这个问题很严重,因为它会抑制经济增长,且不利于创新。

这份报告来自高盛,这是很讽刺的(也是令人钦佩的),高盛

---

a slew of 大量的   withdrawal n. 提款   concierge n.(公寓或旅馆的)主要守门人;管理人员
mortgage n. 抵押   damp economic growth 抑制经济增长

banks—Morgan Stanley, UBS—is putting its future bets on wealth-management services catering to rich individuals rather than the masses. Banks would say this is because the cost of doing business with regular people has grown too high in the wake of Dodd-Frank regulation. It's true that in one sense, new regulations dictating how much risk banks can take and how much capital they have to maintain make it easier to provide services to the rich. That's one reason why, for example, the rates on jumbo mortgages—the kind the wealthy take out to buy expensive homes—have fallen relative to those of 30-year loans, which typically cater to the middle class. It also explains why access to credit cards is constrained for lower-income people compared with those higher up the economic ladder.

Regulation isn't entirely to blame. For starters, banks are increasingly looking to wealthy individuals to make up for the profits they aren't making by trading. Even without Dodd-Frank, it would have been difficult for banks to maintain their precrisis trading revenue in a market with the lowest volatility levels in decades. (Huge market shifts mean huge profits for banks on the right side of a trade.) The market calm is largely due to the Federal Reserve Bank's unprecedented $4 trillion money dump, which is itself an effort to prop up an anemic recovery.

All of this leads to a self-perpetuating vicious cycle: the lack of access to banking services, loans and capital fuels America's growing wealth divide, which is particularly stark when it comes to race. A May study by the Center for Global Policy Solutions, a Washington-based consultancy, and Duke University found that the median amount of liquid wealth (assets that can easily be turned into cash) held by African-American households was $200. For Latino households it was $340.

---

wealth-management n. 金融理财　　jumbo adj. 巨额的　　the economic ladder 经济阶梯
precrisis n. 经济危机前　　volatility level 市场波动性　　dump n. 转储
prop up 支撑　　anemic recovery 举步维艰的经济复苏
self-perpetuating adj. 能使自身永久存在的

The median for white households was $23,000. One reason for the difference is that a disproportionate number of minorities (along with women and younger workers of all races) have no access to formal retirement-savings plans. No surprise that asset management, the fastest-growing area of finance, is yet another area in which big banks focus mainly on serving the rich.

In lieu of forcing banks to lend to lower-income groups, something that is being tried with mixed results in the U.K., what to do? Smarter housing policy would be a good place to start. The majority of Americans still keep most of their wealth in their homes. But so far, investors and rich buyers who can largely pay in cash have led the housing recovery. That's partly why home sales are up but mortgage applications are down. Policymakers and banks need to rethink who is a "good" borrower. One 10-year study by the University of North Carolina, Chapel Hill, for example, found that poor buyers putting less than 5% down can be better-than-average credit risks if vetted by metrics aside from how much cash they have on hand. If banks won't take the risk of lending to them, they may eventually find their own growth prospects in peril. After all, in a $17 trillion economy, catering to the 1% can take you only so far.

(*Time*, 2014.9)

而普通白人家庭的平均流动资产是 23 000 美元。造成这种差距的原因之一在于无法享受正式退休储蓄计划的少数族裔(含妇女和各种族的青年工人)的人数失衡。毫不奇怪的是,在另一个业务板块,即金融业发展最快的资产管理板块中,大银行把焦点放在为富人提供服务上。

在英国,政府没有强迫银行借钱给低收入人群,目前的效果喜忧参半,那么应该怎么做? 我们可以从更灵活的住房政策着手。大多数美国人仍把大部分钱投资在房子上。但是从目前看来,主要靠现金买房的投资者和富人刺激了房地产业的复苏。这就是房地产销售额虽然上升,抵押款申请数量却下降的部分原因。政策制定者和银行需要重新考虑谁才是优质的借方。比如,北卡罗来纳大学教堂山分校的一项持续了十年的研究发现,如果不考虑手头有多少现金,经指标审查后,首付低于 5% 的拮据型购房者,其信用风险会优于平均水平。如果银行不愿意承担风险贷款给他们,他们可能会最终发现自己的发展前景很危险。毕竟,在一个 17 万亿的经济体中,迎合 1% 的人只能到此为止。

长难句解析

① 本句为主从复合句。主句的主干结构为 wealthy individuals enjoy the extras。句中 while 此处译为"当……时候",故其引导的是时间状语从句;provided by banks 作后置定语修饰宾语;which 引导的非限制性定语从句修饰 banks。

While most of us struggle to keep our balances high enough to avoid a slew of extra fees for
　　　　　　　　　　　　　　　　　时间状语从句
everything from writing checks to making ATM withdrawals, wealthy individuals enjoy
　　　　　　　　　　　　　　　　　　　　　　　　　　　　主语　　　　　谓语
the special extras　provided by banks, which increasingly seem more like high-end concierges
　宾语　　　　　　　　后置定语　　　　　　　　　非限制性定语从句
than financial institutions.

---

in lieu of 作为(……的)替代　　　vetted by 经由……的审查　　　metric *n.* 度量

②本句为主从复合句。主句的主干结构为 A report found that...。句中 by the Goldman... Institute 作后置定语修饰 report;the public-policy unit of the finance giant 作 the Goldman... Institute 的同位语;that 引导的宾语从句作 found 的宾语,该宾语从句中还嵌套了一个 while 引导的比较状语从句。

A recent report　by the Goldman Sachs Global Markets Institute, the public-policy unit of the
　主语　　　　　　　　　后置定语　　　　　　　　　　　　　　　　同位语
finance giant, found　that while the rich have ample access to credit and banking services six
　　　　　　　谓语　　　　　　　　　　　　　　宾语从句
years on from the financial crisis, low-and medium-income consumers do not.

Text 3　The Euro Zone: Take One for the Team
欧元区:为了集体利益,牺牲个人利益

Inflation in Germany exceeded 2% in April. If the Bundesbank's latest forecasts prove right, it could soon reach 4% for the first time in nearly 30 years. Inflation angst is rising among the country's monetary hawks. The exigencies of the pandemic muted German grumbling about the European Central Bank's ultra-loose monetary policy. But as inflation rises, so will reflexive German demands that the bank should taper its bond-buying.

Such clamouring would be misguided. Europe's recovery is more subdued than America's, making the odds even better that the inflation spike will prove temporary. ①And the interests of the weaker members of the currency union, still crawling their way back to health, should come first.

德国 4 月份的通货膨胀率超过了 2%。如果德国央行的最新预测证明是正确的,那么通货膨胀率可能很快会在近 30 年来首次达到 4%。货币政策鹰派的通胀焦虑正在与日俱增。疫情的紧急平息了德国对欧洲央行超宽松货币政策的抱怨。但随着通货膨胀率的上升,德国人也会本能地要求央行减少债券购买。

这样的呼声可能是误导的效果。欧洲的复苏比美国要疲软得多,这使得通货膨胀的飙升更有可能是暂时的。①而欧元区经济较弱的成员国仍在艰难地恢复,应该把他们的利益放在首位。

angst n. 焦虑;担心
exigency n. 紧急;紧急事件
grumble vi. 抱怨;嘟囔
reflexive adj. 本能反应的;考虑自身影响的
taper vt. 逐渐变弱(或减轻);(中央银行)缩减资产购买
clamour vi. 吵闹;强烈要求
crawl vi. 爬行;缓慢行进

hawk n. 鹰;鹰派人物
mute vt. 减弱……的声音;缓解
ultra-loose adj. 超宽松的

subdued adj. 冷清的,低迷的

The hyperinflation of the 1920s etched inflation-phobia deep into the German psyche. After the second world war the Bundesbank earned a fearsome reputation by being the first to tame the inflationary beast. In the early 2000s, shortly after the birth of the euro, Germany restrained wage costs and the southern European economies lost competitiveness against it. ② As the southerners recovered from their debt crises, they narrowed the gap by clamping down on their own labour costs, while Germany did too little to adjust. That set the euro zone on a demand-deficient, deflationary path. The area's economy has never fully recovered, even as the ECB has used up most of its ammunition.

That lost decade is one reason why spiralling wages and prices in Europe are vanishingly unlikely, even as overheating is a possibility in America. What is more, the hit from the pandemic in Europe has been worse. Output in the euro zone fell further than in America last year. Despite this, its fiscal stimulus looks stingy compared with the Biden administration's largesse. The EU's new €750bn ($919bn) recovery fund will take years to be disbursed fully. Investors expect inflation in five years' time to languish below the ECB's target of "close to, but below 2%". Expectations in America, by contrast, are above 2%.

Further reassurance can be gained from peering into the mechanics of Germany's inflation spike. As in America, it reflects some transitory global factors, including the oil-price collapse last spring which depressed the base used to calculate the

20世纪20年代的恶性通货膨胀把通胀恐惧深深烙印在德国人的心里。"二战"后，德国央行因第一个驯服通胀这只怪兽而赢得了极大的声誉。21世纪初，就在欧元诞生后不久，德国控制了工资成本，南欧经济体失去了对抗欧元的竞争力。②随着南欧国家从债务危机中恢复过来，他们通过压缩自己的劳动力成本来缩小差距，而德国却没有做什么调整。这使得欧元区走上了需求不足、通货紧缩的道路。即使欧洲央行（ECB）已经用尽了大部分弹药，该地区的经济也从未完全恢复。

"失落的十年"是欧洲工资和物价几乎毫无可能螺旋上升的原因之一，即使在美国经济过热也是一种可能。更重要的是，这次疫情对欧洲的打击更为严重。去年欧元区的产出下降幅度超过美国。尽管如此，与拜登政府的慷慨相比，它的财政刺激仍显得很吝啬。欧盟新发行的7 500亿欧元（9 190亿美元）复苏基金将需要数年时间才能全额拨付到位。投资者预计，五年内通胀率将会低于欧洲央行设定的"接近但低于2%"的目标。美国的通胀率预期值则恰好相反，超过2%。

深入研究德国通胀飙升的机制，可以进一步消除疑虑。就像在美国一样，它反映了一些短暂的全球因素，包括去年春天石油价格的暴跌，压低了用于计算年增长率的基数。

---

hyperinflation n. ［经］恶性通货膨胀
inflation-phobia n. 通货膨胀恐怖病
deflationary adj. 通货紧缩的
vanishingly adv. 难以察觉地；趋于零地
largesse n. 慷慨的赠予
languish vi. 变得衰弱；失去活力
transitory adj. 短暂的，暂时的

etch vt. 蚀刻；鲜明地描述；铭记
tame vt. 驯养；制服
spiral vi. 螺旋形上升
stingy adj. 吝啬的，小气的
disburse vt. 支付；支出
reassurance n. （能消除疑虑等的）肯定；安慰

annual rate. Strip out food and energy prices, and inflation in Germany was only about 1% in April. Some temporary country-specific issues are also in play. A carbon charge has pushed up prices, and an emergency cut to value-added taxes last year will arithmetically boost inflation later this year. Look along the supply chain and you might take fright at Germany's producer-price inflation, of more than 5% in April. But this should ease as factories and suppliers respond to a surge in orders.

Perhaps the biggest reason why Germany should tolerate a period of above-target inflation is that the euro area's health depends on it. Activity is resuming across the zone, as vaccines are administered and lockdown restrictions lifted. Germany has less lost ground to make up than most. ③It suffered a deep downturn last year, with the economy shrinking by 5%, but it fared far better than France, Italy and Spain, where output fell by nearly twice as much. Unemployment in Germany remains low, at 4.5%. Its reliance on manufacturing and exports has been a boon. Other countries, by contrast, must pray that spending on tourism, retail and hospitality returns to the levels of the old days. Goldman Sachs, a bank, reckons that Spain and Italy have twice as much economic slack as Germany.

The ECB sets monetary policy for the currency union as a whole, not its largest member alone. And so Germany must seek to keep its economy humming along while the others catch up and the stimulus is withdrawn. That is the price of being one of the strongest members of a currency union. After a lost decade, the euro zone has learned from some of the mistakes of the past crisis. The pursuit of balanced budgets and austerity has been abandoned for the time being. The EU is

---

strip out 剔除
surge *n.* 急剧上升；激增
lost ground 股市下跌；处于不利的地位
withdraw *vt.* 撤销；收回

arithmetically *adv.* 算术上；[数] 用算术方法
administer *vt.* 给予（药物等）；管理
hum *vi.* 发嗡嗡声；活跃；繁忙
austerity *n.* 紧缩

64

on the verge of issuing common debt to finance its recovery fund. Both shifts were possible because of a change of thinking in Berlin. A recognition that the German economy must run hot is the missing link in restoring confidence throughout the euro zone.

(*The Economist*, 2021.5)

发行共同债券,为其恢复基金而融资。这两种转变之所以成为可能,是因为柏林方面的想法发生了改变。承认德国经济必须保持强劲增长,是整个欧元区恢复信心所缺少的一环。

长难句解析

①本句为简单句。句子的主干为 the interests should come first,是主谓结构,介词短语 of the weaker members of the currency union 是修饰主语的后置定语,still… health 为后置定语修饰 the weaker members。

And the interests of the weaker members of the currency union, still crawling their way
　　　主语　　　　　　后置定语1　　　　　　　　　　后置定语2
back to health, should come first.
　　　　　　　谓语

②本句为 while 连接的并列复合句。As 引导一个时间状语从句。while 在句中表示对比的关系,介词短语 by clamping down on their own labour costs 作方式状语。

As the southerners recovered from their debt crises, they narrowed the gap by clamping
　　　　　时间状语从句　　　　　　　　　　　主语1 谓语1　宾语1
down on their own labour costs, while Germany did too little to adjust.
　　　方式状语　　　　　　　　　主语2　谓语2　　状语

③本句为 but 连接的并列复合句。but 前面的句子为主谓宾结构,介词短语 with the economy shrinking by 5%作伴随状语;but 后面的句子为主谓结构,far better than…为比较状语,最后为 where 引导的非限制性定语从句,修饰 France, Italy and Spain。

It　　suffered　a deep downturn　last year, with the economy shrinking by 5%, but
主语1 谓语1　　宾语1　　　　时间状语　　　　　伴随状语
it　　fared far better than France, Italy and Spain, where output fell by nearly twice
主语2 谓语2　　　比较状语　　　　　　　　　非限制性定语从句
as much.

Text 4 America's Economy 美国经济

Eight out of ten voters told exit pollsters in November that they were worried about the economy. ① That is one reason why the new Congress, which starts sitting next week, is dominated by Republicans. Yet there is mounting evidence that the benefits of the economic recovery—long concentrated among the rich—are spreading to ordinary Americans.

On December 23rd GDP growth for the third quarter was revised up to 5%—its fastest pace since 2003—having grown by a nearly-as-impressive 4.6% in the second quarter. To be sure, America is making up for ground lost in the first quarter, when GDP actually shrink because the weather was awful and companies cut inventories. For the past 12 months GDP is up 2.7%: respectable but not amazing. Forecasters surveyed by *The Economist* think America will grow 3% next year.

Economists have projected similar growth rates since the recovery began, only to be disappointed. Growth has averaged just 2.3% since the recovery began in July 2009. But this time they have hard evidence on their side. Some 321,000 jobs were created in November, compared with a monthly average of 194,000 during 2013. Despite this, inflation has fallen. The Federal Reserve can thus continue to keep monetary policy unusually loose, and asset prices are soaring. The DowJones Industrial Average passed 18,000 for the first time shortly before Christmas.

11月的出口民调显示,80%的投票者称他们对美国经济表示担忧。①这是共和党在下周开始运行的新一届国会中占主导地位的原因之一。但是越来越多的证据表明,经济复苏的益处——此前长期集中于富人当中——正在向美国普通民众扩展。

12月23日公布的第三季度GDP增速上调至5%——这是其自2003年以来最快的增速——接近第二季度4.6%的增长,这一增长令人印象深刻。可以肯定的是,美国正在收复2014年第一季度的失地,实际上,美国的GDP在2014年第一季度因受恶劣的天气和企业库存减少的影响而有所萎缩。过去的12个月内美国GDP增加了2.7%:表现不错,但并不令人吃惊。接受《经济学人》调查的预测者们认为,下一年美国经济将会增长3%。

经济学家们在美国经济开始复苏时曾经做出过类似的预测,但结果令人失望。自2009年7月经济复苏开始以来,平均增速仅为2.3%。而这一次他们掌握了支持他们的确凿证据。2014年11月就业岗位增加了32.1万。相比之下,2013年平均每月仅增加了19.4万。尽管如此,通胀水平却出现了下降。美联储因此得以继续维持超常宽松的货币政策,而资产价格也一路飙升。圣诞节来临之际,道琼斯工业平均指数第一次突破了18 000点。

Republican n. 共和党人 mounting evidence 确凿证据 be revised up 上涨
shrink vi. 缩小,收缩 inventory n. 库存 monetary policy 货币政策
DowJones Industrial Average 道琼斯工业平均指数(道琼斯指数),即道琼斯股票价格平均指数

Consumer sentiment has grown jollier in recent months—as jolly as it has been since before the recession, according to the University of Michigan. For several reasons, the good mood is likely to last into 2015. One is the composition of recent growth: it is the result of solid household spending, the most important component of demand. It grew at a 3.2% annual rate in the third quarter, and may grow 4% or more in the current quarter, reckons Morgan Stanley, a bank.

Two powerful tailwinds are helping. The first is the big drop in the price of oil, from $110 per barrel in June to below $60. Cheaper petrol holds down inflation and leaves American consumers with more money to spend on other things. (Although America produces more oil and imports less of it than five years ago, it remains a net importer.) Saudi Arabia seems willing to tolerate even lower prices to protect its market share, so the boost may last.

The other, even stronger, tailwind is growing incomes. Job growth is accelerating, and there are signs, albeit faint, of an uptick in wages. America's underlying potential growth rate has slipped in recent years, from 3% or more a decade ago to around 2%, thanks to a slower-growing workforce and lack lustre productivity. So any growth rate above 2% helps to use up spare capacity. Labour market data confirm this: non-farm employment grew faster in 2014 than in any year since the 1990s, and unemployment has fallen to 5.8%. On current trends, it could drop close to 5% within a year, less than many estimates of the natural rate of unemployment (at which a labour shortage puts upward pressure on wages and prices).

据密歇根大学的调查,最近数月消费者信心逐渐提高——已经达到经济衰退前水平。在几个因素的作用下,这种乐观情绪有可能持续至2015年。其中一个是近期经济增长的构成要素:它源于稳固的家庭支出,这是需求的最重要部分。据摩根士丹利银行预计,第三季度家庭支出年增长速度为3.2%,当前季度(2014年第四季度)的增速将达4%或以上。

两个强有力的因素起着作用。第一个就是油价的大幅下跌,每桶油价从6月的110美元跌至当前的低于60美元。更便宜的原油价格抑制了通货膨胀,也令美国消费者有更多资金购买其他物品。(与5年前相比,美国的原油产量虽有所上升,进口量也有所下降,但美国仍然属于原油净进口国家。)沙特阿拉伯似乎愿意为保护其市场份额而忍受更低的油价,所以油价走低对美国经济的提振或将持续。

另一个更有力的因素是收入增长。就业岗位数量正在加速上升,且有迹象表明,薪资有所增加,尽管这种迹象很微弱。近年来,由于缓慢增长的劳动力以及缺乏创造性的生产力,美国潜在经济增速从十年前的3%或更多下滑至2%左右。因此任何高于2%的经济增速都有助于充分利用闲置产能。劳动力市场的数据证实:自20世纪90年代以来,2014年非农业就业人口的增长速度最快,而失业率则跌至5.8%。按照目前的趋势,失业率有可能在一年内降至5%,低于不少人对美国失业率的预期(劳动力短缺将对薪资和物价上涨产生压力)。

---

reckon vt. 估计,测算
net importer 净进口国
lack lustre 缺乏新意的

tailwind n. 顺风
albeit conj. 虽然,尽管

inflation n. 通货膨胀
uptick n. 增大;提高

The median household's real income is up 1.2% for the first 11 months of the year, according to Sentier Research, a private firm, a marked acceleration from the previous two years. That barely dents the 8% drop in median incomes between 2008 and 2011, but it does suggest that the expansion is finally reaching ordinary households.

Thanks to cheaper oil, the Federal Reserve now thinks inflation will end next year around 1.3%, according to projections released on December 17th, and will not return to 2%, its target, before 2018. As a result, rates could either rise later, or more slowly, than currently expected. The Fed promises to be "patient" about tightening monetary policy. ②Janet Yellen, the Fed's boss, told reporters that she would like to see unemployment fall below its long-run natural rate, in the hope that this might nudge wages and prices higher. A combination of robust underlying growth and a patient central bank is catnip to investors—hence the buoyant Dow. It is a cocktail reminiscent of 1998, when the Asian crisis sent both oil prices and bond yields down sharply, which goosed American growth and stock prices. What hurt the world helped America.

For the past six years Republicans in Congress have argued that America must cut public spending to bring dangerous deficits and alarming public debt under control. Now, the budget deficit has fallen below its average of the past 40 years (as a share of GDP) and perkier growth is making the national debt look more manageable. Republicans are still arguing for spending cuts, of course, but now they have to convince voters that smaller government is better.

据一家私营企业 Sentier Research 称,美国 2014 年前 11 个月的家庭平均实际收入上升了 1.2%,较前两年有显著上升。这几乎无法抵消 2008 年至 2011 年平均收入高达 8%的降幅,但这确实表明经济扩张最终普及到了普通家庭中。

据 12 月 17 日公布的预期显示,由于油价下降,目前美联储认为美国通胀将于今年年底结束。通胀率大约为 1.3%,在 2018 年前,其目标通胀率不会回升至 2%。因此,与当前预计相比,利率将更晚或更迟缓地上涨。美联储承诺对收紧货币政策"保持耐心"。②美联储主席珍妮特·耶伦向记者表示,她希望失业率低于长期自然失业率,以推动薪资及物价上涨。强健的潜在增速与颇具容忍度的中央银行,这种组合对投资者来说是个诱惑,也因此带动了道琼斯指数的上涨。这不禁令人想起了 1998 年的情景,那时亚洲金融危机导致原油价格和债券收益跳水,并推高美国经济增速和美股行情。这一做法重创了世界其他地区,却给美国带来了益处。

在过去六年里,共和党人在国会争论,称美国必须削减公共开支以控制危险的赤字和公共债务。如今,预算赤字(占 GDP 比重)已经低于过去 40 年的平均水平,而更高的经济增速使得国家债务看起来更加可控。共和党人当然还在主张削减开支,但如今他们必须说服选民:规模较小的政府机构更好。

---

dent vt. 削弱,削减　　　　nudge vt. 推进　　　robust underlying growth 强劲的潜在增长
catnip n. 诱惑,原意为猫薄荷(其香气吸引猫)　　buoyant adj. 看涨的
reminiscent of 令人回忆起　　　　　　　　　goose vt. 推动;鼓励

It may seem obvious that a stronger economy would rob Republicans of one of their best arguments for change in the White House in 2016, and give Democrats a boost as they gear up for the election. But the political effects of a stronger economy are unpredictable. Plenty of candidates have lost despite, rather than because of, their party's recent economic record.

Hitherto, an economy that has delivered soaring corporate profits but done little for median wages has fired up Democratic activists and tempted them to push for a populist platform in 2016. As the benefits of recovery finally start to spread, however, a campaign based on economic disillusion looks less like a winner.

(*The Economist*, 2015.1)

很明显,一个强劲的经济会让共和党人在 2016 年白宫中失去为改变而争论的最佳理由之一,并在民主党为总统竞选做准备时给予他们一臂之力。但是经济强劲所产生的政治影响无法预计。尽管许多竞选人落败,但其原因却不在于他们党派近期的经济成绩。

迄今为止,一个令企业利润大幅攀升但在提升平均工资方面却收效甚微的经济形势已经惹恼了民主党的激进分子,并促使他们在 2016 年大选中奋力争取一个平民主义的平台。但随着经济复苏带来的益处开始向民众扩展,一场基于经济幻灭而组织的大选胜算不大。

长难句解析

① 本句为主从复合句。主句的主干结构为 That is one reason。句中 why 引导的定语从句修饰先行词 reason,其中包含 which 引导的非限制性定语从句,修饰先行词 the new Congress。

That is one reason why the new Congress, which starts sitting next week, is dominated by Republicans.
主语 系动词 表语　　定语从句　　非限制性定语从句
定语从句

② 本句为主从复合句。主句的主干结构为 Janet Yellen told reporters that…。told 后面跟双宾语;同位语从句解释说明目的状语中 hope 的内容。

Janet Yellen, the Fed's boss, told reporters that she would like to see unemployment fall below its long-run natural rate, in the hope that this might nudge wages and prices higher.
主语　　同位语　　谓语　间接宾语　　直接宾语(宾语从句)
　　　　　　　　　　　　　目的状语　　　同位语从句

---

gear up 为……做好准备　　populist *adj.* 平民主义的　　disillusion *n.* 幻灭

Text 5   The Guardian View on Apple's Valuation: A Digital Milestone
《卫报》对苹果公司的价值的看法：一个数字里程碑

Apple is now valued at more than a trillion dollars on the New York stock exchange. It is not the first company to be so huge if inflation is taken into account; but it is the first that is not in the oil business. The other ground-breaking fact about its wealth is that it employs only about a quarter as many people as PetroChina, which is probably the world's largest company. These two facts taken together suggest the direction of the digitalised economy: fewer people are going to make more money. It is still too early to see the ultimate destination, just as it would have been impossible to foresee all the effects of the oil economy in 1918. Transport was obviously going to be revolutionised then but who at the time could have foreseen the world transformed by plastics?

The oil revolution accelerated the shrinkage of the physical world that coal-powered transport—steamships and railways—had started in the 19th century. Air travel and motor transport transformed peacetime economies and the means of waging war. They changed the way we understood the physical world, since distance on its own now no longer meant that anywhere was hard to reach. The digitalisation revolution seems to have abolished social distance in a similar way. But social distance has not been replaced by social closeness. Instead, we have an abrasive and anxious proximity with strangers around the world. In the world of social media we are all up in one another's faces.

Apple has profited from this revolution in two rather contradictory ways. It was the company that

---

take sth. into account 把某事考虑在内
PetroChina 中国石油
abolish vt. 废除

shrinkage n. 收缩
abrasive adj. 生硬粗暴的

ground-breaking adj. 开拓性的
wage vt. 发动
proximity n. 接近

invented the smartphone. Without the smartphone and its ravenous screen it is very hard to imagine the modern social media scene. So Apple bears some responsibility for our present state of constant distraction and confused excitability in which everything is sensational but nothing really matters. But in recent years it has also started to sell the ability to cut oneself off from the online world, at least in bursts. The Silicon Valley elite have long distrusted the effects of smartphones on their own children, however much they wanted to sell them to the rest of the world. So Apple's phones now offer to limit the time you spend on any particular website while its web browser makes ad blocking easier.

Both these can be understood as ways to strike against rival tech giants that make their money from advertisements, primarily Facebook and Google. But they are also examples of Apple's focus on user experience, which has been one of the foundations of its fortune. Sometimes this corresponds to nothing visible to the outside world. Just as cars are sold as an expression of the buyer's personality, Apple products have been sold as a story about the user: one who thinks differently—and spends rather more. But it has also often reflected a real elegance and ease of use difficult to imitate elsewhere. In the end, one reason why Apple is so immensely profitable is that it makes things people really want to buy, and to go on buying.

Apple has more in common with other digital companies than divides them. All use remarkably few workers to generate their enormous profits. All operate an internal class system, which concentrates power in very few hands. None have any unions worth speaking of. All rely on the unglamorous work being done far from California, usually by

---

ravenous *adj.* 贪婪的;渴望的;狼吞虎咽的
sensational *adj.* 轰动的
correspond to 相当于

excitability *n.* 兴奋性,应激性;可激发性
ad blocking 广告拦截
unglamorous *adj.* 乏味的

subcontractors. ①All shuffle their profits around the world in an endless game of "Find the lady" with national tax authorities—a factor that should not be overlooked when it comes to asking why they are so immensely profitable. If this is the model of the company of the future, it will have consequences we have not yet learned how to manage.

The downside of the oil-based economy is now obvious all around us. The symptoms of apparently uncontrollable climate change have become undeniable. Cities are choked with polluting traffic while the seas are choked with plastics made from oil. Whole countries have been devastated by oil riches. The digital revolution seems, so far, much more benign. ②But the loss of trust that social media both causes and exploits may one day be seen as another form of unforgivable pollution.

(*The Guardian*, 2018.8)

的地方完成的乏味的工作，这些工作通常是由分包商完成的。①所有公司在与国家税务当局进行无休止的"三牌赌皇后"游戏时，都已将世界各地的利润进行洗牌——当问及他们为何能获得如此巨大的利润时，这个因素不应被忽视。如果这是未来公司的模式，那么将会产生我们还不知道该如何处理的后果。

如今，以石油为基础的经济弊端已经显而易见。气候变化带来的问题已经不可否认，这种变化显然是无法控制的。城市被交通污染堵塞，海洋被用石油制作的塑料堵塞。整个国家都被石油财富所摧毁。到目前为止，数字革命似乎要温和得多。②但是，社交媒体在造成信任缺失的同时又在利用这一点，信任的缺失，有一天可能会被视为另一种不可原谅的污染。

长难句解析

① 本句为主从复合句。主句的主干结构为 All shuffle their profits—a factor that…。that 引导定语从句修饰 a factor；why 引导宾语从句，作 asking 的宾语。

All	shuffle	their profits	around the world in an endless game of "Find the lady" with
主语	谓语	宾语	状语1

national tax authorities—a factor that should not be overlooked when it comes to asking
　　　　　　　　　　　　同位语　　　　　定语从句　　　　　　　　　　状语2

why they are so immensely profitable.
　　　宾语从句

② 本句为主从复合句。主句的主干结构为 the loss of trust may be seen as another form of…。that 引导定语从句修饰主语。

But	the loss of trust	that social media both causes and exploits	may	one day	be seen as
	主语	定语从句	情态动词	状语	谓语

another form of unforgivable pollution.
　　宾语

---

subcontractor *n.* 分包者　　　　shuffle *vt.* 洗牌　　　　downside *n.* 负面，缺点；下降趋势
choke with 阻塞　　　　　　　　benign *adj.* 温和的

Text 6

UK Losing Millions in VAT from Non-EU Sellers on Amazon and eBay
英国在亚马逊和 eBay 的非欧盟卖家中损失了数百万的增值税

The UK is expected to lose tens of millions of pounds in VAT avoidance and evasion this Christmas as a growing number of non-EU sellers, including hundreds from China, increasingly dominate sales of popular gifts on Amazon and eBay.

"There has been a huge increase in this trade which is very difficult to control," a senior Brussels source told *The Guardian*. "The system is so complicated it's open to abuse."

Customs officers are aware that some overseas sellers are under-declaring the value of goods shipped to the UK and other European destinations in order to qualify for VAT exemptions on low-value packages.

"You're getting packages which the (online) customer might have paid €100 for. And they're coming in through customs identified as €20, or as gifts. And that's the abuse," said the source, who has close knowledge of the subject. This deception benefits the seller because lower-value goods—less than €22 in most EU member states and £15 in the UK—are exempt from VAT.

① Growing numbers of businesses from China are using Chinese-run warehouses in UK port cities as staging posts, allowing them to offer eBay and Amazon shoppers rapid delivery as well as competitive prices.

In many instances, sellers are not disclosing VAT numbers in their eBay and Amazon listings. When asked by a customer for a VAT receipt, several have simply replied that they do not apply the tax.

今年圣诞节期间,英国预计会因增值税的避税和逃税损失数千万英镑,因为越来越多的非欧盟卖家(包括几百家中国卖家)已经逐渐占据亚马逊和 eBay 上流行礼品销售的主导地位。

来自布鲁塞尔的资深内部人士告诉《卫报》:"网上交易量正在激增,这一状况很难控制,且网上交易的保税体系十分复杂,很容易被有心人利用。"

海关人员已经意识到一些海外卖家会故意报低进入英国和其他欧洲国家的商品价值,以此享受欧盟对于低价货物的增值税减免优惠。

对于该问题有深入了解的内部人士说道:"有些包裹(网上)的报价是 100 欧元,而过关价格只有 20 欧元,有的干脆就作为免费赠送的礼物进关。这就是明显利用关税漏洞的行为。"卖家以虚报价格来获益,因为低价物品(进入大多数欧盟成员国的价格低于 22 欧、进入英国的价格低于 15 英镑)是可以免收增值税的。

①越来越多的中国卖家,把中国人运营的位于英国港口城市的仓库作为中转站,以此为 eBay 和亚马逊的买家提供快速的送货服务和具有竞争力的商品价格。

在通常情况下,卖家在 eBay 和亚马逊上注册时不显示其增值税号。如果顾客索要增值税收据发票,不少卖家就直接回复他们并没有申请增值税。

VAT *abbr.* 增值税(Value Added Tax)　　evasion *n.* 逃税　　under-declare *vt.* 报低价
exemption *n.* 豁免　　abuse *n.* 滥用　　exempt *adj.* 被免除的　　receipt *n.* 发票

All overseas businesses selling on eBay and Amazon must apply VAT on their UK sales from the moment they start selling to customers in Britain, regardless of how low their turnover is in the UK.

VAT can be avoided only if items are sold from outside the EU, are genuinely low-value and are imported in small packages already addressed to individual consumers.

"eBay reminds all its users of their need to comply with their legal obligations and we also provide helpful guidance on VAT through our policies and help pages," the company said. "If eBay sellers are found to be breaching UK VAT compliance rules, we will cooperate with HMRC in all cases where HMRC provides evidence of underpayment of taxes."

Amazon said sellers on its site were "independent businesses responsible for complying with their own VAT obligations". It added: "We don't have the authority to review their tax affairs."

Amazon argued that sellers using its site were not required to post their business details or VAT numbers on Amazon.co.uk. Instead they can meet EU seller disclosure rules by making the information available in an email to customers or in a paper invoice delivered with goods bought.

Brussels sources disagreed, insisting EU rules required that customers be informed of seller details before making a purchase. "In practice, for sales via online marketplaces, the information must be provided on the website," one source said.

Both eBay and Amazon said they had no obligation to police VAT compliance by sellers using their sites, and no liability in cases in which sellers are found to have committed VAT fraud.

---

turnover *n.* 营业额
underpayment *n.* 缴付不足
genuinely *adv.* 确实
police *vt.* 监督
breach *vt.* 违反
liability *n.* 责任

Richard Allen of Ravas, a tax fairness campaign group which represents UK small traders, said: "The systematic abuse of the VAT system results in damaging price distortions that drive legitimate UK businesses to the wall, and workers out of their jobs." His members have spent months cataloguing evidence of suspected VAT abuses and have passed on their findings to senior Whitehall and Brussels officials.

Brussels sources told *The Guardian* that out-of-date VAT rules were too complex and ill-suited to the internet age. An overhaul including the removal of low-value exemption is planned, but it will be years before some changes come into force.

About a dozen member states are understood to have informally clubbed together to explore interim measures they can take to cope with the rapid rise of non-EU sellers, many offering VAT-free prices.

British customs officers have tried to increase scrutiny of small package imports in the last year, but they are under pressure to prioritise the monitoring of imports for terrorism threats, drugs and counterfeit goods.

Official estimates suggest the number of small packages shipped into Europe more than quadrupled from 26m in 2000 to 115m two years ago. The figure is thought to have climbed further since then, in line with e-commerce which grew by an estimated 14% last year.

②A report for the European commission in May estimates that more than €500m a year is being lost to member states because of the huge volumes of packages qualifying for the low-value VAT exemption. This estimate did not factor in the possibility many importers might be under-declaring the value of goods. As a result, the true losses to governments could be much higher.

Ravas（一家代表英国小交易商的税务公平推行组织）的理查德·艾伦表示："大量利用增值税系统漏洞会引发严重的价格扭曲，这将会把合法经营的英国企业逼上绝路，也会使大量工人失业。"Ravas 的员工们在过去几个月归整了卖家疑似违反英国增值税系统的诸多证据，并提交给了英国政府和布鲁塞尔的高级官员。

来自布鲁塞尔的内部人士告诉《卫报》，增值税的现行规则已经过时且过于复杂，不适合互联网时代。增值税系统的全面改革已列入计划，其中包括删除对低价商品的增值税减免优惠，但还需数年才能付诸实践。

十几个欧盟成员国已开展非正式合作，即在可能的范围内尝试采取权宜性措施来应对非欧盟卖家的快速崛起，其中很多非欧盟卖家的报价是免增值税的价格。

去年，英国海关加强了对于进关的小型包裹的审查，但他们更不能放松对可能构成恐怖威胁的商品、非法药物和假货的检查。因此他们倍感压力。

官方预计，进入欧盟的小型包裹数量将从 2000 年的 2 600 万激增到两年前的 11 500 万，增加了三倍多。而随着当前电子商务的蓬勃发展（据测算，去年电子商务的发展速度高达 14%），该数据还会继续走高。

②欧盟委员会五月的报告预测道，大量的符合低价商品的增值税减免优惠将致使欧盟成员国一年的损失超过 5 亿欧元。该数字还没考虑许多进口商会故意报低商品价值的因素。因此，欧盟的真正损失额可能更高。

---

distortion *n.* 扭曲　　catalogue *vt.* 归整　　overhaul *n.* 大改
interim *adj.* 短暂性的　　counterfeit goods 假货　　factor *vt.* 把……因素考虑进来

"Already this is a problem that is there and it's a problem that's getting bigger," said the Brussels source.

eBay sales of items ranging from Android phones and balance scooters to iPad covers and bike lights are already dominated by Chinese sellers, according to the latest sales analytics data. Figures for Amazon are harder to obtain, but UK sellers believe Chinese sellers are leading the field in many product lines on its site, too.

(*The Guardian*, 2015.11)

布鲁塞尔的内部人士称:"避税问题已经存在,而且在不断恶化。"

eBay最新的销售分析数据显示,中国卖家已占据半壁江山,从安卓手机到电动平衡车,从iPad保护壳到自行车灯,销售物品种类繁多。亚马逊的数据更难获得,但英国卖家相信,中国卖家在亚马逊的诸多商品线上也是一枝独秀。

长难句解析

① 本句为主谓宾结构,谓语用了 use...as... 的结构,动名词结构 allowing... 作伴随状语。

> Growing numbers of businesses from China [主语] are using [谓语] Chinese-run warehouses [宾语] in UK port cities [地点状语] as staging posts [宾语补足语], allowing them to offer eBay and Amazon shoppers rapid delivery [伴随状语] as well as competitive prices.

② 本句为主从复合句。主句的主干结构为 A report estimates that...。that 引导宾语从句,该宾语从句中还包含 because of 结构,作原因状语。

> A report [主语] for the European commission in May [后置定语] estimates [谓语] that more than €500m a year is being lost to member states [宾语从句] because of the huge volumes of packages qualifying for the low-value VAT exemption [原因状语].

Text 7　Google Is fined €4.3 bn in the Biggest-ever Antitrust Penalty
谷歌被罚款43亿欧元——有史以来最大的反垄断罚款

"The making of a big tech reckoning," blared one typical headline earlier this year. "The case for breaking up Amazon, Apple, Facebook and

今年早些时候一个典型的标题渲染道:"对大型科技公司进行清算的时刻到来了。"另外一个标题吹嘘

---

reckoning *n.* 清算　　　　　　　　blare *vt.* 高声发出

Google," touted another. Based on media coverage alone it might seem as if the tech titans are in trouble. Add in the news, on July 18th, of a record €4.3 bn fine for Google by the European Commission and that impression is strengthened. ①But if you look hard at where the regulatory rubber is actually hitting the road, the techlash seems much less brutal. Notwithstanding this week's fine—which amounts to just over $5bn and is the biggest antitrust penalty ever—the online giants are nowhere near being reined in.

To be sure, the mood has changed. In America a survey for Axios, a news website, found that between October and March the favourability ratings of Facebook, Amazon and Google had fallen by 28%, 13% and 12%, respectively. Republicans such as Ted Cruz, a senator, now employ anti-tech rhetoric. Last month the Federal Trade Commission (FTC) announced that it will, starting in September, hold hearings on "competition and consumer protection in the 21st century".

The shift in sentiment started earlier and has gone further in Europe, both because none of the companies have headquarters there and because of the region's sensitivities in regard to privacy and data protection. Google had already battled the commission, and lost, in "the shopping case", so called because it involves sites that involve comparison-shopping services. The firm was accused of having discriminated against rivals by downgrading their search results and putting its own on top; last year the commission levied a €2.4bn fine and told Google to treat all comparison-shopping results equally.

The case that led to this week's fine carries even more weight, in part because it echoes another famous battle. The commission says that Google is

道:"分解亚马逊、苹果、脸书和谷歌的案例。"仅从媒体报道来看,科技巨头似乎陷入了困境。7月18日谷歌被欧洲委员会处以创纪录的43亿欧元罚款的新闻更是增强了人们的这一感觉。①但如果你认真看监管机构的实际行动,你就会觉得科技抵制潮似乎并没有那么残忍。尽管本周的罚款略高于50亿美元且是有史以来最大的反垄断罚款,但这些科技巨头仍然远未受到控制。

当然,人们的态度发生了变化。在美国,新闻网站Axios的一项调查发现,从去年10月到今年3月,脸书、亚马逊和谷歌的支持率分别下降了28%、13%和12%。像参议员泰德·克鲁兹这样的共和党人现在开始使用反科技的言辞。上个月,美国联邦贸易委员会(FTC)宣布,从9月开始,将举行关于"21世纪的竞争和消费者保护"的听证会。

态度的转变在欧洲开始得更早一些,这种转变也更深远,这既是因为这些公司没有在欧洲设立总部,也是因为该地区在隐私和数据保护方面的敏感性。谷歌已经在"购物事件"中败给了委员会,之所以称为"购物事件"是因为它涉及与比较购物服务相关的网站。谷歌被控告通过降低对手的搜索结果,并将自己搜索结果放在首位而歧视对手;去年该委员会对谷歌处以24亿欧元的罚款并要求谷歌对所有比较购物的结果一视同仁。

本周罚款的事件造成了更深远的影响,部分原因在于它仿效另外一场有名的战斗。欧盟委员会称谷歌现

---

tout *vt.* 吹嘘　　titan *n.* 巨人　　fine *n.* 罚款　　look hard at 认真看
techlash *n.* 科技抵制潮　　brutal *adj.* 野蛮的　　rein in 严格控制
rhetoric *n.* 言辞　　comparison-shopping 比较购物
discriminate *vi.* 歧视　　levy *vt.* 征收(税等)　　carry weight 有影响

doing pretty much what Microsoft did in the late 1990s: tying together pieces of software to cement its dominance. This case involves Android, Google's mobile operating system, and all sorts of related software and services, including Google Play, its app store, internet search and a suite of other apps.

In essence, Google gives smartphone-makers and telecoms operators an all-or-nothing choice: if they want to install any of these programs on their devices, they have to install them all and show the icons in prominent positions. Since firms need at least the app store to make their products commercially viable, they have no choice but to comply. Nor does Google allow them to install competing versions of Android on any of their models. These practices deny "rivals the chance to innovate and compete on the merits" and "consumers the benefits of effective competition," said Margrethe Vestager, the competition commissioner.

Google has clever ripostes. In the shopping case it argued that it wants to give consumers quick access to relevant information, rather than forcing them to click through to another search engine. ②Indeed, the commission was widely criticised in that case for failing to show that consumers were denied a superior service as a consequence of Google's actions.

In the Android case the search firm insists that the restrictions are needed to make open-source platforms a success. The needs of everyone who uses them—not just consumers, but developers, device-makers and Google itself—have to be "painstakingly" balanced, in the words of Sundar Pichai, Google's boss, in a blog post published after the commission's ruling. The decision, he said, risks tearing apart this healthy open-source ecosystem by causing Android to fragment into incompatible versions and by making it less profitable for Google to invest in the software.

---

pretty much 几乎,差不多
riposte n. 回答
incompatible adj. 不相容的

cement vt. 巩固
tear apart 使分裂

all-or-nothing adj. 孤注一掷的
open-source 开放源代码的

But the commission is on firmer ground. Being the provider of both internet search and of related services, with substantial market shares across the board, Google will always have an incentive to discriminate against rival offerings, notes Damien Geradin of Tilburg University. And few will sympathise with Mr Pichai's warning on fragmentation. An open-source ecosystem is tricky to manage, but this does not entitle Google to stymie alternative ecosystems. Rules telling device-makers exactly where to place app icons seem draconian. Their aim, to protect Google's search service from competition, seems clear. And its restrictions have had an impact, for example in the case of Amazon's Fire phones, whose failure owed something to Google.

(*The Economist*, 2018.7)

但是委员会的立场更加坚定。蒂尔堡大学的达米安·格瑞丁指出,作为互联网搜索和相关服务的提供商,谷歌拥有巨大的市场份额,因此总是有歧视竞争对手的动机。很少有人会同情皮查伊关于分裂的警告。一个开放源代码生态系统是很难管理的,但是这并不能成为谷歌阻止其他可供替代的生态系统的借口。告诉设备制造商正确放置应用图标的规则看似苛刻,但他们的目标似乎很明确,即保护谷歌的搜索服务免受竞争。谷歌的限制也产生了影响,比如亚马逊的 Fire 手机,它的失败在一定程度上是由谷歌造成的。

长难句解析

① 本句为主从复合句。主句的主干结构为 the techlash seems much less brutal。if 引导条件状语从句,其中包含一个 where 引导的宾语从句。

But if you look hard at	where the regulatory rubber is actually hitting the road,	the techlash
条件状语从句	宾语从句	
seems much less brutal.		
主语+连系动词+表语		

② 本句为主从复合句。主句的主干结构为 the commission was widely criticised in that case。for failing to show that…为 for 引导的原因状语从句,该从句中 that 引导宾语从句,介词 as 引导的短语作宾语从句的原因状语。

Indeed,	the commission	was widely criticised	in that case	for failing to show	that consumers
插入语	主语	谓语	宾语	原因状语	
were denied a superior service as a consequence of Google's actions.					
宾语从句					

---

on firm ground 立场坚定　　incentive *n.* 动机　　stymie *vt.* 阻挠
draconian *adj.* 苛刻的

Text 8 Google and Facebook Can't Count on Consumers Saving Them
谷歌和脸书不能指望消费者来拯救

The scrutiny of giant technology companies and the inevitable anxiety that follows are now so commonplace that they have become rote. Once terms like "techlash" become household words, it's easy to become numb.

But truly, Monday was a noteworthy day. The attorneys general of 48 U.S. states, the District of Columbia and Puerto Rico announced an antitrust investigation into Google parent company Alphabet Inc. For those in need of a civics lesson, that is nearly every possible top lawyer from a U.S. state. The lone exceptions are those from California and Alabama.

The substance of their investigation is not surprising, but when a red-state attorney general from Texas and his blue-state counterpart from the District join forces, you know something weird is happening. Antipathy about giant tech companies may be the single bipartisan issue that can unite people like President Donald Trump and Elizabeth Warren, the Democratic presidential candidate.

Already, the U.S. Department of Justice, the Federal Trade Commission, U.S. congressional committees, Europe's anti-monopoly authority and a different batch of state watchdogs are looking into whether Alphabet, Facebook Inc. and other tech superpowers are using their influence to unfairly advantage themselves over competitors and give people worse products and services or fewer alternatives. I would call this a laundry list of government investigations into the American tech giants, but no one's wardrobe is this big.

---

rote n. 机械式的过程；死记硬背
wardrobe n. 全部服装；衣柜

watchdog n. 监察委员会；监察员

①It's easy to brush off the announcement by the attorneys general as just another version of the semi-permanent regulatory background noise that won't materially hurt the tech companies. Google has been through the antitrust investigations merry-go-round for the better part of the last decade, including a long federal antitrust inquiry that ended in 2013 without significant adverse findings.

②It's hard to prove that Google's mixed track record in state, federal and international legal investigations has hurt its standing with the public or significantly dented a company with an $830 billion stock market value.

What's different this time is the persistence and volume of these various government inquiries combined with the tech giants' huge size and the public's souring feelings about them. That stew of forces could make these fresh investigations sting even if no one finds a smoking gun.

Regulators and particularly elected officials are divining rods of the public mood. Their willingness to poke and prod the tech giants shows they think it's not just policy makers who wonder whether big tech is too powerful and too unaccountable. The existence of the investigations is another sign that public trust in tech giants isn't ironclad, and headlines about the investigations or subsequent revelations from them could form a feedback loop that further contributes to the erosion of consumer trust.

That matters for Silicon Valley and beyond because tech companies can thrive only if people trust them. The more people think twice and ask themselves why they're getting a particular answer from Google, why Facebook thinks they should join a specific online group, why Amazon suggests they buy a certain bath towel, or why they should track health information with the Apple app, the worse it is

①总检察长很容易忽略这个声明,认为这只是半永久性的监管背景噪声的另一个版本,不会对科技公司造成实质性伤害。在过去十年的大部分时间里,谷歌已经经历了一连串的反垄断调查,包括在2013年结束的漫长的联邦反垄断调查,其没有明显的负面调查结果。

②很难证明谷歌在州、联邦和国际法律调查中的不同纪录损害了其在公众中的地位,或是严重削弱了这家市值8 300亿美元的公司的实力。

这次的不同之处在于政府各种调查的持久性和数量,加上科技巨头的巨大规模和公众对他们的不满情绪。这些混杂的力量也会让这些新调查刺痛人心,即使没有人找到确凿的证据。

监管机构,特别是当选官员正在揣测公众情绪。他们仔细检查科技巨头的意愿表明,他们认为不只有政策制定者怀疑大科技公司是否过于强大和过于不负责任。调查的存在表明另一个迹象,即公众对科技巨头的信任并不是牢不可破的,关于这些调查的头条新闻或监管者后续揭露的事可能会形成一个反馈循环,进一步侵蚀消费者的信任。

这对硅谷及其他地方至关重要,因为只有在人们信任科技公司的时候,他们才能繁荣发展。人们越是再三思考和追问为什么他们要从谷歌那里得到一个特定的答案,为什么脸书认为他们应该加入一个特别的线上群体,为什么亚马逊认为他们应该买某一款浴巾,或者为什

---

brush off 不理睬;拒绝
dent *vt.* 损害;对……产生不利影响;削弱
smoking gun (尤指犯罪的)确凿证据
poke and prod 仔细检查;钻研

merry-go-round 一连串的繁忙活动
stew *n.* 混杂
divine *vt.* 猜测;预言
ironclad *adj.* 打不破的;坚固的

for tech companies. Those rapidly firing human neurons are not good.

It's both good and bad for Google, Facebook and the others that government investigations can drag on and on. Political winds can shift, and outrage may move to other areas. More likely, though, America's tech superpowers will need to figure out how to survive now that they're regarded not with a special affection by the public but with the same kind of lukewarm -at-best feelings they have about more conventional companies. Big tech, in short, needs to learn to live with the same level of public affection as airlines or banks.

(*Bloomberg*, 2019.9)

么他们应该用苹果应用程序追踪健康信息，就越不利于科技公司。那些快速刺激人类神经元的是不好的。

对谷歌、脸书和其他公司来说，政府调查可能一直拖延下去，这是好事，也是坏事。政治风向可能改变，愤怒可能蔓延到其他地区。但更有可能的是，美国的科技巨头需要弄清楚如何生存下去，因为他们没有受到公众的特别喜爱，而是受到与其自身对更传统的公司所持有的同样的冷淡之情。简而言之，大型科技公司需要学会与航空公司或银行一样，得到公众的喜爱。

长难句解析

① 本句主干为主系表结构，it 为形式主语，真正的主语是不定式短语 to brush off...。by the attorneys general 为方式状语；as just another...介词短语作宾语 announcement 的宾语补足语；that 引导的是定语从句，修饰 another version。

> It's easy　to brush off the announcement　by the attorneys general　as just another
> 主系表　　　真正的主语　　　　　　　　　方式状语
> version of the semi-permanent regulatory background noise　that won't materially
> 　　　　　　　宾语补足语　　　　　　　　　　　　　定语从句
> hurt the tech companies.

② 本句主干为主系表结构，it 为形式主语，真正的主语是不定式 to prove that...。that 引导的从句作 prove 的宾语，or 连接宾语从句中的并列谓宾结构 has hurt its standing...和 dented a company...；with 介词短语作 company 的后置定语。

> It's hard　to prove that Google's mixed track record in state, federal and international
> 主系表　　　　　　　　真正的主语
> legal investigations has hurt its standing with the public or significantly dented a company
> with an $830 billion stock market value.
> 　　　　后置定语

---

outrage *n.* 愤怒　　　　　　lukewarm *adj.* 冷淡的；微温的；不够热心的

Text 9   A Strong U.S. Consumer Is a Lagging Indicator
强大的美国消费者是一个滞后标志

① Investors who are optimistic about the outlook for the U.S. economy and financial markets due to reports of healthy consumer spending, retail sales and an unemployment rate that held near a 50-year low in August need a history lesson.

Even though consumer spending accounts for about two-thirds of the economy, it was a poor predictor of the last two recessions, which occurred from March to November 2001, and from December 2007 to June 2009. A slowdown in spending coincided with the start of the first recession and lagged behind in the second.

Although consumers should be viewed as critical to the pace of economic growth, their spending patterns should not be relied upon to provide guidance on the timing of a recession. As such, the strong 0.6% rise in consumer spending for July cannot be taken to mean the economy is on solid ground. This seemingly paradoxical conclusion has important implications for investors.

Economists divide a country's gross domestic product into four components: expenditures by consumers, investment spending by companies, government outlays and net exports. Of these, consumer spending is by far the most important in the U.S., historically between 65% and 70% of the total. This is why U.S. growth has held up relatively well despite the adverse impact on capital spending stemming from the uncertainties of President Donald Trump's trade policies.

Experience from the Great Recession shows that there is a lag of a several months before adverse consumer sentiment gets translated into reduced

①由于8月份良好的消费支出和零售额,以及50年来失业率最低的报告而对美国经济和金融市场前景持乐观态度的投资者,需要吸取一个历史教训。

尽管消费支出约占经济总量的三分之二,但对过去两次经济衰退来说,它是一个非常差的预测指标,这两次经济衰退发生在2001年3月至11月,以及2007年12月至2009年6月。消费的放缓恰逢第一次经济衰退的开始,以及第二次经济衰退之后。

尽管消费者应被视为经济增长至关重要的因素,但不应依赖他们的消费模式来预测经济衰退的时间。因此,7月份消费支出强劲增长0.6%并不意味着经济稳固。这个看似矛盾的结论对投资者具有重要意义。

经济学家将一个国家的国内生产总值分为四个部分:消费者支出,企业投资支出,政府支出和净出口。其中,消费者支出是美国最重要的消费支出,占历史上总消费支出的65%至70%。这就是尽管唐纳德·特朗普总统的贸易政策的不确定性对资本支出产生了不利影响,但美国经济增长仍相对较好的原因。

大萧条的经验表明,经过几个月的滞后期后,不良的消费情绪才会转化为支出减少。(不良)情绪一直高

---

paradoxical *adj.* 自相矛盾的 　　　　　　　　implication *n.* 暗示;含义

spending. Sentiment was still rising until January 2008, but then began to decline before bottoming in November 2008.

Why have consumers largely shrugged off the pessimism toward trade shown by manufacturers? A key reason is that spending is closely tied to movements in equity prices. Equities form a bigger component of retail investors' portfolios than bonds, and consumer optimism rises and falls with the stock market. The S&P 500 index reached a record high in March 2000, while it's high in 2006 came in December, both occurring 12 months before the onset of recessions.

The latest escalation in the trade war, with additional tariffs imposed by both the U.S. and China as of Sept.1, will have a large impact on consumers. Imported food, clothing, footwear and consumer electronics are among the products whose prices will rise once in the U.S. to take account of the new tariffs. Further levies on consumer products are set to become effective on Dec.15.

②Signs of weakness among consumers will become clearer by the start of the new year, meaning U.S. companies will have to decide how much of the price increases they will absorb and how much they will pass on to consumers. Neither option is likely to be positive for share prices. By the middle of 2020, the vicious cycle of consumers on strike and reduced corporate profitability should be in full bloom. That may mark the beginning of the next recession.

(*Bloomberg*, 2019.9)

---

shrug off 认为某事不屑一顾
portfolio *n.* 投资组合
escalation *n.* 扩大,增加
electronics *n.* 电子设备;电子工业;电子学
vicious *adj.* 恶性的;有恶意的

movement *n.* 走势;变动
onset *n.* 开始
footwear *n.* 鞋类
take account of 考虑到,重视
profitability *n.* 盈利(能力)

长难句解析

① 本句为主从复合句,主句的主干为 Investors need a history lesson。who 引导定语从句修饰主语 investors;due to... unemployment rate 为原因状语;that 引导定语从句修饰 an unemployment rate。

Investors who are optimistic about the outlook for the U.S. economy and financial
主语   定语从句1
markets   due to reports of healthy consumer spending, retail sales and an unemploy-
              原因状语
ment rate that held near a 50-year low   in August   need a history lesson.
              定语从句2   时间状语   谓宾结构

② 本句为主从复合句,主句的主干为 Signs of weakness will become clearer,by... new year 为时间状语。动名词短语 meaning... 作状语,其中包含两个由 and 连接的宾语从句。

Signs of weakness   among consumers   will become clearer   by the start of the new year,
主语   定语   系表结构   时间状语
meaning U.S. companies will have to decide   how much of the price increases they will
              状语   宾语从句1
absorb   and   how much they will pass on to consumers.
                          宾语从句2

Text 10 Everywhere in (Supply) Chains
遍布供应链

"The time that I went into the camp and I looked, I was shocked. Where all my expectations and my happiness all got destroyed, that was the minute that it happened." So testified Sony Sulekha, one of the plaintiffs in the largest human-trafficking case ever brought in America. He and around 500 other Indians had been recruited in 2005 to work in the Signal International shipyard in Mississippi. Each had paid at least $10,000 to a local recruiter working

"当走进营帐四处张望时,我感到十分震惊。我所有的期待和快乐顷刻之间被破坏殆尽,一切就发生在那一瞬间。"索尼·苏库拉在法庭上如此控诉,他是美国规模最大的人口贩卖案的原告之一。2005 年,位于密西西比的 Signal 国际造船厂雇用了他和其他 500 名左右的印度人。每人至少向 Signal 公司在当地的招聘人员支付了 1 万美金的费用,期待可以因此得到一份报酬丰厚的工作,

---

plaintiff n. 原告　　　　　　　　　　human-trafficking n. 人口贩卖

for Signal, expecting a well-paid job and help in getting a green card. Instead they laboured in inhumane conditions, lived in a crowded camp under armed guard and were given highly restricted work permits. Last month a jury awarded Mr. Sulekha and four others $14m in damages against Signal and its recruiters. Verdicts in other cases are expected soon. Signal says it will appeal.

A few days earlier Apple said that if it found that a supplier was using recruiters who charged potential employees fees, it would insist that they were repaid. Workers typically raise the cash by taking on debts that tie them to employers—a modern-day version of the ancient practice of bonded labour. The firm has now made suppliers reimburse around $4m collected in 2014 from some 4,500 workers, and has brought in checks to make the policy stick.

Estimates of the number of workers trapped in modern slavery are, inevitably, sketchy. The International Labour Organization (ILO), an arm of the UN, puts the global total at around 21m, with 5m in the sex trade and 9m having migrated for work, either within their own countries or across borders. Around half are thought to be in India, many working in brick kilns, quarries or the clothing trade. Bonded labour is also common in parts of Pakistan, Russia and Uzbekistan—and rife in Thailand's seafood industry. A recent investigation by Verité, an NGO, found that a quarter of all workers in Malaysia's electronics industry were in forced labour.

Until recently campaigners paid most attention to victims who had been trafficked across borders to work in the sex industry. An unlikely alliance of right-wing Christians and left-wing feminists

以及在公司的帮助下获得美国绿卡。事与愿违的是，他们在非人的艰苦环境下出卖苦力，住在武装警卫把守的拥挤的营帐中，所获得的劳工证的数量极为有限。上个月，陪审团给予了苏库拉先生和其他四位雇员1 400万美金的损失费，以褒奖他们反抗Signal公司及其招聘人员的行为。其他相关案件也很快就会有裁决结果。Signal公司声称将会上诉。

几天前，苹果公司表示，如果发现其供应商的招聘人员有向应聘人员收取费用的，必会敦促其尽快返还。工人通常筹集现金的方式是向他们的雇主借钱，这简直就是古代抵债性劳动的现代版本。迄今为止，苹果公司已促使供应商返还了它们在2014年向大约4 500名员工收取的约400万美金的费用，并且引入了审查机制，以确保政策能够持续。

当然，全球范围内究竟有多少工人受困于现代奴隶制度，很少有人能给出精确的统计数据。据联合国下属的国际劳工组织(ILO)估算，全球大约有2 100万工人在忍受现代劳动奴役，其中500万人从事性交易，外出打工的有900万人(在国内工作或出国工作)。其中有将近一半的人被认为在印度，他们中的许多人在砖瓦厂、采石场或制衣厂里劳动。抵债性劳动在巴基斯坦、俄罗斯和乌兹别克斯坦的部分地区也十分常见，泰国的海产产业里充斥着这种性质的劳动。非政府组织"维泰"最近的一项调查发现，马来西亚电子行业中有四分之一的工人都在遭受强制性劳动。

在此之前，发起运动的人都主要关注被跨境贩卖到性产业工作的受害者。右翼的基督信徒和左翼的女权主义者也因此暂时摒弃往日的意见不合，联合呼

---

verdict n. 判决　　raise the cash 筹款　　reimburse vt. 赔偿　　sketchy adj. 粗略的
arm n. 部门　　　　brick kiln 砖窑　　　　quarry n. 采石场

argued that prosecuting sex workers' customers would be the best remedy. But the focus is now widening to the greater number of people in other forms of bonded labour—and the proposed solutions are changing. Campaign groups and light-touch laws, backed up by the occasional high-profile prosecution, aim to shame multinationals into policing their own supply chains.

①In December Pope Francis and the grand imam of Egypt's al-Azhar mosque, together with several other religious leaders, launched the Global Freedom Network, a coalition that tries to press governments and businesses to take the issue seriously. The ILO has launched a fair-recruitment protocol, intended to cut out agents, which it hopes will be ratified by national governments. A pilot project will soon start in Jordan's clothing industry. Last month the British Retail Consortium, a trade group, published guidelines for supply chains, including recommendations on working conditions.

Two new philanthropic funds are also being established. ②The Global Fund to End Slavery, which is reported to have substantial seed money from Andrew Forrest, an Australian mining magnate, will seek grants from donor governments and part-fund national strategies developed by public-private partnerships in countries in which bonded labour is common. The Freedom Fund, launched in 2013 by Mr. Forrest (again), Pierre Omidyar (the founder of eBay) and the Legatum Foundation (the charity of Christopher Chandler, a billionaire from New Zealand), finances research into ways to reduce bonded labour.

---

prosecute *vt.* 起诉　　　　　remedy *n.* 解决方法　　　　　bonded labour 抵债性劳动
light-touch *adj.* 宽松的　　　protocol *n.* 草案；协议　　　philanthropic *adj.* 博爱的；仁慈的
magnate *n.* 巨头

The Freedom Fund's first schemes include assessments of efforts to free bonded labour in the Thai seafood industry, the clothing industry in southern India and—a harder problem, since the customers are rarely multinationals—in brick kilns in the Indian states of Uttar Pradesh and Bihar. Arguably, the lack of evidence about what works is the main obstacle to reducing the prevalence of modern slavery.

America made human trafficking illegal in 2000, after which it started to publish annual assessments of other countries' efforts to tackle it. But it has only slowly turned up the heat on offenders within its borders. Australia and Britain have recently passed light-touch laws along the lines of a law requiring transparency in supply chains that was adopted by California in 2010. This requires manufacturers and retailers that do business in the state and have global revenues of at least $100m to list the efforts they are taking to eradicate modern slavery and human trafficking from their supply chains. A firm can comply by simply reporting that it is doing nothing. But it seems few are willing to admit this, lest it upset customers or staff, meaning that the issue is forcing its way on to managers' to do lists.

Ending bonded labour will require economic as well as legal measures, says Beate Andrees of the ILO. Those desperate enough to get into debt for the chance of a job need better options and long-standing recruitment practices must change. But she also hopes to see some "strategic litigation". Nick Grono of the Freedom Fund thinks one of the multinational construction firms preparing Qatar to host the 2022 football World Cup could be a candidate. There is evidence of "willful blindness" to the terms on which migrant construction workers are being recruited, he says. A successful prosecution could be salutary.

(*The Economist*, 2015.3)

---

arguably *adv.* 可能，大概　　eradicate *vt.* 根除　　salutary *adj.* 有益的

长难句解析

① 本句为主从复合句。together with 是介词短语作伴随状语；a coalition 为宾语 the Global Freedom Network 的同位语；that 引导的定语从句修饰先行词 a coalition。

> In December Pope Francis and the grand imam of Egypt's al-Azhar mosque, together with several other religious leaders, launched the Global Freedom Network, a coalition that tries to press governments and businesses to take the issue seriously.
> 时间状语　主语　伴随状语　谓语　宾语　同位语　定语从句

② 本句为主从复合句。主语为 The Global Fund to End Slavery，which 引导的非限制性定语从句修饰主语；an Australian mining magnate 作 Andrew Forrest 的同位语；谓语为 will seek；宾语为 grants 和 part-fund national strategies。

> The Global Fund to End Slavery, which is reported to have substantial seed money from Andrew Forrest, an Australian mining magnate, will seek grants from donor governments and part-fund national strategies developed by public-private partnerships in countries in which bonded labour is common.
> 主语　非限制性定语从句　同位语　谓语　宾语1　状语　宾语2　后置定语　定语从句

Text 11　Why African Firms Create So Few Jobs?
为何非洲的公司创造的就业机会如此之少？

African businesses are reluctant employers. A given firm in Sub-Saharan Africa typically has 24% fewer people on its books than equivalent firms elsewhere, according to a recent paper from the Centre for Global Development (CGD), a think tank based in Washington, DC. Given the links between employment and development, economists want to figure out the reasons for the shortfall.

非洲公司的老板不愿意过多雇用员工。根据一家位于华盛顿特区的智库，即全球发展中心，近期所做的一项调查显示，非洲撒哈拉以南地区的某一家公司所登记的员工数量通常比其他地方的类似公司的员工数量少24%。考虑到就业与经济发展之间的联系，经济学家们想要找出产生这一差额的原因。

---

given *prep.* 鉴于；考虑到　　　　shortfall *n.* 差额

The study calculates the missing jobs by crunching information on 41,000 formal businesses globally from a World Bank survey. The data capture only a sliver of what actually happens in Africa: nine in ten workers have an informal job. Shunned by the formal sector, workers turn to below-the-radar employment—toiling on family farms or otherwise beyond the government's reach. But a big informal sector makes it harder for Africa to reduce poverty, even when economic growth is strong. Increases in income on the production side of the economy translate weakly into higher wages for workers. Indeed the relationship between economic growth and poverty reduction is weaker in Africa than any other developing region.

Several factors explain African bosses' reluctance to take on new workers. One is that firms tend to be younger than elsewhere, but even older one shave fewer employees. More broadly, Africa's business climate discourages hiring. Government officials in search of taxes and bribes tend to chase large firms, rather than small ones, says Vijaya Ramachandran of CGD, because they are considered more likely to cough up. The managers of Nigerien and Liberian firms with more than 100 employees spend 14% longer dealing with government officials than smaller peers. A recent study from South Africa revealed that bosses there were desperate to dodge the attentions of bureaucrats and thus avoided taking on new workers.

High unit labour costs are also culpable. Employing people in Africa should be cheap, given that many of its countries have rock-bottom income levels. Yet in half of African countries labour costs are higher because workers are less productive. They are nearly 80% higher

---

crunch information 处理信息   shun vt. 避开   below-the-radar adj. 不引人注意的
toil on 辛苦劳作   cough up 付钱   dodge vt. 躲避
culpable adj. 负有责任的

in Africa than those in other countries at similar levels of income. That lowers competitiveness and makes hiring less likely.

Economists disagree about the possible causes of this. Red tape and unionisation may be responsible, though on average indicators of labour-market regulation are no different in Africa than elsewhere. Nonetheless there are horror stories. ① A 2012 report on South Africa, which lays the blame on greedy unions, calculates that the average employee at Eskom, a stateowned electricity utility, earns 40% more in terms of purchasing-power parity than a German professor.

Africa's commodity-driven export models may be another cause of low formal employment. Four-fifths of the continent's export revenues are from commodities. That can lead to overvalued exchange rates if their prices rise. That hurts firms' competitiveness, curbs their growth and thus discourages hiring. (Africa's big inflows of aid also contribute to higher real exchange rates because they result in upward pressure on prices for goods and services that are not traded internationally.)

Changing labour-market dynamics could exacerbate the job problem. Some 250m people are expected to join the African workforce between 2010 and 2050. In the short term many will go into farming, which employs 65% of the African labour force. The agricultural sector struggles to create enough jobs. In the 1990s donors lost interest in using their aid dollars for agricultural investment. Shame: better farming techniques could bring unproductive land into use and help Africa shift into higher-value-added crops. According to a report by McKinsey, a consulting firm, that could create 6m extra jobs by 2020.

---

red tape n. 繁文缛节　　unionisation n. 工会化　　commodity-driven n. 商品驱动
curb vt. 抑制　　exacerbate vt. 激化

But agricultural improvement can also free up labour to work in more productive sectors—if the jobs are available. ②Africa is embracing structural reform: a recent report from the World Bank shows that of the 20 economies worldwide making the most progress in improving business regulation, nine are in Sub-Saharan Africa. Without further improvement, employment growth in Africa's formal sector will remain depressingly stunted.

(*The Economist*, 2014.3)

但是,农业的进步也可以解放劳动力,使其转而投入生产效率更高的领域——如果有工作岗位的话。②非洲正在推行结构改革:世界银行近期发布的报告显示,在全球商业监管取得最大成效的20个经济体中,9个来自非洲撒哈拉以南。如果不进一步改善劳动力市场,非洲正规就业率的增长仍会停滞不前。

长难句解析

① 本句为主从复合句。主句的主干结构为 A report calculates that…。宾语由从句充当,其中解释说明 Eskom 的同位语将宾语从句分割开来。

A 2012 report on South Africa, which lays the blame on greedy unions, calculates that the
　　　主语　　　　　　　　　　非限制性定语从句　　　　　　　谓语　宾语从句
average employee at Eskom, a stateowned electricity utility, earns 40% more in terms of
　　　　　　　　　　同位语　　　　　　　　　　　宾语从句
purchasing-power parity than a German professor.

② 本句为并列复合句,前后两个句子由冒号隔开。两个句子均为主谓宾结构;冒号后句子中的 that 从句作 shows 的宾语,其中 of 引导的较长的介宾结构实际作从句主语 nine 的定语。

Africa is embracing structural reform: a recent report from the World Bank shows that
主语1 谓语1　　　宾语1　　　　　　　　　主语2　　　　　　　谓语2
of the 20 economies worldwide making the most progress in improving business regulation,
　　　　　　　　　　　宾语2(宾语从句)
nine are in Sub-Saharan Africa.

---

stunted *adj.* 发展受阻碍的

Text 12 G7 Tax Accord Is a Game-Changing Opportunity
七国集团税改协议是一次改变游戏规则的机会

For four decades, global corporate tax rates have fallen in an international "race to the bottom", allowing big multinationals to reduce their burden by funnelling profits through low-tax jurisdictions. This weekend's deal between G7 finance ministers offers a game-changing opportunity to reverse that process—and ensure companies are visibly making a fair contribution to the post-pandemic recovery. For it to succeed, the world's largest economies more broadly will need to sign up. But it is in their own interest to do so.

The accord overturns a century of tax practice, where profits are taxed only where companies have a physical presence. ①Instead, any countries where the world's largest and most profitable businesses have sales would have taxing rights over "at least 20 percent of profit exceeding a 10 percent margin". Finance ministers also committed to a global minimum tax of at least 15 per cent, on a country by country basis.

②The agreement also represents a revival of multilateral cooperation and constructive US leadership after the Trump years—even if it suits the Biden administration's efforts to fund its spending plans by raising its domestic corporate tax rate. US companies could otherwise have made further moves to tax havens. If implemented, the accord lifts the

40年来,全球企业税率一直在一场国际"逐底竞赛"中下降,这使得大型跨国公司能够通过低税收管辖区获取利润,从而减轻自己的负担。七国集团财长上周末达成的协议,提供了一个改变游戏规则的机会,可以扭转这一进程,并确保企业明显地为疫情暴发后的复苏做出适当贡献。该协议要想成功,将需要更多全球大型经济体签署,而这样做也符合他们自己的利益。

该协议推翻了一个世纪以来的税收惯例,即只有在企业有实体存在的情况下,才对利润征税。①而根据该协议,凡是全球规模最大、利润率最高的企业有销售额的国家,都将对利润率超过10%的利润,拥有至少20%的征税权。财长们还承诺,各国征收的全球最低税率至少为15%。

②该协议也代表着特朗普执政后美国多边合作和建设性领导力的复兴——尽管它符合拜登政府通过提高国内企业税率为其支出计划融资的努力。否则,美国企业可能会进一步转向避税天堂。如果得以实施,该协议将解除美国

---

funnel *vt.* 传送(资金、商品、信息等)
game-changing *adj.* 改变游戏规则的
accord *n.* 正式协议;条约
practice *n.* 惯常做法,惯例
revival *n.* 复兴;复活

jurisdiction *n.* 管辖地域;管辖范围
reverse *vt.* 颠倒;撤销;反转
overturn *vt.* 推翻;倾覆
physical *adj.* 物质的;有形的;实物的
lift *vt.* 解除(法律限制或决定、禁令)

threat of US tariffs against European countries planning unilateral taxes on US tech giants.

Any compromise has imperfections and disappointments. Cross-border profit reallocation for tax purposes will be confined to the 100 largest global companies, and those making "super" profits. Yet even that limited scope will capture many of the US tech giants targeted by the Europeans. The 10 percent margin will require complex rules to be defined and agreed. The one-fifth of profits above that level open to international taxation will be relatively small, though it will be an improvement on the situation today. And what is crucial is the shift in principle to allow taxation by countries where companies have sales, not just where they are based. More can potentially be built on this foundation in the future.

The 15 percent global minimum tax is well below the 21 percent the Biden administration proposed in April; campaign groups say it is too low. But the "at least" formulation allows countries to adopt higher rates. Vital, too, is the agreement to apply it "on a country by country basis". That means companies cannot pay an average minimum rate by routing some profits through higher-tax countries and some through zero- or low-tax regimes. ③Instead, if a business paid less than the minimum in any individual country, its home country could make up the difference to reach the global floor or whatever that country had legislated for.

If enough large economies agreed to do the same, there would be no incentive for companies to put business through low-tax locations. Tax havens would have no effective power of veto,

---

unilateral *adj.* 单边的
reallocation *n.* 再分配
margin *n.* 利润, 盈利; 利润率
regime *n.* 政权, 政体; 社会制度
legislate *vi.* 立法; 制定法律

compromise *n.* 妥协, 和解
capture *vt.* 夺得, 占领; 获得; 吸引
formulation *n.* 制订, 规划
floor *n.* 最低额, 底价
veto *n.* 否决权

and the zero-tax business model would collapse. An agreement at G20 level might be enough to achieve this—but the "country by country" provision would have to remain in the deal.

These rules make sense for big economies to embrace, including the two largest. China might balk at its own multinationals having to pay some tax elsewhere. But it is in its own interest to receive revenues from, say, Apple, and to have a stable global tax system. For the US, too, giving up some tax revenue from American corporates abroad can open the way to collect much more from them at home— reluctant Republicans in Congress take note . No one wins from a Wild West tax system where everyone is trying to make gains at another's expense. The chance to reform that system should not be lost.

(*The Economist*, 2021.6)

溃。20国集团层面达成的协议或许足以实现这一点，但协议中必须保留"逐国"这一条款。

这些规则对于大型经济体来说是有意义的，其中包括两个最大的经济体。中国可能不愿意让自己的跨国公司在其他地方缴税。但从苹果等公司获得收入，并拥有一个稳定的全球税收体系，符合其自身利益。对美国而言也是如此，放弃一些来自海外美国企业的税收收入，可以为在国内从它们那里获得更多税收开辟道路——国会中不情愿的共和党人请注意这一点。在"蛮荒西部"的税收体系中，每个人都试图以牺牲别人的利益为代价来获利，没有人是赢家。我们不应错失改革这一体制的机会。

长难句解析

① 本句为主从复合句。主句的主干是 any countries would have taxing rights,为主谓宾结构。where 引导定语从句修饰 any countries；介词短语 over...作 taxing rights 的后置定语。

Instead, any countries where the world's largest and most profitable businesses have sales
主语　　　　　　　　　定语从句
would have taxing rights over "at least 20 percent of profit exceeding a 10 percent margin".
谓语　　　宾语　　　　　　　　　　后置定语

② 本句为主从复合句。主句的主干是 The agreement represents a revival,为主谓宾结构。介词短语 of...作后置定语，修饰 revival；after the Trump years 为时间状语；破折号后为 even if 引导的让步状语从句，介词短语 by raising...作方式状语。

The agreement also represents a revival of multilateral cooperation and constructive
主语　　　　　谓语　　宾语　　　　　　后置定语
US leadership after the Trump years—even if it suits the Biden administration's
时间状语　　　　　　让步状语从句
efforts to fund its spending plans by raising its domestic corporate tax rate.
方式状语

---

collapse *vi.* 突然失败；崩溃；倒闭　　　　balk at 回避，畏缩
reluctant *adj.* 不情愿的；勉强的　　　　　take note 注意到

③本句为主从复合句。主句的主干是 its home country could make up the difference，为主谓宾结构；if 引导的是条件状语从句，不定式 to reach...作目的状语，其中包含一个 whatever 引导的宾语从句。

Instead, if a business paid less than the minimum in any individual country, its home country could make up the difference to reach the global floor or whatever that country had legislated for.

状语 | 条件状语从句 | 主语 | 谓语 | 宾语 | 目的状语

Text 13 Finding the Perfect Pace for Product Launches
为产品发布找准节奏

Early this fall, if tradition holds, Apple will introduce one or more new iPhones—an unveiling that's among the year's biggest events in consumer electronics. The smartphone helped make Apple the world's most valuable company, even though Samsung and other rivals introduce new products much more frequently. That paradox led V. Kumar, a marketing professor at Georgia State University, and his colleagues Amalesh Sharma and Alok Saboo, to wonder: If a company wants to maximize shareholder value, what's the optimal number of new products to launch in a given time frame? Does it matter whether the launches are spread out or bunched together, and whether a new product is similar to the rest of the company's current product portfolio?

Managers don't need an academic study to recognize that launches take a toll on many parts of a company, from design and development to manufac-

如果历年传统不变，今年早秋，苹果将推出一款或多款新款 iPhone——这将是今年消费电子产品领域最重大的事情之一。智能手机使得苹果公司成为世界上市值最高的公司，尽管三星及其他竞争对手更频繁地推出新产品。这一矛盾情况使得佐治亚州立大学的市场营销学教授 V.库马尔和他的同事阿马莱什·夏尔马、阿洛克·撒布感到好奇：如果一家公司想将股东价值最大化，那么在既定时限内发布新产品的最佳数量是多少呢？是分期发布还是一次性发布，以及新产品是否与公司现有产品系列的其他部分相似，这些重要吗？

管理者不需要通过学术研究就能认识到，从设计、开发到生产、营销，公司的许多部门都会受到产品

---

unveiling n. 公开　　　　　　optimal adj. 最佳的　　　　spread out 把……分散
portfolio n.（产品或设计的）系列　　　　take a toll on 给……造成重大伤亡(或损失)

turing and marketing. Firms that launch many new products incur high costs, which may hurt stock returns. (Indeed, it's not uncommon for companies announcing disappointing earnings to blame product launches.) And clustering launches can stretch people and systems too thin. But on the basis of previous research into how companies can quickly incorporate learning from product launches, Kumar's team believed its questions involved more than just costs and resource constraints. "Firms introducing products at a rapid pace have little time to evaluate their products, learn from them, assimilate their experiences, and deploy them to commercial ends," they write. In theory, optimal pacing allows firms to use the lessons from one launch to improve subsequent ones, which should boost shareholder returns. And if that's true, the researchers believed, they could prove it empirically.

To do so, they looked to the pharmaceutical industry, where new products are especially important to growth in revenue and market value. Using various databases and studying 73 publicly traded U.S. firms from 1991 to 2015, they identified when each of 1,904 new drugs was introduced. They then calculated the pace of the launches (the average number of products introduced over a period of time) along with the irregularity in pacing (the variance in timing between launches). ①They also looked at whether each new drug fit into a therapeutic class and treated a specific ailment already represented in the company's product portfolio or whether it was outside the firm's existing scope. They gathered data

---

incur *vt.* 招致　　　　　　stock returns 股票收益　　incorporate *vt.* 把……吸收；使并入
assimilate *vt.* 吸收　　　　deploy *vt.* 利用　　　　　end *n.* 目的
empirically *adv.* 以经验为主地　　　　　　　　　　　pharmaceutical *adj.* 制药的
variance *n.* 变化　　　　　therapeutic *adj.* 治疗的　　ailment *n.* 微恙

97

on company stock prices and compared the returns to industry benchmarks. To isolate the effect of product launches, they controlled for a host of variables, including the strength of each firm's patents, whether the new product faced competition, the media attention paid to the launch, and each firm's size, age, and financial health.

The results largely confirmed the researchers' hunches. ②Firms that launched many new products saw their increase in value diminish over time, as did those introducing products just loosely related to their current offerings. Companies whose launches came at irregular intervals did worse than the industry average: They saw their market value fall, and the drop was greater in the case of complex products and for firms with large R&D budgets relative to their marketing budgets. "Our results indicate that there is an optimal level of pace and scope of product introductions that managers must consider," the researchers write. "Managers need to spend time learning from the products they have already introduced and incorporate these insights into their subsequent products."

This research doesn't specify exactly how a particular firm can calculate the optimal pace, spacing, and scope of its launches. But it does provide statistics and equations that can help managers understand whether a different pace might increase value. More important, it provides evidence that an optimal pace exists and that firms should be wary of exceeding it. The researchers also offer some estimates of the significant gains in value that can be realized by establishing a more rational cadence of product introductions. For example, their calculations suggest that the average firm in the study—one with a market value of $5.6 billion—could increase its market value by $702 million if it reduced the irregularity of its launches by 10%. The study puts a spotlight on the importance of process research in launching products, not just in developing them.

---

benchmark *n.* 衡量基准　　isolate *vt.* 区别看待　　hunch *n.* 预感　　loosely *adv.* 宽松地
specify *vt.* 详细说明　　equation *n.* 等式　　wary *adj.* 谨慎的　　cadence *n.* 节奏

Kumar recognizes that managers face numerous pressures—from investors, customers, the media, and competitors—to introduce products faster. But he says the perceived need for speed is often misguided. "Our study highlights the importance of looking at the entire portfolio instead of focusing only on the next product," he says. It's also a mistake to focus too much on when competitors will launch products. ③ Kumar likens companies that launch a product quickly in the hope of beating competitors to investors who try to time the market—which, research has shown, usually backfires. "There's something to be said for spacing out launches," he says. "You need to make sure you've learned enough from the last one and that you're not constrained by lack of resources."

(*Harvard Business Review*, 2018.8)

库马尔认识到,管理者面临着来自投资者、客户、媒体和竞争对手的巨大压力,这些压力迫使他们更快地推出产品。但他表示,人们对速度的感知往往是被误导的。"我们的研究强调关注整个系列的重要性而非只关注下一代产品。"他说道。过分关注竞争对手什么时候发布产品同样是错误的。③库马尔把快速发布产品以期打败竞争对手的公司比作试图抓住市场的投资者,研究表明,这通常会事与愿违。"对于拉开发布产品的时间间隔,我有话要说,"他说,"你需要确保你已经从上次的发布中学到了足够的东西,且没有因缺乏资源而受限。"

长难句解析

① 本句为主从复合句。主句的主干结构为 They also looked at whether…。whether 引导宾语从句,or 连接两个宾语从句。

> They also looked at whether each new drug fit into a therapeutic class and treated a
> 主语　　谓语　　　　　　　宾语从句1
> specific ailment already represented in the company's product portfolio or whether it
>
> was outside the firm's existing scope.
> 　　　　宾语从句2

② 本句为主从复合句,主句的主干结构为 Firms saw their increase in…。as 引导方式状语从句。

> Firms that launched many new products saw their increase in value diminish over time,
> 主语　　定语从句　　　　　　　　谓语　　　宾语　　　　　　　状语
> as did those introducing products just loosely related to their current offerings.
> 　　　　　　　方式状语从句

③ 本句为主从复合句。主句的主干为 Kumar likens… to…。that 引导定语从句修饰 companies;who 引导定语从句修饰 investors;which 引导非限制性定语从句修饰主句。

---

perceived *adj.* 感知的
backfire *vi.* 适得其反

liken *vt.* 比拟
space out (使)间隔开

Kumar likens companies that launch a product quickly in the hope of beating competitors
主语　谓语　宾语1　　　　　　　　　　　　　　　定语从句1
to investors who try to time the market—which, research has shown, usually backfires.
宾语2　　　　定语从句2　　　　　　　　　非限制性定语从句

Text 14 Facebook's $5 Billion Penalty Misses the Point
脸书的50亿美元罚款错失了重点

No one will ever feel sorry for Facebook Inc. Its history of deceptiveness, obfuscation and sheer blundering indiscretion has no modern peer. ①Even so, it's fair to ask whether the Federal Trade Commission got it right this week by imposing a record-smashing $5 billion penalty on the company—and to wonder what this might portend for the rest of the tech business.

The payment resulted from a year-long probe into whether Facebook had misled its users about how it handles their personal information, in violation of a previous FTC order in 2012. In a press release, the commission said the deal would impose "unprecedented new restrictions on Facebook's business operations" and "change Facebook's entire privacy culture." Really?

In one way, the settlement was indeed strict. ②It levied the largest such penalty in the FTC's history, established an independent privacy committee on Facebook's board, created new oversight positions, demanded that executives certify their compliance every quarter, and insisted that the company conduct a privacy

没有人会对脸书感到抱歉。它欺骗世人、混淆视听和完全浮躁轻率的历史在现代社会找不到第二个。①即便如此，询问美国联邦贸易委员会本周对该公司处以50亿美元创纪录罚款的做法是否正确是合理的——同时对这一做法可能给其他科技企业带来的警示感到好奇也是合理的。

这笔款项起源于一项长达一年的调查，即脸书是否在其如何操控用户个人信息方面误导了用户，而违反了2012年联邦调查委员会之前的一项条令。在一个新闻发布会上，该委员会称该政策将对脸书的业务运营实施"前所未有的新限制"并"改变脸书所有的隐私文化。"真的吗？

从某种意义上说，该解决方式确实很严格。②因为联邦贸易委员会此次征收的该类罚款是其有史以来最多的，而且在脸书董事会上建立了一个独立的隐私委员会，创建了新的监督职位，并要求高管每季度都要证明他们的合规性，还坚持要求公司对每个新产品进行隐私审查。

---

obfuscation *n.* 混淆；困惑
blundering *adj.* 浮躁的
portend *vt.* 预示；给……以警告

sheer *adj.* 完全的
indiscretion *n.* 欠考虑，轻率

review of every new product. For good measure, the Securities and Exchange Commission added a $100 million imposition of its own.

And yet the deal creates no significant new limitations on how Facebook collects, stores or shares data. It will have little to no effect on the company's advertising business. And all that added scrutiny and oversight? In practice, it's likely to amount to some added paperwork and bureaucracy that a company of Facebook's means can weather with ease. As for that headline-grabbing penalty, that's hardly going to hurt.

So why does Facebook always seem to get away with it? Not because of a "lack of will" on the FTC's part, as lawmakers sometimes claim. It's because by and large the company's business practices are entirely legal. The U.S. has no comprehensive national privacy law; even imposing these latest penalties required the FTC to take an expansive interpretation of its own powers. Facebook does what it does because it can.

Congress professes to be unhappy with all this. Legislators of both parties have expressed operatic dismay that the FTC's settlement didn't go far enough. But there's only one place to point the finger for this failure: Congress itself. This is a debate that must necessarily be handled by legislators, not farmed out to unelected regulators attempting to intuit popular sentiment or deduce congressional preferences.

Of course, there are good ways and bad ways to regulate privacy. But if Congress thinks that Facebook's data practices are evil, it can outlaw them. If it thinks they're merely abusive or excessive, it can rein them in. And if

---

for good measure = in addition 另外
weather *vt.* 经受住,平安地渡过(困难)
headline-grabbing *adj.* 吸引注意力的;极受媒体关注的
point the finger 公开指责

means *n.* 资源;金钱

operatic *adj.* 戏剧性的;夸张的
outlaw *vt.* 宣布……为非法;禁止

it thinks that the consumer benefits of a free social-media service outweigh the drawbacks of Facebook's misconduct, it can leave well enough alone.

What it shouldn't do is express ambiguous dissatisfaction and then expect the technocrats to sort it out. That's not just irresponsible. ③It could lead to a patchwork of quasi-legal precedents —stitched together fine by fine, company by company—that would only lead to confusion, uncertainty and court challenges down the road.

The right approach is for Congress to specify what behavior it thinks is objectionable, then codify a set of best practices and a system of certification—perhaps along with other incentives—for companies that comply. That would allow consumers to make informed choices about what services to use, and give companies clearer rules of the road. This may be less satisfying than imposing billion-dollar penalties. But writing rules for the digital economy shouldn't be outsourced. It's a job for Congress.

(*Bloomberg*, 2019.7)

一个免费的社交媒体服务给消费者带来的利益大于脸书不当行为带来的弊端，它可以不干预。

国会不应该表达出模棱两可的不满，然后期望技术专家去解决。这不只是不负责任的表现。③这可能会导致拼凑出一系列准法律先例——由一项项罚款、一家家公司拼凑在一起——这在将来只会导致混乱、不确定性和对法庭的质疑。

正确的方法是让国会明确其认为令人反感的行为，然后为符合要求的公司编纂一套最佳实践和认证体系——可能再加上其他激励措施。这将使消费者能够对使用何种服务作出有依据的选择，并为公司提供更清晰的发展规则。这可能不如开数十亿美元的罚款那么令人满意。但是，编写数字经济规则不应该假借他手，这是国会的工作。

长难句解析

① 本句为主从复合句。句首的 it 为形式主语，真正主语是不定式 to ask…和 to wonder…; to ask 后为 whether 引导的宾语从句，介词短语 by imposing…为方式状语; to wonder 后为 what 引导的宾语从句。

Even so, it's fair　to ask　whether the Federal Trade Commission got it right　this week
　主系表　　　　　　　　　　　宾语从句1　　　　　　　　　　时间状语
by imposing a record-smashing $5 billion penalty on the company — and　to wonder
　　　　　方式状语
what this might portend for the rest of the tech business.
　　　　　宾语从句2

technocrat *n*. 技术专家；专家政治论者
precedent *n*. 先例
codify *vt*. 把……编成法典；编纂

quasi-legal 准法律
down the road = in the future 将来

② 本句虽然很长，但句式不复杂，是由多个并列谓宾结构构成的。句首的 it 为代词，指代前文提到的内容；第 4 个和第 5 个谓宾结构中都包含一个 that 引导的宾语从句。

<u>It</u> <u>levied</u>   <u>the largest such penalty</u>   <u>in the FTC's history</u>, <u>established</u>   <u>an independent</u>
主语　谓语1　　　　宾语1　　　　　　　状语　　　　　　谓语2
<u>privacy committee on Facebook's board</u>,   <u>created</u>   <u>new oversight positions</u>,   <u>demanded</u>
　　　　　　宾语2　　　　　　　　　　　谓语3　　　　　宾语3　　　　　　　　谓语4
<u>that executives certify their compliance every quarter</u>,   <u>and</u>   <u>insisted</u>   <u>that the company</u>
　　　　　　　宾语从句1　　　　　　　　　　　　　　　　　　　　　　谓语5
<u>conduct a privacy review of every new product</u>.
　　　　　　宾语从句2

③ 本句为主从复合句。It 为指代词，指代本段首句内容。破折号中间为插入语；that 引导的是定语从句，修饰 a patchwork of quasi-legal precedents。

<u>It</u>   <u>could lead to</u>   <u>a patchwork of quasi-legal precedents</u> — <u>stitched together fine by</u>
主语　　谓语　　　　　　　　宾语　　　　　　　　　　　　　　　　　　插入语
<u>fine, company by company</u> — <u>that would only lead to confusion, uncertainty and court</u>
　　　　　　　　　　　　　　　　　　　　　定语从句
<u>challenges down the road</u>.

第三部分 文化教育类

SECTION THREE

Text 1

Grad School, a Leg Up—in Debt
研究生院,债务占了上风

It's fitting that the College Board released its trends in college pricing just before Halloween. It's frightening what many families are paying to help their children realize the American dream of a middle-income-or-better lifestyle.

The average annual sticker price for tuition and fees at public four-year colleges and universities increased 4.8 percent, to $8,655 over the past year. Prices increased 4.2 percent, to $29,056, at private nonprofit four-year schools. That's not including room and board.

One chilling fact in the report often gets overlooked because there is so much focus on the cost of an undergraduate education.

In 2011-12, 67 percent of the $51.7 billion in student aid received by graduate students came from federal loans, yet federal loans accounted for just 38 percent of the $185.1 billion in aid received by undergraduates. This means graduate students—those enrolled in master's or doctoral programs and those in fields such as law and medicine—are much more dependent on student loans.

And those graduate students taking out new loans from the federal government won't be getting the same subsidized help they've have had access to in the past. The change is part of the federal government's efforts to cut costs and reduce the deficit.

Students get a better deal under federal student loan programs than they do from other lenders. Federal Stafford loans have been either unsubsidized or subsidized. In the case of a subsidized Stafford loan—awarded based on financial need—the federal

在万圣节前这个合适的时机,大学委员会公布了大学的收费状况。令人毛骨悚然的是,许多家庭为了帮助孩子实现过上中产阶级或更好生活的美国梦,需要支付巨额的费用。

四年制公立大学的学杂费平均每年上涨了4.8%,去年达到了8 655美元。四年制私立非营利性大学学费上涨了4.2%,达到29 056美元,其中还不包含食宿。

大家的关注点都落在大学本科教育的花费上,然而却常常忽视报告中另外一个令人寒心的事实。

在2011—2012年,虽然517亿美元的研究生补助中的67%都来自联邦贷款,然而在1 851亿美元的本科生补助中,联邦贷款仅占据了其中的38%。这就意味着研究生(此处指的是攻读硕士或者博士学位,以及像法律和医学这些专业领域的学生),更大程度上需要依靠学生贷款来缴付费用。

而且这些从联邦政府手中拿到新贷款的研究生,拿到的补贴比以前要少。产生这样的转变是由于联邦政府为了削减花费和减少财政赤字而造成的。

学生向联邦政府贷款比从其他地方贷款要好。联邦斯坦福贷款分为无补贴和有补贴两种。有补贴的斯坦福贷款是基于财政需要授予资助贷款的项目,由联邦政府来为这些

---

room and board 食宿　　　chilling *adj.* 令人寒心的　　　in aid 补助

government pays the interest while the student is enrolled in school. ①With an unsubsidized loan, the student is responsible for the interest payments, which begin to accrue immediately, unless the borrower decides to defer these interest payments until after graduation. Most students take the latter option, in which case the interest is tacked onto the loan. This, of course, increases the loan's cost.

As of July 1, new federal Stafford loans taken out by graduate students will all be unsubsidized. Graduate students can borrow $20,500 per academic year. Unless you make interest payments while you're in school, the federal loans will accrue interest at a fixed rate of 6.8 percent.

②"While many graduate students, particularly those in the sciences and engineering, complete graduate school with little or no debt, the data indicate that a growing number of graduate students are not that fortunate," says a report by the Council of Graduate Schools. "The increased reliance on student loans to finance graduate education, combined with the elimination of subsidized Stafford loans for graduate students, increases in tuition and fees, and decreasing or stagnant support for higher education in many states suggest that debt levels will continue to rise. Many graduates are already entering the workforce saddled with debt that exceeds their annual salaries, and without changes to existing financial aid policies, more graduates will be in this position."

In its report, the council recommended that the federal government, state governments, universities and businesses work together to help students earn advanced degrees without incurring massive debt. For example, the organization has recommended a tax break that would encourage employer-provided assistance for graduate studies.

Until there are policy changes, if you're a recent college graduate loaded down with a lot of

---

accrue vt. 积累   defer vt. 推迟   be tacked onto 被附加到……
stagnant adj. 停滞不前的   incur vt. 招致

undergraduate loans and no good job prospects, the default move shouldn't be, "I'll just go to graduate school."

Think of the expression, "When you are in a hole, stop digging." Don't accumulate more loans. Investigate first whether a graduate degree in your field of study and in the job market is worth the debt load you'll amass.

If you're working, save up the cash for graduate school. Yes, I'm aware this will take time. But take the time unless you are prepared to burden yourself with decades of debt. Or look for an employer who will fully fund your graduate education or help subsidize some of your studies.

In the current job market and economy, an undergraduate degree is often not enough education for many fields. I get this. But I also know from the numerous e-mails and conversations I have with people that a graduate degree doesn't always produce a big enough increase in salary to offset the scary debt many graduate students take on.

(*The Washington Post*, 2012.10)

助学贷款,又没有好的工作前景,还不能违约的话,"那么我想我会去读研究生。"

有这么一种说法,"如果你在洞里,就别再挖了"。言外之意是说别去积攒更多的债务。考研之前,先要了解清楚,在你的专业领域和工作前景中,一个研究生学位是否值得你为之负债累累。

如果你工作了,可以考虑存钱读研究生。这个确实需要时间,但是慢慢来。倘若你自己决定了让自己负债累累,或者你的雇主愿意为你的研究生学习付全额学费或部分资助的话,就另当别论了。

从目前的经济和就业市场来看,很多领域的工作需要本科以上学历。我知道这个情况。但从我与大家不计其数的邮件和交谈来看,我也了解到,研究生学历带来的工资涨幅并不总是足以抵消他们担负的巨额债务。

长难句解析

① 本句为主从复合句。句中 which 引导的非限制性定语从句修饰 interest payments。

With an unsubsidized loan, the student is responsible for the interest payments,
　　　状语　　　　　　　　　　主语　　系表结构　　　　　　宾语
which begin to accrue immediately, unless the borrower decides to defer these interest
　　非限制性定语从句　　　　　　　条件状语从句
payments until after graduation.

② 本句为"直接引语+says someone"结构。引号中的内容为直接引语,可看作主句的宾语。直接引语中包含 while 引导的让步状语从句, that 引导的宾语从句作 indicate 的宾语。

"While many graduate students, particularly those in the sciences and engineering,
　　让步状语从句　　　　　　　　　　　　　　插入语
complete graduate school with little or no debt, the data indicate that a growing number
　　让步状语从句　　　　　　　　　　　　　　主语2　谓语2　　宾语从句
of graduate students are not that fortunate," says a report by the Council of Graduate Schools.
　　　　　　　　　　　　　　　　　　　谓语1　主语1　　　　　状语

---

default *n.* 违约　　　　　　amass *vt.* 积聚　　　　　　offset *vt.* 抵消

Text 2 A Turning Point for a Polish Ballet Company
波兰芭蕾舞公司的转机

"In the future we will say, before 'Artifact' and after 'Artifact'," said Krzysztof Pastor, the director of the Polish National Ballet, in a speech at the reception that followed the opening of a triple bill by the company at the stately Wielki Theater this week.

① Mr. Pastor was signaling an important moment for his company, which has existed, in one form or another, since 1785, when King Stanislaus Augustus formed the 30-strong group of "His Majesty's National Dancers." In the 19th century the company ranked high among European troupes (both Filippo Taglioni and Enrico Cecchetti were directors), but Poland's traumatic 20th-century wars and their consequences for the country have meant a low artistic profile on the dance front—and, for the most part, modest artistic ambitions.

Yet how quickly things can change. Two decades after the end of Communism, and eight years after joining the European Union, the Polish National Ballet is performing a program as international and as challenging as any major company today.

Called "Echoes of Time," it features the brand-new "Century Rolls," by the British choreographer Ashley Page; a 2008 work, "Moving Rooms," by Mr. Pastor; and William Forsythe's seminal "Artifact Suite," taken from his 1984 full-length "Artifact," and still a thrilling primer for the development of post-Balanchine classical ballet.

"在未来,我们会说,《神器》之前和《神器》之后,"波兰国家芭蕾舞团负责人克利兹托夫·帕斯特,在Wielki剧场三人芭蕾舞开场舞后招待会上的讲话中说道。

①帕斯特先生预示公司将迎来一个重要的时刻。自1785年斯坦尼斯洛斯·奥古斯都国王精选30名优秀的舞蹈演员组成"皇室国家舞者"舞蹈团以来,这个公司便一直以这样或那样的形式存在着。在19世纪的时候,这个公司在欧洲的舞蹈团里都是数一数二的(菲利波·塔里奥尼和恩里科·切凯蒂都担任过负责人)。但是由于20世纪波兰的战争,国家文化进程遭受了严重破坏,舞蹈的艺术性降低,最重要的是很多人对艺术没有了激情。

但是事态变化迅速。在共产主义结束的20年和加入欧盟8年后,波兰国家芭蕾舞团的表现有着能媲美当今任何大公司的国际水准和挑战性。

《时光的回响》以英国编舞者阿什利·佩吉新编的《世纪轰鸣》、2008年帕斯特先生编著的《移动空间》,以及摘自威廉·弗塞斯1984年的作品《神器》中的《神器套房》为特色,完美演绎了古典芭蕾舞剧的发展。

---

choreographer n. 编舞者

Together the works form a pretty good picture of what contemporary ballet looks like today: the fleet athleticism, the tricky, intricate partnering, the play with point of view through lighting and stagecraft. But those are just the common denominators; as theatrical experiences, these works are wildly different.

Mr. Page's "Century Rolls" is the second work he has made this year to the music of John Adams (the other, "Guide to Strange Places", was for the San Francisco Ballet); he obviously likes the infectiously dancey propulsion of Mr. Adams's compositions, and their joyful exuberance. "Century Rolls," a piano concerto written in 1996 for Emanuel Ax, is inspired by the 1920s technology of piano roll music and the way it transformed the sound of the instrument—something that Mr. Adams evokes in the clattering sounds of the score.

②That idea of technology as artistic fodder is also suggested in the ballet's front curtain, a reproduction of a painting, "Abstract Speed, (The Car Has Passed)," by the Futurist painter Giacomo Bello, and in Tatyana van Walsum's ingenious backdrop—a slowly scrolling, hugely magnified piano roll through which light shines, creating shifting, abstract patterns that sometimes look like far-off cityscapes.

The score cites Gershwin, Fats Waller and Conlon Nancarrow with as much relish as Debussy, Rachmaninoff and Satie, and Mr. Page responds to its jazzy rhythmic complexities with deft musicality. The piece is arranged around three couples, with each getting a major duet and many minor ones, as well as a single woman (the imposing Marta Fiedler) pursued and accompanied by two leaping men (Bartosz Anczykowski and Oskar Switala) and an ensemble of six women.

这些作品营造了一副当代芭蕾的美好画面：动感的舞姿，天衣无缝的配合，灯光和舞台特技对剧情的烘托。这些还只是共同特性，从戏剧体验的角度，这些作品无与伦比。

佩吉先生的《世纪轰鸣》是他当年为了向约翰·亚当斯的音乐致敬的第二部作品（另一个作品《陌生之地指南》是为旧金山芭蕾舞团创作的）。他显然喜欢亚当斯先生淡淡推进、颇具感染力且不失欢快的作曲风格。《世纪轰鸣》是为伊曼纽尔·艾克斯而作的一首钢琴协奏曲，写于1996年，受20世纪20年代钢琴摇滚乐及其改变乐器发声方式的启发。这正是亚当斯先生在铿锵作响的配乐中试图唤起的情感。

②把科技作为艺术素材的理念也在芭蕾舞的前幕得到展现，它复制了未来派画家贾科莫·贝罗创作的绘画《抽象的速度》（车已通过）；这一理念也在塔季扬娜·范·瓦尔苏姆的独创性背景中得到展现，一架缓慢转动、高度放大的钢琴卷帘，在灯光照耀下营造出变幻莫测的、有时看起来像遥远的城市景观的抽象图像。

这个乐曲引用了格什温、菲茨·华勒和康伦·南卡罗、德彪西、拉赫玛尼诺夫和萨蒂的曲风。佩吉先生配以爵士乐的音律来配合灵巧的节奏。这个曲子分为三组，每一组都有一个主要的二重奏和许多次要的节拍，有一个单独的女（气宇轩昂的玛尔塔·费德勒）伴奏和两个男（巴尔托什和奥斯卡）伴奏，还有六个女生的合奏。

---

contemporary *adj.* 当代的
denominator *n.* 共同特性
artistic fodder 艺术素材
deft *adj.* 灵巧的

intricate *adj.* 错综的
propulsion *n.* 推进
magnified *adj.* 放大的
duet *n.* 二重奏

stagecraft *n.* 舞台特技
concerto *n.* 协奏曲
cityscape *n.* 城市景观

Mr. Page's most interesting material is for his soloists —the couples and Ms. Fiedler flash on and off the stage, jumping, turning, whirling, sliding over and under each other's bodies—while the ensemble forms mostly contrapuntal, slightly dutiful contrast. The effect is often exhilarating, particularly in the sections for Yuka Ebihara and Sergey Popov, and Mr. Page weaves his patterns with skill and considerable choreographic invention. But the relentless pace of the music and the rapid, kaleidoscopic shifts of the dancers is, by the end of the long first movement, a bit numbing.

There is a beautiful duet for Ms. Ebihara and Mr. Popov in this section, its slow, off-balance leanings and extensions seen through a scrim and evoking moody poetry. But the third movement returns, musically and choreographically, to the perky brightness and speedy rhythms of the first, and if Mr. Page doesn't quite escape a certain monotony of tone by the end, he does evoke a sheer, pure pleasure of dance.

Mr. Pastor's "Moving Rooms," created for the Dutch National Ballet, where he has been a resident choreographer since 1998, provides a dramatic contrast to the untroubled cheeriness of "Century Rolls." (Mr. Pastor is still a resident choreographer at Dutch National, and is also the ballet director at the Lithuanian National Opera; presumably he never sleeps.)

Dark, literally and imaginatively, "Moving Rooms" opens with the jagged violin strains of the Cadenza from Schnittke's "Concerto Grosso No. 1" as a lone man (Carlos Martín Pérez) in black reaches and lunges in a square of light. He is gradually joined by 12 more dancers in flesh-colored leotards, who form symmetrical lines across the stage in their

---

soloist *n.* 独奏者
dutiful *adj.* 呼应的
choreographically *adv.* 舞蹈艺术地

contrapuntal *adj.* 复调音乐的
kaleidoscopic *adj.* 千变万化的
symmetrical *adj.* 对称的

own boxes of light, before dissolving into the darkness. To the dramatic "Rondo," the black-clad Maria Zuk and Vladimir Yaroshenko dance with plunging dramatic intensity, then mutate into a langorous tango as the music slows with unexpected playfulness.

The mostly overhead lighting, by Bert Dalhuysen, alternately imprisons the dancers in brilliant cages, or swallows them in blackness, adding greatly to the enigmatic world that Mr. Pastor has created onstage.

The use of lighting as a powerful theatrical element has been one of William Forsythe's major contributions to ballet over the last few decades. But it is only one of the many ways in which Mr. Forsythe has influenced the art form.

In "Artifact Suite," he shows many of the elements that choreographers like Mr. Page and Mr. Pastor have absorbed into an idea of what contemporary ballet can be: the give-and-take partnering, in which the man is as dynamically implicated as the woman; the unexpected extensions of ballet technique beyond its conventional lines and shapes; the initiation of movement from different points on the body; the transposition of shape from one part of the body to another.

"Artifact Suite," set to the sublime Chaconne from Bach's "Partita No. 2 for solo violin in D minor," and to a piano score by Eva Crossman Hecht, is a hugely demanding work for any company. ③It demands both a rigor of execution and a visceral, to-the-limit, force of performance, and it is to the great credit of Kathryn Bennetts, who staged the piece, that it looked as good as it did on a company that has never previously performed Mr. Forsythe's work. (It will undoubtedly look even better as the dancers absorb the through-the-body dynamics over time; this isn't movement you can learn by rote.) "Artifact" undoubtedly marks a pivotal

---

mutate into 变成
enigmatic *adj.* 神秘的
langorous *adj.* 没精打采的
visceral *adj.* 发自内心的
tango *n.* 探戈舞

moment for 20th-century ballet. As Mr. Pastor pointed out, it signals one for the Polish National Ballet too.

(*The New York Times*, 2012.11)

长难句解析

① 本句为主从复合句。句中 which 引导的非限制性定语从句 1 修饰 company；when 引导的非限制性定语从句 2 修饰 1785。

> Mr. Pastor was signaling an important moment for his company, which has existed, in one form or another, since 1785, when King Stanislaus Augustus formed the 30-strong group of "His Majesty's National Dancers."
> 主语　谓语　宾语　状语　非限制性定语从句1
> 状语　非限制性定语从句2

② 本句为主从复合句。主句的主干结构为 That idea is suggested。同位语 1 作状语 1 中 the ballet's front curtain 的同位语，解释说明芭蕾舞的前幕是什么；同位语 2 是同位语 1 的同位语，解释说明同位语 1 的画作名称；同位语 3 是状语 3 中 backdrop 的同位语，描述这一背景；其中 which 引导的定语从句 1 修饰 piano roll，through 为介词，与关系词 which 一起提前；creating...patterns 结构作伴随状语，其中，that 引导的定语从句 2 修饰先行词 patterns。

> That idea of technology as artistic fodder is also suggested in the ballet's front curtain, a reproduction of a painting, "Abstract Speed, (The Car Has Passed)," by the Futurist painter Giacomo Bello, and in Tatyana van Walsum's ingenious backdrop — a slowly scrolling, hugely magnified piano roll through which light shines, creating shifting, abstract patterns that sometimes look like far-off cityscapes.
> 主语1　后置定语　谓语　状语1
> 同位语1　同位语2　状语2
> 状语3　同位语3
> 定语从句1　伴随状语
> 定语从句2

③ 本句为并列复合句，由 and 连接。and 前的句子包含两个并列宾语，由 both...and...连接。and 后的句型结构为 it is...that...强调句型，强调 to the great...piece 这部分内容；who stayed the piece 为非限制性定语从句修饰 Kathryn Bennetts；that 引导的定语从句修饰 company。

> It demands both a rigor of execution and a visceral, to-the-limit, force of performance, and it is to the great credit of Kathryn Bennetts, who staged the piece, that it looked as good as it did on a company that has never previously performed Mr. Forsythe's work.
> 主语　谓语　宾语
> 强调句
> 强调句　定语从句

Text 3 A New Language for Pakistan's Deaf
巴基斯坦聋哑人的新语言

Karachi, Pakistan—With one national language, Urdu, four provincial tongues (Sindhi, Punjabi, Pashto and Balochi), and nearly 300 regional dialects, Pakistan's linguistic diversity is like a beautiful carpet, interwoven with threads ancient and young. The regional languages developed over thousands of years, while Urdu came from northwestern India in the 12th century. Then, in 1947, English was made an official language as a legacy of British rule in India.

Now a small group of educators of the deaf intends to add one more language—this one not spoken. It is called Pakistan Sign Language, and its creators just may succeed in spreading its use across the country.

Schools for the deaf have existed in Pakistan since the 1980s; one of the largest in Karachi is the Absa School and College for the Deaf, where initial research was conducted to develop Pakistan Sign Language, or P.S.L., as it is known here. ①A Pakistan Association of the Deaf, with chapters in many cities and towns, was formed in 1987, when deaf people in Pakistan were not just misunderstood; often they were shunned or ostracized by people who considered them mentally handicapped and unsuited for normal life.

In the same decade, Richard Geary Horwitz, an American, and his wife, Heidi, from the Philippines, moved to Pakistan from India and added a new dimension to deaf education. They are the parents of a boy who had been born deaf, and for years they had worked with the deaf in the

卡拉奇市,位于巴基斯坦——拥有一种国家性语言(乌尔都语),四种省会语言(信德语、旁遮普语、普什图语、俾路支语),以及将近三百种地区方言,巴基斯坦多样化的语言就像一张美丽的地毯,由古代和现代的线交织而成。地区性的语言在过去几千年不断发展,而乌尔都语起源于12世纪的印度西北部。随后在1947年,印度沿用了英国统治时期的语言,使英语成为本国的官方语言。

现在一小部分教授聋哑人的教育者想要再增加一种语言——一种并非口头表达的语言。人们称作巴基斯坦手语,它的创造者或许可以成功地在全国范围内将其推广开来。

20世纪80年代,巴基斯坦就开设了聋哑人学校。卡拉奇市最大的一个聋哑人学校就是爱巴萨聋哑人学院,最初就是在这里研究巴基斯坦手语,当地人称之为P.S.L.。①巴基斯坦聋哑人协会成立于1987年,在全国各城镇都有分会。当时巴基斯坦的聋哑人总被误解或是遭到排斥,因为人们认为他们有智力障碍,无法适应正常生活。

在同一时期,美国人理查德·吉尔里·霍维茨和他来自菲律宾的妻子海蒂从印度搬到了巴基斯坦,给巴基斯坦的聋哑人教育带来了新的视角。他们的儿子天生失聪,同时,他们夫妇多年来在菲律宾和新德里致力于聋哑人的教育。

Urdu n. 乌尔都语
(be) interwoven with 与……交织
linguistic diversity 语言多样性
ostracize vt. 排斥
dimension n. 视角

Philippines and in New Delhi. While visiting Karachi in 1984, they learned that their expired Indian visas would not be renewed. So they stayed here and started a program called Deaf Reach in a small classroom with 15 children from Karachi's slums as well as their son, Michael. From it grew the Family Education Services Foundation, a network of seven schools that now stretches across Karachi, Hyderabad, Rashidabad, Sukkur and Nawabshah in the province of Sindh, as well as Lahore in Punjab.

Today, Pakistan's Deaf Reach schools educate nearly 1,000 students, and additional foundation programs offer vocational and technical training, parent training and teacher education.

It is, of course, not enough. There are an estimated 1.25 million deaf children in Pakistan, and Deaf Reach schools educate a small fraction of them. Still, the project is considered a success when measured against Pakistan's bleak educational landscape. It is, after all, a nonprofit network with its own curriculum that delivers high-quality education to a specialized community. Pakistani companies and foreign aid organizations have enthusiastically donated money, and U.S.A.I.D. donated $250,000 last year to help build the Deaf Reach school in Rashidabad.

Inside the Deaf Reach schools, an emotional and social revolution is on view every day. Students are treated not as "special," but as normal. The one thing that sets a Deaf Reach classroom apart is that the lessons take place in complete silence. Students and their teachers—half of whom are deaf themselves—communicate in sign language, a graceful ballet of hands synchronized with moving lips and lively facial expressions.

One key to their success is the invention of Pakistan Sign Language. Another is the use of digital media.

---

synchronized with... 与……同步   digital media 数字媒体

A common Indo-Pakistan sign language was in use across the subcontinent long before the 1980s, but many words and concepts in Urdu and other regional languages had no place in it. Pakistan Sign Language grew out of this need, but by the late 1990s the books and guides developed by Absa were deemed outdated and went out of print. So the family education foundation worked with deaf instructors in Punjab and Sindh, and with Rubina Tayyab, the head teacher at the Absa School, to develop a new online lexicon that now contains 5,000 words and phrases. On its website, a new video each day shows men, women, girls and boys signing a phrase with its meaning repeated in English and Urdu. ②Aaron Awasen, the foundation officer in daily charge of the PSL project, describes this lexicon not as a definitive dictionary, but as "a portal through which Pakistan Sign Language can continue to develop."

The PSL tools imprint three languages—Urdu, English and PSL—on the children's brains at the same time. They also enable relatives and others to learn PSL even if they can't attend regular training sessions. ③Meanwhile, a publicity campaign called "Don't Say It, Sign It" shows Pakistani celebrities like the filmmaker Sharmeen Obaid-Chinoy and the cricket star Shahid Afridi signing simple phrases in short online video clips, in an effort to remove the stigma of "otherness" and incapacity from the common perception of the deaf.

In a country like Pakistan, where so many other languages and communities jostle for space, and a walk down any street reveals a modern-day Tower of Babel, what does it mean to give an entire community its own language? If "a loss of language is a loss of culture," as Mr. Awasen says, then the gain of a language is a gain in culture. So empowering the deaf can only strengthen Pakistan's social fabric; the deaf community will be proud to take its rightful position within the constellation of diversity that is one of Pakistan's greatest assets.

(*The New York Times*, 2015.4)

---

subcontinent *n.* 次大陆　　　　lexicon *n.* 词典　　　　stigma *n.* 成见；烙印
the gain of... ……的获得　　　constellation *n.* 星群；一群，一组

长难句解析

① 本句为并列复合句,由分号隔开,两个分句的主干部分均为被动语态。分号前的句子中,when 引导的非限制性定语从句修饰 1987;分号后的句子中,who 引导的定语从句修饰 people。

A Pakistan Association of the Deaf, with chapters in many cities and towns, was formed in 1987, when deaf people in Pakistan were not just misunderstood; often they were shunned or ostracized by people who considered them mentally handicapped and unsuited for normal life.

② 本句为主从复合句。句中 the foundation officer 为 Aaron Awasen 的同位语;in daily charge of the PSL project 为后置定语修饰 the foundation officer;宾语补足语部分为 not...but...连接的并列结构;which 引导的定语从句修饰 a portal,其中,介词 through 与关系词 which 一并提前了。

Aaron Awasen, the foundation officer in daily charge of the PSL project, describes this lexicon not as a definitive dictionary, but as "a portal through which Pakistan Sign Language can continue to develop."

③ 本句为简单句。句中过去分词结构 called...作后置定语修饰 campaign;like...and...为 Pakistani celebrities 的后置定语;signing simple phrases in short online video clips 作宾语 Pakistani celebrities 的补足语。

Meanwhile, a publicity campaign called "Don't Say It, Sign It" shows Pakistani celebrities like the filmmaker Sharmeen Obaid-Chinoy and the cricket star Shahid Afridi signing simple phrases in short online video clips, in an effort to remove the stigma of "otherness" and incapacity from the common perception of the deaf.

Text 4 It's a Boy Thing (Or Is It?) 这是男孩的问题(是吗?)

① The economic recession of the late 2000s, and the slow economic growth that followed it, have drawn particular attention to the declining

① 21世纪初的经济衰退及其引发的经济增速放缓,对低收入和工人阶层的影响尤为显著,他们遭到上述

fortunes of low-income and working-class men, who were particularly hard hit by these economic trends. Concern about the fate of non-college educated men has led some analysts and authors to focus on the role of the K-12 system. Authors such as Richard Whitmire, Christina Hoff Sommers and Peg Tyre note that, on a range of indicators, boys are struggling more in school than girls are. Boys' academic achievement in reading trails that of girls. Boys are more likely to be suspended, retained in grade or placed in special education. They are less likely to graduate from high school or enroll in and graduate from college than girls are.

That's the bad news. The good news is that boys' academic achievement and educational attainment have improved over the past decade. In the elementary and middle grades, boys are achieving at higher levels in reading and math than at any time since 1971. And the percentage of both men and women over age 25 who hold a bachelor's degree is also at a record high.

Nearly a decade ago, I reviewed the data on boys' and girls' achievement and educational attainment and concluded that boys weren't falling behind. In fact, boys were doing better than ever on a range of educational indicators. But girls' achievement was improving faster, causing girls to pull ahead of boys.

A new report from the Brookings Institution, released last week, largely affirms this analysis. It also finds something new: Boys are starting to catch up. From 2004 to 2012, boys at all grade levels made significant gains in reading. As a result, boys are narrowing the reading gap in the elementary grades. While high school girls today read about as well as they did in 1971, high school boys today do better in reading than they did in the early 1970s.

What should we make of this?

Among the variety of educational achievement gaps that exist in the United States, gender gaps are

---

(be) suspended （被）暂停　　　　attainment n. 造诣

uniquely perplexing. When it comes to achievement gaps by race, ethnicity and socioeconomic status, we know that children from different groups are raised in different families and often attend different schools than peers from other groups, and that these differences in home and school experiences account for a large portion of the achievement gap. Gender gaps are particularly vexing because boys and girls are raised in the same families and attend the same schools as one another.

② This leads to two possible lines of thinking about gender gaps: Either they represent innate differences in boys' and girls' abilities, or they reflect biases in how schools and families treat boys and girls that translate into differences in outcomes.

Do gender gaps in reading reflect inherent differences in boys' and girls' ability? Research consistently shows that, on average, women perform more strongly in tests of verbal skills than men do. But it's not clear if this finding reflects nature or nurture. The fact that gender gaps favoring girls in reading exist across all developed countries is a potential point in favor of the innate difference theory. The huge variation in the size of these gaps across countries is not. Moreover, as Brookings reports, gender gaps in reading disappear in adulthood.

Are schools biased against boys? Hoff Sommers concludes that "misguided feminism," and efforts schools put in place in the 1980s and 1990s to improve educational equity for girls, have had a negative impact on boys' learning. But the timing here is off. Boys' achievement and other outcomes haven't gotten worse during the period when girls have made educational gains, they've gotten better, if not as quickly as those of girls.

---

ethnicity *n.* 种族渊源 socioeconomic status 社会经济地位 vexing *adj.* 令人烦恼的
bias *n.* 偏差 nurture *n.* 培养；熏陶
(be) biased against 对……有偏见

③ A more subtle argument is that the way public schools operate today places boys at a systematic disadvantage, not because of any animus towards boys, but because teachers, the majority of whom are women, make decisions about curricular content, behavior management and the structure of the school day that ignore boys' interests, experiences and tendencies. This has led to efforts to make school more "boy friendly," but many of these strategies are based on dubious science, and there is little evidence on their effectiveness.

Differences in average male and female abilities pale in comparison to the variation within each group. As a result, designing educational approaches and interventions based on gender is likely to be far less effective than designing them based on the needs of individual students. A teacher who is struggling to improve learning for boys in her class will not get much help from learning about structural differences in male and female brains. What she really needs are effective reading curricula, tools for diagnosing students' reading difficulties and research-based interventions for struggling readers. She also needs tools to help differentiate instruction to student abilities and needs. And she needs effective behavior management strategies, as well as research-based approaches to help children develop their self-regulatory skills and ability to focus.

These tools will help her address many of the areas in which boys commonly struggle, but they'll also benefit girls who face similar challenges. And plenty of squirmy, energetic little girls face the same struggles commonly associated with boys in school. I was one of them.

We may never be able to fully understand and explain the causes of gender gaps in reading, but that might be OK. Sometimes, treating the symptom is actually more effective than treating the cause.

(*U.S. News & World Report*, 2015.4)

③一种更精确的说法是,目前的公立学校运作模式将男生置于体系中弱势的一方,这并不是因为学校对男生抱有敌意,而是因为大部分老师都是女性,所以在做出课程内容、行为管理和教学结构方面的决策时,会忽视男生的兴趣、体验和倾向。这使得学校努力"对男生友好",但这些策略很多都缺乏科学依据,因此收效甚微。

男女平均能力的差异在同性别群体的个体差异面前显得毫无意义。因此,基于性别来设计教育方法和干预措施远远没有基于学生个人需求所设计的教学法好。一个想要提高班上男生成绩的教师,从男女大脑结构差异的认识中得不到帮助。她真正需要的是有效的阅读课程体系、诊断学生阅读障碍的工具和有研究依据的干预措施,来帮助有阅读障碍的学生。她还需要能够辅助她对不同能力和不同需求的学生进行区别化指导的工具。她还需要有效的行为管理策略以及有研究依据的教学法,来帮助孩子发展自律能力和专注能力。

这些工具可以在男生普遍不擅长的领域中助老师一臂之力,也能使不擅长该领域的女生受益。很多好动、精力充沛的小女生面临着这个经常困扰着男生的问题。我曾是其中一员。

我们或许永远无法完全理解和解释阅读中性别差距的原因,但这没太大关系。有时候,处理症状实际上比处理病因更有效。

---

dubious *adj.* 可疑的　　curricula *n.* 课程体系　　self-regulatory *adj.* 自律的
squirmy *adj.* 好动的

长难句解析

① 本句为主从复合句。主句的主干结构为 The recession and the growth have drawn attention to…。主语是由 and 连接的两个并列成分，主语 2 中还包含一个定语从句 that followed it，修饰 growth；the declining…作介词 to 的宾语；who 引导的定语从句修饰 low-income and working-class men。

> The economic recession of the late 2000s, and the slow economic growth that followed it, have drawn particular attention to the declining fortunes of low-income and working-class men, who were particularly hard hit by these economic trends.

② 本句为并列复合句。冒号前的句子主干结构为 This leads to…。冒号后的句子是 either…or…连接的两个并列句，解释说明 two possible lines 的内容；or 后的分句中，介宾结构 in how…作后置定语修饰 biases；that 引导的定语从句修饰 biases。

> This leads to two possible lines of thinking about gender gaps: Either they represent innate differences in boys' and girls' abilities, or they reflect biases in how schools and families treat boys and girls that translate into differences in outcomes.

③ 本句为主从复合句。主句的主干结构为 A argument is that…。that 引导的表语从句作主句的表语，该从句中 public schools operate today 为定语从句修饰 the way；该表语从句包含两个并列的表原因的结构，即 not because of…but because…；because 引导的原因状语从句中嵌套了一个 whom 引导的非限制性定语从句，修饰 teachers；原因状语从句中还有一个 that 引导的定语从句，修饰 decisions。

> A more subtle argument is that the way public schools operate today places boys at a systematic disadvantage, not because of any animus towards boys, but because teachers, the majority of whom are women, make decisions about curricular content, behavior management and the structure of the school day that ignore boys' interests, experiences and tendencies.

Text 5 The Diplomatic Power of Art
文化外交力量

① Even as cultural property faces immediate peril today in conflict zones like Syria and Mali, there is anecdotal evidence that some nations are awakening to the diplomatic and foreign policy benefits that can flow from the repatriation of cultural patrimony.

While on a different scale from World War II, historic structures, religious monuments, and other priceless antiquities continue to suffer collateral damage and exploitation in armed conflict. Antiquities have been stolen, smuggled and sold in what is a reported multibillion dollar underground market. They have become the illicit prizes of private collectors and the subject of legal claims against museums.

So it goes in Syria, where wartime damage to World Heritage Sites, such as Krak des Chevaliers, seems intractable. In northern Mali, too, religious strife has brought ruin to centuries-old, historic shrines in Timbuktu. Where is the constructive potential of cultural property?

Some nations are beginning to exploit the power of antiquities as diplomatic and foreign policy tools outside of armed conflict. In 2010, Peru came to an understanding with the Peabody Museum at Yale University over Inca artifacts that had been the subject of dispute for nearly a century. More recently, the planned return of smuggled sarcophagi from Israel to Egypt reflects the strength of cultural property as a medium for cooperation between nations of conflicting ideologies.

Admittedly, cultural property also can complicate foreign relations. The disputed ownership and possession of the bust of Nefertiti has caused tension between Egypt and Germany for nearly a century. The case, however, remains a viable opportunity

①在叙利亚和马里等纷争地区,文化财产面临着迫在眉睫的危险。然而,即便如此,有传闻表明一些国家正在逐渐意识到外交和外交政策的益处,这可以从文化遗产的遣返中窥探一二。

然而从第二次世界大战的不同规模来看,历史建筑、宗教纪念碑和其他珍贵文物还在遭受武装冲突带来的间接伤害和掠夺。文物被盗取、走私,并在一个据报道(成交额)高达数十亿美元的地下市场被贩卖。它们已经成为私人收藏家的非法珍藏和公然对抗博物馆的主体。

在叙利亚也是如此,在战争期间,大量世界遗产遭受破坏,如"骑士堡教堂"等,这些似乎是很棘手的问题。在马里北部的廷巴克图,宗教冲突导致许多历史悠久的名胜古迹被损毁。文化财产的建设性潜力在哪里?

一些国家已经开始利用文物的力量作为武装冲突以外的外交和外交政策工具。2010年,秘鲁与耶鲁大学皮博迪博物馆就印加工艺品达成共识,两方因为该文物已经争执了近一个世纪。最近,按计划从以色列遣返埃及的走私石棺反映了文化财产的力量,其作为一种媒介,能够促进有冲突意识形态的国家之间的合作。

无可否认,文化财产也能使外交关系复杂化。有关奈费尔提蒂半身像所有权的争议导致埃及和德国紧张的外交关系持续了近一个世纪。无论如何,这种情况仍然能够

---

anecdotal *adj.* 传闻的 patrimony *n.* 遗产 antiquity *n.* 文物;古物
intractable *adj.* 棘手的 sarcophagi *n.* 石棺 bust *n.* 半身像

to strengthen relations between the two nations.

Turkey continues to up the political power of cultural property by withholding loans of objects until foreign museums fulfill requests for repatriation. ②As in return of the "Lydian Hoard" from the Metropolitan Museum of Art in New York in the 1980s, Turkey is seeking the return of cultural patrimony—objects that hold traditional or historical signi-ficance for the heritage of a group or nation—as exhibits for a planned "super museum" in Ankara. In the process, Turkey has confronted renowned museums in England, France, Germany, and the United States.

Nigeria also has a history of succeeding in repatriation. In August, All Africa reported that the director general of the National Commission for Museums and Monuments reiterated the resolve of the nation to secure the return of Benin Bronzes that remain abroad. Other nations may draw inspiration from the successes, as the problem of smuggling in stolen antiquities remains a persistent one.

The arrest of Subhash Kapoor last year exposed a history of smuggling of Indian artifacts and sale of stolen objects to museums in Europe, Canada, Australia, and the United States on a multimillion-dollar scale. In August, *The Times of India* reported on representatives of the Hindu community who made a global call for the return of illicitly acquired Hindu art. In July, Pakistani police seized a container of Gandhara artifacts in Karachi, uncovering a smuggling ring that may have supplied antiquities to collectors worldwide. In August, The News International indicated that academics in Mardan initiated an appeal to the federal government for the return of artifacts to the north-west province of Khyber Pakhtunkhwa.

The potential of an emerging trend toward repatriation may seem small in the face of the multidimensional threats, but it is increasing the strategic value of antiquities in diplomacy. As in the case of Peru, the United States government has demonstrated an interest in pursuing the return of artifacts to "source nations." Since February, for example, U.S.

为加强两国之间关系提供可行机会。

通过扣压对方的贷款直到国外的博物馆履行遣返请求,土耳其将继续提高其文化财产的政治权力。②在20世纪80年代,当纽约的大都会艺术博物馆将"吕底亚藏品"还回土耳其之时,土耳其也正在寻求把这些遣返的文物——这些文物是一个群体或民族层面的遗产,承载着传统或历史意义——作为正在规划中的安卡拉"超级博物馆"的展品。在这个过程中,土耳其与英国、法国、德国、美国的著名博物馆进行了对峙。

尼日利亚也有成功遣返的记录。8月,泛非通讯社报道,国家委员会的博物馆及古迹总干事重申了该国誓将收回仍在国外的贝宁青铜器的决心。其他国家可以从这一事件的成功中受到鼓舞,毕竟走私失窃文物仍然是一个反复出现的问题。

去年苏巴斯·卡普尔的逮捕暴露了印度文物的走私史——许多被盗文物被卖往欧洲、加拿大、澳大利亚和美国的博物馆,成交额达到数百万美元。8月,《印度时报》报道了印度教社区的代表,在全球范围内呼吁归还非法所得的印度艺术品。7月,巴基斯坦警方在卡拉奇市没收了一箱犍陀罗时期的文物,揭露了一个可能向世界各地古物收藏家提供货物的走私团伙。8月,(巴基斯坦)国际新闻报表示,马尔丹的学者开始呼吁联邦政府促使文物遣返开伯尔·普赫图赫瓦省的西北部地区。

在多种威胁面前,遣返趋势增长的可能性显得很小,但它在外交中增加了文物的战略价值。例如,在之前提到的秘鲁(这一事件)的这种情况下,美国政府已经表明有意将物品返还给"来源国家"。又如,2月以来,美国政府一直在努力

---

reiterate *vt.* 重申

multidimensional *adj.* 多面的

authorities have been working on behalf of Cambodia to reclaim a statue of a mythical warrior that had been scheduled for auction in New York.

The United States is not alone among "collecting nations" in following this trend. In the United Kingdom, British border police regularly intercept illicitly imported cultural property, such as artifacts from Afghanistan. In August, the British Museum played a role in returning hundreds of antiquities to the National Museum in Kabul.

Proactive repatriation on the part of collecting nations demonstrates the significance of cultural property in foreign policy. There are implications for the private sector, too. As museums and auction houses take on roles as agents of diplomacy, private collectors may reflect on their own engagement in foreign relations. Museum directors and owners of private collections can wait to be challenged on the provenance of artifacts of foreign cultural heritage—or realize an opportunity for strengthening relations with the source nation.

(*U.S. News & World Report*, 2012.11)

帮助柬埔寨收回已定于在纽约拍卖会上拍卖的神秘武士雕像。

美国并不是这些"收集的国家"中的唯一一个遵循这种趋势的国家。在英国，边境警察经常会拦截到非法出口的文化财产，比如来自阿富汗的文物。8月，大英博物馆在将数百件文物返还喀布尔的国家博物馆中发挥了一定的作用。

部分收集(文物)国家的主动遣返证明了文化财产对于外交政策的重要意义。这也对私营部门造成了影响。由于博物馆和拍卖行在承担外交代理的角色，私人收藏者可能会反省自己在外交关系上的参与。博物馆的董事和私人收藏者在外国文物来源方面将受到挑战——或得到加强与来源国家关系的机会。

长难句解析

① 本句的主句为 there be 结构，主干结构为 there is evidence that…。that 引导的同位语从句解释说明 evidence 的内容；that 引导的定语从句修饰 diplomatic and foreign policy benefits。

Even as cultural property faces immediate peril today in conflict zones like Syria and Mali, （让步状语从句）
there is anecdotal evidence that some nations are awakening to the diplomatic and foreign
（there be 结构）   （同位语从句）
policy benefits that can flow from the repatriation of cultural patrimony.
                （定语从句）

② 本句为主从复合句。句中破折号中间内容为插入语，其中 objects 为 cultural patrimony 的同位语，that 引导的定语从句修饰 objects；as exhibits for…为方式状语。

As in return of the "Lydian Hoard" from the Metropolitan Museum of Art in New York in the
（时间状语）
1980s, Turkey is seeking the return of cultural patrimony—objects that hold traditional or
（主语） （谓语）   （宾语）   （同位语） （定语从句）
historical significance for the heritage of a group or nation—as exhibits for a planned "super
                                                （方式状语）
museum" in Ankara.

Text 6 *Maps to the Stars* Shows an Oscar Winner's Untamed Side
《星图》展现了奥斯卡得主野性的一面

If Oscars were handed out for exertion, Julianne Moore would have just picked one up—not for her exquisitely controlled performance in *Still Alice* but for the far wilder *Maps to the Stars*. ①Moore won the Best Actress Oscar and wide acclaim for her tasteful role as an Alzheimer's sufferer, but she shows off a taste for mania in director David Cronenberg's new film, which, after an awards qualifying run last year, opens nationally Feb. 27. The star plays a perpetually panicked actor whose bad behavior includes celebrating a competitor's tragic misfortune with a dance to "Na Na Hey Hey Kiss Him Goodbye." It's the latest iteration of an established pattern: Cronenberg showing us a familiar performer's dark side.

The Canadian director, 71, has spent an entire career working outside the Hollywood system (*Maps to the Stars* is the first film he has shot partly within the U.S.) and has elicited defining performances from several stars by moving them past the recognizable. "Once you're on set with the actor," Cronenberg says. "it's as if you've never seen this person before."

Moore, whose work in *Maps* won her the Best Actress prize at the Cannes Film Festival last year, is untethered from her past personas and from reality. Her character, Havana Segrand, is a second generation actor desperate to land the leading role in a remake of her late mother's signature film, all while being haunted by her mother's ghost (played by Sarah Gadon). Havana's frantic mental state reflects the precariousness of her fame. "After the age of 40, they're gone," Cronenberg says of actresses

如果奥斯卡颁奖典礼依照努力来评奖，那么朱丽安·摩尔只能获得一座小金人——不是由于她在《想念我自己》中收放自如的精湛演技，而是在《星图》中的狂野表现。①因很好地饰演了一个阿尔茨海默症患者的角色，摩尔获得了奥斯卡最佳女主角奖并获得了广泛好评，但她在导演大卫·柯南伯格的新片中展示了自己对躁狂症的尝试，该片在去年角逐各项大奖后，于2月27日开始在全国上映。摩尔扮演一个长期陷入恐慌的演员，该角色在片中有许多不良行为，包括伴着"娜娜嘿嘿吻别"跳舞，来庆祝竞争对手的悲惨遭遇。这是一个既定格局的最新迭代：柯南伯格展示了一个我们熟悉的演员的阴暗面。

这位71岁的加拿大导演的整个职业生涯都脱离开好莱坞系统（《星图》是其第一部在美国境内拍摄的影片），他颠覆了几位明星的固有荧幕形象。"一旦你在片场见到这个演员，"柯南伯格说，"你会感觉你从来没见过这个人。"

摩尔在《星图》中的表现为她赢得了去年的戛纳电影节最佳女演员奖，她脱离了过去的角色和现实中的人物性格。她所扮演的哈瓦那·希尔格莱德，是一位星二代，渴望在已故母亲成名作的电影翻拍版中扮演主角，这期间被她母亲的鬼魂（由莎拉·加顿饰演）纠缠。哈瓦娜疯狂的精神状态反映了她名气的不稳定性。"40岁之后，她们走了，"柯南伯格对主流荧幕中的女

---

iteration *n.* 迭代
frantic *adj.* 狂乱的

elicit *vt.* 引出
precariousness *n.* 不稳定

(be) untethered from 脱离

in mainstream cinema. "The phone stops ringing. And for them, it's kind of a predeath."

Cronenberg, who began his career in horror, with creature features like Shivers and The Fly, is the go-to director for stars who want to push themselves almost too far. ② He turned Viggo Mortensen into a terse Russian gangster, a role that earned him an Oscar nomination, in Eastern Promises (2007) and took Keira Knightley to the brink of madness on screen in A Dangerous Method (2011). But for all the accolades he's brought his actors, Cronenberg has stayed out of the limelight. The director, who turned down opportunities to direct Flashdance and Top Gun, has lived in Toronto his entire life. In Canada, he says, "you're not in the flood. You're in a creek coming off the flood."

Saturday Night Live producer Lorne Michaels and Ghostbusters director Ivan Reitman were among Cronenberg's friends in the 1970s Toronto scene, and both eventually found massive success by heading south. But staying outside Hollywood has allowed Cronenberg something perhaps more precious—his ability to indulge his taste for extremity and to amass a cult of fans while doing so. Those fans include Josh Trank, the director of the forthcoming adaptation of Fantastic Four, who has said his film will be influenced by Cronenberg's themes. Cronenberg is unimpressed. Comic-book films, he says, are "very limited as to what they can say as creative endeavors."

With Maps to the Stars, Cronenberg has proved his mastery at shifting between horror, social commentary and a laugh or two. The Oscars may not have honored Maps, but Moore's hairpin turns between emotions will endure. "I like it," the director says. "when all the tones you've put out there are heard, and heard the way they should be."

(Time, 2015.3)

---

terse adj. 精练的　　gangster n. 黑帮老大　　nomination n. 提名　　accolade n. 荣誉
creek n. 小溪　　indulge vt. 满足　　a cult of 对……的崇拜

长难句解析

① 本句为 but 连接的并列复合句。but 前后句子主干均为主谓宾结构。but 后的句子中，which 引导的非限制性定语从句修饰 new film。

Moore won the Best Actress Oscar and wide acclaim for her tasteful role as an Alzheimer's
主语1 谓语1　　宾语1　　　　　　　　　　　　状语1
sufferer, but she shows off a taste for mania in director David Cronenberg's new film,
　　　　　主语2 谓语2　　宾语2　　　　　　状语2
which, after an awards qualifying run last year, opens nationally Feb. 27.
非限制性定语从句

② 本句包含由 and 连接的两个并列谓语结构。句中 a role 为 a terse Russian gangster 的同位语；that 引导的定语从句修饰 a role。

He turned Viggo Mortensen into a terse Russian gangster, a role　that earned him an Oscar
主语 谓语1　　宾语1　　宾语补足语1　　　　　同位语　　　定语从句
nomination, in *Eastern Promises*（2007）and took Keira Knightley to the brink of madness
　　　　　状语1　　　　　　　　　谓语2　　宾语2　　　宾语补足语2
on screen in *A Dangerous Method*（2011）.
状语2

Text 7　*The Guardian* View on Librarians: Guides to Life, Not Just to Books
《卫报》对图书管理员的看法：人生向导，而不仅仅是图书向导

　　It is often only when we lose things, or risking them, that we realise how much we value them. ①As public library budgets have shrunk and doors have closed—with around 500 branches shut in England since 2010, and around the same number handed over to volunteers—people who had not given libraries much thought have been stirred to action. High-profile campaigns against closures have been fought, and in some cases won. Cressida Cowell, the new children's laureate, is urging that

　　我们总是要等到失去或将失去什么东西的时候，才意识到它们的重要性。①由于公共图书馆预算的缩减和多家图书馆的倒闭——自2010年以来，英国约有500家分店关门，且约有500家交给志愿者负责——那些过去不太重视图书馆的人已经采取行动。备受关注的反对关闭图书馆的运动一直在进行，有一些获得了胜利。克瑞西达·科威尔，新的儿

---

hand over（把某事）交给……负责
stir *vt.* 使……奋起而做……
laureate *n.* 荣誉获得者；获奖者

give sth. much thought 把某种因素考虑进去
high-profile *adj.*（人或事件）引人注目的，备受关注的

school libraries be made a statutory requirement. But the fate of librarians has largely escaped notice.

This is a mistake, because they are the guides and curators without whom a library, whether standalone or in a school or institution, is simply a collection of books. At their best they can reshape not only the skills and knowledge of users, but their whole perspective: "How many times I've been told about a librarian who saved a life by offering the right book at the right time," the American author Judy Blume has said.

Yet 10,000 jobs in council libraries have been lost since 2005, with about 15,000 remaining. Technology has displaced some, with the creation of unstaffed branches, and has transformed the role of others; computer access is now an important aspect of the service, and librarians routinely help people with online benefits applications.

There is no reason why libraries should not offer this kind of support, as long as staff have sufficient resources and training. The baby and book groups, homework and play clubs, English and IT lessons hosted by libraries are a positive extension of their role. ②But such activities must not come at the expense of the librarian's task of championing books and literacy, which is even more important in an age of information overload and fake news.

Shrunken budgets inevitably make this service harder to deliver: when libraries no longer have budgets to buy new publications, readers can't access them, which may in part explain a recent fall in lending. Such cuts affect all sorts of people, but are particularly damaging when children cannot find books to suit them. ③This year marks the 20th anniversary of the Summer Reading Challenge, a scheme offering incentives to children

---

statutory *adj.* 法定的
standalone *adj.* （企业、组织等）独立的
champion *vt.* 拥护，支持

curator *n.* （博物馆或美术馆等的）管理者，馆长
unstaffed *adj.* 无人值守的
literacy *n.* 读写能力；素养

who sign up to read a book a week during the holidays; especially valuable to those who don't go away or have shelves full of books at home. It is also a reminder of the kind of one-on-one engagement that has become a rarity. The ideal librarian is a skilled maker of recommendations.

Librarians can be much more than book experts. Libraries are community as well as knowledge hubs, and should promote and harness civic activism. The 50,000 people now volunteering in English libraries have much to offer. But any government with a serious commitment to expanding educational opportunities for young and old would invest, not only in libraries, but in the people who work in them.

(*The Guardian*, 2019.7)

这对那些不出门或家里书架上堆满书的人来说尤其有意义。这也提醒人们，一对一的服务已经变得罕见。理想的图书管理员是一个出色的建议提供者。

图书管理员不仅仅是图书专家。图书馆既是知识中心，也是社区，应该促进和管理公民行动。现在在英国图书馆做志愿者的5万人可以贡献更多。但是，任何认真致力于为年轻人和老年人扩大教育机会的政府，不仅会投资于图书馆，还会投资于图书馆的工作人员。

长难句解析

① 本句为主从复合句。As 引导的是原因状语从句；破折号中间 with 介词短语作状语；who 引导的定语从句修饰 people。

As public library budgets have shrunk and doors have closed—with around 500 branches shut in England since 2010, and around the same number handed over to volunteers—people who had not given libraries much thought have been stirred to action.

② 本句为主从复合句。主句的主干结构为 such activities must not come。which 引导的非限制性定语从句修饰前面整个主句。

But such activities must not come at the expense of the librarian's task of championing books and literacy, which is even more important in an age of information overload and fake news.

---

one-on-one *adj.* 一对一的　　much more than 不仅仅……；远远超过……
harness *vt.* 管理

③ 本句为主从复合句。主句的主干结构为 This year marks the 20th anniversary of the Summer Reading Challenge。a scheme offering...作 Summer Reading Challenge 的同位语；两个 who 引导的定语从句分别修饰 children 和 those。

This year	marks	the 20th anniversary of the Summer Reading Challenge,	a scheme
主语	谓语	宾语	同位语

offering incentives to children　who sign up to read a book a week during the holidays;
　后置定语1　　　　　　　　　　定语从句1

especially valuable to those　who don't go away or have shelves full of books at home.
　后置定语2　　　　　　　　　定语从句2

Text 8　The Favre Connection
　　　　　　法佛尔情结

　　It's not that I didn't believe; I just needed to see it for myself. And there it was, bobbling square on the church windowsill. ①Before this year's NFC Championship Game between Brett Favre's Green Bay Packers and the New York Giants, I traveled to Green Bay to try to capture the singular bond between Favre, the legendary quarterback who announced his retirement on March 4, and the NFL's company town, where Packer football is more than a Sunday pastime. Driving along Packerland Drive in the -7°F (-22°C) chill, I pulled into the parking lot of Beautiful Savior Lutheran Church, to glean some insight into whether football really is religion in Green Bay and Favre the heavenly Father. I sat in the office of an avuncular pastor, Steve Witte, who shared some concerns that fans had called a reverse on their priorities. There were the shuffled services and the canceled choir practices to accommodate Packer kick off times. But Pastor Witte knows whence he serves. On his sill stood two sacred bobble heads: one of Martin Luther, the other of Brett Favre.

　　并不是我不相信，只是需要自己去亲眼见证。从教堂的窗台上望去，是跳动的广场。①在今年美国橄榄球联会冠军赛绿湾包装工队(布雷特·法佛尔所在队)对纽约巨人队的比赛开始之前，我来到了绿湾，试图寻找这个全国橄榄球联盟公司所在的小镇与3月4日宣布自己即将退役的传奇四分卫法佛尔之间的某种独特联系。在小镇上，包装工队的橄榄球不仅仅是一种假日休闲活动。在零下22℃的天气里，我沿着帕克兰的街道开下去，最后把车停到了美丽的路德教会教堂的停车场，想去看看橄榄球这项运动在这个地方是否有那么神圣，还想看看神圣的法佛尔。我坐在慈爱的牧师史蒂夫·威特的办公室里，他分享了一些他对那些球迷的看法——认为他们颠倒轻重。为了配合绿湾包装工新赛季的准备工作，教堂唱诗班的活动已经被取消了，但是史蒂夫·威特知道他是为谁而服务的。在他的窗台上摆着两个神圣的头像摆件：一位是马丁·路德，另一位是布雷特·法佛尔。

---

bobble *vi.* 跳动　　　windowsill *n.* 窗台　　　glean *vt.* 费力搜集　　　avuncular *adj.* 慈爱的
pastor *n.* 牧师　　　whence *adv.* 从何处

We'll probably never see this relationship in pro sports again. Big-league teams aren't owned by the community, as the Packers are, and don't play in small market towns like Green Bay, an icy industrial city of 100,000 nestled in northeast Wisconsin. Big-league quarterbacks don't throw like Brett Favre—for 275 straight games (including the playoffs) over 16 years, an all-time record 61,655 yds. He threw it hard and threw it wild—a record 288 career interceptions—through searing pain, prescription drug and alcohol addiction, deaths in the family. We'll never forget Monday Night Football, 2003, 399 yds. On the day after his dad died, a memorial of spirals.

Big-league players and tiny towns don't bear-hug each other the way Favre and Green Bay did. On the field, Favre gave Green Bay thrills, chills and a Super Bowl. Off the field, his foundation helped disadvantaged kids in the place where he worked and in his home state of Mississippi. Post-Katrina, groups of Green Bay volunteers have trekked down to Favre's hometown of Kiln to assist in the rebuilding effort there. "For a boy from the South, he was one of us," says Jo-Ann Mikulsky, 55, a Green Bay homemaker. "He was our quarterback. He gave us all the leadership you can ask for."

As he holsters that arm, it's fair to ask if Cheesehead love for Favre was overripe. "No, I don't think so," said Irene Olson, 86, who wore a glittered Packer sweater to church the morning of the Packers-Giants tilt. "Especially since I'm one of the ones going overboard." Dawn Bugos, a Milwaukee resident I had met at the New York City airport gate, slipped me three separate, impeccably hand-written notes describing her feelings for Favre. "Fierce. Passionate. Hilarious. No ego included—ever." read one of the missives. In January an SI.com columnist had said that a La

---

yds n. 码数
bear-hug vt. 包容

interception n. 拦截
overripe adj. 过熟的

spiral n. 旋涡
impeccably adv. 完美地

Crosse, Wis. man named Robert Ruprecht actually dreamed about going shopping with Favre. I called Ruprecht to assess his mental state. "Believe me, if Freud were still alive," says Ruprecht, "I would call him myself to analyze it." ②Michael Holton, who grew up in Milwaukee and now lives in Atlanta, built a Packer-themed vacation house across the street from the team's home at Lambeau Field, replete with a flat-screen TV that permanently displays a picture of the stadium. That TV sits above a urinal in his bathroom. "I'm in love with Brett Favre, O.K." Holton says. "He's a different breed from what's been developed over the last 10 years."

Sure, it could all pass as creepy at times. But in today's sports world, in which athletes are harder to admire, you have to envy the connection between Cheeseheads and Favre. Football, and sports, are worse off now that he's gone. And though the Giants had a riveting run to the championship, I wish I could have soaked up Green Bay on a night that Favre led the Packers to a Super Bowl. I mean, is anyone less deserving of a more horrid final moment than Favre? His last fling sailed right into the hands of Giants cornerback Corey Webster, setting up New York's shocking win.

Long after that game was over, past midnight, I wandered over to a Green Bay sports bar, expecting tears on tap. But you never would have known the Packers had lost: fans in Favre jerseys were drinking, dancing, carrying on. Green Bay can accept a loss. "Title town" bid goodbye to the great Bart Starr once; it will move on without Favre. It'll be odd though. "I can't imagine the Packers without him," said Olson, the nice lady from church who has been following the team for 76 years. "Can you?"

(*Time*, 2014.3)

---

cornerback *n.* 美式橄榄球侧卫　　　jersey *n.* 球衣　　　odd *adj.* 奇怪的

长难句解析

① 本句为主从复合句。句中 the legendary quarterback 为 Favre 的同位语；who 引导的定语从句修饰 the legendary quarterback；where 引导的非限制性定语从句修饰 the NFL's company town。

Before this year's NFC Championship Game between Brett Favre's Green Bay Packers and the New York Giants, I traveled to Green Bay to try to capture the singular bond between Favre, the legendary quarterback who announced his retirement on March 4, and the NFL's company town, where Packer football is more than a Sunday pastime.

② 本句为主从复合句。句中 who 引导的非限制性定语从句修饰主语 Michael Holton；that 引导的定语从句修饰 a flat-screen TV。

Michael Holton, who grew up in Milwaukee and now lives in Atlanta, built a Packer-themed vacation house across the street from the team's home at Lambeau Field, replete with a flat-screen TV that permanently displays a picture of the stadium.

Text 9 Does Birth Order Affect Personality?
出生顺序会影响人格吗？

In spite of sharing genes and environments, siblings are often not as similar in nature as one might think. But where do the supposed differences come from? ① Alfred Adler, a 19th-and early 20th-century Austrian psychotherapist and founder of individual psychology, suspected that birth order leads to differences in siblings.

尽管有相同的基因和环境，兄弟姐妹在本质上并不像人们想象的那样相似。但所谓的差异是从何而来的呢？① 19世纪末20世纪初奥地利心理治疗师和个体心理学的创始人阿尔弗雷德·阿德勒怀疑是出生顺序导致了兄弟姐妹之间的差异。

---

sibling n. 兄弟姐妹   psychotherapist n. 心理治疗师

Adler considered firstborns to be neurotic, because they don't have to share their parents for years and are essentially dethroned once a sibling comes along. He also considered oldest children dutiful and sometimes conservative. According to Adler, the youngest children are ambitious, while middle children are optimally positioned in the family and are characterized by emotional stability. Adler himself was the second of seven children.

②American psychologist Frank J. Sulloway, who, in the mid-1990s, combed history books for leading figures who were firstborns and rebellious ones who were born later, saw a similar trend. Among the later borns, he found lateral thinkers and revolutionaries, such as Charles Darwin, Karl Marx and Mahatma Gandhi. Among firstborns, he discovered leaders such as Joseph Stalin and Benito Mussolini. His explanation? Every child occupies a certain niche within the family and then uses his or her own strategies to master life. Firstborn and single children had less reason to quarrel with the status quo and identify more strongly with the worldview of their fathers and mothers. Younger siblings are less sure of their parents' view and therefore more often choose alternative paths in life.

Such categorizations are popular because they're rather intuitive, and one can always find an example of the sensible big sister or the rebellious young brother in their circle of acquaintances. As such, Adler's words still appear regularly in educational guides and continue to reverberate in the minds of parents.

阿德勒认为头胎子女是有点神经质的,因为他们一开始的几年不需要(和其他兄弟姐妹)分享父母,一旦有了兄弟姐妹,他们基本上就不能独享父母的爱了。他还认为最年长的孩子本分守己,有时很保守。根据阿德勒的说法,最小的孩子是雄心勃勃的,而中间的孩子在家庭中处于最有利的位置,其特点是情绪稳定。阿德勒本人是七个孩子中的第二个。

②20世纪90年代中期,美国心理学家弗兰克·J.苏洛威对关于头胎出生的领导人物和非头胎出生的叛逆者的历史书籍进行了梳理,他也看到了类似的趋势。在非头胎出生者中,他发现了横向思想家和革命家,如查尔斯·达尔文、卡尔·马克思和圣雄甘地。在头胎出生者中,他发现了约瑟夫·斯大林和贝尼托·墨索里尼等领导人。对此,他的解释是什么呢?每个孩子在家庭中都有特定的位置,然后使用自己的策略来掌控生活。头胎和独生子女有更少的理由反对现状,反而会更加认同他们父母的世界观。年幼的兄弟姐妹对父母的看法不太认同,因此经常会选择其他生活方式。

这种分类之所以受欢迎,是因为它们非常直观,而且在熟人圈子里总能找到一个像明智的大姐姐或叛逆的小弟弟这样的例子。因此,阿德勒的话仍经常出现在教育指南中,并在父母的脑海中回荡。

---

neurotic *adj.* 神经过敏的
optimally *adv.* 最佳
rebellious *adj.* 反抗的
niche *n.* 合适的职位
reverberate *vt.* 使回响

dethrone *vt.* 罢免;废黜(国王或女王)
comb *vt.* 梳理
lateral *adj.* 横向的
acquaintance *n.* 熟人

Furthermore, some studies confirmed the idea that sibling position can shape personality. For example, a 1968 study showed that, compared with later borns, first borns are less likely to participate in dangerous sports because of fears of physical injury. And a 1980 study of 170 female and 142 male undergraduates showed lower anxiety and higher ego in firstborns, as measured by the Howarth Personality Questionnaire.

"It is quite possible that the position in the sibling sequence shapes the personality—but not in every family in the same way," says Frank Spinath, a psychologist at Saarland University in Germany. "In other words, there may be an influence but not a systematic one. Nevertheless, other influences weigh more heavily when it comes to the differences in character of siblings. In addition to genes, the so-called undivided environment also plays a role. For siblings who grow up in the same family, this includes the respective circle of friends, for example." Further, parents do not treat their children the same regardless of their birth rank. Studies show that parents react sensitively to the innate temperament of their offspring and adapt their upbringing accordingly.

On average, firstborns enjoy a small IQ advantage over their younger siblings. Those born first also tend to complete their education with a higher degree and opt for traditionally prestigious careers, such as medicine or engineering.

How does this intellectual advantage come about? Adler may be right that the undivided attention given to the first child in early life promotes cognitive abilities. This advantage is already apparent by the age of two. Norwegian researchers Petter Kristensen and Tor Bjerkedal cleverly showed that the difference in intelligence is not linked to biological factors. They tested children whose older siblings had died early. The researchers'

---

sequence *n.* 顺序

prestigious *adj.* 享有声望的

temperament *n.* 性格, 性情, 气质

assumption was that although these children were biologically younger siblings, they assumed the role of the firstborn in the family. Compared with other younger siblings, they achieved better results in intelligence tests.

(*Scientific American*, 2019.8)

子是生物学上年纪较小的兄弟姐妹，但他们承担了家庭中长子（长女）的角色。与其他年纪较小的兄弟姐妹相比，他们在智力测验中取得了更好的成绩。

长难句解析

① 本句为主从复合句，主句的主干为 Alfred Adler suspected that…。a 19th-and early 20th-century…psychology 作主语的同位语；that 引导的是宾语从句。

Alfred Adler, a 19th-and early 20th-century Austrian psychotherapist and founder of individual psychology, suspected that birth order leads to differences in siblings.
主语 / 同位语 / 谓语 / 宾语从句

② 本句为主从复合句，主句的主干为 American psychologist Frank J. Sulloway saw a similar trend。who 引导的非限制性定语从句修饰主句主语；定语从句1修饰 leading figures；定语从句2修饰 rebellious ones。

American psychologist Frank J. Sulloway, who, in the mid-1990s, combed history books for leading figures who were firstborns and rebellious ones who were born later, saw a similar trend.
主语 / 非限制性定语从句 / 后置定语1 / 定语从句1 / 后置定语2 / 定语从句2 / 谓语 / 宾语

Text 10 Snow Flower and the Not-So-Secret Metaphor
雪花和并不隐秘的隐喻

① Fans of Lisa See's bestselling novel, *Snow Flower and the Secret Fan*, can't have been surprised when the book was made into a film. A tale of sworn friendship between two women in 19th century China, it's got enough plague, death, revolution and foot-binding to warrant a proper screen

① 邝丽莎的畅销小说《雪花秘扇》被翻拍成了电影，书迷们并不感到惊讶。《雪花秘扇》讲的是在19世纪的中国，两个女人宣誓结为密友的故事。为了保证史诗般的影视效果，电影拍摄中有相当一部分瘟疫、死亡、

---

plague *n.* 瘟疫

epic. But the book's admirers might be surprised to discover that Ms. See's plot takes up just half of the running time. Unlike the novel, Wayne Wang's screen adaptation intercuts between the 19th century and the 21st, when viewers meet two more Chinese women with their own issues to contend with, from exam fraud to listening to Hugh Jackman crooning in Mandarin.

According to press materials, this new material was crowbarred in at the behest of Mr. Wang, the director. "Wayne's vision was to make the story much more relatable to women today, by pursuing parallel stories, one in the Old China and one in the New China," says the film's producer, Wendi Murdoch. What next, you might ask? How else might period dramas be made "much more relatable" to today's audiences? Perhaps a film about the Holocaust could compare the massacre of several thousand Parisian Jews to an American journalist's uncertainty about her marriage 70 years later. Maybe a film about Wallis Simpson and Edward VIII could intercut the abdication with a strand about a hip New York art dealer with her own marriage problems.

Far-fetched (and dreadful) as those scenarios might seem, both of them exist already. ②The Holocaust drama is *Sarah's Key*, starring Kristin Scott Thomas, which comes out on DVD in late November. The Wallis Simpson biopic is Madonna's *W.E.*, which is due in January. Both films promise to leave viewers with the same queasy feeling I had after watching *Snow Flower and the Secret Fan*.

These films have several things in common. In each case the scenes set in an old days are much more dramatic than those set in the present,

---

epic *n.* 史诗 intercut *vt.* 使(镜头)交切 croon *vi.* 低唱
crowbar *vt.* 撬开 at the behest of 在……要求下 abdication *n.* 退位
queasy *adj.* 呕吐的; 心神不定的

which suggests that the film-makers are embarrassed by the triviality of modern life. The message is that workaday bourgeois concerns need to be spiced up by the horrors of a more turbulent time in order to be interesting on screen. But the dual narratives also belittle the past. They imply that previous lives don't matter unless they illuminate our own. Foot-binding can't be shocking in and of itself, it seems: it's only worth mentioning if we, too, feel as if our feet are metaphorically bound. There's yet more narcissism in the fact that the films' contemporary characters are all writing books or researching projects about the historical incidents we're shown, just as the films' own screenwriters must have done. In essence, the film-makers are writing themselves into the story. "The stuff I've dug up on the Holocaust is all very interesting," they're saying. "But let me tell you what I was going through while I was digging …"

That doesn't mean that the technique is never worthwhile. When the counterpointing is done with care and insight, in literary fiction such as Michael Cunningham's *The Hours* and A.S. Byatt's *Possession*, the strands weave together into a rich tapestry. But novels can slip between time periods far more easily than films can. On a practical level, a 400-page book has more room to fit in multiple narratives than a two-hour film does.

The main effect of the back-and-forthing in *Snow Flower and the Secret Fan* is to insult the audience. It assumes that we don't have the imagination to sympathise with people from a pre-iPhone era. Apparently we need intermediaries to remind us of how we're all connected. How else could the film be "relatable to women today"? But what about men today? Maybe Mr. Wang should have stuck in a third strand, in which a bunch of men sit

---

spice up 加香料
tapestry *n.* 织锦
narcissism *n.* 自我陶醉
back-and-forthing *n.* 反反复复
in essence 本质上

and watch the film, and chat about how they, too, feel as if they're having their feet bound. When working with a good metaphor, perhaps it is best to not be too subtle.

(*The Economist*, 2011.11)

王颖导演应该在电影中发展第三条线:一群男人坐下来看这部电影并且探讨如果他们的感受,就像他们也被缠足了一样。如果我们想利用隐喻的手法取得好的效果,那么最好不要让它过于精巧微妙。

长难句解析

① 本句为主从复合句。句中 of Lisa See's bestselling novel 作后置定语修饰 Fans; *Snow Flower and the Secret Fan* 为 Lisa See's bestselling novel 的同位语; when 引导时间状语从句。

Fans of Lisa See's bestselling novel, *Snow Flower and the Secret Fan*, can't have been
主语   后置定语   同位语   系动词
surprised when the book was made into a film.
表语   时间状语从句

② 本句为主从复合句。句中现在分词作表语的后置定语; which 引导的非限制性定语从句修饰表语 *Sarah's Key*。

The Holocaust drama is *Sarah's Key*, starring Kristin Scott Thomas, which comes out
主语   系动词 表语   伴随状语   非限制性
on DVD in late November.
定语从句

Text 11 Universities: Pile Them High
大学:多多益善

Steep tuition fees are not deterring most students. But the attempt to create a market in higher education is off track.

Asking students to pay more for their education was supposed to encourage competition among universities, not just lighten the load on taxpayers. That was the idea in December 2010, when Parliament voted to let English universities charge tuition fees of up to £9,000 from this September, almost treble the existing limit. But

大多数学生并没有被飙升的大学学费吓退,但建立高等教育市场的尝试却在偏离轨道。

让学生为他们受的教育多付钱的本意是鼓励大学间的竞争,而不仅仅是为了减轻纳税人的负担。当 2010 年 12 月议会表决通过,允许英国各大学从今年 9 月起收取高达 9 000 英镑/年的学费时,人们就是这样想的,这个学费几乎是现在上限的三倍。但对高等教育的需求

---

tuition *n.* 学费   off track 偏离轨道   treble *vt.* 使……增为三倍

demand for higher education is so great, and the fee increase so ringed with restrictions, that universities are not competing for students and responding to market demand. Instead, students are competing for places.

At first glance, statistics seem to tell a different story. ①The number of British people who applied for a full-time university course fell by 8.7% this year, according to figures published by the Universities and Colleges Admissions Service on January 30th. But the decrease was mainly among older folk, who may have been unwilling to quit hard-won jobs. And fewer people are leaving school in 2012. Adjusting for that decline, applications by school leavers were only 1% lower than last year, when a bumper crop dashed off to university to avoid the fee increase. High youth unemployment has encouraged many to seek shelter in higher education, taking applications to their third-highest level ever.

There are a few signs that higher fees have encouraged marginal decision-making, even if they haven't stopped young people applying altogether. Arts and social-science subjects have attracted fewer applicants than last year. The lack of jobs has concentrated students' minds on employment prospects, according to Ross Renton, dean of students at the University of Hertfordshire. But they seem unfazed by the expense itself. "The first question is never 'How much?' Students want to know what the course is like and what facilities we have," he says.

In the past students have also proven surprisingly calm about rising prices. Just before tuition fees of £1,000 were introduced in 1998, many people cancelled gap years to avoid paying. The number of applicants fell slightly when the fees kicked in, but then recovered strongly. The same thing happened when fees

如此之大，而提高收费又受到诸多限制，所以并不是大学在抢生源或响应市场需求，相反是学生在竞争进入大学学习的机会。

乍一看，统计数字似乎与此不符。①根据"英国高等院校入学服务机构"1月30日公布的数字，今年英国申请攻读全日制大学课程的人数下降了8.7%。但这一下降的趋势主要发生在年龄较大的申请者中，他们可能不愿放弃来之不易的工作。并且2012年的中学毕业生人数本来就少。根据这一减少进行调整之后，中学毕业生的申请人数只比去年减少了1%，而去年曾有许多人抢在学费增加之前申请，这导致大学申请人数剧增。居高不下的青年失业率也促使许多人借继续学习深造暂避一时，令高校申请人数达到有史以来第三高的水平。

有几个迹象表明，尽管高额学费并没有完全阻止年轻人申请大学，但还是让一些人在做决定时更多地考虑边际效应。申请文科与社会科学专业的人数低于去年。赫特福德大学教务长罗斯·仁顿认为，由于缺少工作岗位，学生们在选专业时更注重就业前景，但他们似乎对读大学所需费用本身并不感到担忧。他说："首要问题从来就不是'学费的多少'，学生们想知道的是专业课程的内容，还有我们有哪些设施。"

人们过去就曾见识过学生对学费的日益增长表现出的惊人冷静。就在1998年第一次实行每年1 000英镑的收费标准之前，许多人为避免交费而取消了空档年，直接进入大学学习。收费规定开始实施后申请人数略有下降，但随即强烈反弹。2006年学费上涨两倍后

---

bumper crop 丰收　　　　dashed off 急忙离开　　　　marginal adj. 边缘的
unfazed adj. 不担忧的

trebled in 2006. The enduring popularity of higher education is such that demand now significantly outstrips supply, and the chances of applicants gaining a university place has been falling for years.

Alas for ambitious school leavers, universities cannot expand to accommodate them. That fact, as well as the cap on tuition fees, albeit at a higher level, has stymied the development of a higher-education market. ②Because the Treasury must lend students the funds to pay their fees and because not all graduates clear their debts, the state limits not only how much universities charge but also how many students they can admit. During the boom years, adding places was affordable. Now it is not. A temporary expansion of places in England announced in 2010 is about to end. In Scotland, Wales and Northern Ireland, where devolved administrations keep fees down for local and EU students, expansion is equally unaffordable.

Moreover, reforms intended to make universities more responsive to student demand look increasingly bizarre. English institutions recruiting students who gain good grades at A-level will be allowed to take as many as they wish. But historically most high-fliers go to Oxford, Cambridge and a handful of other elite universities which prefer to retain their exclusivity and their present size. So David Willetts, the universities minister, will also let some institutions that charge £7,500 or less expand at the expense of others. The outcome will be determined not by student demand but by a committee comprised of dons and administrators.

Libby Hackett of Universities Alliance, which represents many middle-ranking universities, decries the opportunities lost. "At a time when our global competitors are increasing the number of graduates in the workforce to increase their capacity for economic growth, how can Britain justify a reduction in university places?" she asks.

---

outstrip *vt.* 超过　　　accommodate *vt.* 容纳　　　don *n.* 大学教师
decry *vt.* 责难

She is not alone. Matt Grist of Demos, a think-tank, argues that anyone who wants to study and is qualified should be allowed into higher education. Too little capacity hampers social mobility more than high tuition fees. Mr. Grist reckons the government should increase the interest on student loans and make the debt harder to forgive in order to finance more places.

Britain could benefit if it did. Graduates not only contribute more to the economy than less-qualified people but also pay more tax, enjoy better health and are more politically active. Poor youngsters would have a better shot at university in future, and the coalition's school reforms may swell the numbers of those qualified to get in. Future taxpayers might be thankful too: the Treasury is set to lose 30%-40% of the money lent under the current arrangements. Perhaps Mr. Willetts should tinker some more with the ivory towers.

(*The Economist*, 2012.2)

与她意见相同者大有人在。智囊公司(Demos)的马特·格里斯特认为,应该让任何有资格又想读大学的人接受高等教育。大学容纳量过小对社会阶层间的流动造成的损害更甚于高额学费。格里斯特认为,政府应提高学生贷款的利息,严格债务免除要求,这样才能资助更多的大学生就读。

如果这样做的话,英国确实能从中受益。与学历较低者相比,大学毕业生不但对经济的贡献更大,他们也缴纳更多的税款,身体更加健康,政治上更为活跃。贫困青年将来会有更多机会上大学,联合政府的学校改革可能会增加有资格读大学者的人数。将来的纳税人也可能会心存感激:因为在现行制度下,财政部大概会有30%~40%的贷款无法收回。威列茨先生或许应该进一步修补这座象牙塔。

长难句解析

① 本句为主从复合句。句中 who 引导的定语从句修饰先行词 British people。

> The number of British people who applied for a full-time university course fell by 8.7% this year, according to figures published by the Universities and Colleges Admissions Service on January 30th.
>
> 主语 / 定语从句 / 谓语 / 状语1 / 状语2 / 状语3 / 后置定语

② 本句为主从复合句。句中包含两个并列的原因状语从句,均由 because 引导,由 and 连接;how much 引导的宾语从句1 和 how many 引导的宾语从句2 由连词 not only... but also... 连接,表示并列,共同作 limits 的宾语。

> Because the Treasury must lend students the funds to pay their fees and because not all graduates clear their debts, the state limits not only how much universities charge but also how many students they can admit.
>
> 原因状语从句1 / 原因状语从句2 / 主语 / 谓语 / 宾语从句1 / 宾语从句2

---

hamper *vt.* 妨碍　　swell *vt.* 使……膨胀　　tinker *vt.* 修补

Text 12 Flipping the Floppers
轻惩假摔

"A flail, a spin and fall to the floor." In a video released before the start of this year's National Basketball Association (NBA) season, league officials announced a crackdown on "flopping", or embellishing minor (or non-existent) contact in order to fool referees into calling a foul. ①With examples from the previous season—including the aforementioned flop by Danilo Gallinari of the Denver Nuggets, which also featured "apparent demonstration of injury" for good measure, according to the unimpressed voice-over—the league announced a series of escalating fines for convicted floppers.

Violations are now judged via post-game video by the league's front office. The first incident draws a warning; subsequent flops attract fines that start at $5,000 and rise to $30,000 for the fifth infraction, with suspensions kicking in after that. No longer will the NBA suffer from the rampant diving and play-acting that bedevils professional football, according to the policy's supporters. If successful, its approach may also inspire other leagues to eradicate "simulation" in the same way.

Less than a week into the season, the league issued its first warnings for flopping. JJ Barea of the Minnesota Timberwolves and Donald Sloan of the Cleveland Cavaliers earned these dubious honours in two clear-cut cases of over-embellishment. A

---

spin *n.* 旋转
foul *n.* 犯规
bedevil *vt.* 长期搅扰

crackdown *n.* 制裁
aforementioned *adj.* 上述的
over-embellishment *n.* 过度修饰

flopping *n.* 假摔
rampant *adj.* 猖獗的

few more warnings, perhaps a fine or two and... problem solved?

The NBA's haste in enforcing its new rule is an encouraging sign. ② Other leagues have similar rules for retrospective punishments against flopping—including football's Serie A in Italy, A-League in Australia and Major League Soccer in the United States—but rarely enforce them. Giving referees the power to punish floppers during play—via technical fouls in international basketball, yellow cards in football or two-minute penalties in the National Hockey League—is also an imperfect solution. The speed of modern sports makes detecting dives exceedingly difficult on the fly; the fear of a false positive (judging a foul as a flop) makes most referees err on the side of caution.

If, then, post-game video evidence is the least-bad solution to identifying floppers in the NBA, the league should not be shy about calling players out. The size of the fines is irrelevant in a league where the average annual salary is $5m, although the stigma of being labelled a serial flopper may act as a mild deterrent (not least because referees may judge convicted floppers more harshly than others). The timing of announcements is crucial, particularly if suspensions are at stake late in a season or during the playoffs; the warnings for Messrs Barea and Sloan were announced three days after the incidents took place. ③ Violations against the league's biggest stars, some of whom already boast extensive lowlight reels, would also show that the NBA is serious about the integrity of the game, and is not offering just a mere semblance of action against behaviour that drives fans mad.

The risk is that the NBA's anti-flopping fanfare will soon fizzle. After all, the league failed to introduce similar punishments in 2008, after a particularly flop-filled season. The histrionics were

---

haste *n.* 匆忙   retrospective *adj.* 回顾的   deterrent *n.* 威慑   timing *n.* 时机的掌握

already widespread by then; the popular narrative blames the influx of foreign players, with Vlade Divac of Serbia often cited as patient zero. The truth is that the rewards of "one down man ship" greatly outweigh the costs, and athletes of all types have long been in on the act. A retroactive suspension is a small price to pay if flopping helps a team win the deciding game of a playoff series, for example.

A swift and reliable means of punishing flops during a game is the only true solution. Unfortunately, the broad scope for interpretation of fouls in an intensely physical sport like basketball makes this nearly impossible. Television time-outs and the growing number of instant-replay reviews for other situations already disrupt the flow of NBA games to an uncomfortable degree. The difficulty of making summary judgments on marginal flopping calls would add yet another interruption, particularly since more than 40 fouls are whistled during a typical game.

If applied forcefully, the NBA's anti-flopping rule makes the best of a bad situation. At the least, official recognition of the most egregious flops will serve as a perverse sort of endorsement. The audacity of Mr. Sloan's flailing, spinning fall is admirable, in a way—there are few better examples of the elaborate "heliflopter" move, even if true connoisseurs consider the "double flop" as the pinnacle of achievement in the dark arts.

(*The Economist*, 2012.11)

长难句解析

① 本句为主从复合句。句中状语1作主句的状语;状语2是破折号中间的非限制性定语从句中的状语;which 引导的非限制性定语从句修饰先行词 flop;for convicted floppers 作后置定语修饰 fines。

---

influx *n.* 流入　　　　　　　　　retroactive *adj.* 反作用的
instant-replay *n.* 即时回放　　　endorsement *n.* 认可
connoisseur *n.* 行家　　　　　　pinnacle *n.* 极点

With examples from the previous season—including the aforementioned flop by Danilo
状语1　　　　　　　　　　　　　　　　　　　后置定语1
Gallinari of the Denver Nuggets, which also featured "apparent demonstration of injury" for
　　　　　　　　　　　　　　　非限制性定语从句
good measure, according to the unimpressed voice-over—the league announced a series of
　　　　　　　　状语2　　　　　　　　　　　　　　主语　　　谓语
escalating fines for convicted floppers.
　宾语　　　　后置定语2

② 本句中包含两个并列的谓语,由 but 连接,主语均为 other leagues。介宾结构 for...作后置定语修饰 rules;against flopping 作后置定语修饰 punishments;including... 作后置定语修饰 leagues。

Other leagues have similar rules for retrospective punishments against flopping—including
　主语　　 谓语1　　宾语1　　　　后置定语1　　　　　　　　　后置定语2
football's Serie A in Italy, A-League in Australia and Major League Soccer in the United
　　　　　　　　　　　　　　　　　后置定语3
States—but rarely enforce them.
　　　　　　　　谓语2　　宾语2

③ 本句为主从复合句。句中 against the league's biggest stars 作后置定语,修饰主语 violations;whom 引导的非限制性定语从句修饰先行词 stars;that 引导的宾语从句作 show 的宾语,该宾语从句中包含两个并列的系表结构,由 and 连接,主语均为 the NBA;句末 that 引导的定语从句修饰先行词 behaviour。

Violations against the league's biggest stars, some of whom already boast extensive lowlight
　主语　　　　后置定语　　　　　　　　　非限制性定语从句
reels, would also show that the NBA is serious about the integrity of the game, and is not
　　　　谓语　　　　　宾语从句
offering just a mere semblance of action against behaviour that drives fans mad.
　　　　　　宾语从句　　　　　　　　　　　　　　　定语从句

Text 13

Why So Little Chinese in English?
英语中的汉语借用词为何如此之少？

On Twitter, a friend asked "Twenty years from now, how many Chinese words will be common parlance in English?" I replied that we've al-

有个朋友在推特上问我:"二十年内,有多少汉语词汇会成为英语常用词呢?"我回答道,邓小平同志

---

parlance n. 用语

ready had 35 years since Deng Xiaoping began opening China's economy, resulting in its stratospheric rise—but almost no recent Chinese borrowings in English.

Many purported experts are willing to explain China to curious (and anxious) westerners. And yet I can't think of even one Chinese word or phrase that has become "common parlance in English" recently. The only word that comes close might be guanxi, the personal connections and relationships important to getting things done in China. Plenty of articles can be found discussing the importance of guanxi, but the word isn't "common in English" by any stretch.

① Most Chinese words now part of English show, in their spelling and meaning, to have been borrowed a long time ago, often from non-Mandarin Chinese varieties like Cantonese. Kowtow, gung ho and to shanghai are now impeccably English words we use with no reference to China itself. Kung fu, tai chi, feng shui and the like are Chinese concepts and practices westerners are aware of. And of course bok choy, chow mein and others are merely Chinese foods that westerners eat; I would say we borrowed the foods, and their Chinese names merely hitched a ride into English.

Given China's rocket-ride to prominence, why so little borrowing? We import words from other languages that are hard for English-speakers to pronounce. We borrow from languages with other writing systems (Yiddish, Russian, Arabic). We borrow from culturally distant places (India, Japan). We borrow verbs (kowtow) and nouns (tsunami) and exclamations (banzai! oy!). We borrow concrete things (sushi) and abstract ones (Schadenfreude, ennui). We borrow not only from friends, but from rivals and enemies (flak from German in the Second World War, samizdat from Russian during the cold war, too many words to count from French during the long Anglo-French rivalry).

---

stratospheric *adj.* 同温层的
hitch a ride 搭顺风车
by any stretch 无论如何
prominence *n.* 突起
impeccably *adv.* 无可挑剔地
exclamation *n.* 感叹词

So perhaps China's rise is simply too new, and we just need another 20 years or so. We've seen a similar film before. Japan's sudden opening to the world, a world war, and then forty years of an economic boom put quite a few Japanese words and concepts into the Anglophone mind: kamikaze, futon, haiku, kabuki, origami, karaoke, tycoon, tsunami, jiu-jitsu, zen and honcho are all common English words that nowadays can be used without any reference to Japan. Add to that the more specifically Japanese phenomena well known to the English-speaking world: karate, judo, sumo, bonsai, manga, pachinko, samurai, shogun, noh and kimono, say, not to mention foods from the bland (tofu) to the potentially fatal (fugu). Of course, Japanese borrowed some of these words from Chinese, like zen (modern Mandarin chán) and tofu (dòufu). But English borrowed them from Japanese, not Chinese.

It seems likely English will borrow from Chinese, too, as trade, cultural and personal connections between China and the west grow. ② Whether future Chinese borrowings will be new edibles, cultural items or even philosophical terms will depend on China's development and how the West responds.

(*The Economist*, 2013.6)

高射炮,冷战时期引自苏联的地下出版物,还有在漫长的英法对峙时期,引自法语的许多词汇)。

也许是因为中国崛起的时间太过短暂,我们可能还要再过20年左右才能从汉语中引进更多词汇。类似的情况在一部电影中也出现过。日本突然实施对外开放,发动世界大战,又经历了四十年的经济腾飞,这一系列的事件使相当一部分日语词汇和概念汇聚到以英语为母语的人的头脑中,比如神风特攻队、蒲团、俳句、歌舞伎、折纸、卡拉OK、大亨、海啸、柔道、禅以及老板,这些词汇现在都是英语中的常用语,在应用时无须注释出自日本。除此之外,还有英语国家熟知的独特的日本文化概念:空手道、柔道、相扑、盆栽、日本漫画、弹球盘、武士、将军、能剧以及和服,此外还有食物名称,不论是清淡的(如豆腐)还是含有剧毒的(如河豚)。当然,日语中的一些词汇是从汉语中引入的,比如禅(现代汉语"禅")和豆腐(现代汉语"豆腐")。但是这些词汇是由日语转化成英语的,而非汉语。

随着中国与西方贸易往来的日益密切、文化交往的日益频繁和民间交流的日益加深,英语中可能也会出现汉语借用词。②将来中国的语言输出是新型食品还是文化元素抑或是哲学术语,都将取决于中国的发展水平以及西方社会对其的回应。

长难句解析

① 本句为简单句,句子的主干结构为 Most Chinese words show。句中 now part of English 作后置定语,修饰 Chinese words;like Cantonese 作 non-Mandarin Chinese varieties 的后置定语。

Most Chinese words now part of English show, in their spelling and meaning, to have
　主语　　　　　后置定语1　　谓语　　　　　状语
been borrowed　a long time ago,　often from non-Mandarin Chinese varieties
　谓语　　　　时间状语　　　　　地点状语
like Cantonese.
后置定语2

---

edible *n.* 食物

② 本句为主从复合句，主干结构为 whether… or… will depend on…。句中 whether… or… 结构的主语从句为该句主语，宾语部分由名词短语 China's development 和 how 引导的宾语从句构成。

Whether future Chinese borrowings will be new edibles, cultural items or even philosophical terms will depend on China's development and how the West responds.
主语从句　　　　　　　　　　　　　　　　　谓语　　　　　　宾语　　　　　　　宾语从句

Text 14 A Grim Half-Century 糟糕的半个世纪

① For Europe, as Ian Kershaw notes in this magisterial history, which came out in Britain in September and is just being published in America, the 20th century was a game of two halves. The first saw a cataclysm that brought down empires, plunged the continent into a deep slump and culminated in the horrors of the Second World War. At least for Western Europe, the second was, in contrast, a triumph of peace and prosperity. That distinction may explain why Mr. Kershaw has sensibly divided his original assignment to write the 20th century volume in the Penguin "History of Europe" series into two books, of which this is the first.

His broad picture of what went wrong in Europe in the 20th century is built around four related points. First was the rise of ethnic nationalism, something that helped to doom the multinational empires of Austria-Hungary, Russia and the Ottomans. Next were demands for territorial revision, between France and Germany, in central and eastern Europe and all over the Balkans. Third was class conflict, as workers and a nascent socialist movement

①对欧洲而言，正如伊恩·科修在这部9月份已在英国上市、目前正在美国印刷的权威历史书中所言，20世纪是上下半叶之间的一场博弈。在上半叶中，我们经历了一场灾难，使帝国崩溃、令这块大陆深陷低潮、最后在第二次世界大战的恐怖中达到了极点。与之相比，下半叶，至少对西欧来说，是一场和平与繁荣的胜利。这种区别可能正好解释了科修先生明智地将其原来打算写成一册的企鹅"欧洲史"丛书20世纪卷分为上下两册的原因，而此书则为上册。

他从四个方面概括了20世纪欧洲的败落。一是使奥匈帝国、沙俄帝国和奥斯曼土耳其帝国等多民族帝国走向末日的民族国家主义的兴起；二是法德之间、中欧和东欧各国以及所有巴尔干国家对于重新划分领土的要求；三是随着工人阶层和初生的社会主义运动为了向资本家和传统贵族统治阶层展示力量而

---

magisterial *adj.* 有权威的　　　　　　　cataclysm *n.* 灾难　　　　　　　culminate *vi.* 达到顶峰
ethnic nationalism 民族国家主义　　　　Austria-Hungary *n.* 奥匈帝国
Ottomans *n.* 奥斯曼土耳其帝国　　　　territorial revision 领土修订
Balkans *n.* 巴尔干半岛地区　　　　　　nascent *adj.* 初期的

flexed their muscles against bosses and the traditional aristocratic ruling class. And fourth was the crisis of capitalism, which struck home in the early 1930s and contributed hugely to the rise of Nazism.

Mr. Kershaw, an acknowledged expert on Germany and author of the best biography of Adolf Hitler, naturally places the two world wars at the heart of his narrative, with Germany standing condemned as the main cause of both. That is a more controversial position to take for the first than the second, but on the whole Mr. Kershaw justifies his claim. ②He also delineates cogently and chillingly the way in which the collapse of the tsarist empire, brought about to a large extent by Russia's military and political setbacks during the First World War, led to the Bolshevik triumph and the creation of the Soviet Union.

The author shows how the failings of that first war's victors—the reparations fiasco, the Versailles treaty, America's withdrawal into isolationism—laid the ground for a path that led inexorably to the second. But he also insists that the path was not inevitable. The Locarno treaty of 1925 between Germany, France, Britain, Belgium and Italy, and the entry of Weimar Germany into the League of Nations, could, just about, have led to something rather like the rehabilitation of West Germany in the 1950s. What really took Europe back to the horrors that culminated in another war was economic collapse after 1929. Just as after the recent financial crisis of 2007-08, it was the political right, not the left, that benefited most from this collapse. In Europe that ultimately meant a snuffing out of democracy and the rise of the extreme right in Spain, much of central Europe and, above all, in Germany.

---

flex one's muscles 展示力量
delineate vt. 描写；解释
reparations fiasco 赔款失败
inexorably adj. 不可阻挡的

aristocratic adj. 贵族的
cogently adv. 中肯地
the Versailles treaty 凡尔赛和约
Weimar Germany 魏玛共和国

Nazism n. 纳粹主义
chillingly adv. 冷淡地

rehabilitation n. 复原

Mr. Kershaw's focus on Germany inevitably means a few weaknesses elsewhere. He has little to say on Turkey: no mention of Field-Marshal Allenby nor T.E. Lawrence, little on Kemal Ataturk. His treatment of the military story of the two world wars is succinct almost to the point of cursoriness, but this ground is well-tilled in other books. It is also obvious from his narrative that he is more interested in politics and war than in social, demographic and cultural changes, though he dutifully covers these too.

As in previous volumes in the series, the editors have decided to dispense with footnotes and sources (though there is a useful bibliography). That may be understandable in a history aimed more at the general public than at fellow academics, but it is still annoying. Yet this is a worthy, impressive and well-written addition to a series that has become the definitive history of Europe for our times—and one that whets the appetite for his next volume.

(*The Economist*, 2015.11)

科修先生对德国的重点关注, 不可避免地意味着在其他方面的不足。他对土耳其着墨不多: 没有提及艾伦比元帅、托马斯·爱德华·劳伦斯, 对凯末尔·阿塔蒂尔克的描述也只有只字片语。他对两次世界大战战事的描述简明扼要, 一带而过, 好在另外几本书已对该部分做了较好的阐述。从他的叙述来看, 他对政治和战争的兴趣明显超过了对社会变迁、人口变动以及文化变革的兴趣, 尽管他也忠实地论述了这些内容。

正如这套丛书中的前几卷那样, 编辑们已经决定不加注释和来源说明(尽管有一个有用的参考书目)。对一套以普通读者而不是专家学者为对象的历史丛书来说, 也许这是可以理解的, 但是, 仍然会让人感到有些不适。然而, 对一套已经毫无疑问成为当代欧洲权威史丛书而言, 该书是一个极具价值、令读者印象深刻, 且文笔优美的补充——同时它也是能吊起读者对下册的胃口的一本书。

长难句解析

① 本句为主从复合句。主句的主干为 the 20th century was a game。句中 which 引导的非限制性定语从句 2 修饰先行词 magisterial history, 该定语从句中包含两个并列的谓语结构, 由 and 连接, 主语均为 which; of two halves 作后置定语修饰 game。

For Europe, as Ian Kershaw notes in this magisterial history, which came out in Britain in September and is just being published in America, the 20th century was a game of two halves.
状语1 / 非限制性定语从句1 / 非限制性定语从句2 / 主语 系动词 表语 后置定语

② 本句为主从复合句。句中 in which 引导的定语从句修饰先行词 the way, 该从句主干为 the collapse of the tsarist empire led to the Bolshevik triumph and the creation of the Soviet Union; 该定语从句中, brought about... 作后置定语修饰 collapse。

---

succinct *adj.* 简洁的 cursoriness *n.* 疏忽 well-tilled *adj.* 阐述得很好的
dutifully *adv.* 忠实地 whet *vt.* 刺激

He also delineates cogently and chillingly the way in which the collapse of the tsarist empire, brought about to a large extent by Russia's military and political setbacks during the First World War, led to the Bolshevik triumph and the creation of the Soviet Union.

主语 谓语 状语 宾语 定语从句
后置定语 时间状语
定语从句

Text 15 The $1-a-Week School
每周一美金的学校

Across the highway from the lawns of Nairobi's Muthaiga Country Club is Mathare, a slum that stretches as far as the eye can see. Although Mathare has virtually no services like paved streets or sanitation, it has a sizeable and growing number of classrooms. Not because of the state—the slum's half-million people have just four public schools—but because the private sector has moved in. Mathare boasts 120 private schools.

This pattern is repeated across Africa, the Middle East and South Asia. The failure of the state to provide children with a decent education is leading to a burgeoning of private places, which can cost as little as $1-a-week.

The parents who send their children to these schools in their millions welcome this. But governments, teachers' unions and NGOs tend to take the view that private education should be discouraged or heavily regulated. That must change.

Chalk and fees

Education in most of the developing world is shocking. Half of children in South Asia and a third

内罗毕的玛萨瑞贫民窟就在穆海咖乡村俱乐部的高速公路对面，贫民窟一直向前延伸至视野尽头。虽然玛萨瑞实际上连铺好的路和卫生设备都没有，但这里的学校数量却很可观，且仍在不断增多。可大多数学校却不是国家建设的，而是借私人部门之力建成——这个50万人口的贫民窟只有4个公立学校。现在，玛萨瑞因拥有120所私立学校而自豪。

这种办学模式在非洲、中东和南亚屡见不鲜。因国家无法为儿童提供良好的教育，所以私立学校涌现，每周学费甚至低至1美元。

千千万万把孩子送到私立学校的家长们对此自是欢迎。然而政府、教师联盟和非政府组织则倾向于阻止或严管私立教育。他们的这种态度必须改变。

教学与费用

大多数发展中国家的教育现状令人震惊。在南亚和非洲，分别有一

---

slum n. 贫民窟   NGO 非政府组织

of those in Africa who complete four years of schooling cannot read properly. In India 60% of six- to 14-year-olds cannot read at the level of a child who has finished two years of schooling.

Most governments have promised to provide universal primary education and to promote secondary education. But even when public schools exist, they often fail. In a survey of rural Indian schools, a quarter of teachers were absent. In Africa the World Bank found teacher-absenteeism rates of 15%-25%. Pakistan recently discovered that it had over 8,000 non-existent state schools, 17% of the total. Sierra Leone spotted 6,000 "ghost" teachers, nearly a fifth the number on the state payroll.

Powerful teachers' unions are part of the problem. They often see jobs as hereditary sinecures, the state education budget as a revenue stream to be milked and any attempt to monitor the quality of education as an intrusion. The unions can be fearsome enemies, so governments leave them to run schools in the interests of teachers rather than pupils.

The failure of state education, combined with the shift in emerging economies from farming to jobs that need at least a modicum of education, has caused a private school boom. According to the World Bank, across the developing world a fifth of primary-school pupils are enrolled in private schools, twice as many as 20 years ago. So many private schools are unregistered that the real figure is likely to be much higher. A census in Lagos found 12,000 private schools, four times as many as on government records. Across Nigeria 26% of primary-age children were in private schools in 2010, up from 18% in 2004. In India in 2013, 29% were, up from 19% in 2006. In Liberia and Sierra Leone around 60% and 50% respectively of secondary-school enrolments are private.

---

teacher-absenteeism *n.* 教师缺勤　　　sinecure *n.* 闲职　　　intrusion *n.* 侵入
fearsome *adj.* 可怕的　　　census *n.* (官方)的统计

By and large, politicians and educationalists are unenthusiastic. Governments see education as the state's job. Teachers' unions dislike private schools because they pay less and are harder to organise in. NGOs tend to be ideologically opposed to the private sector. The UN special rapporteur on education, Kishore Singh, has said that "for-profit education should not be allowed in order to safeguard the noble cause of education".

This attitude harms those whom educationalists claim to serve: children. The boom in private education is excellent news for them and their countries, for three reasons.

First, it is bringing in money—not just from parents, but also from investors, some in search of a profit. Most private schools in the developing world are single operators that charge a few dollars a month, but chains are now emerging. Bridge International Academies, for instance, has 400 nursery and primary schools in Kenya and Uganda which teach in classrooms made from shipping containers. It plans to expand into Nigeria and India. Mark Zuckerberg, Facebook's founder, Bill Gates and the International Finance Corporation, the World Bank's private sector arm, are among its investors. Chains are a healthy development, because they have reputations to guard.

Second, private schools are often better value for money than state ones. Measuring this is hard, since the children who go to private schools tend to be better off, and therefore likely to perform better. ①But a rigorous four-year study of 6,000 pupils in Andhra Pradesh, in southern India, suggested that private pupils performed better in English and science than public school pupils, and at a similar level in maths and Telugu, the local language. The private schools achieved these results at a third of the cost of the public schools.

---

rapporteur *n.* 报告员

Lastly, private schools are innovative. Since technology has great (though as yet mostly unrealised) potential in education, this could be important. Bridge gives teachers tablets linked to a central system that provides teaching materials and monitors their work. Such robot-teaching may not be ideal, but it is better than lessons without either materials or monitoring.

Critics of the private sector are right that it has problems. Quality ranges from top-notch international standard to not much more than cheap child care. But the alternative is often public school that is worse—or no school at all.

Those who can

Governments should therefore be asking not how to discourage private education, but how to boost it. ②Ideally, they would subsidise private schools, preferably through a voucher which parents could spend at the school of their choice and top up; they would regulate schools to ensure quality; they would run public exams to help parents make informed choices. But governments that cannot run decent public schools may not be able to do these things well; and doing them badly may be worse than not doing them at all. Such governments would do better to hand parents cash and leave schools alone. Where public exams are corrupt, donors and NGOs should consider offering reliable tests that will help parents make well-informed choices and thus drive up standards.

The growth of private schools is a manifestation of the healthiest of instincts: parents' desire to do the best for their children. Governments that are too disorganised or corrupt to foster this trend should get out of the way.

(*The Economist*, 2015.8)

---

top-notch *adj.* 拔尖的   subsidise *vt.* 给予补助金   voucher *n.* 代金券
manifestation *n.* 显示   foster *vt.* 促进

长难句解析

① 本句为主从复合句。主干结构为 a study suggested that...。句中 that 引导的宾语从句为谓语 suggested 的宾语；同位语解释说明宾语从句中的 Telugu。

But a rigorous four-year study of 6,000 pupils in Andhra Pradesh, in southern India, suggested that private pupils performed better in English and science than public school pupils, and at a similar level in maths and Telugu, the local language.

② 本句为并列复合句，由分号隔开。第一个分号前的分句中，which 引导的定语从句修饰先行词 voucher；后两个分句都使用了动词不定式结构作状语，表目的。

Ideally, they would subsidise private schools, preferably through a voucher which parents could spend at the school of their choice and top up; they would regulate schools to ensure quality; they would run public exams to help parents make informed choices.

Text 16 Schools Get Permission to Skip Standardized Tests
学校获得准许跳过标准化考试

The Education Department has made an exception to its requirement that states administer annual exams this year and given the District's public and charter schools permission to skip federally mandated standardized tests. It cited "specific circumstances" that make it impossible for the school district to administer the exams, according to a letter the department sent to city officials.

教育部打破惯例，今年不再要求各州组织例行年度考试，并准许学区的公立和特许学校跳过联邦政府法定的标准化考试。该部门在发给市政府官员的信件中提及"特殊情况"，使得学区无法组织标准化考试。

exception n. 例外；除外
charter school 特许学校
standardized tests 标准化考试
administer vt. 施行，实施（法律、考核等）
mandated adj. 依法的；按法律要求的

It said that "the vast majority of students in the District of Columbia (88 percent) are receiving full-time distance learning as of March 20, 2021, and most students receiving hybrid instruction are in school for only one day per week. As a result, very few students would be able to be assessed in person this spring."

①The Biden administration has rejected calls to waive the annual exams, permission that former education secretary Betsy DeVos granted in 2020 to all states that did not want to give the tests after school buildings closed.

A number of states asked for waivers this year, saying conditions made it too hard to administer tests that would produce credible results. But the department said that while states could change the timing of tests, shorten them and administer them remotely, students still had to take them. Exceptions could be made in certain places because of the pandemic. Public schools are required to give annual standardized exams in math and English language arts under the federal 2015 Every Student Succeeds Act, which replaced the 2002 No Child Left Behind law. In a letter this week approving the District's waiver, Ian Rosenblum, the Education Department's deputy assistant secretary for policy and programs, wrote that "we must also recognize that we are in the midst of a pandemic that requires real flexibility."

To protect students' identities, the city might not be able to release data, Rosenblum said, because so few students would be able to be assessed

该部门称,"截至2021年3月20日,哥伦比亚特区的绝大多数学生(占比88%)一直在接受全日制远程教育,大多数接受混合教学的学生每周只在学校上一天课。所以,今年春季能够亲自参加评估测试的学生屈指可数。"

①2020年,美国前教育部部长贝特西·德沃斯对所有不想在封校后组织考试的州予以"考试豁免权",但是拜登政府否决了这种"不强求组织年度考试"的呼吁。

今年很多州要求"考试豁免权",说当前的条件使得组织可信度高的考试很困难。但教育部说,各州可以更改、缩短考试时间,组织远程考试,但学生仍必须参加考试。由于疫情盛行,一些地方可以有例外。2015年联邦颁布的《让每个学生成功法》(该法案取代了2002年颁布的《不让一个孩子落后法》)要求公立学校每年都要组织数学和英语语言艺术两门标准化考试。本周,教育部政策和项目副助理部长伊恩·罗森布鲁姆在授予学区"考试豁免权"的一封信中写道,"我们也必须意识到,我们正处于疫情中,需要真正的灵活性。"

罗森布鲁姆说,为了保护学生的身份信息,该市可能不会公开信息,因为能参加春季考试评估的学生太少,

---

full-time distance learning 全日制远程教育
as of 在……时;截至
instruction n. 教学;讲授
waive vt. (在特定情况下)不强求执行(规则等)
grant vt. (尤指正式地或法律上)同意,准予,允许
condition n. 状态,条件
shorten vt. 使变短,缩短
flexibility n. 灵活性
release vt. 公开;公布

hybrid adj. 混合的
reject vt. 拒绝接受,不予考虑

credible adj. 可信的;可靠的
approve vt. 批准;通过
identity n. 身份;本身

in the spring and subgroups could be very small. In addition to tests in English language arts and math, the District also tests students in science, though that is not part of the federal mandate. Rosenblum said the science tests did not have to be given either. However, the District will administer exams intended to measure the proficiency of students designated as English language learners.

②The decision to grant D.C. an exemption may rankle states that want a testing waiver but can't get one, said Bob Schaeffer, acting executive director of the National Center for Fair and Open Testing, a nonprofit known as Fair Test that works to prevent the abuse of standardized tests.

"Perceived inconsistencies in USDOE's 'standardized' policy for standardized testing waivers will certainly anger states whose similar requests have been rebuffed (either denied or urged to edit and resubmit)," he said in an email.

The Office of the State Superintendent of Education—which administers the federal standardized exams to the city's students—said in a statement that it believes the assessments help advance student learning. "But given our unique circumstances in D.C. this year, we appreciate the U.S. Department of Education's approval on our assessment waiver," Interim Superintendent Shana Young said. "We look forward to resuming statewide assessments next year as we continue to support recovery efforts for our students, families and school communities."

(*The Washington Post*, 2021.4)

---

subgroup *n.* 小组;(团体中的)部分
designate *vt.* 选定,指定
inconsistency *n.* 前后矛盾;不一致
superintendent *n.* 主管人;负责人

proficiency *n.* 熟练;精通
rankle *vt.* 使人发怒;激起怨恨
resubmit *vt.* 重新提交
resume *vt.* 使重新开始;使继续进行

长难句解析

①该句是主从复合句,主句的主干是 The Biden administration has rejected calls,为主谓宾结构,to waive the annual exams 为不定式短语作后置定语修饰 calls;permission 是 to waive the annual exams 的同位语;that 引导的定语从句 1 修饰 permission,其中还包含一个 that 引导的定语从句 2 修饰 states,after school buildings closed 为时间状语从句。

The Biden administration has rejected calls to waive the annual exams, permission that former
     主语   谓语   宾语   后置定语   同位语   定语从句1
education secretary Betsy DeVos granted in 2020 to all states that did not want to give the tests
                           时间状语   状语   定语从句2
after school buildings closed.
     时间状语从句

②该句是主从复合句。主句的主干是…said Bob Schaeffer,为倒装的主谓宾结构,宾语是 The decision… can't get one,为省略 that 的宾语从句,该宾语从句中包含一个 that 引导的定语从句 1 修饰 states;acting executive director… Testing 为 Bob Schaeffer 的同位语;a nonprofit 为 the National Center… Testing 的同位语;known as Fair Test 为后置定语修饰 a nonprofit;that 引导的定语从句 2 修饰 a nonprofit。

The decision to grant D.C. an exemption may rankle states that want a testing waiver but
   主语2   后置定语1   谓语2   宾语2   定语从句1
can't get one, said Bob Schaeffer, acting executive director of the National Center for Fair
           谓语1   主语1   同位语1
and Open Testing, a nonprofit known as Fair Test that works to prevent the abuse of
              同位语2 后置定语2   定语从句2
standardized tests.

Text 17   Thanks but No Thanks
心领了,但不用了

David Stern did his best to up the ante. ①The commissioner of the National Basketball Association (NBA) warned the league's players, who have been locked out by its owners for over four months, that the clubs' latest proposal for a new collective-bargaining agreement (CBA) would be

大卫·斯特恩尽其最大努力来营造气势。①NBA(美国国家篮球协会)总裁警告那些遭到老板雪藏四个月的联盟球员:球会最近一次提议的劳资协议将会是他们所能提供最好也是最后的机会。此

---

ante n. 赌注   collective-bargaining n. 劳资双方代表进行的谈判

their best and last. Moreover, if the union rejected it, he said, the owners would revert to a previous and much less favourable offer. The league then launched a publicity blitz to try to get public opinion on its side.

The players did not blink. On November 14th Billy Hunter, the head of the National Basketball Players Association, declared that the union would leave the owners' take-it-or-leave-it proposal, and try its luck in court. It will attempt to disband and have its members file an antitrust suit against the owners, setting the stage for months or even years of legal wrangling. Of the six months of the 2011-12 season, one has already been lost. Mr Stern called the situation a "nuclear winter" for the league.

The owners made great fanfare of the concessions they had made to the players over months of bargaining. Compared with their original proposal, they have dramatically increased the share of the league's income players would be allowed to keep. They also dropped demands for a hard cap on individual team payrolls and the right to wriggle out of contracts with unproductive players.

However, the offer they are using as a baseline was essentially a management wish list, which had no chance of being accepted. Relative to the CBA that expired after last season, the league's latest proposal would still impose big losses on the players. Their share of revenues would drop from 57% to 50%, a gap worth $280m. And although a few loopholes in the current salary-cap system would remain, they would be sharply curtailed. ②Teams whose payrolls exceed a given threshold would be subject to a punitive tax and prevented from taking advantage of most exceptions to the cap, making it all but equivalent to a firm ceiling. The union has vowed never to accept such restrictions.

---

blitz *n.* 闪电式行动　　　fanfare *n.* 大肆宣扬　　　wriggle out of 设法逃脱
salary-cap *n.* 工资上限　　curtail *vt.* 缩减　　　　　punitive *adj.* 惩罚性的

Mr. Stern, for his part, cannot offer much more without risking a revolt among club owners. The players seem willing to accept a 50-50 split of revenue, enough to make the teams profitable as a group even by the clubs' own contested figures. But that would do nothing to narrow the gap between the league's rich and poor teams. The have-nots would lose less money than they have in the past. But they would still probably remain in the red, and would have little hope of winning a championship over their better-heeled rivals.

The other big North American sports leagues have addressed such inequalities through revenue sharing. But rich teams like the New York Knicks and Los Angeles Lakers fiercely oppose expanding the NBA's modest sharing scheme, which would reduce their franchise values. The owners note that their proposal would triple the amount of money the league currently shares between teams. But the resulting system would still be far smaller as a proportion of total league turnover than that of the National Football League (NFL), National Hockey League or Major League Baseball. Barring even more revenue sharing, the only way to improve competitive balance is a de facto limit on team payrolls with real teeth. That is anathema to the union.

With the parties at an impasse, the lockout will now be contested in court. ③Taking a page from the NFL Players Association (NFLPA), which also faced a lockout earlier this year, the union will attempt to dissolve itself and become a mere trade association, freeing the players to negotiate with clubs individually. They will then accuse the owners of violating antitrust law by colluding to prevent them from working, seeking an injunction to force the resumption of play and damages worth three times their losses, as the law permits. In response, the league will call the union's

---

have-nots *n.* 一无所有的人   barring *prep.* 除……之外   de facto *adj.* 实际上的
real teeth 实际可行的措施   anathema *n.* 令人厌恶者   impasse *n.* 僵局
collude *vi.* 勾结

disbandment a sham . The owners also warn that currently guaranteed contracts might no longer be valid if it is upheld .

The outcome of such a suit is difficult to predict. The NFLPA has prevailed in such cases in the past, and won one antitrust claim against the owners earlier this year. However, that victory was overturned on appeal. The two sides then reached an agreement, rendering the case moot . The Supreme Court has not addressed the matter directly since 1972. And that case involved baseball, which unlike basketball is legally exempt from federal antitrust law.

It will be months before a district court issues a ruling. Once it does, appeals can take years to exhaust. The two sides will have to find a solution at the bargaining table before then. The union's strategy is simply to gain extra leverage by filing suit, and perhaps by scoring some preliminary legal victories. Now that the parties have broadly agreed on a 50-50 revenue split , they differ only on the flexibility of restrictions on team payrolls and player movement between clubs. That might not sound like much. But it seems to be sufficient to put the entire 2011-12 season in jeopardy.

(*The Economist*, 2011.11)

解散是一个骗局。球会老板们也警告说,如果法院判球员胜诉,那么现有保障合同可能会失效。

很难预料这场官司的最终结果。国家足球联盟球员协会曾在类似的诉讼中获得成功,而且今年早先对球会老板的反垄断控告也一度告捷,但在上诉中却没有继续吹响胜利的号角。劳资双方之后达成和解,宣布该官司无效。最高法院自1972年之后就没有直接审判过类似诉讼。然而1972年的审判是关于棒球的,与篮球不一样,其并不受到联邦反垄断法的管制。

地方法院要花上几个月的时间来进行判决。一旦宣判,各类上诉流程下来可能需要几年时间。那时双方必须重新在谈判桌上找到一个解决方案。工会的策略很简单,通过提出诉讼来获得多余筹码,在一些初审中获胜也可能有所助益。现在双方已经一致同意将收入五五分成,唯一的分歧在于球队薪资限制以及球员转会这两方面的灵活性。这听上去似乎没什么大不了,但是这足以危及整个2011—2012年赛季。

长难句解析

① 本句为主从复合句。主句的主干结构为 The commissioner warned the players that…。句中 who 引导的非限制性定语从句修饰先行词 the league's players;that 引导的宾语从句作谓语 warned 的直接宾语。

| The commissioner of the National Basketball Association (NBA) | warned | the league's players, |
| 主语 | 谓语 | 间接宾语 |

who have been locked out by its owners for over four months, that the clubs' latest
非限制性定语从句　　　　　　　　　　　　　　　　　　　直接宾语(宾语从句)
proposal for a new collective-bargaining agreement (CBA) would be their best and last.

② 本句为主从复合句。主句的主干结构为 Teams would be subject to… and prevented from…。句中包含两个并列的谓语结构,由 and 连接,主语均为 Teams;whose 引导的定语从句修饰先行词 Teams。

---

sham *n.* 骗局　　　　　uphold *vt.* 维持(原判)　　　　moot *adj.* 无实际意义的
revenue split *n.* 收益分成

Teams whose payrolls exceed a given threshold would be subject to a punitive tax and
主语　　　　定语从句　　　　　　　　　　　　　　　　　谓语1　　　　　宾语1
prevented from taking advantage of most exceptions to the cap, making it all but equivalent
　谓语2　　　　　　　宾语2　　　　　　　　　　　　　　　　　　　结果状语
to a firm ceiling.

③ 本句为主从复合句。句中which引导的非限制性定语从句修饰先行词the NFL Players Association（NFLPA）。

Taking a page from the NFL Players Association (NFLPA), which also faced a lockout
　　　　条件状语　　　　　　　　　　　　　　　　　　　非限制性定语从句
earlier this year, the union will attempt to dissolve itself and become a mere trade association,
　　　　　　　　　主语　　　谓语　　　目的状语
freeing the players to negotiate with clubs individually.
　　　伴随状语

Text 18　The Guardian View on Creative Workers: Britain Needs Them
《卫报》对创造性工作者的看法：英国需要他们

This week came the news that acts at this year's Womad had been cancelled, owing to artists' difficulties in obtaining visas under the Home Office's "hostile environment." This is not an issue confined to the world music festival. It has been causing problems for British cultural organisations for years. ① Applying for visas is often a humiliating strain for artists and a time-consuming nightmare for the festivals and venues that have invited them for no other reason than the pleasure and enrichment of British citizens. It took Scotland Street Press five months to help Belarusian poet Tania Skarynkina get a visa to appear at this month's Edinburgh international book festival: time that could have been better spent on the work of publishing authors—and contributing to the UK's economy.

本周有消息称，今年世界音乐与舞蹈节的表演已被取消，原因是艺术家们在内政部的"敌对环境"下难以获得签证。这个问题不仅出现在世界音乐节上，多年来，它一直给英国文化组织带来问题。①申请签证对艺术家们来说往往是一个带有羞辱性的问题，对于邀请他们的活动和举办场所来说，这也是一场耗时颇久的噩梦，主办方邀请他们是为了给英国公民带来快乐和丰富他们的生活。苏格兰街道出版社花了5个月的时间，帮助白俄罗斯诗人塔尼亚·斯卡林金娜获得参加本月爱丁堡国际图书节的签证；而他们本可以把时间花在出版作家书籍的工作上，并为英国经济做出贡献。

Womad n. 世界音乐与舞蹈节
humiliating adj. 丢脸的；羞辱性的
venue n. 举办场所
Home Office（英国）内政部
strain n. 问题
Belarusian adj. 白俄罗斯的

Things could get much worse. The government's Brexit white paper is desperately vague on possible arrangements for mobility for those in the cultural sector after leaving the EU. There are fears of more Womad-style chaos, spread across the entire creative industries, especially in the case of a no-deal Brexit, which the Bank of England chief Mark Carney warned today was an "uncomfortably high" risk.

This is not just a matter of artists visiting the UK, though that is in itself important. No: this is also about how the British economy works. It is about bringing in the highly specialised skills that make the British company Jellyfish Pictures the firm of choice to create the visual effects for the Star Wars films. This is about the 25% of architects in Britain who are EU, non-UK nationals, or the over 20% who work in video games, or the 15% of employees at the British Museum. British creative industries generated almost £92bn in 2016 and grew at twice the average of the UK economy—in large part because of their ability to attract the very best talent from Europe.

European employees of British organisations are the tip of the iceberg. According to the Creative Industries Federation, more than a third of creative workers are self-employed—compared with 15% across the economy. That's violinists, artists, ballet dancers, film editors, lighting designers, curators, fashion photographers, authors, games designers, and a host of other British workers whose success depends on their ability to take a short-term contract in Germany or Italy, or to appear at festivals in the Netherlands or France. Many British orchestras are made up of freelance players. Were they faced with a European tour that involved acquiring visas for each country they wished to visit it could utterly debilitate them. That's not to mention artists, designers and musicians who study or work in Liverpool or Glasgow, contributing to the cultural life of

---

creative industriy 创意产业
curator *n.* 馆长；监护人；管理者
debilitate *vt.* 逐步削弱，削弱……的力量

in itself 本身；就其本身而言
orchestra *n.* 管弦乐队

our cities, making them better places for everyone to live and work.

②It is crucial that mobility arrangements for cultural workers do not default to the rest-of-the-world model, which is so evidently ill-suited to the specific needs of the creative economy. Arrangements must be put in place allowing the quick and easy sponsorship of freelancers coming to the UK, perhaps on a "creative freelance visa". Reciprocal agreements for the creative sector must be made with the EU27. Above all, the government should apply thought and intelligence, and listen hard to arts organisations and industry bodies. The vague pronouncements in the white paper give little indication that it understands the problems, let alone is ready to address them seriously. But if it fails to do so, the UK is at risk of losing one advantage that it indisputably has at present: an edge in the creative economy.

(*The Guardian*, 2018.8)

我们各个城市的艺术生活做出了贡献，让城市成了更适合所有人生活和工作的地方。

②至关重要的是，文化工作者的流动安排不应遵照世界上其他人的模式，这种模式显然不适合创造性经济的具体需求。流动安排必须落实到位，允许自由职业者能够快速方便地前往英国，或许可以通过"创造性自由职业者签证"解决这一问题。同时还必须与欧盟 27 国达成创意部门的互惠协议。最重要的是，政府应该运用思想和智慧，认真听取艺术组织和行业组织的意见。白皮书中含糊的声明几乎表明它没有理解这些问题，更不用说准备认真地解决这些问题了。但如果不能做到这一点，英国就有可能失去目前无可争议的一个优势：创意经济优势。

长难句解析

① 本句为主从复合句。主句的主干结构为 Applying for visas is a… and a…。that 引导的定语从句修饰 festivals and venues；for no other reason than 意为"只是因为"。

```
Applying for visas  is     often     a humiliating strain for artists and a time-consuming
    主语           系动词  程度副词           表语1                       连词
nightmare for the festivals and venues that have invited them for no other reason than the
        表语2                          └──────────────────────┬──────────────────────┘
                                                         定语从句
pleasure and enrichment of British citizens.
```

② 本句为主从复合句。主句的主干结构为 It is crucial that…。It 为形式主语，真正的主语是 that 引导的主语从句；which 引导非限制性定语从句。

```
It        is    crucial that mobility arrangements for cultural workers do not default to
形式主语 系动词   表语              真正的主语
the rest-of-the-world model, which is so evidently ill-suited to the specific needs of the
└──────────────────────┬──┘                非限制性定语从句
creative economy.
```

default *vi.* 默认；设置　　　　ill-suited *adj.* 不合适的　　　put in place 落实到位
sponsorship *n.* 赞助；发起　　reciprocal *adj.* 互惠的；相互的　indisputably *adv.* 无可争议地
edge *n.* 优越之处；优势，上风

第四部分 科学技术类

SECTION FOUR

Text 1

Advances in Neuroscience Raise Medical Hopes, Social Questions
神经科学的进步燃起了医学希望，也引发了社会问题

She suffered a stroke at the age of 42, and for nearly a decade after, she was unable to move or communicate beyond shaking her head. Such patients usually experience little improvement, but today, thanks to a neural implant that links her brain to a computer, she has used her mind to control a keyboard and move a robotic arm.

Leigh R. Hochberg, a neuroengineer and doctor who specializes in brain-computer interface systems, told her story at a AAAS Capitol Hill briefing to illustrate how advances in neuroscience may transform once-futuristic ideas into better lives for soldiers, accident victims, and others. "We're hoping to develop technologies that will restore the ability to communicate and restore the ability to move," Hochberg said.

The briefing focused on the military applications of neuroscience, and the presentations reflected the sense that today's advances could have far broader future impact. But with the benefits of enhanced brain function will become critical social and ethical issues.

"These issues are emerging now and will only get more prominent over time," said moderator Alan I. Leshner, the chief executive officer of AAAS and executive publisher of *Science*.

About 100 congressional staff and others attended the 90-min briefing, held 26 July in cooperation with the House Armed Services Committee and with financial support from The Dana Foundation. The AAAS Office of Government Relations has scheduled a second neuroscience briefing—on

---

neural implant 神经植入物
once-futuristic adj. 曾经幻想的
brain-computer interface system 人脑-电脑交互系统
briefing n. 简报

possible links between cell phones and brain tumors—for 7 September. The final briefing in the series, on traumatic brain injury, will be held in October.

In areas such as "shell shock" and brainwashing, neuroscience has long been a military interest. Today, the military is exploring new realms of neuroscience to make soldiers safer and more effective. Jonathan D. Moreno, an historian and ethicist at the University of Pennsylvania, detailed the Pentagon's 2011 neuroscience investments: U. S. Army, $55 million; Navy, $34 million; Air Force, $24 million; and the Defense Advanced Research Projects Agency (DARPA), more than $240 million.

Martha J. Farah, director of Penn's Center for Neuroscience & Society, said a key military interest is cognitive enhancement. Research is assessing newer drugs to keep soldiers alert or neutralize the effects of wartime fatigue, stress, and trauma. Another area of interest, Farah said, is noninvasive brain stimulation in which a weak current is directed into a targeted area of the brain. ①Such techniques have been found to affect attention, learning, memory, decision-making, and mood, and some believe that the effects could extend to visual perception, reaction time, and even social behavior.

Given the legion of war casualties from Iraq and Afghanistan, research into prosthetics is acutely important. Hochberg, who has appointments at Brown and Harvard universities and the Providence VA Medical Center, is focused on technology that may allow people with tetraplegia to move robotic limbs.

When a spinal injury leaves someone paralyzed, he explained, the brain still generates a signal to move the arm, but the signal never arrives. ②At scientific meetings, he has described early research

---

traumatic *adj.* 外伤的   brainwashing *n.* 洗脑   legion *n.* 军团
war casualties 战争中的伤亡   tetraplegia *n.* 四肢瘫痪

in which tiny arrays are implanted in the brain's motor cortex; the array picks up that signal, conveys it through a thin wire into a computer, and then to external devices.

Almost inevitably, however, neuroscience research raises social and ethical questions. Newer drugs developed for sleep disorders and attention deficit hyperactivity disorder are increasingly misused now by travelers, students, and others battling fatigue, Farah reported. Meanwhile, said Moreno, military research has developed a "robo-rat" that can be controlled through electrodes in its brain—and other creatures could be used as living robots too, he said.

For now, though, the potential benefits provide powerful motivation for further research. Hochberg said the stroke victim with whom he's worked sent a video message last year to a Society for Neuroscience conference. Using an on-screen keyboard, her intentions guided the cursor, letter by letter, to type a simple message: "There is hope."

(*Science*, 2011.8)

然而,神经科学研究不可避免地引发了一些社会和伦理问题。法拉在报告中称,为治疗睡眠障碍和注意力缺陷多动症而研发的新药,正日益被旅客、学生和其他对抗疲劳的人滥用。同时,莫雷诺说,军队已经研发出了一种"机器鼠",人们可以通过在其大脑内植入电极来控制它;其他生物也可被当作活的机器人使用。

然而,现在,潜在的益处给未来的研究提供了强劲的动力。霍茨伯格说,他的一位中风患者去年给神经科学协会的一场会议发送了一则视频消息,她用的是屏幕上的键盘,用注意力引导光标,一个字母一个字母地打出了一则简单的消息:"有希望。"

长难句解析

① 本句为并列复合句。and 前句子的主干结构为 Such techniques have been found to affect…,其中动词不定式作被动语态中动词 found 的实际宾语 Such techniques 的补足语;and 后的句子中,that 引导的宾语从句作 believe 的宾语。

> Such techniques have been found to affect attention, learning, memory, decision-making,
> 主语1   谓语1   宾语补足语
> and mood, and some believe that the effects could extend to visual perception, reaction
>   主语2 谓语2   宾语从句
> time, and even social behavior.

② 本句为并列复合句。分号前句子的主干结构为 he has described early research;in which 引导的定语从句修饰宾语 early research;分号后的句子并列了两个谓语动词;宾语3 指代 that signal,为避免重复,此处用 it 代替;into a computer 和 to external devices 为两个表示方向的状语。

---

array *n.* 阵列　　electrode *n.* 电极　　cursor *n.* 光标

At scientific meetings, he has described early research in which tiny arrays are implanted
　地点状语　　　　主语1　谓语1　　　宾语1　　　　定语从句
in the brain's motor cortex; the array picks up that signal, conveys it through a thin wire
　　　　　　　　　　　　　主语2　谓语2　　宾语2　　谓语3 宾语3　　方式状语
into a computer, and then to external devices.
　　状语1　　　　　　　　状语2

Text 2 The Newly Discovered, Very Important Ice Mountains of Pluto
最新重要发现：冥王星上存在冰山

Something is heating up the dwarf planet, NASA scientists announced on Tuesday. And that could change our understanding of other rocks in the cosmos.

Ice mountains as tall as the Rockies loom high above Pluto's surface. They are made of water so cold as to be like rock, and they rise out of a surface of frozen methane and nitrogen. About every 150 hours, a brilliant star rises from behind the peaks. The star is no larger than a dot—not really bigger than any pinprick in the sky—but it shines with the brightness of tens of thousands of full moons.

On Wednesday, NASA scientists announced the very first findings captured by the agency's New Horizons probe. ①The spacecraft completed a gravitational dance with the tiny world and its moon, Charon, on Tuesday morning, but it was so occupied with observing the two orbs that it only began beaming back the very first and most compressed images hours later.

美国国家航空航天局的科学家周二宣布，矮行星上的某些物质正在升温。这将改变我们对宇宙中其他岩石行星的了解。

冥王星表面隐约可见跟落基山脉一样高的冰山。它们的主要成分是水，因为太冷，以至于看起来像冰岩，在布满甲烷冰和氮冰的行星表面隆起。大约每隔150小时，一颗灿烂的星星会从山峰后面升起。这颗星星比一个点还小（在天空中看起来还没有针孔大），但它的亮度却相当于几万个满月的亮度。

周三，美国国家航空航天局的科学家公布了该机构"新视野"号探测器的首个发现。①周二上午，航天器完成了与这个小星球及其卫星"卡戎"的引力舞蹈，但是，由于太忙于观察这两个星球，它在几小时后才开始发回最初的也是最重要的压缩图像。

Pluto n. 冥王星
dwarf planet 矮行星，或称"侏儒行星"，体积介于行星和小行星之间，围绕太阳运转，质量足以克服固体引力以达到流体静力平衡（近于圆球）形状，没有清空所在轨道上的其他天体，同时不是卫星
methane n. 甲烷　　　nitrogen n. 氮　　　pinprick n. 针孔　　　orb n. 球体
compressed adj. 压缩的

NASA released two historic new images. The first is the highest-resolution photo of Charon ever, capturing the full disk of the moon. The second is a close-up on Pluto's surface. Both were full of surprises: It was the kind of press conference where giddy scientists chuckle and repeat, "I don't know" over and over again.

Both images were also very, very exciting. One even suggests a new understanding of how geology might work on the universe's many small, icy objects.

The first image reveals that Charon has some but not many craters. This is perplexing, because scientists would expect to see many on its surface. (Think about how many there are on Earth's own, much larger moon.) The lack of them suggests that evidence of previous asteroid collisions has been erased by changes on the moon's surface—by, in other words, geological activity.

There were zero craters in the newly observed region. Again, scientists would expect to see many of them—the complete lack indicates that Pluto is almost certainly geologically active. And that throws entire ideas of how space rocks work into question.

Pluto is the first small, icy world that humankind has closely observed that isn't orbiting a much larger planet, like Neptune or Saturn. Moons attached to a large planet might be subject to tidal heating, a process in which the force of the giant's gravity deforms and heats the smaller one. ② Triton, Neptune's largest moon, is geologically active—it has volcanoes and surface change—and scientists hypothesized that the giant blue planet might be stirring up most of that energy.

There's only one problem. "This doesn't look

---

highest-resolution photo 最高分辨率图像
giddy adj. （高兴或激动得）发狂的
perplexing adj. 令人费解的   Neptune n. 海王星

close-up n. 特写镜头
crater n. 坑；火山口
tidal heating 潮汐加热

like Triton, which up to now is what we thought was the most similar object in the solar system to Pluto," said Alan Stern, the principal investigator on the New Horizons mission, at the press conference Tuesday.

And Pluto sure looks geologically active—but, also unlike Triton, it's not subject to tidal heating. Its energy must be coming from somewhere else, but scientists aren't sure where yet. In the press conference, they hypothesized that its activity might be due to radioactive energy building up inside the planet. The dwarf planet might also hide a vast, frozen ocean beneath its surface, which could be gradually melting and expanding the world.

We just don't know.

"I would never have believed that the first close-up shot of Pluto didn't have a single impact crater on it," said John Spencer, a space scientist at the Southwest Research Institute. "There's something very different about Plutonian geology."

And that, in turn, is important, because humanity's search for exoplanets—planets beyond the solar system—has just begun. So far, we've found 1,932 of them. Some are gas giants, a few seem to be rocky worlds in their star's habitable zone. What seems likely, though, is that there are many worlds like Pluto: small, round, and distant from their suns.

If all those objects are geologically active, we might be living in a far more active universe than we thought. Suddenly, the many thousands of small objects beyond Neptune look like they could have cryovolcanoes on them, too. The entire cosmos might have many more volcanoes and earthquakes than we thought.

"I know we've tended to think of those worlds, those types of objects, as candy-coated lumps of ice," said Spencer. "I think they could be equally amazing if we ever get a spacecraft there."

---

cryovolcano *n.* 冰火山

It will take many years before scientists understand the full import of the science that New Horizons did on Tuesday. The images received on Wednesday were heavily compressed, and it will be more than a year until NASA receives the full raw data set . But on Wednesday, scientists seemed exhausted, surprised, and overjoyed.

"Pluto is something wonderful," said Stern. "This is what we came for."

Cathy Olkin, another lead scientist with the program, added: "This exceeds what we came for."

(*The Atlantic*, 2015.7)

可能需要很多年，科学家才能理解"新视野"号周二的探索结果对于科学研究的全部意义。周三我们接收到的图像资料是大比例压缩过的，得需要一年多的时间，美国国家航空航天局才能接收到完整的原始数据集。但是，周三，科学家们似乎筋疲力尽，十分惊讶又狂喜万分。

"冥王星是神奇的，"斯特恩表示，"这就是我们要探索它的初衷。"

本项目的另一位带头科学家凯茜·奥金补充道："这超越了我们要探索它的初衷。"

长难句解析

① 本句为并列复合句，由转折连词 but 连接的两个分句构成。but 前句子的主干结构为 The spacecraft completed a dance；句中 Charon 为同位语，补充说明 its moon；but 后句子的主干结构为 it was so occupied with… that…，句中包含一个 so… that…结构。

```
The spacecraft  completed  a gravitational dance  with the tiny world and its moon, Charon,
   主语1          谓语            宾语                        状语                     同位语
on Tuesday morning, but    it      was      so occupied with observing the two orbs
    时间状语          主语2   系动词            表语
that it only began beaming back the very first and most compressed images hours later.
                             结果状语从句
```

② 本句为并列复合句。and 之前句子的主干结构为 Triton is active；Neptune's largest moon 作 Triton 的同位语；破折号中间的部分可看作插入语；and 后句子的主干结构为 scientists hypothesized that…；that 引导的宾语从句作 hypothesized 的宾语。

```
Triton, Neptune's largest moon, is geologically active —it    has  volcanoes and surface
  主语1       同位语            系动词     表语       主语2  谓语2       宾语
change—and scientists  hypothesized  that the giant blue planet might be stirring up most of
              主语3        谓语3                      宾语从句
that energy.
```

---

raw data set 原始数据集

Text 3　The Internet of Everything Holiday Shopping Guide
万物联网——假日购物指南

After all, Cisco believes the Internet of Everything (tech cognoscenti call it the "IoE") is a $14 trillion-dollar opportunity and General Electric says it will transform entire industries. The regular old Internet has relied on humans connecting to machines. The IoE is about machines—computers, phones, toys, appliances, robots, drones—connecting to humans and to each other. Since there are exponentially more machines than people, the IoE will end up being like the Internet on crystal meth.

①On a more prosaic and personal level, the IoE is already solving some really big problems—for example, it can let you know whether your dog is getting enough exercise, or signal your smartphone when you're running out of eggs.

With the IoE bearing down on us, I enlisted the help of gadget guru Greg Harper of Harpervision Associates, who scours the earth for newfangled connected devices, to present the First Annual Too-Much-Expendable-Income IoE Gift Guide.

For the executive who is too busy to keep anything alive: The IoE is all about the convergence of a bunch of tech trends: tiny sensors that can measure things; ubiquitous wireless connections; cloud computing; devices like smartphones that can collect data and use it in an app.

One popular IoE product, for example, is the Fitbit. Wear it on your wrist, and it tracks activity and displays your patterns on a phone app. Now, let's say you have a dog, and you suspect that while you're at the office all day, the dog doesn't even bother to expend the energy to bark at the UPS man. Well,

毕竟，思科公司认为万物联网（技术行家称之为"IoE"）是一个14万亿美元的机会，并且美国通用电气公司表示，它将改变整个行业。普通旧互联网依赖人类连接到机器。IoE与机器相关——电脑、手机、玩具、电器、机器人、无人机——它们与人类相连接，彼此之间也有连接。因为机器显然比人多，IoE最终将会成为像互联网冰毒一样的东西。

①从一个更平淡无奇的个人层面来说，IoE已经解决了一些"非常大"的问题，例如，它可以让你知道你的狗是否得到了足够的锻炼，鸡蛋吃完了也给你的手机发提示。

在IoE向我们铺天盖地地袭来时，我在"Harpervision联营"的插件大师格雷格·哈珀的帮助下，完成了《第一本年度过多可支配收入的IoE礼品指南》，哈珀曾满世界地寻找最新式的连接设备。

对于忙于让所有东西都保持活跃状态的高管们来说，IoE是关于一大堆技术的集合：可以用于测量的微小传感器，无处不在的无线连接、云计算等一些像智能手机那样能够收集数据并在应用程序中使用的设备。

例如，一个流行的IoE产品，健身手环。将它戴在你的手腕上，就能跟踪显示你的活动并在你手机上的应用程序上展示出来。现在，假设你有一只狗，你怀疑当你在办公室的时候，你的狗发现陌生人时甚至都不叫。嗯，这时

---

cognoscenti *n.* 行家　　　　exponentially *adv.* 以指数方式　　　crystal meth 冰毒
prosaic *adj.* 平庸的　　　　newfangled *adj.* 最新式的　　　　　　convergence *n.* 集合
sensor *n.* 传感器　　　　　cloud computing 云计算　　　　　　　 Fitbit *n.* 健身手环

you can get the Whistle ($99.95), which is basically a Fitbit for dogs. It can tell your smartphone if the dog is walking, playing, or sleeping. This way, you can enjoy your dog right from your desk chair.

Hyperbusy executives can also be very good at killing plants. One solution is the Parrott Flower Power ($59.99), a system of wireless sensors that you push into a plant's soil. Each sensor measures levels of water, light and nutrients, and talks to a phone app to call for help. "Basically, your plants are tweeting you," Harper says.

For the person who can't keep track of stuff: Billy Crystal's new autobiography is titled, *Still Foolin' 'Em: Where I've Been, Where I'm Going, And Where Are My Keys?* ② Someone should tell him there's an emerging category of IoE products designed to let you know what you've got and where it is—just in time for the millions of baby boomers losing their short-term memories.

Some of these devices, like Tile, seem to be more useful than others, but here are two that don't seem to be useful at all: Behold the Egg Minder, billed as The Smart Egg Tray ($69.99). As the website says: "In-tray indicate the oldest egg, while push notifications alert you when you're running low." In its overapplication of technology, this takes me back to the 1970s and Ronco's inside-the-egg scrambler.

Or there's the smart piggy bank, called—cue the groans—Porkfolio ($69.99). It tracks how many quarters go in and out, and talks to an app that, the site says, lets you "track your balance and set financial goals from afar." Perfect for that little nephew who wears a suit to kindergarten and already plans to work at Goldman Sachs.

---

hyperbusy *adj.* 特别忙的　　autobiography *n.* 自传　　overapplication *n.* 超额核销
inside-the-egg scrambler 卵内扰频器

For the person who eats too much and lets his or her teeth rot: HAPIfork ($99.99) is a Bluetooth-enabled fork that can tell when, how much and how fast you eat—just in case your spouse isn't already informing you. If you're eating too fast, the HAPIfork starts vibrating, which of course makes it harder to keep eating.

Once you've given up trying to eat because food is jumping off your fork, pick up a Beam networked toothbrush ($24.99). This will keep track of how often and how long you brush, and report back to an app. If Orwell only knew.

For the faded high school sports star who still obsesses over his or her performance: Data is transforming sports. Sensors and software allow professional teams to measure stuff no one could ever measure before, like how fast each player runs during a soccer game.

Sports sensor technology is moving down to consumers. The basketball nut might enjoy the 94Fifty ball ($295). The ball can measure shot speed, dribble speed, backspin, and shot arc, and feed it to a phone app that can then tell you how to play better—for instance, by increasing the arc on your shot. In 2003, I wrote about some inventors who built an incredibly complex machine just to measure basketball shot arc and sold it to the Dallas Mavericks. This is a better version of the same machine, in your pocket.

For baseball, tennis, or golf, try the Zepp Labs training system ($150). Stick a tiny square device on the end of a bat, racket or club, and it tracks speed and motion and sends 1,000 data points per second to an app. It can also measure the speed of your bat as you use it to smash your HAPIfork into tiny pieces.

By themselves, none of these IoE gadgets seem like anything that could ramp up to a $14 trillion opportunity. But it's worth remembering that when

---

vibrate *vi.* 振动　　　dribble speed 运球速度　　　backspin *n.* 下旋　　　smash *vt.* 粉碎

electricity was new, one of the first household applications was the doorbell, invented in 1831. Imagine people giggling at the notion that a door knocker wasn't good enough.

As Harper notes, today's HAPIfork and Whistle point the way to a new kind of household. The IoE will change daily life, much as electricity once did. Better start saving with your Porkfolio so you can pay for it.

(*Newsweek*, 2013.12)

出现的时候,第一个家庭应用程序是 1831 年发明的门铃。想象一下人们对于门环还不够好这一说法嘲笑不已的画面吧。

哈珀指出,今天的减肥叉子和哨子指出了一条新的家庭模式道路。IoE 将改变人们的日常生活,就像电的发明那样。最好开始用智能存钱罐来走上储蓄之路,这样你才能有钱买它。

长难句解析

① 本句为并列复合句。破折号前句子的主干结构为 the IoE is solving problems;破折号后句子的主干结构为 it can let you know…,其中 whether 引导的宾语从句作 know 的宾语。

> On a more prosaic and personal level, the IoE is already solving some really
> 　　　　状语　　　　　　　　　　主语1　　　　谓语1　　　宾语1
> big problems—for example, it can let you know whether your dog is getting
> 　　　　　　插入语　　　主语2 谓语2 宾语2　　　　宾语从句
> enough exercise, or signal your smartphone when you're running out of eggs.
> 　　　　　　　　　　　　　　　　　　　　时间状语从句

② 本句为主从复合句。主句的主干结构为 Someone should tell him…,其中宾语从句作 tell 的直接宾语;what 引导的宾语从句 2 和 where 引导的宾语从句 3 为并列结构,作 know 的宾语;后置定语 1 修饰 IoE products;后置定语 2 修饰 baby boomers。

> Someone should tell him there's an emerging category of IoE products
> 　主语　　谓语　　间接宾语　　直接宾语(宾语从句1)
> designed to let you know what you've got and where it is—just in time for the
> 　　　后置定语1　　　　　宾语从句2　　　宾语从句3　　　　状语
> millions of baby boomers losing their short-term memories.
> 　　　　　　　　　　后置定语2

Text 4　The Call of Mars
来自火星的呼唤

When I view the Moon, there are times when I feel like I'm on a time machine. I am back to a

当我看见月球的时候,我有时感觉我就在一个时光机上。我回到一

cherished point in the past—now nearly 45 years ago—when Neil Armstrong and I stood on that bleak, but magnificent lunar landscape called the Sea of Tranquility.

While we were farther away from Earth than humans had ever been, the fact is that we weren't alone. An estimated 600 million people back on Earth, at that time the largest television audience in history, watched us plant our footprints on the Moon.

Fast forward to today. ①Now I see the Moon in a far different light—not as a destination but more a point of departure, one that places humankind on a trajectory to homestead Mars and become a two-planet species.

It is time to lay the groundwork for effective global human exploration of space.

NASA's Apollo program adopted a get-there-in-a-hurry, straightforward space race strategy that left the former Soviet Union ithe lunar dust. Doing so meant don't waste time developing reusability. Let's close that chapter in the space exploration history books.

I am calling for a unified international effort to explore and utilize the Moon, a partnership that involves commercial enterprise and other nations building upon Apollo. Let me emphasize: A second "race to the Moon" is a dead end. America should chart a course of being the leader of this international activity to develop the Moon. The United States can help other nations do things that they want to do, a fruitful avenue for U.S. foreign policy and diplomacy.

②A step in the right direction is creating an International Lunar Development Corporation, customized to draw upon the legacy of lessons learned from such endeavors as the International Geophysical Year (whose purpose was to get scientists allover the world to focus on the physics and

---

bleak *adj.* 荒凉的
reusability *n.* 可重用性
trajectory *n.* 轨迹
fruitful *adj.* 富有成效的

atmosphere of the Earth), the International Space Station program, as well as model organizations such as Intelsat and the European Space Agency. Space collaboration should be the new norm, including the tapping of talented Chinese, Indian and other space experts from around the globe.

In my view, U.S. resources are better spent on moving toward establishing a human presence on Mars. I envision a comprehensive plan that would lead to permanent human settlement on Mars in the next 25 years. To get under way, the International Space Station can serve as a test bed for long-duration life support and for technologies that can safely, reliably and routinely transport crews to the distant shores of Mars. I've championed the creation of spacecraft to be placed on continuous loops between Mars and Earth, thereby putting in place a pathway to sustainability that forever links the two planets.

Going to Mars means staying on Mars—a mission by which we are building up a confidence level to become a two-planet species. ③At Mars, we've been given a wonderful set of moons—one of which, perhaps Phobos, can act as an offshore world from which crews can robotically preposition hardware and establish radiation shielding on the Martian surface to begin sustaining increasing numbers of people. To succeed at Mars, you cannot stop with a one-shot foray to the surface.

My passion for space exploration is guided by two principles: a continuously expanding human presence in space, and retention of U.S. leadership in space. To move forward, what's required is what I term as a Unified Space Vision for America that is predicated on exploration, science, development, commerce and security. To reach beyond low Earth orbit requires a suite of missions that are the foundation for such a Unified Space Vision. Putting in place and staying on track with this unified approach must begin now.

---

envision *vt.* 想象　　continuous loop 连续循环　　foray *n.* 侵略；短暂访问(新地方)
retention *n.* 保留　　a suite of 一系列

I call for an international effort to further explore and utilize the Moon. It would be a partnership that involves commercial enterprise and other nations building upon the Apollo legacy. But the real calling is Mars.

By implementing a step-by-step vision—just as the United States did with the single-seat Mercury capsule, followed by the two-person Gemini spacecraft that made Apollo possible—humankind can push outward to the distant dunes of Mars.

Our Earth isn't the only world for us anymore. It's time to seek out new frontiers.

(*The New York Times*, 2013.6)

我呼吁通过国际合作，来进一步开发和利用月球。这种合作形式包括在阿波罗计划基础上引入商业公司和其他国家。但是真正的目标是火星。

通过执行步骤分明的计划——就像美国执行的只能承载一人的水星计划，紧随着的是使得阿波罗计划成为可能的双人双子号宇宙飞船——人类可以朝着更远的火星沙丘发展。

地球再也不是我们赖以生存的世界，是时候去寻找新的家园了。

长难句解析

① 本句为主从复合句。主句的主干结构为 I see the Moon；句中 not as a destination but more a point of departure 为宾语 the Moon 的补语；one 为 a point of departure 的同位语；that 引导的定语从句修饰 one。

Now I see the Moon in a far different light—not as a destination but more a point of departure, one that places humankind on a trajectory to homestead Mars and become a two-planet species.
状语1　主语　谓语　宾语　　状语2　　　　　宾语补足语
同位语　　　　　定语从句

② 本句为主从复合句。主句的主干结构为 A step is creating an… Corporation；in the right direction 作后置定语修饰 a step；customized 分词短语作后置定语修饰宾语；learned from…作后置定语修饰 lessons；whose 引导的定语从句修饰 the International Geophysical Year，起补充说明的作用。

A step in the right direction is creating an International Lunar Development Corporation, customized to draw upon the legacy of lessons learned from such endeavors as the International Geophysical Year (whose purpose was to get scientists all over the world to focus on the physics and atmosphere of the Earth), the International Space Station program, as well as model organizations such as Intelsat and the European Space Agency.
主语　后置定语1　谓语　宾语
后置定语2　后置定语3
补语（定语从句）
后置定语3
后置定语3

dune *n.* 沙丘　　　　　　　　　　frontier *n.* 边界，边疆

③ 本句为主从复合句。主句的主干结构为 we've been given moons；句中 of which 引导的定语从句修饰 one；Phobos 为 one 的同位语；from which 引导的定语从句修饰 world，该从句中还包含由 and 连接的两个并列的谓语结构。

At Mars, we've been given a wonderful set of moons—one of which, perhaps
状语　主语　　谓语　　　　　宾语　　　　　　　　　定语从句1
Phobos, can act as an offshore world from which crews can robotically preposition
同位语　　　　定语从句1　　　　　　　　　　定语从句2
hardware and establish radiation shielding on the Martian surface to begin sustaining
　　　　　　　　　　　　　　　定语从句2
increasing numbers of people.

Text 5 Apple's Privacy Rules Force Marketers to Find New Ways to Target Ads
苹果的隐私条例迫使营销商另寻新径精准投放广告

Online shoppers often feel they are being watched. Put an item in your basket but fail to buy it, and it may follow you plaintively around the Internet for days. Announce your engagement on social media and you will be hit with adverts for the honeymoon. As you turn 40, expect the attention of elasticated -trouser merchants.

On April 26th Apple, which supplies one-fifth of the world's smartphones and around half of America's, introduced a software update that will end much of this snooping. Its latest mobile operating system forces apps to ask users if they want to be tracked. Many will decline. It is the latest privacy move forcing marketers to rethink how they target online ads.

网购者常常感觉自己被监视着。把一件商品加入购物车却没买，之后这件商品就会在网络上苦苦地纠缠你好几天。在社交媒体上宣布订婚消息后，你会被蜜月广告轮番轰炸。当你刚年满40，预计弹力裤商人就会关注你。

占据全球20%和美国约50%智能手机市场份额的供应商苹果公司于4月26日推出了一款更新软件，很大程度上将终止这种隐私窥探。苹果最新的手机操作系统强制手机应用咨询用户是否想被追踪。许多用户将会拒绝。这个最新的隐私举措迫使营销人员重新思考怎样精准投放在线广告。

---

plaintively *adv.* 悲伤地，哀怨地
advert *n.* 广告；宣传；（电视上的）广告时间
elasticated *adj.* 有松紧性的；有弹力的
snoop *vi.* 窥探；打探；探听
rethink *vt.* 重新考虑

engagement *n.* 订婚；婚约
expect *vt.* 预计；预期
introduce *vt.* 引进；推行
decline *vi.* 谢绝；婉言拒绝

① By micro-profiling audiences and monitoring their behaviour, digital-ad platforms claim to solve advertisers' age-old quandary of not knowing which half of their budget is being wasted. In the past decade digital ads have gone from less than 20% of the global ad market to more than 60%, according to GroupM, the world's largest media buyer.

Stronger privacy protections may make their ads less effective. In 2018 the EU imposed its General Data Protection Regulation (GDPR) and America's most-populous state introduced the California Consumer Privacy Act. Both made it harder to harvest users' data. Since 2020 Apple's Safari web browser has blocked the "cookies" that advertisers use to see what people get up to online. Google has similar plans for its more popular Chrome browser.

Apple's latest change makes explicit an option that was previously hidden deep in its phones' settings. Users can forbid apps to access their "identifier for advertisers" (IDFA) code, which singles out their device, and from tracking their activity across other firms' apps and websites. It amounts to a "seismic shift" in in-app advertising, says Jon Mew, head of the Internet Advertising Bureau, an industry body.

The inability to share data is forcing advertisers to come up with new ruses. One is to bypass rules banning data transfers between ad-tech com-panies by consolidating. In February AppLovin, a mobile-software firm, acquired Adjust, which provides mobile-ad attribution, reportedly for $1bn. Another is to ask users to "sign in", which lets an app monitor their behaviour with no need for IDFAS. And instead of targeting individuals, marketers

①数字广告平台声称,通过微观描述网络用户画像并对其网络行为进行监控,可以解决广告商存在已久的困惑——自己的哪一部分预算正在打水漂?据全球最大的媒介采购公司群邑集团(GroupM)的数据显示,过去十年,数字广告在全球广告市场的份额从不到20%上升至60%以上。

加强隐私保护可能会使广告效果打折扣。2018年,欧盟强制实行了《通用数据保护条例》,美国人口最多的加利福尼亚州出台了《加州消费者隐私法案》。这两项举措都增加了获取用户数据的难度。从2020年开始,苹果手机的Safari网络浏览器屏蔽了广告商用来追踪用户上网痕迹的cookies。谷歌对其更受欢迎的Chrome浏览器也有类似计划。

苹果公司的最新转变让一个手机选项变得清晰明朗,之前它一直隐秘地藏在手机设置里。用户可以禁止应用程序访问"广告标识符"进而识别他们的设备,也可以阻止某一应用程序利用跨公司的应用程序和网站跟踪自己的网络活动。行业机构网络广告局的负责人乔恩·缪表示,这对应用内嵌广告来说,相当于"地震级别的转变"。

不能共享数据正迫使广告商想出新的招数。一是广告科技公司通过整合绕过禁止"互相传输数据"的规定。今年2月,移动软件公司AppLovin据传以10亿美元的价格收购了提供移动广告归属的Adjust。二是要求用户"登录",这样应用程序就可以在不需要广告标识符的情况下监控用户的行为。市场营销人员可

---

profile *vt.* 扼要介绍;描……的轮廓
impose *vt.* 强制实行;推行
block *vt.* 阻碍;堵塞
explicit *adj.* 明确的;清楚明白的
seismic *adj.* 地震的;影响深远的
attribution *n.* 归因;属性

quandary *n.* 困惑;进退两难;困窘
harvest *vt.* 收割(庄稼等);收获
cookie *n.* 网络跟踪器(记录上网用户信息的软件)
identifier *n.* 标识符,标识号
ruse *n.* 诡计;骗术
sign in 签到,登记

can target broader interest groups—coffee lovers, *Daily Mail* readers, and so on—much as they did in the pre-internet age. It's "back to the future", says Mr Wieser.

Stripped of accurate ways of measuring their impact, "direct-response ads" that require consumers to take an action (like clicking) lose their appeal. Advertisers will again have to gauge ads' effectiveness by looking for a rise in sales in a region where an ad ran but not elsewhere. ② Because campaigns that promote general awareness of a brand never benefited as much from tracking, platforms which mostly attract brand advertising will not feel much difference. Snap, whose social network, popular with teenagers, belongs to that group, posted a year-on-year rise in revenues of 66% in the first quarter.

The less advertisers know about their audience, the costlier advertising will become. Facebook has argued this will hurt small businesses. It is probably right, thinks William Merchan of Pathmatics, a data company. Digital ads promise to cut waste in media buys, he says. Now that advertisers are again in the dark about which half of their budget is wasted, they are "going to have to just spend more".

(*The Economist*, 2021.5)

以瞄准更广泛的兴趣群体,如咖啡爱好者、《每日邮报》读者等,而不是针对个人——就像他们在前网络时代所做的那样。维瑟说,这是"返回未来"。

"直接反应广告"要求消费者进行诸如点击页面这样的操作,在被苹果新规剥夺了精确计算广告效力的方法后,失去了吸引力。广告商将不得不再次观测销售额在特定区域(而不是其他区域)的增长,进而衡量广告效力。②因为提升品牌知名度的活动从没有在追踪数据中获益颇多,所以主要吸引品牌广告的平台并没受多大影响。Snap 就属于这一类公司,其社交网络深受青少年欢迎,今年第一季度收入同比去年增长了66%。

广告商对其受众了解越少,广告的成本越大。脸书公司认为这对小企业非常不利。数据公司 Pathmatics 的威廉·麦臣认为这一看法有可能是正确的。他说,数字广告承诺能减少媒体购买方面的浪费。既然广告商再次陷入"摸瞎"状态,对哪里浪费了一半预算一无所知,他们"将不得不花更多的钱"。

长难句解析

①本句为主从复合句。主句的主干为主谓宾结构;of not knowing…作后置定语修饰quandary,该后置定语中包括 which 引导的宾语从句,作 knowing 的逻辑宾语。

By micro-profiling audiences and monitoring their behaviour,	digital-ad platforms	claim
方式状语	主语	谓语
to solve advertisers' age-old quandary	of not knowing	which half of their budget is being wasted.
宾语	后置定语	宾语从句

②本句为主从复合句。主句的主干是 platforms will not feel much difference,为主谓宾结构;Because 引导一个原因状语从句,其中包含一个 that 引导的定语从句修饰 campaigns,as much from tracking 作比较状语;which 引导一个定语从句修饰先行词 platforms。

---

strip *vt.* 剥夺;掠夺
gauge *vt.* (用仪器)测量;估计;估算
audience *n.* (同一事物的)观众,听众

appeal *n.* 吸引力;感染力;魅力
campaign *n.* (社会、政治)运动,活动
promise *vi.* 承诺;保证;答应

> Because campaigns that promote general awareness of a brand never benefited as
>   原因状语从句
> much from tracking, platforms which mostly attract brand advertising will not feel
> 比较状语   主语   定语从句   谓语
> much difference.
> 宾语

Text 6　Time to Build a More Secure Internet
是时候建立一个更安全的网络环境了

The internet was designed in a way that would allow it to **withstand** missile attacks. That was cool, but it resulted in an unintended side effect: it made it more vulnerable to **cyberattacks**. So now it may be time for a little renovation. The roots of the Internet's design come from the network built by the Pentagon's Advanced Research Projects Agency to enable research centers to share computer resources. The ARPANET, as it was called, was packet-switched and looked like a fishnet. Messages were broken into small chunks, known as packets, that could **scurry** along different paths through the network and be reassembled when they got to their destination. There were no centralized hubs to control the switching and routing. Instead, each and every **node** had the power to route packets. If a node were destroyed, then traffic would be routed along other paths.

These ideas were conceived in the early 1960s by a researcher at the Rand Corp., whose motive was to create a network that could survive a nuclear attack. ① But the engineers who actually devised the traffic rules for the ARPANET, many of whom were graduate students **avoiding the draft** during the Vietnam War,

网络的构建方式就是让它能够承受攻击。这确实很酷。但是也造成了一种出乎意料的反面效应：它使得网络攻击变得更加容易。所以也许现在是时候实行一场微改革了。网络设计来源于美国国防部高级研究计划署，其目的是让研究中心能共同分享电脑资源。高级研究计划署网络，人称ARPANET，是数据包交换网络，看起来就像一张渔网。信息被切割成小块的数据包，通过网络快速穿梭在不同的路径，并在抵达终端时聚合起来。这种网络并不需要中央系统来控制交换和路径。相反，每一个节点都有自己的路由项，如果一个节点被损坏，就会选择其他的路径。

早在20世纪60年代，美国兰德公司的研究人员就已经有这些想法了，这些想法的目的是创造一个可以经受得住核能袭击的网络。①但是实际进行操作的工程师中许多都是越战期间逃兵役的

---

withstand *vt.* 承受　　　cyberattack *n.* 网络攻击　　　scurry *vi.* 急赶
node *n.* 节点　　　avoid the draft 逃兵役

were not focused on the military uses of the Net. Nuclear survivability was not one of their goals.

Anti-authoritarian to the core, they took a very collaborative approach to determining how the packets would be addressed, routed and switched. Their coordinator was a UCLA student named Steve Crocker. He had a feel for how to harmonize a group without centralizing authority, a style that was mirrored in the distributed network architecture they were inventing. To emphasize the collaborative nature of their endeavor, Crocker hit upon the idea of calling their proposals Requests for Comments (RFCs), so everyone would feel as if they were equal nodes. It was a way to distribute control. The Internet is still being designed this way; by the end of 2014, there were 7,435 approved RFCs.

So was the Internet intentionally designed to survive a nuclear attack? When *Time* wrote this in the 1990s, one of the original designers, Bob Taylor, sent a letter objecting. Time's editors were a bit arrogant back then (I know, because I was one) and refused to print it because they said they had a better source. That source was Stephen Lukasik, who was deputy director and then director of ARPA from 1967 to 1974. The designers may not have known it, Lukasik said, but the way he got funding for the ARPANET was by emphasizing its military utility. "Packet switching would be more survivable, more robust under damage to a network," he said.

Perspective depends on vantage point. As Lukasik explained to Crocker, "I was on top and you were on the bottom, so you really had no idea of what was going on." To which Crocker replied, with a dab of humor masking a dollop of wisdom, "I was on the bottom and you were on the top, so you had no idea of what was going on."

研究生，他们在为 ARPANET 设置运行规则的时候，并没有将重点放在网络的军事用途上。能否经受得住核考验不在他们的目标之内。

他们的核心是反独裁，并一起确定了数据包将如何处理、寻找路径和转换。他们的协调员是加利福尼亚大学洛杉矶分校的一个学生，叫作斯蒂芬·克罗克。他知道如何在不用中央集权的情况下，使一个组织中的各个成员和谐相处，而这一方式充分体现在他们正在创造的分布式网络体系中。为了强调他们研究的协作性，克罗克想到把他们的意见统称为"征求意见文档"，这样每个人都能感觉到他们是平等的。这是一种分布控制的方法。网络也是按照这个方式来设计的。到2014年年底，已经有了7 435 份有效征求意见文档。

所以网络到底是不是故意设计来抵挡核能攻击的呢？《时代周刊》在20世纪90年代提出这个疑问之时，网络原始创造者之一鲍勃·泰勒致信否认此事。《时代周刊》的编辑当时有些不满（这我知道，因为我就是其中之一）并拒绝将其刊登，因为他们说收到了更好的资源。这个资源就是史蒂芬·鲁卡席克，他是 ARPA 的代理董事，于1967 至 1974 年期间任董事长。设计者们可能对此并不知情，但鲁卡席克说只有通过强调互联网的军事作用他们才能获得开发ARPANET的资金。"在面对网络攻击时数据包的调换会更具有生存能力、更加强大。"他说。

观点因人而异。鲁卡席克向克罗克解释道："我是领导者，你是实施者，所以你根本不知道会发生什么。"对此，克罗克机智幽默地回应道："我是实施者，你是领导者，所以你也不知道发生了什么。"

Requests for Comments（RFCs）征求意见文档　　　　vantage point 有利位置

Either way, the Net's architecture makes it difficult to control or even trace the packets that dart through its nodes. ② A decade of escalating hacks raises the question of whether it's now desirable to create mechanisms that would permit users to choose to be part of a parallel Internet that offers less anonymity and greater verification of user identity and message origin.

The venerable requests-for-comments process is already plugging away at this. RFCs 5585 and 6376, for example, spell out what is known as Domain Keys Identified Mail, a service that, along with other authentication technologies, aims to validate the origin of data and verify the sender's digital signature. Many of these techniques are already in use, and they could become a foundation for a more robust system of tracking and authenticating Internet traffic.

Such a parallel Internet would not be foolproof. Nor would it be completely beneficial. Part of what makes the Internet so empowering is that it permits anonymity, so it would be important to keep the current system for those who don't want the option of being authenticated.

Nevertheless, building a better system for verifying communications is both doable and, for most users, desirable. It would not thwart all hackers, perhaps not even the ones who crippledSony. ③ But it could tip the balance in the daily struggle against the hordes of spammers, phishers and ordinary hackers who spread malware, scarf up credit-card data and attempt to lure people into sending their bank-account information to obscure addresses in Nigeria.

(*Time*, 2015.1)

无论网络以哪种方式搭建,都很难控制或者跟踪数据包的交换。②10年间不断升级的黑客问题导致了现在这个问题的出现,即是否还有必要建立一套可让用户选择是否联入一个平行的网络的机制,该平行网络不太允许匿名并更多地要求用户身份验证和消息来源确认。

这个严肃的认证请求也致力于此。例如,征求意见文档5585号和6376号都表明了什么叫作域名密钥识别邮件标准——这是一项利用其他认证技术的服务,目标是验证数据的来源以及证实发送者的数字签名。这其中的许多技术都已被应用,因此可以为更强大的追踪和验证网络传输系统奠定基础。

这样的平行网络并不是使用简单的,也不是尽善尽美的。网络如此强大的一部分原因正是允许匿名,所以对那些不想选择身份验证的人来说,保护现在的系统是十分重要的。

然而,对于大多数人来说,建立一个更好的系统来验证交流,是可行的,也值得一做。它并不需要去阻拦所有的黑客,即便是攻击了索尼网站的黑客。③然而,在对付日常的麻烦时,天平可以稍微倾斜,比如,垃圾邮件发送人、钓鱼者、传播恶意软件或试图盗取用户信用卡信息或者诱导人们将银行账号信息发到尼日利亚的模糊地址的黑客们。

长难句解析

① 本句为主从复合句。主句的主干结构为 the engineers were not focused on the uses;句中 who 引导的定语从句和 whom 引导的非限制性定语从句都修饰主语 the engineers。

Domain Keys Identified Mail 域名密钥识别邮件标准
thwart *vt.* 拦截　　　spammer *n.* 垃圾邮件发送者
authenticate *vt.* 验证
phisher *n.* 钓鱼者

> But the engineers who actually devised the traffic rules for the ARPANET, many of whom were graduate students avoiding the draft during the Vietnam War, were not focused on the military uses of the Net.

② 本句为主从复合句。主句的主干结构为 hacks raises the question；句中 of 结构作 question 的后置定语，whether 引导的宾语从句作 of 的宾语；that 引导的定语从句 1 修饰 mechanisms；that 引导的定语从句 2 修饰 a parallel Internet。

> A decade of escalating hacks raises the question of whether it's now desirable to create mechanisms that would permit users to choose to be part of a parallel Internet that offers less anonymity and greater verification of user identity and message origin.

③ 本句为主从复合句。主句的主干结构为 it could tip the balance；句中 who 引导的定语从句修饰 ordinary hackers。

> But it could tip the balance in the daily struggle against the hordes of spammers, phishers and ordinary hackers who spread malware, scarf up credit-card data and attempt to lure people into sending their bank-account information to obscure addresses in Nigeria.

Text 7　Google Car's Computer Got Smarter in 2015
谷歌车载电脑在 2015 年变得更智能

Google says the computer brain inside its self-driving car is getting smarter fast, with the number of times human test drivers had to take over for the autonomous vehicle decreasing sharply in recent months.

谷歌表示其无人驾驶汽车内的智能系统正迅速变得更智能，在近几个月的测试中，驾驶员必须接管自主驾驶系统的次数也在锐减。

In its latest mandatory autonomous-car report to the California Department of Motor Vehicles, and its first on the subject of "disengagements of autonomous mode," Google reported its cars handed over control to the driver seven times less frequently in the fourth quarter of 2015 than in a similar period in 2014.

"What's encouraging is that the numbers are going down," Chris Urmson, Google self-driving car project lead, told *USA Today*. He noted that of 13 incidents in which Google test drivers suddenly took control of the car, five happened over the course of 370,000 miles in 2015. That's down from eight within 53,000 miles of driving in 2014.

①The disengagements, which Google reported in a blog post Tuesday, were grouped into two categories: failure of the autonomous system due to unfamiliar road parameters, which alerted the driver who then took over control (272 incidents), and unanticipated human actions taken before the computer could react (69).

Urmson says that by using modeling software, Google's self-driving car engineers were able to play out those 69 incidents in which the driver suddenly took over to see if there would have been any contact had the human not intervened. Contact would have occurred in 13 of the 69 events, either with another motorist or in some cases traffic cones.

②Of the 272 instances in which the car's computer alerted the driver that he or she needed to take the wheel, the gap between these events decreased in recent months to once every 5,300 autonomous miles, as compared to once every 785 miles a little over a year ago.

One watchdog group that has been a vocal critic of Google's driverless approach expressed concern about the new data. "How can

---

disengagement *n.* 脱离　　modeling *n.* 建模　　cone *n.* 圆锥体
vocal critic 直言不讳的批评家

Google propose a car with no steering wheel, brakes or driver when its own tests show that over 15 months the robot technology failed and handed control to the driver 272 times and a test driver felt compelled to intervene 69 times?" John M. Simpson, Consumer Watchdog's Privacy Project director, said in a statement.

Urmson notes that the Google car's software currently is "set conservatively" for testing purposes, meaning it is designed to err on the side of being easily triggered so engineers can refine and upgrade the system.

Over the past six years, the company's fleet of sensor-packed Lexus SUVs and prototype pod-cars have logged 1.3 million miles on public roads in Mountain View, Calif, and in Austin, Texas.

Self-driving car tech has fast become a small obsession with a range of traditional automakers. ③ Ford and Kia recently announced at the Consumer Electronics Show that they are beefing up their autonomous car plans, while Volvo, Audi, Tesla and Mercedes-Benz are quickly growing the number of driver-assist features that edge close to autonomous driving but require drivers to stay engaged in the process.

In all these instances, the automobiles will retain their steering wheels and pedals. In contrast, Google has made clear that its cars will be two-passenger machines will lack those features. "We have always believed that fully self-driving is the right path," Urmson says, noting that the more a car can handle driving chores the less alert its driver would be to the possibility to taking back the wheel. "It is challenging to maintain vigilance if you're untrained" in terms of taking back control from an autonomous car.

But Urmson doesn't believe Google's car will be alone on the roads one day, but rather just "one part of many solutions to a changing transportation

---

err *vi.* 犯错　　　　trigger *vt.* 触发　　　　refine *vt.* 优化　　　　prototype *n.* 原型
vigilance *n.* 警觉

landscape." He is excited about the growing number of players in the space. "The more the merrier. It's a technology that's important. The more of us out there trying to solve this, the faster we can get this out there and hopefully save some lives."

If there is one thing that drives Urmson and his team, it is in fact statistics on deaths caused by automobiles. The news there isn't good. U.S. traffic deaths jumped 14% in the first half of 2015, according to the National Safety Council. Around 14,000 people lost their lives in that period.

"That's the equivalent of a 737 full of passengers falling out of the sky every weekday, yet we seem to accept (that) as the price of our mobility," Urmson wrote in his blog post. "Self-driving cars have the potential to reduce those numbers, because they eliminate the driver inattention that leads to thousands of collisions, injuries and deaths."

(*USA Today*, 2016.1)

部分。"他很高兴越来越多的人参与到这一领域。"多多益善。它是一项很重要的技术。越多的人参与进来并试图解决它,我们就可以更快地得到它,进而希望拯救一些人的生命。"

如果还有一个原因推动了乌尔逊和他的团队,那么则是由汽车引起的死亡统计数据。这条消息令人不安。根据国家安全委员会统计,美国交通死亡率在2015年上半年大幅上涨14%,大约1.4万人丧命。

"这相当于每个工作日就有一架满载乘客的波音737客机从天空坠落,然而我们就如同将其视作出行的代价一样,似乎也接受了这件事,"乌尔逊在其博客中写到,"自动驾驶汽车有希望应对这种情况,因为他们可以消除驾驶员注意力不集中现象,而这会导致数以千计的碰撞、受伤和死亡。"

长难句解析

① 本句为主从复合句。冒号后的内容为宾语 two categories 的同位语,是由 and 连接的两个并列成分。冒号前句子的主干结构为 The disengagements were grouped into two categories。which 引导的非限制性定语从句1修饰主语 The disengagements; taken before the computer could react 作 unanticipated human actions 的后置定语。

```
The disengagements, which Google reported in a blog post Tuesday, were grouped into
   主语              非限制性定语从句1                              谓语
two categories: failure of the autonomous system due to unfamiliar road parameters, which
   宾语                          同位语1                                          非限
alerted the driver who then took over control (272 incidents), and unanticipated human
制性定语从句2           定语从句                              同位语2
actions taken before the computer could react.
          后置定语
```

② 本句为主从复合句。主句的主干结构为 the gap decreased; in which 引导的定语从句修饰先行词 instances,该从句中还嵌套了一个 that 引导的宾语从句,作 alerted 的直接宾语; as compared to... ago 作状语。

---

merrier *adj.* 更快乐的 equivalent *n.* 等价物 collision *n.* 碰撞

Of the 272 instances in which the car's computer alerted the driver that he or she needed to take the wheel, the gap between these events decreased in recent months to once every 5,300 autonomous miles, as compared to once every 785 miles a little over a year ago.

③ 本句为主从复合句。主句的主干结构为 Ford and Kia announced...，其中 that 引导的宾语从句作 announced 的宾语；while 引导的时间状语从句中还嵌套了一个 that 引导的定语从句修饰先行词 features。

Ford and Kia recently announced at the Consumer Electronics Show that they are beefing up their autonomous car plans, while Volvo, Audi, Tesla and Mercedes-Benz are quickly growing the number of driver-assist features that edge close to autonomous driving but require drivers to stay engaged in the process.

Text 8　The Social Network's Shares Recover as It Fixes Its Search Problem
修复自身搜索问题，该社交网络股价回升

Mark Zuckerberg is trying to spice up things online with some pillar talk. ①Unveiling a revamped search engine on January 15th, the boss of Facebook referred to it as the "third pillar" of the social network alongside its timeline, which lets individual users post what they have been up to, and its news feed, which lets them see what their friends are doing. Facebook's search offering has long been so dire that any improvement to it is a welcome relief. But the company will have to do much more in future if it wants to mount a serious challenge to Google's dominance of the online-search business.

马克·扎克伯格正试图通过用一些关键探讨来增添网络趣味性。①1月15日，脸书推出一款改良后的搜索引擎——总裁扎克伯格称其为脸书的"第三大支柱"，另外两大支柱分别是供用户发布自己动态的时间轴和了解自己朋友实时动态的新闻推送。长期以来，脸书糟糕的搜索功能一直为人们所诟病，因此，任何的改进对于脸书来说都值得一试。不过，面对如今在网络搜索界占主导地位的谷歌公司，想要向它发起实质性的挑战，未来脸书需要做得更多。

spice up 增添趣味　　　　　　　　　　revamped adj. 翻新的

This still accounts for the lion's share of digital advertising. According to eMarketer, a research firm, an estimated $17.6 billion was spent on search ads in America alone last year, with Google pocketing three-quarters of that sum. Facebook has been focused on digital display advertising and its success in winning business has helped its share price rise, phoenix-like, from the ashes of a catastrophic stock market flotation last year. If it can pinch search ads from Google and others too, its shareholders will be even more delighted.

Hence Mr. Zuckerberg's third pillar. Still in its infancy, the new search engine serves up answers to queries by tapping into people's social networks and those of their mates. ②So someone who is, say, thinking of visiting New York can search for "restaurants in New York visited by my friends" to see eateries his pals have raved about there. Lonely hearts can trawl for kindred spirits who happen to know their friends, and job-hunters can more easily track down people who know folk at companies they want to work for. All this should offer plenty of fodder for targeted ads.

Some critics point out that the social network is very late to the search game. "It's unbelievable that Facebook has taken so long to do something that should be table stakes online," says Nate Elliott of Forrester Research. But Face bulls point out that Google, whose Google+ social network is still a shadow of Facebook's, cannot match its rival's prowess in "social" search. ③And they claim that Facebook's move will help it counter the likes of Siri, a voice-activated personal assistant for mobile devices from Apple, which is hoping mobile search ads will boost a share price that dipped below $500 this week, having been more than $700 in September.

---

phoenix-like *adj.* 如凤凰涅槃般的　　flotation *n.* （公司的）发行股份　　pinch *vt.* 捏去
tap into 接上　　trawl *vi.* 搜索　　fodder *n.* 素材
dip below 跌破

Mounting an effective challenge to Google will still be tough, however, because most web searches are for things such as the weather and traffic conditions, where friends' opinions are irrelevant. (Recognising this, Facebook has turned to Microsoft, whose Bing search engine will answer such queries in the social network's service.) Moreover, many Facebookers don't "like" their doctors, dentists, builders and other things that would help make social search more valuable. Without such material, Facebook's new pillar will be built on a shaky foundation.

(*The Economist*, 2013.1)

然而,想要向谷歌发起有效性挑战仍然是件艰难的事情,因为大多数人搜索网页都是为了查询诸如天气、交通等信息,而朋友的意见对这些方面不太有指导意义(意识到这点之后,脸书转向微软寻求帮助,因为微软旗下的必应搜索引擎将会在社交网络服务中给出这类搜索的答案。)此外,许多脸书用户不"喜欢"他们的医生、牙医、建筑商以及其他让社交搜索更有价值的事物。要是没有这些材料,脸书的新支柱恐怕会根基不稳。

长难句解析

① 本句为主从复合句。主句的主干结构为 the boss referred to it as…;alongside 是介词短语作状语,其宾语 its timeline 和 its news feed 由 and 连接;定语从句1 修饰先行词 timeline;定语从句2 修饰先行词 news feed。

> Unveiling a revamped search engine on January 15th, the boss of Facebook referred to it
> 伴随状语　　　　　　　　　　　　　　　　　主语　　　　　　　谓语　宾语
> as the "third pillar" of the social network alongside its timeline, which lets individual users
> 宾语补足语　　　　　　　　　　　　　状语　　　　　　定语从句1
> post what they have been up to, and its news feed, which lets them see what their friends
> 　　　宾语从句　　　　　　　　　状语　　　　　　　定语从句2
> are doing.

② 本句为主从复合句。主句的主干结构为 someone can search for…;句中 say 相当于语气助词;who 引导的定语从句修饰先行词 someone;定语从句2 修饰先行词 eateries,关系词 that 在定语从句中作宾语,故此处省略。

> So someone who is, say, thinking of visiting New York can search for
> 主语　　　定语从句1 插入语　　　定语从句1　　　　谓语
> "restaurants in New York visited by my friends" to see eateries his pals have raved about
> 　　　　　　宾语　　　　　　　　　　目的状语　　　　定语从句2
> there.

③ 本句为主从复合句。主句的主干结构为 they claim…;that 引导的宾语从句1 作 claim 的宾语;a voice-activated personal assistant for mobile devices from Apple 作 Siri 的同位语;which 引导的非限制性定语从句修饰先行词 Apple。

---

shaky foundation 根基不稳

And they claim that Facebook's move will help it counter the likes of Siri, a voice-activated personal assistant for mobile devices from Apple, which is hoping mobile search ads will boost a share price that dipped below $500 this week, having been more than $700 in September.

Text 9

Technology Brought Us All Together. That's Part of What's Holding Us Back
技术使世界互通互联,但也是阻碍我们进步的部分原因

Our connected world has allowed researchers to become so tightly networked that they're falling into the trap of groupthink. ①That might explain why some researchers seeking cures for Alzheimer's disease, for example, have conceded that they've been throwing years of work and billions of dollars toward a single theory that has failed to lead to any treatment—while ignoring promising alternatives.

Sociologist James Evans of the University of Chicago has concluded that what's being lost, at least in biomedical research, is scientific independence. Being able to work independently of other labs allows researchers to come up with fresher insights.

In a new study, Evans and colleagues found that weak studies are more likely to come from labs that share lots of researchers and methods with others, and strong studies come from labs that do things their own way.

Weak studies are not just those that come to the wrong conclusions but those whose conclusions are fragile. If a competitor tries to replicate them,

互通互联的世界使研究人员间的联系变得如此密切,以至于使他们逐渐陷入趋同思维的困境。①比如,这也许可以解释为什么一些寻求阿尔茨海默症治疗方法的研究人员承认,他们为了一个单一理论努力了多年,投入了数十亿美元,却不见成效——同时忽略了有希望的替代方案。

芝加哥大学的社会学家詹姆斯·埃文斯指出,现在的研究失去了科学独立性,至少在生物医学研究领域是这样的。能够独立于其他实验室工作,可以使研究人员提出更新颖的见解。

在一项新研究中,埃文斯及其同事发现,缺乏说服力的研究更可能来自与其他实验室共用大量研究人员和方法的实验室,而有说服力的研究则更可能来自以自己的方式做研究的实验室。

缺乏说服力的研究其结论不仅是错误的,而且容易被推翻。如果竞争对手试图复制它们,研究结果将会有

---

groupthink n. (决策水平低下的)集体决策,趋同思维   replicate vt. 复制

the result will be different, unless conditions and methods are exactly the same. The conclusions of such studies are unlikely to represent broad biological facts, and probably won't be of much use in medicine.

To sort the weak from the strong, Evans and colleagues were able to use a special case where thousands of studies on the interaction between drugs and genes can be re-tested quickly. A machine can now do what's called a high throughput assay to rerun a whole slew of previous studies. And so Evans was able to evaluate more than 3,000 published claims against the results of this mechanical backup, which can not only replay the exact experiments but also test the robustness of the claims by varying the parameters a bit.

Groupthink is well known in politics and media. Where once competing reporters would look into the same events independently and not know the others' results until the next day's papers, now there's an unconscious temptation among journalists to believe the interpretation of the most prominent news outlets, or whoever posts online first.

Scientists are subject to the same human foibles, but groupthink shouldn't be conflated with scientific consensus, which is often based on ideas that are backed up by multiple lines of inquiry. That would include things like the structure of DNA, Einstein's theory of relativity, and the basic physics behind the greenhouse effect. Those are widely accepted now, in part because they were supported by independent, even isolated researchers.

What's rewarded these days is the absolute opposite of those historic claims. While science works best when researchers prove one idea multiple ways, funding agents and journal editors today reward those with only a single line of evidence to

---

be of much use 很有用
assay n. 测定；化验
backup n. 备用物（如设备、计划）
news outlet 大型新闻机构；权威通讯社

throughput n.（确定时间内的）工作量；生产量
rerun vt. 重做；重播，重演   slew n. 大量，许多
parameter n. 参数；系数
foible n. 弱点，小缺点   conflate vt. 合并

support multiple claims. They want bigger claims and are content with lesser evidence.

The technology that's allowed so much connection has of course also been positive, enabling people to collaborate and learn more efficiently. Researchers can sometimes even counteract extraneous noise by harnessing a wisdom-of-the-crowd phenomenon, where many individuals converge on a right answer. But like many technological changes, it's come with unintended consequences. ②The fact that U.S. researchers are producing 1,000 papers a day shows there's a lot of energy out there to be used more productively—if funding encouraged bold exploration.

(*Bloomberg*, 2019.8)

一项证据来证实多个声明的人。他们追求意义重大的声明,也乐于接受证据少的研究。

技术在很大程度上加强了人们之间的联系,这当然也有积极意义,可以使人们更高效地合作与学习。有时研究者甚至能够利用大众智慧现象——许多个人研究者致力于找出一个正确答案——来屏蔽外界噪声。但是,与许多技术变革一样,它带来了意想不到的后果。②美国研究人员每天发表1 000篇论文,这表明有很多精力可以被更有效地利用——如果学术资金鼓励大胆探索的话。

长难句解析

① 本句为主从复合句,主句的主干为 That might explain why…。why 引导宾语从句作主句的宾语;宾语从句中第一个 that 引导宾语从句;第二个 that 引导定语从句,修饰 a single theory;while 后接现在分词作状语,表示伴随。

| That | might explain | why some researchers seeking cures for Alzheimer's disease, for example, have conceded that they've been throwing years of work and billions of dollars toward a single theory that has failed to lead to any treatment—while ignoring promising alternatives. |
| 主语 | 谓语 | 宾语从句 |

（定语从句修饰 a single theory；while ignoring promising alternatives 作状语）

② 本句为主从复合句,主句的主干为 The fact shows…。that 引导同位语从句,解释说明 the fact 的具体内容;there's a lot of…为省略了引导词 that 的宾语从句;to be used more productively 作 energy 的后置定语;if 引导虚拟条件句,表示与现在事实相反。

| The fact | that U.S. researchers are producing 1,000 papers a day | shows | there's a lot of energy out there to be used more productively — if funding encouraged bold exploration. |
| 主语 | 同位语从句 | 谓语 | 宾语从句（含后置定语与虚拟条件句） |

---

extraneous *adj.* 外来的;没有关联的
wisdom-of-the-crowd 大众智慧

harness *vt.* 利用;治理

Text 10 When a New Study Debunks Science, don't Ignore It
当一项新的研究揭露科学的真相时,不要忽视它

In 2008, *Science*, one of the top scientific journals, published a paper by a group of psychologists that claimed to find biological differences between liberals and conservatives. According to the paper, conservatives tended to react more to "sudden noises" and "threatening visual images." This result, which suggests that political liberalism and conservatism spring from deep, indelible sources rather than reactions to the issues of the day, suggests that polarization will never end—that the populace will always be divided into two camps, separated by a gulf of biology.

On its face, that claim should sound a bit fishy. The issues dividing liberals and conservatives change—a century ago, religious fundamentalists argued for more inflation and easy money. Today, they are in a conservative coalition that generally favors hard money. Ideologies and coalitions also differ greatly from country to country—in most nations, for example, social conservatives tend to favor big government. Yet because research seemed to say that political differences are biological, news outlets started to accept the idea as fact.

Fast forward a decade, though, and the claim is unraveling. In a working paper published this month, another team of psychologists attempted to repeat the experiment, and also conducted other similar experiments. They failed to find any evidence linking physical-threat perception with political ideology. But when they tried to publish their paper, *Science* desk rejected it—that is, the editors refused

---

indelible *adj.* 不可磨灭的
fundamentalist *n.* 原教旨主义者;基要主义者
hard money 硬性货币(指价值稳定的货币),硬通货
desk *n.* <美>(报馆中的)编辑部

populace *n.* 民众;平民

unravel *vi.* 崩溃;瓦解

to even send the paper out for peer review, claiming that the replication study simply wasn't noteworthy enough to be published in a top journal. Meanwhile, another team of researchers also recently tried to replicate the original study, and failed. So even though at this point the evidence proving a biological basis for liberalism and conservatism seems to have been invalidated, it's unclear whether this fact will make it into the public conversation.

Traditionally, scientific breakthroughs are imagined as pioneering experiments that conclusively discover important scientific truths. Young students learn a long list of such breakthroughs—the oil drop experiment that determined the charge of the electron, the Michelson-Morley experiment that found that light always travels at a constant speed, and others. The most commonly used tests are designed to deal with a single test of a single hypothesis.

But modern science has moved away from this model. Although early experimenters in physics and chemistry generally had to build one apparatus to test each hypothesis, modern researchers gather large amounts of data and run a large number of tests on it. That increases the chance that the researchers will find false correlations, especially if they choose which tests to perform based on the results of previous tests.

In other words, the mass production of testable hypotheses in modern science makes it very likely that large numbers of false results will gain wide acceptance in the media. The fundamental problem is that scientific journals are too focused on novel ideas. ①In a recent case, some scientists found a gene called 5-HTTLPR that they claimed influenced depression, but even as failed replication efforts piled up, other scientists were getting published and winning acclaim for finding correlations between that gene and all sorts of other social outcomes. The novel findings got more attention than the skeptical follow-ups.

---

apparatus *n.* 仪器；设备

follow-up *n.* 后续行动；后续事物

For science to reform itself, this needs to change. Efforts to replicate old research needs to be given just as much priority, attention and journal publication as claims of original findings. ② The old model of science—a single research team discovering a new phenomenon with a single brilliant experiment—needs to `give way to` the idea of science as a vast `collective` effort, with researchers checking and double-checking each other's results and methods. And the media, for its part, needs to restrain its impulse to broadcast the latest hot result, and wait for a predominance of evidence to pile up.

If changes like these are not made, scientists will find themselves facing a `mounting` crisis of credibility and respectability, as finding after finding `turns out to` have been an illusion. That in turn will make the public less `responsive` to science when it really matters, such as with climate change. For science to `retain` its `air` of professionalism and authority, there must be more emphasis on replication.

(*Bloomberg*, 2019.6)

为了科学可以自主改革,这种情况需要改变。复制旧研究的努力须被给予和首创研究的声明同等的优先权、关注度和期刊发表机会。②科学的旧模式——一个研究团队通过一项出色的实验发现一个新现象——需让位于这样一种看法,即将科学看作许多人员的共同努力,研究人员不断检验彼此的研究结论和研究方法。就媒体而言,他们需克制披露最新热门研究结果的冲动,直到重要的证据积累得足够多。

如果不能做出此类改变,随着一项又一项科学发现被证明是假象,科学家会发现自己面临着愈发严重的信任和尊重危机。这反过来会导致公众在面对真正重要的科学发现(如气候变化)时反应不够积极。为使科学保持其专业和权威的印象,人们必须更加注重复制研究。

长难句解析

① 本句为并列连词 but 连接的并列句。第一个并列分句主干为 some scientists found a gene。that 引导的定语从句修饰 gene,从句中 they claimed 为插入语。but 后第二个并列分句主干为 other scientists were…。even as… 为让步状语从句;for finding correlations between… 为介词短语,在句中做原因状语。

```
In a recent case,   some scientists   found   a gene   called 5-HTTLPR   that they claimed
    状语              主语 1           谓语 1   宾语        定语              定语从句
influenced depression,   but   even as failed replication efforts piled up,   other scientists
                               让步状语从句                                      主语 2
were getting published and winning acclaim   for finding correlations between that gene
          谓语 2                                        原因状语
and all sorts of other social outcomes.
```

② 本句主干为 The old model of science needs to give way to the idea of science。破折号中间为插入语,解释说明 old model 的内容;介词短语 as a vast collective effort 为 science 的补语,对 science 进行补充说明;with researchers checking and double-checking… methods 为

---

give way to 让位于;被……代替 collective *adj.* 全体成员的
mounting *adj.* 上升的;增长的 turn out to be 证明是;结果是
responsive *adj.* 积极响应的 retain *vt.* 保留 air *n.* 印象

伴随状语，对 a vast collective effort 进行解释说明。

> The old model of science—a single research team discovering a new phenomenon
> 主语　　　　　　　　　　　　　　插入语
> with a single brilliant experiment—needs to give way to the idea of science as a vast
> 　　　　　　　　　　　　　　　　　谓语　　　　　　宾语　　　　　　　　　　　补语
> collective effort, with researchers checking and double-checking each other's results
> 　　　　　　　　　　　　　　　　　　伴随状语
> and methods.

Text 11　Mirrors Could Replace Air Conditioning by Beaming Heat into Space
镜面可将热量传送至太空，有望取代空调

A mirror that sends heat into the frigid expanse of space has been designed by scientists to replace air-conditioning units that keep buildings cool on Earth.

Researchers believe the mirror could slash the amount of energy used to control air temperatures in business premises and shopping centres by doing away with power-hungry cooling systems.

Around 15% of the energy used by buildings in the U.S. goes on air conditioning, but the researchers' calculations suggest that in some cases, the mirror could completely offset the need for extra cooling.

①In a rooftop comparison of the device in Stanford, California, scientists found that while a surface painted black reached 60℃ more than ambient temperature in sunlight, and bare aluminium reached 40℃ more, the mirror was up to 5℃ cooler than the surrounding air temperature.

"If you cover significant parts of the roof with this mirror, you can see how much power it can save. You can significantly offset the electricity used for air conditioning," said Shanhui Fan, an expert in photonics at Stanford University who led the development of the mirror. "In some situations the

科学家正在设计一种可以把热量传送到寒冷太空的镜面，用来代替为建筑降温的空调装备。

研究人员认为，该技术可以取代商务场所和购物中心里高能耗的制冷系统，从而大幅降低制冷的能耗。

在美国，空调的耗能量占总建筑物耗能量的15%。而研究人员的计算结果表明，在某些情况下，这种镜面完全可以消除对制冷的额外需求。

①科学家在加利福尼亚斯坦福大学的屋顶设备对比实验中发现，在太阳光照下，黑面板的表面温度比环境温度高60℃，裸铝面板的温度比环境温度高40℃，而镜面的温度比周围温度低了将近5℃。

"如果用镜面来覆盖大部分的屋顶，你就知道它能节省多少电量了。这样做可以有效抵消空调制冷的耗电量，"该镜面研发的带头人、斯坦福大学光电学专家范珊辉说道，"计算结果证明，在某些情况下，它可以完

---

frigid adj. 寒冷的　　　　　　premises n. （企业）营业场所

computations say you can completely offset the air conditioning."

The Stanford mirror was designed in such a way that it reflects 97% of the visible light that falls on it. But more importantly, it works as a thermal radiator. When the mirror is warmed up, it releases heat at a specific wavelength of infrared light that passes easily through the atmosphere and out into space.

To make anything cool requires what engineers call a heat sink: somewhere to dump unwanted heat. The heat sink has to be cooler than the object that needs cooling or it will not do its job. For example, a bucket of ice will cool a bottle of wine because it becomes a sink for heat in the liquid. Use a bucket of hot coals and the result will the very different. The Stanford mirror relies on the ultimate heat sink: the universe itself.

The mirror is built from several layers of wafer-thin materials. The first layer is reflective silver. On top of this are alternating layers of silicon dioxide and hafnium oxide. These layers improve the reflectivity, but also turn the mirror into a thermal radiator. When silicon dioxide heats up, it radiates the heat as infrared light at a wavelength of around 10 micrometres. Since there is very little in the atmosphere that absorbs at that wavelength, the heat passes straight out to space. The total thickness of the mirror is around two micrometres, or two thousandths of a millimetre.

"The cold darkness of the universe can be used as a renewable thermodynamic resource, even during the hottest hours of the day," the scientists write in *Nature*. In tests, the mirror had a cooling power of 40 watts per square metre at ambient temperature.

②Writing in the journal, Fan puts the installed cost of mirrors at between \$20 and \$70 per square metre and calculates an annual electricity saving of 100MWh per year on a three storey building.

---

thermal radiator 热辐射器
radiate *vt.* 辐射

infrared *adj.* 红外线的
thermodynamic *adj.* 热力的

silicon dioxide 二氧化硅

Fan said that the mirror could cool buildings—or other objects—simply by putting it in direct contact with them. Coating the roof of a building with the mirror would prevent heating from sunlight but do little to remove heat from its interior. More likely, the mirror would be used to cool water or some other fluid that would then be pumped around the building.

He ruled out the idea of using the mirrors to slow down global warming. "Roof space accounts for only a small portion of the Earth's surface, so at this point we don't think this would be a geoengineering solution. Rather, our contribution on the green house gas emission issue is simply to reduce electricity consumption," he said.

"I'm really excited by the potential it has and the applications for cooling," said Marin Soljačić, a physicist at MIT. "You could use this on buildings so you have to spend much less on air conditioning or maybe you wouldn't need it at all. You could put it on top of shopping malls. With a large enough surface you could get substantial cooling."

(*The Guardian*, 2014.11)

范珊辉说,使镜面与楼房或其他物体的表面接触,就能达到降温的目的。将镜面覆盖到楼顶上,便可有效阻止太阳辐射的热量,但它对降低室温作用甚微。镜面倒是更可能用来给楼房管道中流动的水或其他液体降温。

他打消了利用该镜面技术延缓全球变暖的念头。他说:"屋顶面积只占地球表面的极小一部分,因此,我们认为,该技术不能提供地球工程解决方案。镜面技术对温室气体减排的贡献,仅仅在于减少耗电量而已。"

"这一技术的发展潜力及其在制冷方面的应用令我感到振奋,"麻省理工学院物理学家马林·索里亚西克说道,"你可以把这种镜面安装在楼顶上,这样空调的耗电量会大大降低,你甚至根本不需要空调制冷了。你还可以把这种镜面安装在商场的屋顶。因为屋顶面积比较大,所以制冷效果会好得多。"

长难句解析

① 本句为主从复合句。主句的主干结构为 scientists found…; found 后是 that 引导的宾语从句;该宾语从句是 while 引导的并列句,主干结构为 while a surface reached 60℃ more… and bare aluminium reached 40℃ more, the mirror was up to…。

In a rooftop comparison of the device in Stanford, California, scientists found that while a surface painted black reached 60℃ more than ambient temperature in sunlight, and bare aluminium reached 40℃ more, the mirror was up to 5℃ cooler than the surrounding air temperature.

② 本句为简单句。句子的主干结构为 Fan puts the cost at… and calculates saving…;句子包含由 and 连接的两个并列的谓语;writing 作伴随状语,与主语为主动关系。

---

geoengineering *n.* 地球工程学　　　　　　　substantial *adj.* 大量的

Writing in the journal, Fan puts the installed cost of mirrors at between ＄20 and ＄70 per square metre and calculates an annual electricity saving of 100MWh per year on a three storey building.

Text 12 Admit It, Older People—You Are Addicted to Your Phones, Too
承认吧，老年人们，你们也对手机上瘾了

My mother likes to sit with her legs crossed on the sofa, glasses balanced on her nose, while she scrolls through her iPhone. I don't know whether she is commenting on a friend's family photo album, crushing candy or liking a meme with the caption: "Tonight's forecast: 99% chance of wine," but I do know that this is not the first time I catch her like this. My father opts for the "I'll be with you shortly" line, which he delivers with a very serious look on his face as he aggressively taps away on his phone. I have learned by now that this is my cue to leave him alone for the next 10 minutes. As much as they don't like admitting it, both of my parents are just as addicted to their phones as I am.

Growing up, we are constantly reminded that young people are the demographic most affected by technology. We are the "antisocial social club," those who prefer to text our friends in the same room rather than having to make eye-contact with them. We are the "digital natives," ruining the English language because we favour using heart-eye emojis to tell someone we fancy them, instead of spelling it out. ①And even though I can recognise myself in some of the never-ending studies that reveal to us the extent of our social media addiction, warning

我的母亲喜欢盘着腿坐在沙发上，端正地戴着眼镜浏览她的苹果手机。我不知道她是在评论一位朋友的全家福相册抑或在粉碎糖果（一款手机游戏），还是在给配着"今晚的预测是99%的葡萄酒！"文字的表情包点赞，但我的确知道这不是我第一次"抓到"她这样。我父亲会说"我很快就去陪你"这句话，这时他正一脸严肃地用力敲着手机屏幕。我现在已经知道这是给我的暗示，让他一个人再待10分钟。尽管他们不愿意承认这一点，但我的父母和我一样沉迷于手机。

在成长的过程中，我们不断地被提醒着，年轻人是受科技影响最大的群体。我们是"不善社交的社会群体"，我们宁愿给共处一室的朋友发短信，也不愿跟他们进行眼神交流。我们是"数字原住民"，正在毁灭英语这种语言，因为我们喜欢用心形眼睛的表情符号告诉别人我们喜欢他们，而不是明确地说出来。①一些无止境的研究揭示了我们沉迷于社交媒体的程度，并警告我们正慢慢变成科

---

meme n. 表情包   caption n.（图片或卡通的）说明文字   aggressively adv. 强有力地
tap away 敲打   demographic n. 特定年龄段的人群   antisocial adj. 不善交际的
digital native 数字原住民   spell out 讲清楚

us that we are slowly turning into tech-zombies, we should at least consider that it's not only us young 'uns any more.

There's the rise of the Instagram mums, who like to post an abundance of cute baby pictures, showcasing their seemingly put-together lifestyles and sharing their many momfeelings along the way. They are the so-called "Facebook mum generation," a growing group of parents that like to overshare and, in the process, are slowly pushing out young people who can't bear to see another one of mum's embarrassing gin-and-tonic-on-a-holiday selfies. While many millennials are slowly leaving Facebook because our timeline seems to only clog up with fake news, dog videos and repetitive memes these days, our parents might see the platform as a way of keeping up with the social lives of their old schoolmates.

And while all of this might be fine, and even a little humorous, new research suggests that parents' technology addiction is negatively affecting their children's behaviour. According to the study, 40% of mothers and 32% of fathers have admitted to having some sort of phone addiction. This has led to a significant fall in verbal interactions within families and even a decline in mothers encouraging their children. "Technoference" is the term used here to describe the increasing trend that sees people switching their attention away from those around them to check their phones instead—one that seems to be infiltrating far beyond friendship circles and now also into family life. ②And by family life, I mean not only young teens and children who are glued to their phones or tablets, but also their parents, who are now joining in on the antisocial fun. What are the consequences if we don't deal with this?

There is no denying that I get annoyed when I receive the "I'll be with you shortly line" from a

---

tech-zombie 科技宅 young 'uns = young ones 年轻人 push out 排挤
gin n. 杜松子酒 tonic n. 滋补品 clog up 堵塞
verbal interaction 语言交流 infiltrate vi. 渗入

parent, when all I want to do is ask one question. But, at the same time, leaving the room to wait until my father is finished with his "serious business" (ie Farmville), has now become the norm. Whether you want to escape your pestering children for a bit, or want to stay up late flicking through Twitter, know that wanting to do all of this is normal. We—your children—know how addictive it can be and how difficult it is to switch off. But before calling us out and telling us to "put our phones away at the table" or even worse, pulling up statistics of how damaging social media can be for us, maybe lead by example and consider how much time you spend on the phone as well as how this is impacting your children and your relationship with them. Maybe in this way we can work on our addiction together.

(*The Guardian*, 2018.7)

长难句解析

① 本句为主从复合句。主句的主干结构为 we should consider that…。前半部分为 even though 引导的让步状语从句,that reveal to us the extent of our social media addiction 为定语从句修饰 studies,warning us that…作伴随状语,that we are slowly turning into tech-zombies 作 warning 的宾语从句。that it's not only us young 'uns any more 作 consider 的宾语从句。

And even though I can recognise myself in some of the never-ending studies that reveal to us the extent of our social media addiction, warning us that we are slowly turning into tech-zombies, we should at least consider that it's not only us young 'uns any more.

② 本句为主从复合句。主句的主干结构为 I mean not only…, but also…。句子中包含两个 who 引导的定语从句,分别修饰 young teens and children 以及 their parents。

And by family life, I mean not only young teens and children who are glued to their phones or tablets, but also their parents, who are now joining in on the antisocial fun.

Farmville 开心农场
flick through 浏览
pester *vt.* 纠缠
lead by example 以身作则

Text 13 Ichthyosaurs and the Bends
鱼龙与减压病

If a diver surfaces too quickly, he may suffer the bends. ①Nitrogen dissolved in his blood is suddenly liberated by the reduction of pressure, just as the gas in a bottle of champagne is released when the cork is popped. The consequence, if the bubbles accumulate in a joint, is crippling pain and a contorted posture—hence the name. If the bubbles form in his lungs or his brain, though, the consequence can be death.

Other air-breathing species also suffer this decompression sickness if they surface too fast: whales, for example. And so, long ago, did ichthyosaurs. That these Mesozoic marine reptiles, contemporaries of the dinosaurs, got the bends can be seen from their bones. What can also be seen is a curious evolutionary tale—for not all ichthyosaurs succumbed.

Bone is a living tissue, and if bubbles of nitrogen form inside it they can cut off its blood supply. This kills the cells in the bone, and consequently weakens it, sometimes to the point of collapse. Fossil bones that have caved in on themselves are thus a dead giveaway, as it were, of an animal that once had the bends.

Bruce Rothschild of the University of Kansas knew all this when he began a study of ichthyosaur bones in order to find out how prevalent the problem was in the past. ②What Dr. Rothschild particularly wanted to investigate was how ichthyosaurs—which, like whales, were descended from terrestrial animals—adapted to the problem of decompression over the 150m years that they roamed the oceans. To this end, he and his colleagues travelled the world's

潜水员如果浮出水面过快,他的身体可能会变弯曲,也就是患上减压病。①由于压强降低,溶解在血液中的氮气会被突然释放出来,就如同打开瓶塞后,香槟酒中的气体会被突然释放出来一样。其后果就是,如果气泡积聚在关节中,就会造成剧痛和身体弯曲——这就是病名的由来。但如果气泡在肺部或大脑中形成,那么后果可能是死亡。

其他呼吸空气的物种上浮过快时也会患这种减压病,比如说鲸鱼。很久以前的鱼龙也是如此。人们可以从它们的骨骼看出,这些与恐龙同存于中生代的海洋爬行动物患上了减压病。人们也能看到一种新奇的进化现象——因为并非所有鱼龙都患上了减压病。

骨骼是活的组织,在骨骼内形成的氮气气泡会切断血液供应,这会杀死骨骼内的细胞,从而削弱骨骼强度,有时甚至可令骨骼断裂。因此,骨骼化石上的凹陷可以说明该动物生前患有减压病。

当堪萨斯大学的布鲁斯·罗斯柴尔德为了找出过去这种病有多么流行而开始研究鱼龙骨骼时,他完全了解这些。②和鲸一样,鱼龙也是从陆地迁往海洋的。罗斯柴尔德博士特别希望弄明白,它们在遨游大洋的1.5亿年间是如何应对这一减压问题的。为此,他与他的同事们走遍了世界各地的自然历史博物馆,总共考察

---

surface *vi.* 浮出水面   liberate *vt.* 释放   crippling pain 常伴有疼痛
contorted *adj.* 扭曲的   decompression *n.* 减压   ichthyosaur *n.* 鱼龙
giveaway *n.* 使真相暴露的事物

natural-history museums, looking at a total of 116 ichthyosaurs from the Triassic period (250m-200m years ago) and 190 from the later Jurassic and Cretaceous periods (200m-145m and 145m-65m years ago, respectively).

When he started, he assumed that signs of the bends would be rarer in younger fossils, reflecting their gradual evolution of measures to deal with decompression, such as the ability found in many whales to store lots of oxygen in their blood. Instead, he was astonished to discover the reverse. More than 15% of Jurassic and Cretaceous ichthyosaurs had suffered the bends before they died, but not a single Triassic specimen showed evidence of that sort of injury.

If ichthyosaurs did evolve an anti-decompression mechanism, then they clearly did so quickly—and, most peculiarly, they subsequently lost it. But that is not what Dr. Rothschild thinks happened. As he reports in *Naturwissenschaften*, he suspects it was evolution in other species that caused the change.

Whales that suffer the bends often do so because they have surfaced to escape a predator such as a large shark. One of the features of Jurassic oceans was an abundance of large sharks, and also of huge marine crocodiles, both of which were partial to ichthyosaur lunches. Triassic oceans, by contrast, were (from the ichthyosaur's point of view) mercifully shark-and-crocodile-free. In the Triassic, then, ichthyosaurs were top of the food chain. In the Jurassic and Cretaceous, they were prey as well as predator—and often had to make a speedy exit as a result.

(*The Economist*, 2012.5)

Triassic *n.* 三叠纪　　Jurassic *n.* 侏罗纪　　Cretaceous *n.* 白垩纪
peculiarly *adv.* 特别地　　mercifully *adv.* （不幸中）幸运地

长难句解析

① 本句为主从复合句。主句的主干结构为 Nitrogen is liberated，其中谓语是被动语态；句中动词过去分词结构 dissolved in his blood 作后置定语修饰主语 Nitrogen；as 引导的方式状语从句中还嵌套了一个 when 引导的时间状语从句。

Nitrogen dissolved in his blood is suddenly liberated by the reduction of pressure,
主语　　后置定语　　　　　　　谓语　　　　　　　方式状语
just as the gas in a bottle of champagne is released when the cork is popped.
　　　　　方式状语从句　　　　　　　　　　时间状语从句

② 本句为主从复合句。主句的主干结构为 What... was how...；主语为 What 引导的主语从句；how 引导的从句在句中作表语；破折号中间 which 引导的定语从句 1 修饰 ichthyosaurs；that 引导的定语从句 2 修饰 the 150m years。

What Dr. Rothschild particularly wanted to investigate was how ichthyosaurs
　　　　　主语从句　　　　　　　　　　系动词　表语从句
—which, like whales, were descended from terrestrial animals—
定语从句1　插入语　　　　　定语从句1
adapted to the problem of decompression over the 150m years that they roamed the oceans.
　　表语从句　　　　　　　　时间状语　　　　　　　　定语从句2

Text 14　Thigh Bone Points to Unexpectedly Long Survival of Ancient Human Ancestors
股骨化石表明古人类祖先长期存在

Partial femur found in the Red Deer Cave might show that a pre-modern species of human may have overlapped with modern humans into the ice age.

红鹿洞里发现的部分股骨说明，前现代人种与冰河世纪的现代人类在时间上有重叠的可能性。

A 14,000-year-old fragment of thigh bone found in a cave in China may represent evidence of the unexpected survival of long-vanished human ancestors.

在中国的一个山洞里发现了有着1.4万年历史的部分股骨，这或许是消逝已久的人类祖先曾经长期存在的证据。

---

femur n. 股骨　　　pre-modern adj. 前现代的，一般指计算机时代以前的工业社会的
long-vanished adj. 早已销声匿迹的

① If so, then right into and through the ice age, a creature that was either Homo habilis or Homo erectus survived alongside the Neanderthals, the unknown humans who left behind some DNA in a cave in Siberia, the mysterious so-called hobbit of the island of Flores in Indonesia, and modern Homo sapiens.

But by the end of this multicultural ice age 10,000 years ago, only one human species survived.

The fossil, a partial femur, had survived unstudied for at least 25 years in a museum in southeastern Yunnan in China. It was one of a set of fossilised remains found in the Maludong Cave—it means Red Deer Cave—in 1989. Darren Curnoe, a paleoanthropologist from the University of New South Wales, and Ji Xueping from the Yunnan Institute of Cultural Relics and Archaeology, report in the *PLoS One* that in their estimation, the bone fragment matched those from species such as Homo habilis or Homo erectus, who first stalked the planet more than 1.5 million years ago.

"Its young age suggests the possibility that primitive-looking humans could have survived until very late in our evolution, but we need to be careful as it is just one bone," said Ji.

Curnoe said: "The new find hints at a possibility that a pre-modern species may have overlapped in time with modern humans on mainland East Asia, but the case needs to be built up slowly with more bone discoveries."

② The find comes too late for reference in a new gallery of human evolution at the Natural History Museum in South Kensington, but Chris Stringer, who heads research into human origins at the museum, greeted the find with caution. "It is an isolated bone. It is not even half a femur," he said. "I am cautious. What we need more than anything is more complete material."

① 如果真是这样，那就说明，直至整个冰河世纪，除了尼安德特人、在西伯利亚的一个山洞里留下DNA的未知人类、印度尼西亚佛罗雷斯岛的神秘霍比特人以及现代的智人外，还有一种人类物种存在，即早期智人或是早期直立人。

但是，在1万年前的多元文化冰河世纪末期，只有一种人类物种生存了下来。

这一部分股骨化石在中国云南省东南部的一个博物馆里被保存了至少25年，人们并未对其进行研究。它是1989年在马鹿洞（又称红鹿洞）里发现的一组遗骨化石之一。新南威尔士州大学的古人类学家达伦·科诺与云南省文物考古研究所的吉学平在《科学公共图书馆·综合》上发表研究称，这一骨片与生活在150多万年前的智人或直立人的骨片相匹配。

吉教授表示："这块遗骨的历史较短，这说明，远古形貌的人类极有可能到人类进化的后期方才灭绝。由于我们只有这一根遗骨，所以鉴定时须格外谨慎。"

科诺表示："该新发现暗示了前现代人种与东亚大陆上的现代人类在时间上有重叠的可能性，但还须发现更多遗骨，才能慢慢建立这个假设。"

② 这一发现来得太晚，无法列入南肯辛顿自然历史博物馆里关于人类进化的新长廊，但博物馆主管人类起源研究的负责人克里斯·斯特林格对此发现持谨慎态度。"这只是一根单独的骨头，甚至算不上半块股骨，"他说，"我对此持谨慎态度。我们现在需要的是更加完整的材料。"

---

paleoanthropologist n. 古人类学家

stalk vt. 偷偷接近

The Natural History Museum gallery displays—either in fossil form or as casts—embrace the whole seven-million-year story of humankind's emergence from primate ancestry, and includes a display of recent and not-so-recent finds that present human evolution as complex network of uncertain relationships and still disputed identities.

They include the "hobbit" Homo floriensis, the fragment of finger and teeth from the Denisova cave in Siberia that seem to have belonged to an unknown species, and evidence of recently identified species from South Africa (Homo naledi) and from Spain (Homo antecessor). The story of human evolution has never been straightforward, and the cast of characters keeps growing. The discoveries in the Red Deer Cave may have made the tale even more tangled.

But even the discoverers are cautious. The thigh bone from the Red Deer Cave indicates an individual who must have been small by ice age standards. He or she would have weighed about 50 kilograms. And as such finds do, it raises more questions than it can answer.

"The riddle of the Red Deer Cave people gets even more challenging now: just who were these mysterious stone age people?" said Curnoe. "Why did they survive so late? And why only in tropical southwest China?"

(*The Guardian*, 2015.12)

自然历史博物馆长廊上以化石或模型形式的展示，涵盖了从人类祖先——灵长类的出现到之后整整700万年间的人类进程，并包括了近期及早期的发现，这些发现展示了人类的进化历程是一个复杂的、不确定的关系网络，并且物种身份仍有争议。

这些包括佛罗雷斯的霍比特人，西伯利亚丹尼索瓦洞里似乎属于某种未知物种的手指及牙齿碎片，以及最近发现的可以证实南非物种（纳莱蒂人）和西班牙物种（史前人）的证据。人类进化的故事从来都不是简单明了的，其复杂性在不断深化。红鹿洞中的发现可能会令这一故事变得更加复杂。

但是，甚至发现者也持谨慎态度。根据冰河时代的衡量标准，红鹿洞中的股骨表明，此人体型很小，大概50公斤。这个发现提出的问题比它能够回答的问题要多得多，此类发现都是如此。

科诺说："如今，解开红鹿洞人之谜更具挑战性。这些神秘的石器时代的人类究竟是谁？他们为何在这么晚的时期依然存活？为何仅出现在中国西南部的热带地区？"

长难句解析

① 本句为主从复合句。主句的主干结构为 a creature survived；从句是 if 引导的省略的条件状语从句。that 引导的定语从句 1 修饰 a creature；alongside…这一介宾短语作状语，其宾语由四个并列的名词性短语组成，即 the Neanderthals, the unknown humans, the mysterious so-called hobbit 和 modern Homo sapiens，其中，定语从句 2 修饰 the unknown humans。

---

ancestry *n.* 祖先
tangled *adj.* 复杂的
straightforward *adj.* 简单明了的
riddle *n.* 谜

If so, then right into and through the ice age, a creature that was either Homo habilis or Homo erectus survived alongside the Neanderthals, the unknown humans who left behind some DNA in a cave in Siberia, the mysterious so-called hobbit of the island of Flores in Indonesia, and modern Homo sapiens.

② 本句为转折连词 but 连接的并列复合句。but 前句子的主干结构为 The find comes；but 后句子的主干结构为 Chris Stringer greeted the find；who 引导的非限制性定语从句修饰 Chris Stringer。

The find comes too late for reference in a new gallery of human evolution at the Natural History Museum in South Kensington, but Chris Stringer, who heads research into human origins at the museum, greeted the find with caution.

Text 15　Wake Up, Humanity! A Hi-Tech Dystopian Future Is Not Inevitable
醒醒，人类！高科技反乌托邦的未来是可避免的

When is the future no longer the future? Only a decade ago, air travel seemed to be moving ineluctably towards giant planes, or "superjumbos". ①But last week Airbus announced it will cease manufacturing its A380, the world's fattest passenger jet, as current trends favour smaller and more fuel-efficient craft. Progress changed course. A more vivid reminder of lost dreams will come in a few weeks: 2 March marks

未来何时不再是未来？就在十年前，航空旅行似乎就不可避免地向巨型飞机或是超级喷气式客机发展。①但是，上周空客宣布其将停止生产 A380 这一全球载客量最大的客机，因为当前的趋势对更小型和更节能的飞机有利。进步改变了发展方向。几周后，一件事情会

---

dystopian adj. 反面乌托邦的，反面假想国的
superjumbo n. 超级喷气式客机

ineluctably adv. 无法躲避地，不能避免地

the 50th anniversary of the maiden flight of Concorde. Once upon a time, all aviation was going to be supersonic. But sometimes, the future is cancelled.

What if what we think is going to be the future right now is cancelled in its turn? We are supposedly on an unstoppable path towards driverless vehicles, fully automated internet-connected "smart homes", and godlike artificial intelligence—but, then, we've been promised flying cars for half a century, and they are still just around the corner. We live in a time when technological change is portrayed as an inexorable, impersonal force: we'd better learn how to surf the tsunami or drown. But as a society, we always have a choice about which direction we take next. And sometimes we make the wrong decision.

For one thing, history is full of technological marvels that were abandoned for reasons that were only reassessed much later. To most people in the late 19th century, when fleets of electric taxis operated in London and Manhattan, the electric car was clearly going to win out over the filthy petrol-driven alternative. But then vast oil reserves were discovered in America, and the future went into reverse. Until, in the late 20th century, global warming and advances in battery technology made electric cars seem like a good idea again. Similarly, vinyl records have enjoyed a major resurgence in the age of the MP3: not necessarily because they are an objectively better sonic format, but because it turned out that people liked owning their culture as physical objects.

Just as we resurrect ideas from the past, we also have the power to bury ideas in the present—whether for business reasons, like Airbus, or for the wider public good. Technology isn't just something that happens to us; it's something we can decide to build and to use, or not. Should we, for example,

---

maiden *adj.* 初次的,首次的
inexorable *adj.* 不可阻挡的;不能变更的
vinyl record 黑胶唱片
sonic *adj.* 声音的;音速的

Concorde *n.* 协和式客机
filthy *adj.* 肮脏的;污秽的
resurgence *n.* 复苏
resurrect *vt.* 使再活跃;使再流行

allow anyone to make inheritable changes in the DNA of humans? One of the inventors of the modern gene-editing method Crispr, Jennifer Doudna, thinks not: she has called for a moratorium on such "germline" editing, because of the potentially disastrous consequences. ② Many thinkers on machine intelligence, meanwhile—led by the philosopher Nick Bostrom—suggest that the supposedly sci-fi scenario of a conscious AI escaping its box and taking over the world represents such an enormous, existential threat to humanity that we ought to be taking steps right now to prevent it happening.

Not much less alarming, and far closer, is the moment when "deep fakes"—computer-generated pictures and video—become indistinguishable from the real thing. Satisfying as it would be to shame some individuals in this way, the wider result would be a total corrosion of trust, not only in news media but in documentary evidence of many kinds.

So, as work continues apace on deep fakes, we are sleepwalking towards a media dystopia in which nothing at all can be trusted, and the only people to benefit will be authoritarian leaders who insist on their own fantastical realities. Therefore, it's hard not to think that researchers building deep-fake technology right now are actively working, whether they realise it or not, to destroy liberal democracy. Should we just sit back and let them, because, you know, technology will always happen anyway?

We should not, and it's time to reject the wider myth that tech is apolitical. We are so used to hearing that technological progress is smooth and inevitable these days that it just seems like common sense. But this idea may not be unrelated to the fact that the people who promote it are mainly the people with a large financial interest in the adoption of new technology. Just as our past futures need not be dead to us, our present future is not compulsory.

(*The Guardian*, 2019.2)

---

moratorium *n.* (行动,活动等的)暂停,暂禁
scenario *n.* 情节;剧本;方案
germline *n.* 生殖(细胞)质
apace *adv.* 飞快地;急速地

长难句解析

① 本句为主从复合句,主句的主干为 Airbus announced…。it will cease…为省略了引导词 that 的宾语从句;两个逗号之间的内容为插入语,解释说明 A380;as 引导的是原因状语从句,解释空客所宣布内容的原因。

But last week Airbus announced it will cease manufacturing its A380, the world's fattest passenger jet, as current trends favour smaller and more fuel-efficient craft.
- But — (无标注)
- last week — 时间状语
- Airbus — 主语
- announced — 谓语
- it will cease manufacturing its A380 — 宾语从句
- the world's fattest passenger jet — 插入语
- as current trends favour smaller and more fuel-efficient craft — 原因状语从句

② 本句为主从复合句。主句主干为 Many thinkers suggest that…。介词短语 on machine intelligence 作 many thinkers 的后置定语;破折号中间为插入语,同样修饰的是 many thinkers;suggest 后为 that 引导的宾语从句,宾语从句的主语为 the supposedly sci-fi scenario of a conscious AI;escaping its…为动名词短语作宾语从句主语的后置定语,宾语从句的谓语为 represents;宾语从句中包含一个 such… that 结构,表示"如此……以至于";that 引导的是结果状语从句。

Many thinkers on machine intelligence, meanwhile—led by the philosopher Nick Bostrom—suggest that the supposedly sci-fi scenario of a conscious AI escaping its box and taking over the world represents such an enormous, existential threat to humanity that we ought to be taking steps right now to prevent it happening.
- Many thinkers — 主语
- on machine intelligence — 后置定语
- meanwhile—led by the philosopher Nick Bostrom — 插入语
- suggest — 谓语
- that the supposedly sci-fi scenario of a conscious AI escaping its box and taking over the world represents such an enormous, existential threat to humanity — 宾语从句
- that we ought to be taking steps right now to prevent it happening — 结果状语从句

Text 16 Chips off the Old Block
机器人也能像监护人一样(照顾孩子)

Paul Wallich usually walks his small son to the bus stop a stone's throw from their Vermont home. But he can use a robot too: a football-sized drone, hovering several metres off the ground, follows a beacon stashed in the little boy's school bag. A smartphone strapped to the device beams back video.

家住美国佛蒙特州的保罗·沃利克经常要步行把小儿子送到附近的汽车站去。但他也可以选择使用机器人:在小男孩的书包里放入一个信标台,足球大小的无人飞机会盘旋在距地面几米高的地方,一直跟着信号。同时,一个智能手机与该设备捆绑,将视频发送回去。

---

drone n. 无人驾驶飞机
(be) strapped to (被)绑在……
beacon n. 信标台
beam vt. 发送

Few parents areas handy as that, but even Luddites like the idea of keeping an electronic eye on the young. An early offering, in 2003, was Wherify, a tracking device which locks to a child's wrist. Devices invented since then protect autistic children, who easily get lost, or into danger. Youngsters on Canadian farms wear radio tags on bracelets to signal their proximity to adults operating heavy machinery.

Longer battery life and miniaturisation are making tracking cheaper and more practical. The easiest way is to use smartphones. Many mobile operators offer child-tracking at extra cost, but the number of free tracking applications is growing fast. Life360 rocketed from 1m registered users in 2010 to nearly 26m now. Berg Insight, a research firm, reckons that 70m Americans and Europeans will be tracking family members by 2016.

These services and devices can provide children's location, or send alerts about their behaviour: when they return home, or stray beyond an agreed boundary, or go out late. Speed detection reveals when somebody is in a vehicle—and whether it is breaking the speed limit.

No devices, so far, have full chaperone functions—such as revealing furtive movements in a stationary vehicle. But some providers do have ingenious extra features. The pocket-sized tracking beacons of Amber Alert GPS, a company based in Utah, carry a microphone to let parents eavesdrop. ① SecuraTrac, a Californian firm, has a product that disables a phone's e-mail and text functions when it is moving: that stops boy-racers from typing while

---

electronic eye 电子眼   autistic *adj.* 孤独症的   bracelet *n.* 手镯   proximity *n.* 距离
miniaturisation *n.* 微型化   ingenious *adj.* 巧妙的   eavesdrop *vi.* 窃听

driving. Life360's maps highlight the addresses of sex offenders.

Parents in Japan and America are the keenest on such gizmos. Europeans, seemingly more relaxed about child safety and with more complex privacy laws, are less enamoured. Some European countries require minors' consent for some kinds of surveillance. Child tracking appeals particularly to middle-class families in South American countries who worry about gang crime and kidnapping, says André Malm, an analyst at Berg Insight.

Public authorities are keen, too. Schools in Osaka began issuing radio frequency identification (RFID) tags to students in 2004. Sensors in school buildings read them to check pupils' attendance and location (though not what they do off the premises). In Dubai the same technology notifies parents when their progeny get on or off school buses. In March last year 20,000 school children in the Brazilian city of Vitoria da Conquista had radio tags sewn into their uniforms to help detect truants.

In August 2012 two schools in San Antonio, Texas, embedded RFID tags in identity badges belonging to their 4,200 students. These help administrators to count students who turn up to class but miss the morning register. Because funding is linked to daily attendance, the system enables schools to claim more taxpayer cash. ②On January 8th a court lifted an earlier injunction halting the expulsion of a child who refused to wear the badge on religious grounds (some Christians liken the devices to the Mark of the Beast, foreseen in the Bible). The family intends to appeal.

---

gizmo n. 小发明　　　　consent n. 同意　　　　surveillance n. 监督
radio frequency identification (RFID) 无线射频识别　　　　sew vt. 缝合
truant n. 旷课者

X marks the child

But what about privacy? Enthusiasts say tracking means more freedom, not less. Parents who know they can easily find their children may be happier to let them roam. Teenagers are spared annoying phone calls. Daisy Ashford, a mother of children aged ten and eight who lives in Ashland, Virginia, says her children like the "James Bond" feel of their Amber Alert trackers. Her military family moves every 18 months, making it hard to develop a protective network of friends and neighbours: the devices are "another set of eyes."

Critics say tracking does not really protect children. Savvy kidnappers will dispose of phones or other devices (implantable tracking chips are, so far, the stuff of spy movies only). And strangers rarely attack children anyway: parents are the most likely murderers, and accidents are a far graver danger than assault. "Location tracking won't stop your child falling into a river," says Anne-Marie Oostveen, who studies surveillance at Oxford University. For fretful parents the new devices may just mean still more grounds for worry.

The same technology also enables snooping on adults. In America mobile subscribers can buy location-tracking services for all users of a family phone plan. Some survivors of domestic violence say this makes it harder to escape. Parents use webcams to keep an eye on their children's carers (generally legal, though the ethics of hidden cameras are contested, and covertly captured audio can break laws on wiretapping). A Saudi government agency that sends men text messages if their children leave the country also helps track wives.

对孩子进行定位追踪

那么隐私怎么办？追踪装置的支持者称追踪意味着更多的自由，而非受到束缚。家长如果知道自己可以轻松找到孩子，那么他们就会更乐意让孩子出去玩耍。孩子则可以摆脱家长打来的恼人电话。家住弗吉尼亚州阿什兰的黛西·阿什福德有两个孩子，一个10岁，一个8岁。她说她的孩子很喜欢Amber Alert追踪器，戴上它有一种"詹姆斯·邦德"的感觉。她们家是军官家庭，每18个月要搬一次家，因此很难在朋友、邻居间建立起孩子的保护网，而追踪装置就像"另一个监护人"一样。

反对者称追踪并不能真正地保护孩子。精明的绑匪会扔掉手机和其他设备（到目前为止，只有间谍片里才会出现植入式的追踪芯片）。而陌生人又很少袭击儿童：最有可能谋杀孩子的是父母，而且比起攻击，意外所带来的后果更加严重。在牛津大学研究"监视"的安妮·玛丽·奥斯特文说："定位追踪无法防止你的孩子掉入河中"。对忧心忡忡的家长来说，新设备可能仅仅意味着更多的担忧。

这种技术还可以用来窥探成年人的隐私。在美国，移动用户可以为家庭用户组的所有成员购买定位追踪服务。一些家庭暴力的幸存者称这使逃跑变得更加困难。一些父母会使用网络摄像机来监视孩子的保姆（通常来说这种行为是合法的，虽然使用隐形摄像头的合法性的确在道德层面上受到了人们的质疑，而暗中录音则更是触犯了窃听法）。在沙特阿拉伯，孩子一出国界，一个政府机构就会发送短信提醒其父亲，这一功能对其妻子也适用。

X mark X 标记　　　dispose of 去掉　　　fretful adj. 焦虑的　　　snoop on 窥探

Others fear that children who submit to tracking in schools will more readily accept state surveillance in adulthood. In August a coalition of American civil-rights outfits advised schools not to make such tracking mandatory. It termed the technology "dehumanising" and said that, where it operates, sensors should be visible.

Small fixes can make tracking by parents more palatable, too. Services that help kids report their location, perhaps by "checking in" as they move around, calm anxious grown-ups with less annoyance for the young. An app called Glympse lets users share their location for a few minutes at a time; WalkMeHome, a Swedish app also available in English, helps people share their where abouts with trusted contacts any time they feel unsafe. A prototype tracker built by Microsoft substituted detailed location data for broader descriptions ("at school", "at home" or "at work"). Such humdrum messages maybe less fun than child-tracking drones—but they are also less alarming.

(*The Economist*, 2013.1)

也有人担心孩子如果在上学时就被追踪，等他们成年后，他们就更容易接受国家监视。8月，一个美国民权联合组织建议学校不要强制规定对学生进行追踪。该组织称这种追踪技术"丧失人性"，如果要进行追踪，那么感应器必须安装在可见范围内。

做一些小的调整也能让孩子更容易接受父母的追踪。有一些服务能让孩子在外出时可以通过登录汇报他们所处的位置，这样父母不必担心，孩子也少了烦恼。用户能通过一个名叫 Glympse 的应用程序每几分钟分享一次他们所在的位置。每当觉得不安全时，人们还可以通过一个名叫 WalkMeHome 的应用软件与信任的人联系，告知自己所处的位置，这款瑞典软件还有英文版可供人们使用。微软公司发明的一款追踪器样机用详细的定位数据替代了概括的描述(如"在学校""在家里""在工作")。比起追踪孩子的无人飞机，这样单调的信息或许少了些趣味，但同时它们也没有那么令人担忧了。

长难句解析

① 本句为并列复合句，冒号连接前后两个分句。冒号前句子的主干结构为 SecuraTrac has a product；that 引导的定语从句修饰先行词 a product；冒号后句子的结构为 that stops sb. from doing sth.，that 指代冒号前的整个句子；while 引导的时间状语从句中省略了 boy-racers 和 be 动词。

> SecuraTrac, a Californian firm, has a product that disables a phone's e-mail and text
> 　主语1　　　同位语　　　　谓语1 宾语1　　　　　　定语从句
> functions when it is moving: that stops boy-racers from typing while driving.
> 　　　　时间状语从句1　主语2 谓语2　宾语2　宾语补足语　时间状语从句2

② 本句为主从复合句。主句的主干结构为 a court lifted an injunction；句中 halting the expulsion of a child 为后置定语，修饰先行词 an earlier injunction；who 引导的定语从句修饰先行词 a child；括号部分补充说明定语从句的内容。

---

outfit *n.* 机构　　　　　　　　　　humdrum *adj.* 无聊的

On January 8th a court lifted an earlier injunction halting the expulsion of a child who refused to wear the badge on religious grounds (some Christians liken the devices to the Mark of the Beast, foreseen in the Bible).

Text 17 A Better Way to Use Satellite Images to Save Lives After Tremors
震后利用卫星图像救生的更有效的方法

When a big earthquake strikes, it does not do equal harm everywhere. Places resting on unstable sediment will shift around a lot and are thus likely to be damaged badly. Those resting on bedrock are normally better off—though not if they are stuck at the end of a rocky promontory that amplifies a quake's vibrations in the manner of a tuning fork. ①Finding the areas most badly damaged, and therefore most urgently in need of assistance, in an area whose geology is not already well understood is thus a high-stakes game of hide-and-seek. It involves experts both on the ground where the earthquake happened, and in faraway laboratories, studying satellite photographs.

Sang-Ho Yun of the Jet Propulsion Laboratory—NASA's outpost in Pasadena, California—hopes to help those seekers by using such photographs more effectively. These days, pretty much all of the Earth's surface has been mapped by a technique called satellite-born synthetic-aperture radar. Crucially for disaster-relief work, radar can see through cloud, so does not require clear skies. Equally crucially, its images include information on altitude, accurate to within a few centimetres. Dr. Yun's plan is to

---

sediment n. 沉积物
outpost n. 前哨基地
vibration n. 震动
synthetic-aperture n. 合成孔径
tuning fork 音叉

compare, automatically, the "before" and "after" shots of a stricken area, to workout which parts have risen or fallen the most, and are thus likely to have suffered most damage. A suitably programmed computer would then colour these in, making them obvious to human users.

On April 25th 2015, as he reports in *Seismological Research Letters*, he got a chance to test his ideas out. An earthquake of magnitude 7.8, the most powerful in the region since 1934, hit central Nepal. It claimed over 8,000 lives and caused widespread damage. Four days after it struck, an Italian satellite called COSMO-Sky Med, which is equipped with a synthetic-aperture radar, flew over the area. Dr. Yun and his colleagues fed the information COSMO-Sky Med's radar collected into their computers and compared it with radar images taken before the disaster.

②Their labours produced wide-area colour-coded maps that showed where the ground had risen or fallen during the earthquake in ways that might damage buildings. Higher-resolution examination of these high-risk areas was then able to pick out buildings that looked as if they had changed in some substantial way. In some cases these buildings had simply gone askew. In others they had collapsed completely.

To double check the accuracy of their conclusions Dr. Yun's team collaborated with one at the United States Geological Survey, led by Kenneth Hudnut. This let them compare their maps with those created independently, after the disaster, by the National Geospatial Intelligence Agency, one of America's groups of spies, and by the United Nations. Both these sets of maps were made by people inspecting high-resolution satellite photographs for damage—a process that took three days. Dr. Yun's

---

high-resolution *n.* 高分辨率

askew *adv.* 歪斜地

maps, the comparison showed, contained almost all of the same information.

　　This test, then, proved that the method works. But Dr. Yun and his colleagues know they still have a long way to go before they can provide such maps quickly enough to be useful. The four days it took an appropriately equipped satellite to come by in the case of the Nepalese earthquake were four days too many for effective disaster relief. ③Such delays are, though, expected to shorten in coming years, as more satellites equipped with synthetic-aperture radar make it into orbit, and more of the agencies operating them realise the value of keeping that radar running all the time, and also of sharing their data as widely and quickly as possible. By 2020, Dr. Yun reckons, the average wait should have dropped to between four and seven hours. That is still a long time to be stuck under a collapsed building. But it is a lot better than the current alternative.

(*The Economist*, 2015.11)

云博士团队绘制的地图与其他两份地图所包含的信息几乎完全一致。

　　这一测试结果证实了该方法是可行的。但云博士及其同事都明白，要想在地震发生后迅速提供这样一份地图使其发挥作用，他们还任重道远。尼泊尔地震发生后，他们花费了四天时间才调到一颗有适当配置的卫星，而四天的时间对于有效的灾后救援工作来说实在是太漫长了。③但这一时间上的延迟有望在未来几年内缩短，因为更多装载着合成孔径雷达的卫星会进入预定轨道，更多机构可以对雷达进行操控，以实现雷达保持不间断运转的真正价值，这类机构还会尽量广泛迅速地实施数据共享。云博士估计，到2020年，灾后救援的平均等待时间会降至4~7个小时。而对于被困在坍塌建筑物中的人来说，这个时间仍然很漫长。但与现在的等待时间相比，这个时间已经短得多了。

长难句解析

① 本句为主从复合句。主句的主干结构为 Finding the areas is a game；主语为动名词结构，most badly damaged... assistance 是后置定语修饰 areas；whose 引导的定语从句修饰先行词 an area。

Finding the areas most badly damaged, and therefore most urgently in need of assistance,
　主语　　　　　　后置定语
in an area whose geology is not already well understood is thus a high-stakes game of
地点状语　　　　　　定语从句　　　　　　　　　　　　系动词　　　　表语
hide-and-seek.

② 本句为主从复合句。主句的主干结构为 Their labours produced maps；that 引导的定语从句1修饰先行词 maps，其中 where 引导的宾语从句作 showed 的宾语；that 引导的定语从句2修饰先行词 ways。

---

stuck *adj.* 卡住的

Their labours produced wide-area colour-coded maps that showed where the
　　主语　　　谓语　　　　　　宾语　　　　　　　 定语从句1　宾语从句
ground had risen or fallen during the earthquake in ways that might damage buildings.
　　　　　　　　　　　　　　　　　　　　　　　　　　　定语从句2

③ 本句为主从复合句。主句的主干结构为 Such delays are expected to shorten；as 引导的原因状语从句是由 and 连接的并列句；后置定语3和后置定语4修饰 the value。

Such delays are, though, expected to shorten in coming years, as more satellites
　主语　　谓语　　　　　谓语　　　　　　　　主语补足语　　　　 原因状语从句
equipped with synthetic-aperture radar make it into orbit, and more of the agencies operating
　　　后置定语1　　　　　　　　　原因状语从句　　　　　　　　原因状语从句　　　　后置定
them realise the value of keeping that radar running all the time, and also of sharing their
语2 原因状语从句　　　　　　后置定语3　　　　　　　　　　　　　　　　后置定语4
data as widely and quickly as possible.

第五部分 能源环境类

SECTION FIVE

Text 1

Cleaning Up Plastic Pollution in Africa
清理非洲的塑料污染

Plastic waste pollution, aggravated by inefficient waste collection and limited recycling capabilities, is prevalent across Africa. However, the continent also has a growing, youthful population that values improving the quality of life and readily adopts technologies toward this end. This makes Africa especially suitable as a testbed to investigate the effectiveness of new technologies for solving environmental problems. In addition to consumers pushing brands to be more environmentally responsible, a business case also exists in Africa that enables brands to invest in technologies that promote a circular economy. As such, a trend for plastic waste remediation efforts in Africa that relies principally on consumer engagement to create a plastics circular economy has emerged.

Over 416 billion plastic bags per month are used globally. In Africa, they litter roads, rivers, boreholes, and sewage systems. In many African countries, increasing plastic pollution has motivated policy-makers to enact legislation to protect the environment from further contamination. Currently, Africa has the highest percentage of countries with plastic bans. For example, in 2008, Rwanda took the global lead in banning nonbiodegradable polyethylene bags. The law prohibits the manufacture, use, import, and sale of nonbiodegradable bags that fall outside its sustainability criteria, and violations are punishable by high fines or jail time. It is strictly enforced at airports and other port entries by agents from the Rwanda Environment Management Authority. Tax incentives in Rwanda are motivating plastic bag manufacturers to consider recycling as a business opportunity. The policy has led to local production of sustainable bags made from local materials, alleviating fears about negative impact on small businesses, jobs, and foreign direct investment.

在整个非洲，塑料废物污染因废物收集效率低下和回收能力有限而加剧。但是，非洲大陆也有越来越多的年轻人重视改善生活质量，并很乐意运用技术达到此目的。这使得非洲尤其适合作为试验台去测试新技术解决环境问题的有效性。除了消费者敦促品牌对环境负责外，非洲还存在一个商业案例，其可使品牌投资于促进循环经济的技术。因此，非洲出现了一种主要依靠消费者参与来治理塑料废物以建立塑料循环经济的趋势。

全球范围内，塑料袋月使用量超过4 160亿个。在非洲，道路、河流、井眼和污水处理系统中到处都是塑料袋垃圾。在许多非洲国家中，越来越多的塑料污染促使政策制定者制定法律，以保护环境免于进一步污染。目前，非洲实行塑料禁令的国家所占比例最高。例如，2008年，卢旺达在禁止非生物降解的聚乙烯袋方面处于全球领先地位。该国法律禁止制造、使用、进口和销售超出其可持续性标准的非生物降解的袋子，违者将被处以高额罚款或监禁。卢旺达环境管理局的代理人在机场和其他港口入境处严格执行该法规。卢旺达的税收鼓励政策正在激励塑料袋制造商考虑将塑料袋回收视为商机。该政策促进了当地生产商使用本地材料制作可持续包装袋，从而减轻了其生产会对小企业、各行业和外商直接投资产生负面影响的担忧。

---

aggravate *vt.* 使恶化　　　　　testbed *n.* 试验台　　　　　remediation *n.* 补救；修复
borehole *n.* 井眼，钻孔　　　　sewage *n.* 污水；污物；下水道
nonbiodegradable *adj.* 非生物降解的　　　　　　　　　polyethylene *n.* 聚乙烯

Some African countries are following Rwanda's lead, albeit with less effective law enforcement. Tanzania is in the second phase of its plastic ban, and Kenya is following a gradual path by taxing plastic bags. Although Kenya implemented a plastic bag ban in 2017, punishable with fines and jail time, enforcement has been difficult. The tax has decreased consumer demand for single-use plastic shopping bags and increased the use of reusable alternatives.

Many of the programs in Africa that limit the production of new, nonbiodegradable plastics have occurred in the last 4 years. Thus, there are few data about the efficacy of these programs and technological efforts to tackle plastic waste, but the engagement and public responses are encouraging. Although efforts to limit plastic use may reduce the introduction of new plastics into the environment, the need to address plastic pollution already present in Africa still remains.

The rapid adoption of information technologies at various points along the plastic waste recycling chain can facilitate the realization of a closed-loop plastic waste ecosystem. ① Regional factors, such as government regulations and consumer motivation to improve African quality of life, play a critical role in the adoption of technologies to tackle plastic pollution in an environment that otherwise lacks a plastics recycling framework.

Recently, application-centered startups in African cities and surrounding areas have spurred plastic waste collection from citizens in exchange for goods ranging from household items to cash. Combined with emerging technologies, this model has been effective in low-income areas in Africa. ②If deployed as a global recycling model, networks that leverage consumer participation will promote the availability of high-quality recycled materials that can be reintroduced into the market and close the plastics life-cycle loop.

(*Science*, 2019.9)

尽管执法效果不佳，一些非洲国家仍在效仿卢旺达。坦桑尼亚正处于塑料禁令的第二阶段，而肯尼亚正在逐步对塑料袋征税。尽管肯尼亚于2017年实施了塑料袋禁令，对违者处以罚款和监禁，但执法难度很大。税收减少了消费者对一次性塑料购物袋的需求，并增加了可再利用替代品的使用。

在非洲，许多限制生产新的非生物降解塑料的计划是在最近4年内实施的。因此，关于这些计划的有效性和为解决塑料废物而进行的技术努力，目前数据很少，但是参与度和公众反应令人鼓舞。尽管限制塑料使用的努力可能会减少向环境中投入的新塑料，但仍然需要解决非洲已经存在的塑料污染问题。

将信息技术迅速运用在塑料废物回收链的各个点上可以促进闭环塑料废物生态系统的实现。①区域性因素，诸如政府法规和消费者改善非洲生活质量的动机，在采用技术解决缺乏塑料回收体系环境下的塑料污染方面，起着至关重要的作用。

最近，在非洲城市和周边地区，以应用程序为中心的初创公司鼓励居民收集塑料废物，以换取从家居用品到现金等各种好处。结合新兴技术，这种模式在非洲低收入地区已产生效果。②如果将其部署为一种全球回收模式，那么利用消费者参与度的网络将使得高质量可回收材料为人所用，这些材料也可重新进入市场并关闭塑料生命周期循环。

长难句解析

① 本句为主从复合句，主句的主干为 Regional factors play a critical role in…。such as…是插入语，是对主语的进一步解释说明；to improve…作 consumer motivation 的后置定语；to tackle…作 technologies 的目的状语；that 引导的定语从句修饰 environment。

---

albeit *conj.* 即使；虽然　　implement *vt.* 贯彻，执行　　efficacy *n.* 效力，效能
spur *vt.* 激励，鞭策　　leverage *vt.* 利用；促使……改变

Regional factors, such as government regulations and consumer motivation to improve African quality of life, play a critical role in the adoption of technologies to tackle plastic pollution in an environment that otherwise lacks a plastics recycling framework.

② 本句为主从复合句,主句的主干为 networks will promote…。if 引导条件状语从句;that 引导的定语从句1修饰主句主语 networks;定语从句2修饰 high-quality recycled materials。

If deployed as a global recycling model, networks that leverage consumer participation will promote the availability of high-quality recycled materials that can be reintroduced into the market and close the plastics life-cycle loop.

Text 2 Is Texas the Greenest State? By One Measure, Maybe
得州是最"绿色"的州？在某种标准下,可能如此

When one thinks of "green energy," one doesn't typically picture Texas. The Lone Star State, is, after all, home to the richest oil barons in the country. And Texans—with our gas-guzzling, smog-spewing pickups—haven't exactly cultivated an image of environmental responsibility.

①But a new report released by Choose Energy, a San Francisco-based company that helps consumers navigate deregulated electricity markets (of which Texas is one) suggests that Texans, when given the choice, are actually choosing green energy in droves.

The report shows that nearly 40 percent of CE's customers in Texas pick electricity plans that rely completely on green energy. Fewer than ten percent of customers in lefty stronghold Connecticut choose green plans, despite the fact that both states

当大家想到"绿色能源"时,没人会特别联想到得克萨斯州。毕竟"孤星之州"是整个国家最富有的石油大亨聚集之地。得克萨斯人,喜欢开着耗油、尾气排放高的皮卡车——他们还没有完全塑造出具有环保责任的形象。

①总部位于旧金山的选择能源公司,主要在无管制的电力市场中为消费者保驾护航(得克萨斯州就是这样一个无管制的电力市场)。其最新公布的报告显示,如果有机会,大批的得克萨斯人实际上会选择绿色能源。

该公司的报告显示,近40%的得克萨斯州客户在用电套餐中完全依赖绿色能源,而在左翼阵营康涅狄格州,只有不到10%的客户选择绿色能源,尽管这两个州的电力市场都不受

---

gas-guzzling *adj.* 耗油的 smog-spewing *adj.* 排放尾气的
deregulated *adj.* 不受管制的 stronghold *n.* 大本营

have deregulated electricity markets. In New York, another state that presents itself as clean and green, fewer than 5 percent of consumers opt for green plans.

So why does Texas, where oil is revered as black gold, lead the nation in green energy consumption?

Because it's plentiful and cheap.

It's plentiful because Texas simply pumps out more energy than any other state. In 2012, the state produced 14,201 trillion BTUs of electricity. Montana, the nation's second-largest producer, produced a measly 9,611 trillion BTUs, by comparison.

And Texas produces more green energy than any other state, too. "We generate a lot of wind power—and a growing amount of solar—but we're a huge wind power state," said Dr. Michael Webber, Deputy Director of the Energy Institute at the University of Texas at Austin. "There are a lot of people who have wind turbines within sight or on their land or near their land, especially in rural west Texas," he said. "So I wouldn't be surprised if people think, 'Well, that's a local resource, it's on my buddy's ranch, so I'll buy green energy.'"

In 2013, Texas's 103 wind power plants produced 35,937 thousand megawatt-hours of electricity. Compare that to the West Coast and Mid-Atlantic, which combined produced 34,590 thousand megawatt-hours last year, according to the U.S. Energy Information Administration.

And, unlike natural gas, Texas's huge supply of green energy isn't subject to wild price fluctuations, which makes it attractive to power producers. ② "Back in 2008, when natural gas prices were really whipping around up and down, companies had already purchased a lot of green energy, which comes at a fixed price, because wind prices don't change from year to year…that fixed

---

black gold 石油　　　BTUs abbr. 英国热量单位(British thermal units, 简称"英热单位"), 一桶石油的燃烧值约为 600 万英热单位　　measly adj. 极少的　　wind turbine 风力涡轮机　　megawatt-hour 兆瓦时　　　　fluctuation n. 波动　　　whip around 绕着

price ended up being a very valuable financial hedge against the price spikes of natural gas," Dr. Webber said.

Third, Texas's energy market is set up in such a way that renewables compete well against traditional "brown" energy there. "The way our market is designed, the competitive bids for the different power generators is done at a marginal cost basis and the marginal cost of wind is zero," Dr. Webber said. "So our deregulated market design happens to line up really well with how renewables compete."

While supply might be plentiful, green energy still isn't cheaper than brown energy in most parts of the state. On average, green energy costs $6.72 more a month than brown energy, data collected by Choose Energy show. So why do Texans go for the more expensive option?

Two reasons: education and—not surprisingly, as it is Texas we're talking about—pride.

③ "In Texas, there is a unique combination of lower priced green energy from the high volume of wind power, and a relatively conservative customer base that is more inclined to opt for non-coal based energy, supporting the energy independence movement," said John Tough, CE's Head of Operations and Business Development. In other words, because green and brown energy are nearly equally priced in Texas, Texans are willing to pay a few cents more a month for green energy's added benefits. In Connecticut, where green energy costs more than 10 percent more than brown energy, consumers are less willing to go green.

(*Newsweek*, 2014.7)

长难句解析

① 本句为主从复合句。主句的主干结构为 a new report suggests that…。非谓语动词结构 released by…作后置定语修饰 report;a San Francisco-based company 为 Choose Energy 的同位语;that 引导的定语从句修饰 company;句末 that 引导的宾语从句作 suggest 的宾语,该宾语从句中还包含一个 when 引导的条件状语从句,该状语从句省略了主语和谓语。

spike of ……的峰值　　brown energy 棕色能源　　marginal cost 边际成本

> But a new report released by Choose Energy, a San Francisco-based company that helps consumers navigate deregulated electricity markets (of which Texas is one) suggests that Texans, when given the choice, are actually choosing green energy in droves.
> 主语 ┗后置定语┛　　　　　　　　　同位语 ┗━━━━━━
> 　　　　　　　　　　　定语从句　　　　　　　　　　谓语
> 　　　　　　　　　宾语从句

② 本句是"直接引语+someone says"句型。省略号前面句子的主干为 companies had purchased a lot of green energy；省略号后面句子的主干为 that fixed price ended up being a financial hedge。

> "Back in 2008, when natural gas prices were really whipping around up and down, companies had already purchased a lot of green energy, which comes at a fixed price, because wind prices don't change from year to year…that fixed price ended up being a very valuable financial hedge against the price spikes of natural gas," Dr. Webber said.
> 状语 ┗━━━━　　非限制性定语从句
> 主语1　谓语1　　　宾语1　　　　　定语从句
> 　原因状语从句　　　　主语2　　谓语2
> 　　宾语2

③ 本句是"直接引语+says someone+同位语"句型，同位语解释说明说话人的身份。直接引语是一个 there be 句型；and 连接两个并列部分 lower priced green energy…和 a…base；现在分词结构 supporting…作伴随状语。

> "In Texas, there is a unique combination of lower priced green energy from the high volume of wind power, and a relatively conservative customer base that is more inclined to opt for non-coal based energy, supporting the energy independence movement," said John Tough, CE's Head of Operations and Business Development.
> 地点状语　　　there be 句型　　　后置定语1　　　　后置定语2
> 后置定语1　　　　　　　　　定语从句
> 伴随状语

Text 3

Numerous States Prepare Lawsuits Against Obama's Climate Policy
多个州准备通过法律途径阻止奥巴马的气候政策

As many as 25 states will join some of the nation's most influential business groups in legal action to block President Obama's climate change reg-

多达25个州将加入一些全国最有影响力的商业团体的法律行动之中，希望能够阻止将于周五正式颁布

ulations when they are formally published Friday, trying to stop his signature environmental policy.

In August, the president announced in a White House ceremony that the Environmental Protection Agency rules had been completed, but they had not yet been published in the government's Federal Register. Within hours of the rules' official publication on Friday, a legal battle will begin, pitting the states against the federal government. It is widely expected to end up before the Supreme Court.

"I predict there will be a very long line of people at the federal courthouse tomorrow morning, eagerly waiting to file their suits on this case," said Jeffrey R. Holmstead, a lawyer for the firm Bracewell & Giuliani who represents several companies that are expected to file such suits.

While the legal brawls could drag on for years, many states and companies, including those that are suing the administration, have also started drafting plans to comply with the rules. That strategy reflects the uncertainty of the ultimate legal outcome—and also means that many states could be well on the way to implementing Mr. Obama's climate plan by the time the case reaches the Supreme Court.

The EPA's climate change rules are at the heart of Mr. Obama's ambitious agenda to counter global warming by cutting emissions of planet-warming carbon pollution. ①If they withstand the legal challenges, the rules could shutter hundreds of polluting, coal-fired power plants and freeze construction of such plants in the future, while leading to a transformation of the nation's power sector from reliance on fossil fuels to wind, solar and nuclear power.

Mr. Obama has also used the rules as leverage in his negotiations to reach a global climate change accord in Paris in December. He hopes to broker a

的气候变化法规,这些法规是奥巴马总统的标志性环保政策。

八月,总统在白宫会议上宣布,环境保护署制定的条例已经完成,但未在政府的《联邦公报》上正式颁布。条例一旦在周五由官方正式颁布,几小时内就会引起法律上的争执,部分州将联合起来对抗联邦政府。大家都希望能由最高法院来解决这个问题。

Bracewell & Giuliani 公司的律师杰佛里·霍姆斯特德代表一些有提交法案念头的公司。他说道:"我估计,明天早上,联邦法庭前将会排着长长的队伍,大家都等着提交自己的提案。"

然而,这类法律争端可以持续很多年,许多州和公司,包括那些正在起诉政府的,都已经开始草拟遵循新条例的法案。这项策略反映出最终法律结果的不确定性,同时意味着,在法案到达最高法院之前,许多州已经在准备执行奥巴马的气候计划。

环保署的气候变化条例是奥巴马雄伟计划的核心,其目的是通过减少二氧化碳排放来对抗全球变暖。①如果它们能承受法律的挑战,那么,这些条例将会使数百家污染环境的煤电厂关闭,并冻结未来类似工厂的建造,最终使国家能源产业从依赖化石燃料转变为依赖风能、太阳能和核能。

奥巴马也已将此条例作为条件,以便其能在 12 月巴黎全球气候变化谈判上达成协议。他希望能说服各

Federal Register《联邦公报》,是美国联邦政府的政府公报,其内容可大概分为美国联邦机构的规则及其拟议中的规则与公告
pit against 敌对　　　file vt. 提出　　　brawl n. 争端　　　drag on 拖延　　　shutter vt. 关闭
leverage n. 杠杆

deal committing every country to enacting domestic climate change policies.

The official publication of the rules will also spur legislative pushback on Capitol Hill, where Senator Mitch McConnell of Kentucky, the majority leader, will introduce two resolutions to block them. The legislation will be introduced under the rarely used Congressional Review Act, which allows Congress to block an executive branch rule within 60 legislative days of its publication.

While the resolutions are likely to pass the Republican-controlled Congress, Mr. Obama would be expected to veto them. ②But by introducing the resolutions, Mr. McConnell hopes to convey to the world that Congress does not support the Obama regulations—a message that could be amplified if the Senate votes on the resolutions before or during the Paris summit meeting.

The Obama administration has sought to ensure that the rules will not come under question before that meeting. By delaying the official publication of the rules until nearly three months after they were announced, for example, the administration appeared to be trying to ensure that no major legal decisions to weaken them would be issued before the Paris meeting.

A broad and powerful coalition of governors, attorneys general, coal companies, electric utilities and business groups such as the United States Chamber of Commerce will file suits contending that the rules, put forth under the 1970 Clean Air Act, represent an illegal interpretation of the law. They will also petition to delay implementation of the rule until the case is argued in federal court.

"The president's illegal rule will have devastating impacts on West Virginia families, and families across

国执行国内气候变化条例。

官方条例颁布也会使美国国会推迟法律的制定，多数党领袖、肯塔基州参议员米奇·麦康诺将会引入两条决议来阻止条例的颁布。法案将在《国会审议法案》的规定下被引入，极少被用到的《国会审议法案》允许议会在行政规定颁布的60天内阻止该规定的实施。

尽管这些决议可能会传递到由共和党控制的议会，但人们还是希望奥巴马能够否决这些决议。②但是，通过引入这些决议，麦康诺先生希望昭告全世界：议会不支持奥巴马的政策。如果参议院在巴黎峰会之前或者期间对这些决议进行投票的话，这一信息还会被放大。

奥巴马政府一直在努力确保会议召开之前条例不会受到质疑。例如，通过把条例的颁布时间推迟了将近三个月，政府似乎正在努力确保，在巴黎峰会之前，不会发布任何会削弱这些条例的重大决议。

政府官员、司法部部长、煤炭公司、电厂和美国商会之类的商业团体形成广泛而有力的联合并将提起诉讼，辩称基于《1970年清洁空气法案》提出的该条例是对法律的错误解读。他们还会请愿延迟执行该条例，直到联邦法院插手这件案子。

"总统的这项非法律性条例会给西弗吉尼亚州的家庭带来毁灭性的影

---

amplify *vt.* 放大　　　come under question 受到质疑　　　coalition *n.* 联合
petition *vi.* 请愿　　　devastating *adj.* 毁灭性的

the country," Attorney General Patrick Morrisey of West Virginia said in a statement. Mr. Morrisey, whose home state's economy is heavily dependent on coal mining, is expected to play a lead role in the multistate lawsuit.

States and companies may be hedging their bets.

In Georgia, Gov. Nathan Deal's administration plans to sue the EPA. At the same time, the governor, a Republican, has also instructed his director of environmental protection, Judson H. Turner, to begin crafting a plan to comply with the rules.

"The governor of Georgia said to me, Whatever action may be taken on the legal front, we'll need to develop a plan that works for Georgia," Mr. Turner said. If Mr. Obama's plan survives the legal challenge, Mr. Turner added, "we'll have the confidence that we'll put a plan for Georgia together that's better than a federal plan."

Similar dynamics are playing out in many other states that are suing over the rules, said Vicki Arroyo, the executive director of the Georgetown University Climate Center, which focuses on state-level climate policies.

"It's really rare to find a state that just says, 'Hell no,'" she said.

The rules assign each state a target for reducing its carbon pollution from power plants, but allow states to create their own custom plans for doing so. That rule is designed to encourage states to make major changes in their electric power sectors—for example, to shut down coal-fired power plants and replace them with wind and solar power. ③It is also designed to encourage states to enact so-called cap-and-trade systems, under which they would place a cap on carbon emissions and create a market for buying and selling pollution credits.

States have to submit an initial version of their plans by 2016 and final versions by 2018. States that

---

instruct vt. 指示   play out 凸显

refuse to submit a plan will be forced to comply with one developed by the federal government.

Republican governors have denounced the rule, particularly its emphasis on pushing cap-and-trade systems; in his first term, Mr. Obama tried but failed to send a cap-and-trade bill through Congress. Since then, the term has become politically toxic: Republicans have attacked the idea as "cap-and-tax." The governors of five states—Texas, Indiana, Wisconsin, Louisiana and Oklahoma—have threatened to refuse to submit a plan of any kind.

But economists and many industry leaders have found that in many cases, the easiest and cheapest way for states to comply would be by adopting cap-and-trade systems.

American Electric Power, an electric utility that operates in 11 states, is among the companies that intend to sue the administration over the rule. At the same time, the company's vice president, John McManus, said: "We think it makes sense for states to at least start developing a plan. The alternative of having a federal plan has risks." And he said that his company could support a cap-and-trade plan. "The initial read is that a market-based app-roach is more workable," he said.

(*The New York Times*, 2015.10)

长难句解析

① 本句为主从复合句。主句的主干结构为 the rules could shutter power plants and freeze construction; while 引导时间状语从句, 该从句的主语与主句主语一致, 因此省略了主语和系动词(the rules are)。

If they withstand the legal challenges, the rules could shutter hundreds of polluting,
条件状语从句　　　　　　　　　　主语　谓语1　宾语1
coal-fired power plants and freeze construction of such plants in the future, while leading
　　　谓语2　　　　　　宾语2　　　　　状语
to a transformation of the nation's power sector from reliance on fossil fuels to wind, solar
　　　　　　　　　时间状语从句
and nuclear power.

toxic *adj.* 有害的　　　　　　　　　　　workable *adj.* 切实可行的

② 本句为主从复合句。主句的主干结构为 Mr. McConnell hopes to convey...that...。句中 that 引导的宾语从句作 convey 的直接宾语，the world 为间接宾语；a message 为 that Congress does not support the Obama regulations 的同位语，并由 that 引导的定语从句修饰，该定语从句中还嵌套了一个 if 引导的条件状语从句。

> But by introducing the resolutions, Mr. McConnell hopes to convey to the world
> 方式状语　　　　　　　　　　　　　主语　　　　谓语　　　　　宾语
> that Congress does not support the Obama regulations—a message that could be amplified
> 宾语从句　　　　　　　　　　　　　　　　　　　同位语　　　定语从句
> if the Senate votes on the resolutions before or during the Paris summit meeting.
> 条件状语从句

③ 本句为主从复合句。主句的主干结构为 It is designed to...。句中 which 引导的非限制性定语从句修饰 cap-and-trade systems；for buying and selling pollution credits 修饰 a market。

> It is also designed to encourage states to enact so-called cap-and-trade systems,
> 主语　谓语　　　　　　　　目的状语
> under which they would place a cap on carbon emissions and create a market
> 　　　　　　　非限制性定语从句
> for buying and selling pollution credits.
> 后置定语

Text 4　Climate Change Forces New Pentagon Plan
气候变化敦促五角大楼新计划

The Arctic is covered with pure driven snow. ①The Department of Defense hopes to keep it that way with a new policy that for the first time addresses how the U.S. will respond to the effects of climate change, which have opened up a veritable treasure trove around the North Pole that until recently was inaccessible.

Defense Secretary Chuck Hagel unveiled the military's new Arctic Strategy Friday afternoon during his trip to Canada. The plan seeks to head off potential tensions in the crowded Arctic

北极覆盖着洁白的积雪。①为了保留这些雪，国防部发布新政，首次谈到美国将如何应对气候变化，这打开了北极这座以前从未被人涉足的名副其实的宝库。

周五下午，在前往加拿大的途中，国防部长查克·哈格尔公布了军方的新北极战略。该计划旨在疏导北极潜在的紧张局势。拥挤的北极居

Arctic n. 北极圈　　　　veritable adj. 真实的　　　　head off 阻止

233

neighborhood among its residents—most notably Russia, but all eager for access to massive oil reserves and newly thawed passages for shipping, fishing and tourism.

"President Obama has said, 'The Arctic region is peaceful, stable, and free of conflict.' Our goal is to assure it stays that way," said Hagel, while speaking at the Halifax International Security Forum in the maritime city.

②The modern world is inexperienced in dealing with the challenges of global climate change, he said, adding this new endeavor will take place over the coming years and decades, not days and months.

"Typhoon Haiyan in the Philippines is a reminder of the humanitarian disaster brought on by nature," said Hagel. "And climatologists warn us of the increased probability of more destructive storms to come."

Warming trends thaw Arctic ice and provide greater access to the Ocean's surface and contents, as well as the oil reserves it covers. The plan will build the framework for military and homeland security responses to national security threats, or more practical contingencies like search and rescue or natural disasters.

Five nations border directly on the Arctic: Russia, Canada, Norway, the U.S. via Alaska and Denmark through Greenland. Russia received special attention in Hagel's remarks, amid a love-hate relationship that has dogged the former Cold War foes.

"We will enhance our cold-weather operational experience and strengthen our military-to-military ties with other Arctic nations," Hagel said. "This includes Russia, with whom the United States and Canada share common interests in the Arctic."

This creates an opportunity to pursue "practical cooperation between our militaries and promote greater transparency," he said.

---

notably *adv.* 显著地　　thawed *adj.* （已）解冻的　　maritime *adj.* 海上的
contingency *n.* 突发事件　　amid *prep.* 在……之间

Most of the U.S.-Russian interaction in this sphere rests with their respective coast guards, says a senior Defense official, who spoke on the condition of anonymity.

"We don't have a lot of interaction with the Russian navy in the Arctic," he said, adding, "That relationship has been quite positive over the years, and we hope to keep it that way."

The Navy's top officer highlighted the Arctic region earlier this year as among America's most important security priorities for the coming decades.

"The Arctic is a challenge. It's a future challenge," said Adm. Jonathan Greenert, the chief of naval operations, at a defense summit in April.

"The natural resources present in the Arctic region are being surveyed currently for exploitation. Virtually every arctic nation has made claims of sovereignty, some quite visible," said Vice Adm. John P. Currier, the vice commandant for the U.S. Coast Guard, at the same event. "They exist on a daily basis and pose a real challenge to our country."

There currently is a "relatively low level of military threat" in the region, according to the Pentagon slideshow detailing the new strategy released Friday. ③The region is bounded by nation states that "have not only publicly committed to working within a common framework of international law and diplomatic engagement, but have also demonstrated the ability and commitment to do so."

To keep it that way, the military will lean heavily on its much-touted relationships with other country's fighting forces, known as "mil-to-mil relations" to help keep the peace.

But the strategy comes at a time of occasional heightened tensions between the U.S. and Russia that echoes Cold War saber rattling. Russia is believed to directly supply the Syrian regime as the U.S. and allies bolsters the struggling rebel forces there. Both countries' warships occasionally cross paths off the Syrian coast.

美国和俄罗斯在这方面的互动主要在于各自的海岸警卫队,一位不愿意透露姓名的高级国防官员如是说。

"在北极地区,我们与俄罗斯海军并没有很多互动,"他补充道,"多年来,这种关系相当不错,我们希望这能继续保持下去。"

海军的最高官员今年早些时候强调,北极地区是美国未来几十年优先考虑的重要问题之一。

"北极是一个挑战,是未来的挑战。"海军上将兼海军作战部部长乔纳森·格林纳特,在今年四月的国防峰会上如是说。

"为了开采北极地区的自然资源,调研工作已在进行中。几乎每一个北极国家都已发表主权声明,有些非常明显,"海军副上将、美国海岸警卫队副指挥官约翰·柯里尔也就此事件说,"他们每天都在挑战我们。"

五角大楼上周五公布了新策略的细节,根据幻灯片的描述,目前该地区"存在军事威胁的程度较低"。③该地区的各国"不仅致力于在同一个国际法律和外交框架内共事,而且显示了这样做的能力与决心"。

为了保持现状,军方将严重依赖备受推崇的"军方—军方关系",即通过与其他国家的战斗部队保持关系来维持和平。

但是,当该策略推出时,美国和俄罗斯之间的紧张局势不时加剧,反映了冷战中的刀刃相见的特征。俄罗斯被认为直接支持叙利亚政权,而美国和其盟国则支持当地的叛军组织。两国军舰在叙利亚海岸边偶尔会有交集。

---

in this sphere 在此领域　　slideshow n. 幻灯片播放　　much-touted adj. 备受推崇的
saber n. 武力　　bolster vt. 支持

The subsequent 1990s thaw also brought both countries closer together. Both conduct joint military exercises and law enforcement exchanges, and the U.S., for example, purchases all of its gas for Afghanistan from Russia.

(*U.S. News & World Report*, 2013.11)

随后20世纪90年代的关系解冻也使两国的关系更加密切。双方进行联合军事演习和执法交流,例如,美国在阿富汗的所有天然气都从俄罗斯购买。

长难句解析

① 本句为主从复合句。主句的主干结构为 The Department of Defense hopes to keep it that way。that 引导的定语从句1修饰 policy,该定语从句中嵌套了一个 how 引导的宾语从句,作 addresses 的宾语;which 引导的非限制性定语从句修饰前面整个句子;that 引导的定语从句2修饰 the North Pole。

The Department of Defense	hopes	to keep	it	that way	with a new policy	that for the first time addresses how the U.S. will respond to the effects of climate change, which have opened up a veritable treasure trove around the North Pole that until recently was inaccessible.
主语	谓语		宾语	方式状语		定语从句1

（宾语从句：how the U.S. will respond to the effects of climate change；非限制性定语从句：which have opened up a veritable treasure trove around the North Pole；定语从句2：that until recently was inaccessible）

② 本句为主从复合句,句子的结构为"间接引语+someone says+伴随状语"。间接引语的主干结构为 The world is inexperienced in dealing with…, adding…部分的内容为伴随状语,adding 后为省略了连接词的宾语从句。

The modern world	is	inexperienced	in dealing with the challenges of global climate change,
主语1	系动词	表语	状语

he said,	adding	this new endeavor will take place over the coming years and decades, not days and months.
主语2+谓语	伴随状语	宾语从句

③ 本句为主从复合句。主句的主干结构为 The region is bound…。因为谓语是 bind 的被动语态,所以 by 后面引出了 bind 这一动作的发出者。句中 that 引导的定语从句修饰 nation states;该定语从句中包含一个 not only…but also…结构,连接两个并列的谓语。

The region	is bounded	by nation states	that "have not only publicly committed to working within a common framework of international law and diplomatic engagement, but have also demonstrated the ability and commitment to do so."
主语	谓语	状语	定语从句

Text 5 Build That Pipeline! 建那条管道!

One way to think about the keystone project —the 2,000-mile (3,220 km) pipeline that would bring oil from the tar sands of Canada to the Gulf of Mexico—is to ask what would happen if it is never built. The U.S. Department of State released an extremely thorough report that tries to answer this question. ①It concludes, basically, that the oil derived from Canadian tar sands will be developed at about the same pace whether or not there is a pipeline to the U.S. In other words, stopping Keystone might make us feel good, but it wouldn't really do anything about climate change.

Given the need for oil in the U.S., Canadian producers would still get Alberta's oil to the refineries on the Gulf of Mexico. There are other pipeline possibilities, but the most likely method of transfer is by train. The report estimates that it would take daily runs of 15 trains with about 100 tank cars each to carry the amount planned by TransCanada. That would be a large increase in traffic from what now goes north to south, but it would hardly be an insurmountable problem. Rail traffic in this corridor is already exploding: the number of carloads of crude oil doubled from 2010 to 2011, then tripled from 2011 to 2012. And remember, moving oil by train produces much higher emissions of CO_2 (from diesel locomotives) than flowing it through a pipeline.

Canada could also transport the oil by train or pipeline west to British Columbia and then on to Asia, where demand is booming. ②Right now that seems a distant and costly prospect, but having visited

---

keystone project 基石项目 thorough adj. 周密的 tar sand 沥青砂
refinery n. 炼油厂 insurmountable adj. 难以对付的 corridor n. 通道
diesel locomotive 柴油机动车

Alberta recently, I can attest that Canadian businesspeople and officials are planning seriously for Asian markets—especially since they have come to regard U.S. energy policy as politicized, hostile and mercurial. Whoever uses the oil, the CO_2 will be released into the atmosphere just the same.

Also, if we don't use oil from Alberta, we will need to get it somewhere to fuel our transportation needs—from Venezuela, Mexico, Saudi Arabia or Columbia. Some of these oils are heavy crude, and processing, refining and burning them is believed to be even more harmful to the environment than using fuels from refracted Canadian oil sands. Switching from oil sands to, say, Venezuelan crude (the most likely alternative) would reduce greenhouse-gas emissions by a minimal amount or not at all. To the extent that this would make us use more coal for electricity generation, it would be a big step backward for the environment. For many of these reasons, the scientific journal *Nature*, long a leader on climate change, argued in an editorial that President Obama should approve Keystone. A decision is expected this spring.

Environmental groups are approaching this project much as the U.S. government fights the war on drugs. They are attacking supply rather than demand. In this case, environmentalists have chosen one particular source of energy—Alberta's tar sands—and are trying to shut it down. But as long as there is demand for oil, there will be supply. A far more effective solution would be to try to moderate demand by putting in place a carbon tax or a cap-and-trade system. Ideally we would use the proceeds to fund research on alternative energy. Washington spends $73 billion on research for defense, $31 billion on health care and just $3 billion on energy. Massive increases in research would make a difference. Targeting one Canadian oil field—or one pipeline company—will not.

attest *vt.* 证明　　　mercurial *adj.* 变化无常的　　　refracted *adj.* 折射的　　　editorial *n.* 社论

Some in the environmental movement seem to recognize that the facts don't really support singling out Keystone, so they have turned to more intangible reasons to oppose it.

Opponents of Keystone say that the specifics are less important in this case and that it is the symbolism that matters. And it does. ③If we block this project—whose source is no worse than many others, rebuffing our closest trading partner and ally and spurning easily accessible energy in favor of Venezuelan or Saudi crude—it would be a symbol, and a depressing one at that. It would be a symbol of how emotion has taken the place of analysis and ideology now trumps science on both sides of the environmental debate.

(*Time*, 2013.3)

环保运动中的一些成员似乎意识到，这些事实不会帮助基石项目脱颖而出，于是，他们转向用更无形的理由来反对它。

基石项目的反对者说，这些细节在基石项目中并没有那么重要，重要的是其所象征的意义。这个项目的确具有象征意义。③如果我们阻止这个项目——该项目的石油来源并不比许多其他的石油来源差，就等于回绝我们最亲密的贸易伙伴和盟友，拒绝更容易获得的能源，而青睐委内瑞拉或沙特原油——这将会是一个令人绝望的信号。这表明情绪已经替代了分析，而且，在环保辩论的双方中，意识形态胜过了科学。

长难句解析

① 本句为主从复合句。主干结构为 It concludes that...。句中 that 引导的宾语从句作 concludes 的宾语；derived from Canadian tar sands 作后置定语修饰 oil；句中还包含 whether 引导的让步状语从句。

It	concludes,	basically,	that the oil	derived from Canadian tar sands	will be developed
主语	谓语	状语	宾语从句	后置定语	宾语从句

at about the same pace　whether or not there is a pipeline to the U.S.
　　　　　　　　　　　　　　　　让步状语从句

② 本句是由转折连词 but 连接的并列复合句。but 前句子的主干结构为 that seems a prospect；but 后句子的主干结构为 I can attest that...，that 引导的宾语从句作 attest 的宾语，句末是 since 引导的原因状语从句。

Right now　that　seems a distant and costly prospect, but having visited Alberta recently,
状语　　　主语1 系动词　　表语　　　　　　　　　　　　　　　伴随状语
I　can attest　that Canadian businesspeople and officials are planning seriously for Asian
主语2　谓语　　　　　　　　　宾语从句
markets—especially since they have come to regard U.S. energy policy as politicized, hos-
　　　　　　　　　　　原因状语从句
tile and mercurial.

③ 本句为主从复合句。主句的主干结构为 it would be a symbol, and a depressing one。句中 if 引导的条件状语从句中嵌套了一个 whose 引导的定语从句，来修饰 project。

---

single out 挑出　　　intangible *adj.* 难以明了的　　　rebuff *vt.* 断然拒绝　　　spurn *vt.* 冷落

If we block this project—whose source is no worse than many others, rebuffing our closest trading partner and ally and spurning easily accessible energy in favor of Venezuelan or Saudi crude—it would be a symbol, and a depressing one at that.

Text 6 EPA Tells BP to Use Less-Toxic Chemicals
美环保署要求英国石油公司使用低毒化学物质

① The U.S. government is ordering energy giant BP to find less-toxic chemicals to break up the Gulf of Mexico oil spill amid evidence that the dispersants are not effective and could actually make the spill more harmful to marine life.

The Environmental Protection Agency said Thursday that BP has to choose an alternative dispersant by today and must begin using it by Sunday. So far, BP has put about 600,000 gallons of the chemical mixture Corexit 9500 on the surface and 55,000 gallons on the sea bottom.

"EPA wants to ensure BP is using the least-toxic product authorized for use," the agency said in a statement. "We reserve the right to discontinue the use of this dispersant method if any negative impacts on the environment outweigh the benefits."

② The chemicals touted as a critical means of attacking the growing spill have questionable value over the long run and may actually slow down the bacteria that biodegrade crude oil, according to a USA Today review of the latest scientific studies and some of the world's top experts.

Just as household detergents break up grease

①美国政府命令能源巨头英国石油公司来寻找毒性更低的化学物质,以分解墨西哥湾泄漏的石油,因有证据显示,分散剂非但没有效果,还会使泄漏的石油对海洋生物造成更大的危害。

周四,美国环保署要求英国石油公司须当日选出分散剂的代替品,并于周日前投入使用。到目前为止,英国石油公司在墨西哥湾的海洋表层与海底,分别投入了约60万加仑和约5.5万加仑的Corexit 9500分散剂。

环保署在一份声明中称:"我们想确保英国石油公司所使用的分散剂是经授权后毒性最低的产品。如果产品对环境造成的任何负面影响大于其所带来的收益,我们有权制止这种分散剂的使用。"

②据《今日美国》一篇综合最新科学研究和一些世界顶尖专家观点的评论,该化学物质曾被视为应对持续泄漏的关键物质,但要长期使用,其价值值得商榷,而且,它实际上有可能降低可生物降解原油的细菌的生长速度。

正如家用清洁剂能分解油脂一

BP abbr. 英国石油公司(British Petroleum)
outweigh vt. 比……更重要
detergent n. 清洁剂

dispersant n. 分散剂
(be) touted as 被吹捧为……
grease n. 油脂

in the wash, dispersants can clear an oil slick by breaking the crude into tiny droplets that fall beneath the water's surface.

However, research shows that much of the oil returns to the surface in as little as a few hours, said Merv Fingas, a Canadian researcher and a leading authority on the chemicals.

Dispersants are toxic, and when mixed with oil can become even more dangerous than either the dispersant or oil alone, according to Fingas and EPA data.

Oil treated with dispersants spreads through the water, more readily coming in contact with delicate fish eggs and other fragile sea dwellers, said Peter Hodson, a specialist in fish toxicology who is director of the School of Environmental Studies at Queen's University in Kingston, Canada.

"You've just added to the toxic cocktail that the ocean has to put up with," said Silvia Earle, an oceanographer who is "explorer in residence" at the National Geographic Society.

BP will not be able to find an alternative dispersant that is not toxic, according to EPA records. All 14 of the approved dispersants listed on the agency's website are toxic to marine life at levels of a few hundred parts per million or less. Tests on all but three of the 14 indicate they are more toxic after being mixed with oil.

The EPA also began posting test results of water where BP has released dispersants. So far, the "data does not indicate any significant effects on aquatic life," the agency said.

BP issued a statement saying it had chosen to use Corexit 9500 because it was available in the large quantities needed to fight the spill, now a month old. The company said it would continue to use only government-approved products. BP spokesman Scott Dean declined to comment on research showing that the dispersants do not perform as the company has claimed. John Schoen,

样,分散剂可将原油分解成细小的油滴,使之从水面潜落,以达到清理水面浮油的目的。

然而,加拿大研究员、化学制品领域的权威代表梅尔夫·芬格丝表示,研究表明,大部分被分解的石油会在短短几小时内返回水面。

芬格丝的研究及环保署的数据表明,分散剂具有毒性,当其与石油混合后会产生更大的危害,此危害远大于分散剂或者泄漏的石油本身。

加拿大金斯顿皇后大学环境研究学院主任、鱼类毒理学研究专家彼得·霍德森表示,被分散剂处理过的石油经水传播后,更易接触脆弱的鱼卵及其他海洋生物。

海洋学家和美国国家地理协会驻校探险家西尔维娅·厄尔表示:"你们加入了海洋不得不忍受的有毒混合物。"

环保署的记录显示,英国石油公司将无法找到可替代的无毒分散剂。在该机构的网站上,所列的14种经批准可使用的分散剂,在几百万分之一或更少的程度上,都对海洋生物有害。对所有14种分散剂进行的测试显示,有3种与石油混合后毒性更大。

环保署也开始公布英国石油公司使用分散剂后的水性检测结果。它声称,到目前为止,"数据并未显示分散剂对水生生物有任何明显的影响"。

英国石油公司发表声明称,他们之所以选择使用Corexit 9500分散剂,是因为该分散剂可以大量供应来应对石油泄漏问题,到目前已投入使用1个月。该公司表示,将继续使用只经政府许可的产品。英国石油公司发言人斯科特·迪安拒绝对分散剂并未如公司声称的那么有效这一研究

---

put up with 忍受　　oceanographer *n.* 海洋学家　　aquatic *adj.* 水生的

a spokesman for Nalco, the company that makes Corexit 9500, also declined to comment.

Though dispersants have been used for decades, it is difficult to determine their chemical makeup. The companies that make them keep their formulas secret, according to EPA data.

Several scientists said they were surprised that the EPA granted BP permission to use the dispersants on the Gulf floor because their use in deep water had never been tried before.

"It's sort of the act of a desperate man," Hodson said. "You get the sense they are throwing everything they have at the problem without a lot of scientific backup."

(*USA Today*, 2010.5)

结果做出评论。Nalco 公司(生产 Corexit 9500 分散剂的厂商)的发言人约翰·舍恩同样拒绝做出评论。

尽管分散剂已使用了数十年,但其化学成分仍难以确定。环保署的资料显示,生产这些分散剂的公司都对其配方保密。

环保署允许英国石油公司在墨西哥湾海底使用分散剂,部分科学家对此表示惊讶,因为此前并未在深海区尝试过类似行为。

"这是一种绝望的人的行为,"霍德森表示,"你会有一种感觉,他们在此问题的解决上倾其所有,却没有太多的科学依据。"

长难句解析

① 本句为主从复合句。主句的主干结构为 The U.S. government is ordering BP to find chemicals to break up the oil spill amid evidence…。句中 that 引导的是同位语从句,作 evidence 的同位语,该从句的谓语部分是由 and 连接的两个并列成分。

The U.S. government | is ordering energy giant BP | to find less-toxic chemicals to break
主语 | 谓语 | 宾语 | 宾语补足语
up the Gulf of Mexico oil spill amid evidence that the dispersants are not effective and
　　　　　　　　　　　　　　　状语　　　　　　　　同位语从句
could actually make the spill more harmful to marine life.

② 本句为主从复合句。主句的主干结构为 The chemicals have value and may slow down the bacteria,主句包含 and 连接的两个并列谓语。touted as a…spill 作后置定语修饰主语 The chemicals;that 引导的定语从句修饰宾语 2 the bacteria;句末的状语中,of the latest…experts 作后置定语修饰 review。

The chemicals | touted as a critical means of attacking the growing spill | have questionable
主语 | 后置定语 | 谓语1　宾语1
value over the long run and may actually slow down the bacteria that biodegrade crude
　　时间状语　　　　　　　　　谓语2　　　　　　宾语2　　　定语从句
oil, according to a *USA Today* review of the latest scientific studies and some of
　　　　　　　　　　　　　　状语
the world's top experts.

---

makeup *n.* 组成　　　　　　　　backup *n.* 支持

Text 7

Japan's Hydra-Headed Disaster
日本灾难重重

That "tsunami" is one of the few Japanese words in global use points to the country's familiarity with natural disaster. But even measured against Japan's painful history, its plight today is miserable. ①The magnitude-9 earthquake—the largest ever in the country's history, equivalent in power to 30,000 Hiroshimas—was followed by a wave which wiped out whole towns. With news dribbling out from stricken coastal communities, the scale of the horror is still sinking in. The surge of icy water shoved the debris of destroyed towns miles inland, killing most of those too old or too slow to scramble to higher ground. The official death toll of 5,429 will certainly rise. In several towns over half the population has drowned or is missing.

In the face of calamity, a decent people has proved extremely resilient: no looting; very little complaining among the tsunami survivors. In Tokyo people queued patiently to meet their tax deadlines. Everywhere there was a calm determination to conjure a little order out of chaos. Volunteers have rushed to help. The country's Self-Defence Forces, which dithered in response to the Kobe earthquake in 1995, have poured into the stricken area. Naoto Kan, the prime minister, who started the crisis with very low public support, has so far managed to keep a semblance of order in the country, despite a series of calamities that would challenge even the strongest of leaders. The government's inept handling of the Kobe disaster did much to undermine Japan's confidence in itself.

Tsunami(海啸)是为数不多的国际通用的日语词之一,由此可见,这个国家对自然灾害是多么习以为常。即使与日本多灾多难的历史相比,日本目前的境地也很悲惨。①这是日本史上最强的9级地震,其威力相当于广岛原子弹威力的3万倍,而接踵而来的海啸将整个市区夷为平地。沿海灾区逐渐传出的消息表明,恐惧仍在加深。冰冷的海水淹没了城市废墟,使海岸线向内陆推移了几英里,很多太老或者来不及爬上高地的人因此而丧生。日本官方公布的死亡人数是5 429人,这个数字必定会继续上升。在有些市县,超过半数的人不是溺亡,就是失踪了。

面对灾祸,素养良好的日本民族表现得极为顽强:没有抢掠;幸存者们也很少抱怨。在东京,市民们耐心地排队交税。到处都保持着一种镇定,在一片混乱中却萌生了一种秩序,像施了魔法一样。志愿者们踊跃伸出援手。日本国家自卫队——曾在1995年神户地震时犹豫不决——也奔赴灾区赈灾。首相菅直人在应对危机之初,民众支持率很低,虽然说,面对这一系列灾祸,即使是最强大的领导集体也会受到挑战,但是,目前在其领导下,日本的秩序得以维持。政府对神户地震的处理失当,在很大程度上打击了日本应对同类事件的信心。

---

plight n. 境况　　　　Hiroshima 广岛市　　　wipe out 彻底摧毁　　dribble out 传出
surge n. 奔涌向前　　debris n. 碎片　　　　　scramble vi. 攀爬　　conjure vt. 变戏法
stricken area 受灾地区　semblance n. 表象　　inept adj. 不适当的　　undermine vt. 破坏

The immediate tragedy may be Japan's; but it also throws up longer-term questions that will eventually affect people all the way round the globe. Stock markets stumbled on fears about the impact on the world's third-biggest economy. Japan's central bank seems to have stilled talk of financial panic with huge injections of liquidity. Early estimates of the total damage are somewhat higher than the $100 billion that Kobe cost, but not enough to wreck a rich country. Disruption to electricity supplies will damage growth, and some Asian supply chains are already facing problems; but new infrastructure spending will offset some of the earthquake's drag on growth.

Those calculations could change dramatically if the nuclear crisis worsens. ②As *The Economist* went to press, helicopters were dropping water to douse overheating nuclear fuel stored at the Fukushima Daiichi plant, where there have been explosions, fires and releases of radiation greater, it seems, than the Japanese authorities had admitted. The country's nuclear industry has a long history of cover-ups and incompetence, and—notwithstanding the heroism of individual workers—the handling of the crisis by TEPCO, the nuclear plant's operator, is sadly in line with its past performance.

Even if the nuclear accident is brought under control swiftly, and the release of radiation turns out not to be large enough to damage public health, this accident will have a huge impact on the nuclear industry, both inside and outside Japan. Germany has already put on hold its politically tricky decision to extend the life of its nuclear plants. America's faltering steps towards new reactors look sure to be set back, not least because new concerns will mean greater costs.

Thus the great nuclear dilemma. For the best nuclear safety you need not just good planning and

目前，这是日本的悲剧，但从长远角度来看，最终也会波及全世界。证券市场担忧这会对日本这个世界第三大经济体造成影响。日本中央银行注入了大量资金后，似乎平息了人们的金融恐慌。神户地震的经济损失可能高达1 000亿美元，初步估计，本次地震可能损失更惨重，但还不足以摧毁一个经济大国。电力的中断会对日本的发展造成影响，一部分亚洲供应链也面临着重重困难，但是，新的基础设施开支将会抵消地震对经济的部分拖累。

如果日本的核扩散危机进一步恶化，这些数据就会急速上升。②就在《经济学人》发稿期间，为了给过热的核反应堆降温，直升机在福岛核电厂上空泼洒冷水。该核电站已经发生过爆炸事件和火灾，核泄漏似乎比日本官方所承认的还要严重。日本的核工业有遮遮掩掩的历史传统，且缺乏能力。尽管个体工人带有英雄主义色彩，但可悲的是，核电厂的运营商东京电力公司在危机处理方面继承了过往的表现。

尽管核事故很快得到控制，且核泄漏量不足以威胁公众健康，但是，这起事故对日本乃至世界的核工业发展都影响巨大。德国颇具政治深意的延长核电站寿命的决定已经被搁置。美国再建核反应堆的踌躇步伐势必也会推迟，尤其是因为新的担心将意味着更多的成本投入。

于是，大的核困境出现了。为了确保核能的安全状态达到最佳，我们需

---

stumble *vi.* 踌躇　　　　wreck *vt.* 破坏　　douse *vt.* 弄湿　　notwithstanding *prep.* 尽管
TEPCO 东京电力公司 (Tokyo Electric Power Co.)　　　　　　　　　　swiftly *adv.* 即刻
faltering *adj.* 踌躇的　　　set back 使……受挫折

good engineering. You need the sort of society that can produce accountability and transparency, one that can build institutions that receive and deserve trust. No nuclear nation has done this as well as one might wish, and Japan's failings may well become more evident. But democracies are better at building such institutions. At the same time, however, democracy makes it much easier for a substantial and implacable minority to make sure things don't happen, and that seems likely to be the case with plans for more nuclear power. Thus nuclear power looks much more likely to spread in societies that are unlikely to ground it in the enduring culture of safety that it needs.

Yet democracies would be wrong to turn their back on nuclear power. It still has the advantages of offering reliable power, a degree of energy security, and no carbon dioxide emissions beyond those incurred in building and supplying the plants. In terms of lives lost it has also boasted, to date, a good record. Chernobyl's death toll is highly uncertain, but may have reached a few thousand people. ③ It remains a reasonable idea for most rich countries to keep some nuclear power in their portfolio, not least because by maintaining economic and technological stakes in nuclear they will have more standing to insist on high standards for safety and non-proliferation being applied throughout the world. But in the face of panic, of sinister towers of smoke, of invisible and implacable threats, the reasonable course is not an easy one.

Back to Tokyo

No country faces that choice more painfully than Japan, scarred by nuclear energy but also deprived of native alternatives. To abandon nuclear power is to commit the country to massive imports of gas and perhaps coal. To keep it is to face and overcome a national trauma and to accept a small but real risk of another disaster.

---

incur vt. 招致　　　　　　　　　　Chernobyl n. 切尔诺贝利

Japan's all too frequent experience of calamity suggests that such events are often followed by great change. After the earthquake of 1923, it turned to militarism. After its defeat in the Second World War, and the dropping of the atom bombs, it espoused peaceful growth. The Kobe earthquake reinforced Japan's recent turning in on itself.

This new catastrophe seems likely to have a similarly huge impact on the nation's psyche. It may be that the Japanese people's impressive response to disaster, and the rest of the world's awe in the face of their stoicism, restores the self-confidence the country so badly needs. It may be that the failings of its secretive system of governance, exemplified by the shoddy management of its nuclear plants, lead to more demands for political reform. As long as Mr. Kan can convince the public that the government's information on radiation is trustworthy, and that it can ease the cold and hunger of tsunami survivors, his hand may be strengthened to further liberalise Japan. Or it may be that things take a darker turn.

The stakes are high. Japan—a despondent country with a dysfunctional political system—badly needs change. It seems just possible that, looking back from a safe distance, Japan's people will regard this dreadful moment not just as a time of death, grief and mourning, but also as a time of rebirth.

(*The Economist*, 2011.3)

长难句解析

① 本句为主从复合句。主句的主干结构为 The earthquake was followed by a wave…。破折号中间的内容为插入语,解释说明主语 The magnitude-9 earthquake;which 引导的定语从句修饰先行词 a wave。

The magnitude-9 earthquake—the largest ever in the country's history, equivalent in power to 30,000 Hiroshimas—was followed by a wave which wiped out whole towns.
主语　　　　　　　　　　　　插入语
　　　　　　　　　　　　　　谓语　状语　　　　定语从句

militarism *n.* 军国主义　　espouse *vt.* 信奉　　psyche *n.* 精神　　awe *n.* 敬畏
stoicism *n.* 坚韧　　　　shoddy *adj.* 劣质的　liberalise *vt.* 使自由化
despondent *adj.* 沮丧的　dreadful *adj.* 可怕的

② 本句为主从复合句。主句的主干结构为 helicopters were dropping water…。As 引导时间状语从句,表示"当……时候";where 引导的非限制性定语从句修饰 Fukushima Daiichi plant;it seems 为插入语。

> As *The Economist* went to press, helicopters were dropping water to douse overheating nuclear
> 　时间状语从句　　　　　主语　　　　谓语　　　宾语　　　　　　目的状语
> fuel stored at the Fukushima Daiichi plant, where there have been explosions, fires
> 　　　　　　　　　　　　　　　　　　　　　非限制性定语从句
> and releases of radiation greater, it seems, than the Japanese authorities had admitted.
> 　　　　后置定语　　　　　插入语　　　　　　比较状语从句

③ 本句为主从复合句。句中 it 为形式主语;动词不定式结构 to keep some nuclear power in their portfolio 为真正主语;原因状语从句中含有非谓语动词 being applied throughout the world 作后置定语来修饰 safety and non-proliferation。

> It   remains a reasonable idea for most rich countries to keep some nuclear power in their
> 形式主语 系动词　　　　　表语　　　　　　　　　　　　　　　　真正主语
> portfolio, not least because by maintaining economic and technological stakes in nuclear they
> 　　　　　　原因状语从句　　　　　　　　　　状语
> will have more standing to insist on high standards for safety and non-proliferation being
> 　　　　　　原因状语从句
> applied throughout the world.
> 后置定语

Text 8　Blooming Horrible 可怕的富营养化

South-east of New Orleans, where the Mississippi empties into the Gulf of Mexico, the North American land mass does not end so much as gently give up. ①Land subsides to welts of green poking up through the water, and the river grows wider and flatter until it meets the ocean, where a solid line divides the Mississippi's brown water from the gulf's blue.

On its long journey south the water has scooped up nutrients such as nitrogen and phosphorus, mainly from the fields of the Midwest. So much so

在美国新奥尔良市的东南部,密西西比河最终流入墨西哥湾,但北美大陆并没有在这里缓缓终结。①陆地下沉,呈现出块块绿洲。河流变得愈加宽阔,河水愈加平缓,最后流入大洋,那里有一条明显的分割线,将密西西比河棕褐色的河水与墨西哥湾蓝色的海水划得泾渭分明。

水一路向南流去,在漫长的途中吸附了氮、磷等营养物质,这些营养物质主要来自中西部的农田。营养

---

empty into 流入　　　scoop up 舀上来　　　nitrogen *n.* 氮　　　phosphorus *n.* 磷

that agriculture's gift to the gulf is a "dead zone". The excess nutrients cause algae to bloom, consuming all the available oxygen in the sea, making it hostile to other forms of marine life. Creatures that can swim away, such as shrimp and fish, do so; those that cannot, die. In the four decades since the dead zone was discovered it has grown steadily. Today it covers 6,700 square miles, an area larger than Connecticut.

This ecological disaster area imperils the region's commercial and recreational fisheries, worth around $2.8 billion a year. One study suggests yearly shrimp-fishery losses of nearly 13%. The dead zone drives shrimp farther out to sea, making it costlier and more time-consuming to catch them. It also makes them smaller.

② Nancy Rabalais, who heads the Louisiana Universities Marine Consortium and has mapped the dead zone each year for nearly three decades, claims that the amount of nitrates flowing into the Gulf of Mexico has increased by up to 300% over that time. Most of this comes from agriculture in the "I"-states (Illinois, Iowa and Indiana) and some from the city of Chicago.

It would be a mistake, though, to think that the problem is confined to the Gulf. The effects of nutrient pollution are increasingly apparent throughout the Mississippi River basin. Environmentalists say that half the streams in the upper Mississippi have too much nitrogen and a quarter have too much phosphorus. This nutrient enrichment damages aquatic life there too, and degrades drinking water. It also causes blooms of toxic algae that have closed beaches, made people ill and killed fish and pets. Nasty green lakes have also damaged tourism, property values and fisheries.

For years green groups have been trying to persuade the Environmental Protection Agency (EPA) to set a limit for the amount of nitrogen and

---

algae *n.* 藻类　　　shrimp *n.* 虾　　　imperil *vt.* 使……处于危险

phosphorus allowed in the states whose rivers feed the Mississippi. Little has happened. So in March members of the Mississippi River Collaborative, an environmental group, filed a lawsuit designed to force all those involved to think about ways to solve the problem.

The EPA refuses to comment while the matter is in litigation. But the Federal Water Quality Coalition, a group composed of industrial and metropolitan water users, has launched its own lawsuit in opposition to the first. It argues that the federal government should play no role in setting limits, and furthermore that the very idea of limits is too simplistic.

Yet it is not just green groups that think limits are helpful. Wisconsin is one of the few states to introduce, in 2010, statewide numerical limits for phosphorus. Joe Parisi, who runs Dane County, says these have spurred the county into working on new measures with the Madison metropolitan sewerage district. ③The idea is to experiment with projects that pay farmers to reduce nutrient pollution, using money that would otherwise have been spent on expensive technology for use by institutions such as municipal water authorities. One scheme is an innovative community biodigester that generates power from cattle manure. Another idea is a low-tech effort to extract phosphorus by using crops which are then harvested.

Whatever the outcome of the nutrient-pollution lawsuits many people seem to believe that strict limits will come anyway, one way or another. One interesting pilot scheme being tried out in Minnesota allows farmers who reduce fertiliser run-off and soil erosion to enjoy an exemption from future state and federal water-quality standards. Elsewhere, the Electric Power Research Institute, an industry think-tank, is creating a programme that would allow the trading of nutrient credits between states. Its Ohio River basin water-quality trading project will allow

---

simplistic *adj.* 过分单纯的   manure *n.* 肥料；类肥   fertiliser *n.* 化肥

those facing high pollution-control costs to buy reduction credits from those whose costs are lower. The first pilot trading will begin at the end of 2012, and again will allow those involved to use any credits against expected obligations in the future.

If that project takes off it could become the world's largest water-quality trading programme, spanning as many as eight states and allowing trading between 46 power plants, thousands of waste water facilities and about 230,000 farmers. But those involved say numerical limits are needed to really push trading forward.

If the upper Mississippi must await progress with limits, what hope is there further down the river? Along the lower Mississippi some have proposed diversions through wetlands as a way to mitigate oxygen starvation. But a network of levees has held the Mississippi back for decades, so it is doubtful how much the river could feasibly be moved; the process of changing the course of America's greatest river is more glacial than alluvial. Those Mississippi shrimpers had better cross their fingers and hope that the wheels of justice turn a bit faster.

(*The Economist*, 2012.6)

长难句解析

① 本句为并列复合句。and 前的句子中，非谓语动词结构 poking up through the water 作后置定语修饰 welts of green；and 后的句子中，where 引导的非限制性定语从句修饰 ocean。

> Land subsides to welts of green poking up through the water, and the river grows
> 主语1 谓语1   状语   后置定语   主语2   系动词
> wider and flatter until it meets the ocean, where a solid line divides the Mississippi's brown
>   表语   时间状语从句   非限制性定语从句
> water from the gulf's blue.

② 本句为主从复合句。主句的主干结构为 Nancy Rabalais claims that…。句中 who 引导的定语从句修饰主语 Nancy Rabalais；that 引导的宾语从句作 claims 的宾语。

---

span *vt.* 横跨　　oxygen starvation 缺氧　　levee *n.* 防洪堤　　glacial *adj.* 冷冰冰的
alluvial *adj.* 淤积的

Nancy Rabalais, who heads the Louisiana Universities Marine Consortium and has mapped
主语　　　　　　　　　　　　　　　非限制性定语从句
the dead zone each year for nearly three decades, claims that the amount of nitrates flowing
　　　　　　　　　　　　　　　　　　　　　谓语　　　　宾语从句
into the Gulf of Mexico has increased by up to 300% over that time.

③ 本句为主从复合句。主句的主干结构为 The idea is to experiment with projects...。主句的表语是不定式结构;that 引导的定语从句 1 修饰先行词 projects;that 引导的定语从句 2 修饰先行词 money。

The idea is to experiment with projects　　that pay farmers to reduce nutrient pollution,
主语　系动词　　　表语　　　　　　　　　　定语从句1
using money that would otherwise have been spent on expensive technology for use by
伴随状语　　　　　　定语从句2　　　　　　　　　　　　　　　　　状
institutions such as municipal water authorities.
语　　　　　　后置定语

Text 9 Japan May Have Lost Race to Save Nuclear Reactor
日本或许未来得及挽救核反应堆

Fukushima meltdown fears rise after radioactive core melts through vessel—but no danger of Chernobyl-style catastrophe.

The radioactive core in a reactor at the crippled Fukushima nuclear power plant appears to have melted through the bottom of its containment vessel and on to a concrete floor, experts say, raising fears of a major release of radiation at the site.

The warning follows an analysis by a leading U.S. expert of radiation levels at the plant. Readings from reactor two at the site have been made public by the Japanese authorities and Tepco, the utility that operates it.

Richard Lahey, who was head of safety research for boiling-water reactors at General Electric

福岛核电站核泄漏事故发生后，放射性核芯穿透安全罩导致恐慌加剧——但不会发生类似切尔诺贝利核电站事件的大灾难。

专家称，受损的福岛核电站的一个反应堆的放射性核芯可能穿透了安全罩的底部，泄漏到混凝土地面上。现场发生大规模泄漏的恐慌日益加剧。

一名核电站辐射值领域的美国权威专家在做出分析之后发出了上述警告。日本政府及核电站运行机构东京电力公司已将现场二号反应堆的资料公之于众。

通用电气在福岛完成设备安装后，任命理查德·莱希作为沸水反应

---

radioactive core 放射性核芯　　　　　　　crippled adj. 瘫痪的

when the company installed the units at Fukushima, told *The Guardian* workers at the site appeared to have "lost the race" to save the reactor, but said there was no danger of a Chernobyl-style catastrophe.

Workers have been pumping water into three reactors at the stricken plant in a desperate bid to keep the fuel rods from melting down, but the fuel is at least partially exposed in all the reactors.

At least part of the molten core, which includes melted fuel rods and zirconium alloy cladding, seemed to have sunk through the steel "lower head" of the pressure vessel around reactor two, Lahey said.

"The indications we have, from the reactor to radiation readings and the materials they are seeing, suggest that the core has melted through the bottom of the pressure vessel in unit two, and at least some of it is down on the floor of the drywell," Lahey said. "I hope I am wrong, but that is certainly what the evidence is pointing towards."

①The major concern when molten fuel breaches a containment vessel is that it reacts with the concrete floor of the drywell underneath, releasing radioactive gases into the surrounding area. At Fukushima, the drywell has been flooded with seawater, which will cool any molten fuel that escapes from the reactor and reduce the amount of radioactive gas released.

Lahey said: "It won't come out as one big glob; it'll come out like lava, and that is good because it's easier to cool."

The drywell is surrounded by a secondary steel-and-concrete structure designed to keep radioactive material from escaping into the environment. But an earlier hydrogen explosion at the reactor may have damaged this.

---

fuel rod 燃料棒　　　　　　　　zirconium n. 锆
drywell n. 干井。一般来讲,任何产出不具有商业价值的油或气的井都可以称为干井
molten fuel 熔化的燃料　　　glob n. 团　　lava n. 火山岩浆
steel-and-concrete adj. 钢筋混凝土的

"The reason we are concerned is that they are detecting water outside the containment area that is highly radioactive and it can only have come from the reactor core," Lahey added. "It's not going to be anything like Chernobyl, where it went up with a big fire and steam explosion, but it's not going to be good news for the environment."

The radiation level at a pool of water in the turbine room of reactor two was measured recently at 1,000 millisieverts per hour. At that level, workers could remain in the area for just 15 minutes, under current exposure guidelines.

A less serious core meltdown happened at the Three Mile Island nuclear plant in Pennsylvania in 1979. During that incident, engineers managed to cool the molten fuel before it penetrated the steel pressure vessel. The task is a race against time, because as the fuel melts it forms a blob that becomes increasingly difficult to cool.

In the light of the Fukushima crisis, Lahey said all countries with nuclear power stations should have " Swat teams " of nuclear reactor safety experts on standby to give swift advice to the authorities in times of emergency, with international groups coordinated by the International Atomic Energy Authority.

The warning came as the Japanese authorities were being urged to give clearer advice to the public about the safety of food and drinking water contaminated with radioactive substances from Fukushima.

Robert Peter Gale, a U.S. medical researcher who was brought in by Soviet authorities after the Chernobyl disaster, in 1986, has met Japanese cabinet ministers to discuss establishing an independent committee charged with taking radiation data from

---

detect *vt.* 检测　　　　　　　millisievert *n.* 毫西弗,衡量辐射剂量的基本单位之一
core meltdown 堆芯熔化　　　penetrate *vt.* 穿透　　　　　blob *n.* 一滴
Swat teams 特殊武装战术部队(Special Weapons and Tactics Teams)
contaminated *adj.* 受污染的

the site and translating it into clear public health advice.

"②What is fundamentally disturbing the public is reports of drinking water one day being above some limit, and then a day or two later it's suddenly safe to drink. People don't know if the first instance was alarmist or whether the second one was untrue," said Gale.

"My recommendation is they should consider establishing a small commission to independently convert the data into comprehensible units of risk for the public so people know what they are dealing with and can take sensible decisions," he added.

(The Guardian, 2011.3)

"②民众目前最担心的是,媒体今天报道饮用水中某物质的含量超标,但一两天后又报道饮用水可以安全饮用。人们不知道,到底是第一则报道在危言耸听,还是第二则报道失实。"盖尔说。

"我的建议就是,他们应该考虑建立一个独立工作的小型委员会。该委员会将采集到的数据描述成民众可以理解的危险程度。这样,人们就能知道他们目前面临何种状况,并由此做出理智的决定。"他补充道。

长难句解析

① 本句为主从复合句。主句的主干结构为 The major concern is that…。句中包含 when 引导的时间状语从句;that 引导的表语从句作 is 的表语;句末的现在分词结构作伴随状语。

The major concern when molten fuel breaches a containment vessel is that it reacts with
  主语   时间状语从句   系动词   表语从句
the concrete floor of the drywell underneath, releasing radioactive gases into the surrounding area.
                                                       伴随状语

② 本句为并列复合句。and 前句子的主干结构为 What…is reports…,主语是 what 引导的主语从句,介词短语 of…limit 作 reports 的后置定语;and 后句子的主干结构为 it's safe to drink。

What is fundamentally disturbing the public is reports of drinking water one day being
          主语从句   系动词 表语   后置定语
above some limit, and then a day or two later it's suddenly safe to drink.
                       状语   主系   表语

Text 10 Carbon Targets, Renewables and Atomic Risks
碳目标、可再生能源与原子能风险

• At issue in your article (*UK Wants Renewable Energy Target Scrapped*, 12 March) is what new EU

• 你在3月12日的文章《英国计划搁置可再生能源目标》中谈到的

---

instance *n.* 事例　　　　　　　　　　　　　alarmist *adj.* 危言耸听的

targets should be put in place for 2030. The UK is one of a number of countries that believe any new targets should be technology-neutral, leaving member states free to determine the most cost-effective energy mix to get the best deal for consumers.

Our communication to the European commission explicitly states that the UK is not in any way "against renewables." Far from it—renewables will play a key role in the future UK energy mix, helping to reduce import dependency and meet our carbon targets. But the consumer will be best served in the long term through all low-carbon energy technologies competing freely to meet our energy needs and emission-reduction targets.

Edward Davey MP
Energy and Climate Change Secretary

• The news that the UK government is secretly lobbying the European commission for the abolition of future EU renewable energy targets sadly comes as no surprise, and merely reveals the scale of the challenge facing supporters of clean, green power.

Coalition ministers have shown little appetite for meeting the UK's 2020 target: indeed, rather than take positive steps to boost, encourage and support burgeoning green technologies, which have created thousands of new jobs and made an important contribution to climate change goals, the government has instead penalised those that have thrived.

Attention has now turned to onshore wind, for which there is huge potential in the UK. Last week the UK government supported ambitious targets in the EU 2050 energy roadmap, but we know from experience that a voluntary, market approach does not give the necessary clarity or impetus for the required investment. "Sign up and hope" is not a policy. We are told that straitened public finances

---

technology-neutral 技术中立   burgeoning *adj.* 增长迅速的   straitened *adj.* 拮据的

mean that subsidies for green energy are no longer affordable, but stepping up our ambition on emission reductions makes sense for our energy policy, and economic sense in terms of green growth and jobs too. Frankly, no other solution will do.

  Jean Lambert MEP
  Green, London
  Keith Taylor MEP
  Green, South East England

• Your report was correct to assume that Lib Dems would oppose allowing nuclear energy to be given parity with renewables for the purposes of meeting European targets, but the situation is more complex than it implies.

When the Lib Dems last had a full debate on nuclear energy, the majority opposed it. However, since then, circumstances have changed. The climate is changing faster than we expected, our progress on replacing fossil fuels with renewable energy systems is slower than hoped for, efficiency measures are not reducing demand fast enough, and fossil fuel supplies are becoming less reliable and more difficult to procure. The party's current stated position is opposition to spending taxpayers' money on nuclear power stations.

The cases for and against another generation of nuclear power stations were debated in the summer 2011 edition of *Challenge*, the journal of the Green Lib Dems (an organisation of party members with a special interest in environmental issues). ① While continuing to believe that increasing the use of renewable energy has to be our primary objective, an increasing number of Lib Dems think that the need to combat climate change is so urgent that we need both renewables and nuclear energy. The development of nuclear and renewable energy technologies were both emaciated by competition from cheap, polluting, unsustainable fossil fuels.

---

procure *vi.* 取得   emaciate *vt.* 使衰弱

We need to look to the future with a set of EU-wide targets that allow the development of renewables and other low-carbon energy production technologies.

The proportion of energy production that each EU member state could reasonably be expected to provide from renewables depends on climate, topography and population density. The next set of EU targets need to further increase the proportion of energy required to be produced from renewables, but to be achievable by all it will have to be lower than the maximum some states could achieve. I would thus support a further requirement for low-carbon energy, which member states could fulfil with further renewables or with other low-carbon sources such as nuclear.

Steve Bolter

Member of Green Lib Dems Executive

• As we approach another drought, (Report, 12 March), consider August 1666, when the Thames at Oxford was reduced to a trickle…The great fire of London started early on 12 September, and the east wind drove the flames before it, burning much of London and spreading smoke as far as Oxford. In 2007 a nuclear power station site was still proposed at Didcot on the Thames; even when in "down mode" a nuclear power station requires around 3 MW of cooling to keep the fuel rods stable.

In August 2011 Dominique Bestion, research director of the French Atomic Energy and Alternative Energies Commission, said he foresaw no new inland nuclear power stations being built because of climate change. He cited the experience of France, where they increasingly have to put their nuclear plants into sleep mode on rivers such as the Loire.

In the summer of 2003, when 15,000 people died in the heatwave in France, three of the Loire plants were shut down and blackouts ensued. In response France installed over 200MW of distributed

---

MW *abbr.* 兆瓦(megawatt)

sleep mode 休眠模式

photovoltaics to meet summer peak demands, when such inland nuclear plants fail to generate. Nuclear energy in a rapidly warming climate, with more extreme weather, is unsafe, whether inland or by the sea. We already have the technology to build a safe and sufficient renewable energy future at much lower costs. The question is, who is actually stopping us doing it?

  Professor Susan Roaf
  Edinburgh

• Your welcome article on Fukushima (Report, 9 March) sadly repeats the mantra that for cumulative doses below 100mSv: "No study has linked cancer development to exposure at below that level." I hope *The Guardian* will not fall for the reassurances of the nuclear industry so easily.

The low-dose radiation debate has a long history, including the pioneering work of the late Alice Stewart, who discovered the link between exposure to diagnostic X-rays in utero and increased risk of childhood cancer. The peer-reviewed open-access journal *Environmental Health* has published two articles of mine (2007, 2009) on radiation risks for cancer mortality in Japanese A-bomb survivors exposed to under 20mSv external doses.

  Greg Dropkin
  Liverpool

• I have just heard that the energy regulator Ofgem has given the energy giant EDF a rap over the knuckles for mis-selling (Report, 9 March). EDF has apparently agreed to pay £4.5m to its vulnerable customers in lieu of a fine. Surely, if this hugely profitable company has been contravening

---

photovoltaics *n.* 光伏发电
reassurance *n.* 再保证
peer-reviewed *adj.* 同行评议的
mantra *n.* 咒语
low-dose radiation 低剂量辐射
cumulative *adj.* 累积的
utero *n.* 子宫

the rules on selling, it should be fined. This "in lieu of a fine" agreement seems to me to let the company off the PR hook and allow them to spin bad practice as a generous gesture to their vulnerable customers.

Last November a French court fined the same company, EDF, £1.3m for spying on Greenpeace in France, sent two senior EDF employees to prison for three years and awarded Greenpeace damages from the company. This seems like an honest and transparent way of dealing with a company that has broken laws.

This weekend, a large number of people are expressing their opposition to plans to build new nuclear reactors in the UK by surrounding the nuclear power station at Hinkley Point on the Bristol Channel. This is the first site where our prime minister recently announced preliminary work would start on a new reactor as part of a joint Anglo-French deal. Guess which energy company will be doing this work? EDF.

②If this company cannot abide by our regulations on fair selling and falls foul of French law when it has concerns about those who oppose its plans, should we really trust it to build and run nuclear plants, which have the potential to experience some of the most hazardous accidents on the planet? I am opposed to further expansion of nuclear power, but if our government insists on this course, surely it should at least go out to competitive tender.

Dr Julia Spragg
Oxford

(*The Guardian*, 2012.3)

长难句解析

① 本句为主从复合句。句中 while 译为"虽然",引导让步状语从句,该从句主语和主句主语一致,因此省略了主语和系动词;that 引导的宾语从句 1 为让步状语从句中 believe 的宾语;that 引导的宾语从句 2 为谓语 think 的宾语;宾语从句 2 中还嵌套了一个 so...that...结构引导的结果状语从句。

Anglo-French 英法

> While continuing to believe that increasing the use of renewable energy has to be our primary
>   让步状语从句   宾语从句1
> objective, an increasing number of Lib Dems think that the need to combat climate change
>   主语   谓语   宾语从句2
> is so urgent that we need both renewables and nuclear energy.
>   结果状语从句

② 本句为主从复合句。主句为反问句，主干结构为 should we really trust it…? 句中 if 引导的条件状语从句中嵌套了一个 when 引导的时间状语从句，时间状语从句中又嵌套了一个 who 引导的定语从句修饰 those；which 引导的非限制性定语从句修饰 plants。

> If this company cannot abide by our regulations on fair selling and falls foul of French law
>   条件状语从句
> when it has concerns about those who oppose its plans, should we really trust   it
>   时间状语从句   定语从句   助动词 主语 状语 谓语   宾语
> to build and run nuclear plants, which have the potential to experience some of the most
>   宾语补足语   非限制性定语从句
> hazardous accidents on the planet?

Text 11　Plastic Fishing in the Southern Ocean
在南太平洋打捞塑料

In one of the remotest places on Earth, a scientist is measuring for the first time the concentration of plastic particles that can float on the sea surface for hundreds or even thousands of years.

Erik van Sebille is looking for something very much out of the ordinary in the Southern Ocean: plastic. He has come to one of the most remote parts of the world—as far as it is possible to go from major concentrations of people—to look for the stuff humans throw away.

Van Sebille, an oceanographer at the University of New South Wales and one of the research leaders on the Australasian Antarctic Expedition, was one of

在地球上最偏远的角落，一位科学家正在首次探测可以在海面上漂浮几百甚至几千年的塑料粒子凝结物。

埃里克·范·赛比耶正在南太平洋寻找一种非同寻常的东西：塑料。他来到地球上最偏远的地方——尽可能地远离人类的聚居地——寻找人类的丢弃品。

新南威尔士大学的海洋学家范·赛比耶是澳大利亚南极考察队研究工作的带头人之一，也是首批

Antarctic Expedition　南极考察

the first to start his scientific work aboard the Shokalskiy. In the morning on our first full day at sea, he threw a two-metre-long plankton net, with a pint-sized jar attached to one end, overboard. After five minutes dragging the assembly behind the ship, he fished out the jar and held in his hands something that looked a bit like pea soup—seawater filled with plankton, krill and, perhaps, bits of plastic. For his research, he will take many more seawater samples at different latitudes, sieving each one to identify the constituent parts.

The plastic he is looking for is the stuff that starts off as consumer goods and ends up in the sea as waste. The plastic is broken down over time, by sunlight, into fragments no more than a millimetre across. These particles can float for hundreds to thousands of years on the surface of the sea. Scientists have identified huge areas of the North Atlantic and Pacific oceans, for example, where the water currents force the plastic particles to accumulate. In some of these places, there seems to be more plastic than plankton on the surface. The particles can attract algae, absorb toxic chemicals and have major impacts on the entire marine food chain.

So far no one has carried out measurements of plastic in the Southern Ocean, partly because it is so remote but also because oceanographers have assumed that the prevailing surface currents would limit any plastic build-up there. Van Sebille is aiming to fill that knowledge gap.

"We want to find out, in a systematic way, how much plastic there is," he tells me. "Especially if, as we go from relatively close to New Zealand and further south, how quickly the amount of plastic actually decreases."

General measurements of the sea also began last night: one of the science teams attached a half-metre-long metal tube, bristling with electronic sensors, to a long rope and plunged it into the sea.

登上绍卡利斯基院士号科考船从事科学研究的专家之一。在海上第一天的早晨，他把一张约两米长的浮游生物网撒到海里，网的一端系有一个小型的罐子。在船尾拖行了五分钟后，他捞起罐子，将液体倒在手上，那是些看起来有点像豌豆汤的液体——充满了浮游生物、磷虾，可能还有一些塑料的海水。他将在不同纬度采集海水水样，并对水样进行筛分，以确定其成分。

他要找的塑料是最终成为海上垃圾的生活消费品。经过长时间的阳光照射，塑料被分解成直径不超过1毫米大小的碎粒。这类粒子能在海面上漂浮数百到数千年。例如，科学家们已经确定，在北大西洋和太平洋的大片海域，海流使这类塑料粒子大量累积。在有些海域，海面上的塑料粒子比浮游生物还要多。这种粒子可以吸引藻类，吸收有毒化学物质，并严重影响整个海洋食物链。

迄今为止，还没有人对南太平洋的塑料粒子进行测量，部分原因在于该海域太过偏远，还因为海洋学家们本认为该海域盛行的表层流可以限制塑料粒子的累积。范·赛比耶要填补这一认识空白。

"我们想系统地了解该海域塑料粒子的数量，"他告诉我，"尤其是想了解，如果我们从离新西兰相对较近的地点出发，一路向南，塑料粒子数量的减少速度会有多快。"

对海水的一般性测量已于昨晚开始。其中一个科考小组准备了一根半米长的布满了电子传感器的金属管，把它系在一根长绳上后抛入海中。

---

plankton n. 浮游生物（总称）   krill n. 磷虾   sieve vt. 筛   millimetre n. 毫米

① Dragged along behind the boat for the duration of the trip to Antarctica, the $25,000 "Exoprobe" will record a range of variables—sea temperature, salinity, pH—every few seconds to build a detailed picture of the Southern Ocean along our route.

On the 1911—1914 expedition that Douglas Mawson led, his team pulled up buckets of sea water a few times and used a thermometer to measure its temperature. The 2013 version can measure the sea's features almost continuously day and night, providing thousands of data points every day. In recent decades, Earth-observation satellites have measured the surface temperature of the ocean from space, but no one has directly probed it in this way for more than a century.

② By lunchtime, the researchers had reeled in the Exoprobe to download its first 12 hours of measurements and, more importantly, to ensure that it was still in one piece and hadn't been bitten by any inquisitive sharks.

Some identified and counted birds from vantage points at the bridge of the ship. Others looked on at the stern deck as expedition leader Chris Fogwill, a glaciologist at the University of New South Wales, began his collection of plankton from the sea surface, using the same set-up of jars and nets that van Sebille was using to find plastic.

"The Southern Ocean, at this time of year, really starts to bloom with huge amounts of biological productivity going on," says Fogwill. "What we're going to do is sieve it and then we'll see what forms of plankton we have in there once we have it all cleaned up and ready to go. We'll do this every day to get the latitudinal variability as we go down."

① 船只驶向南极洲的全程都拖行该设备，这个价值2.5万美元的"远征探索号"设备会记录一系列的变量——海水温度、盐度以及pH值——每隔几秒绘制一幅沿线的南太平洋详细图像。

在道格拉斯·莫森领头的1911—1914年的考察中，考察小组分次用水桶打捞海水，并使用温度计测量海水温度。2013年版的设备可以不分昼夜地对海水指标进行连续测量，每天都能提供数千组数据。近几十年来，地球观测卫星在太空对海洋表面温度进行了测量，但一个多世纪以来，还没有人像这次一样，对海水进行直接测量。

② 到了中午，研究人员收起"远征探索号"，下载了头12个小时的测量数据。更重要的是，他们要确认该设备仍然完好无损，并没有被好奇的鲨鱼咬坏。

一些人在舰桥的有利位置上对鸟类进行识别和数量统计。其他人在船尾的瞭望台上观望。新南威尔士大学的冰川学家克里斯·福格威尔开始收集海面浮游生物，他使用的罐子和网与范·赛比耶收集塑料粒子的装备是一样的。

"每年的这个时候，南太平洋的生物就开始大量繁殖，"福格威尔说，"我们要筛选出它们的种类，一旦我们清理完毕并准备继续前进，我们就会知道这片海域都有哪些种类的浮游生物。这是我们每天必做的工作，一边航行，一边掌握浮游生物在不同纬度海域的变化。"

---

duration n. 期间　　salinity n. 盐度　　reel vi. 摇摇晃晃地挪动　　inquisitive adj. 好奇的
vantage n. 优势　　glaciologist n. 冰川学家

The data Fogwill collects will provide a baseline of information for scientists who want to study the variability of the Earth's climate over millions of years.

"The plankton on the floor of the ocean, you can compare it with tree rings," says van Sebille. "There are layers being formed over millions of years."

As the plankton that lives at the surface of the sea dies, it sinks down to the bottom—what oceanographers call "marine snow." In some places, this can be hundreds of metres deep on the sea bed. Studying what species are present in the different layers can provide insights into past climate. "Sometimes you have tropical species, sometimes sub-tropical," says van Sebille. "To interpret that data you need to have a baseline, you need to know what's at the surface of the ocean right now."

Other scientific research projects—including surveying sea mammals and taking cores of mud and ice—will begin in the coming days. And, very soon, we'll see our first penguins. Meanwhile, as the sun went down (though it never went dark) on the second day, a few passengers reported seeing something beguiling: a pod of dolphins at the bow of the Shokalskiy, leaping and racing our lumbering ship.

(*The Guardian*, 2013.12)

对于那些想要研究地球数百万年来的气候变化的科学家来说，福格威尔收集的数据可以提供基本的信息。

"海底的浮游生物就好比树的年轮，"范·赛比耶说，"分层的形成需要数百万年的时间。"

海面上的浮游生物死亡后会沉入海底，海洋学家将此称为"海雪"。有些海床上的海雪有几百米厚。对不同分层中的物种进行研究，可以更好地了解过去的气候条件。"有时我们会发现热带物种，有时又会发现亚热带物种，"范·赛比耶说道，"要解读这些数据，必须有一个基线，即我们需要知道目前海面上到底有哪些物种。"

其他科学研究项目——包括对海洋哺乳动物的调查以及泥核与冰核的样本采集——也将在今后几天展开。很快我们就能看到企鹅了。此外，当第二天太阳下山的时候（但却从不天黑），一些人看到了有趣的一幕：一群海豚在绍卡利斯基院士号科考船的船头跳跃，并追逐我们缓慢前进的船只。

长难句解析

① 本句为简单句。句首使用了动词过去分词结构 Dragged along… 作状语；sea temperature, salinity, pH 为 variables 的同位语，解释说明 variables 的具体内容。

Dragged along behind the boat for the duration of the trip to Antarctica,	the $25,000
状语1	主语

"Exoprobe"	will record	a range of variables	—sea temperature, salinity, pH—	every
	谓语	宾语	同位语	

few seconds	to build a detailed picture of the Southern Ocean along our route.
状语2	目的状语

---

beguiling *adj.* 有趣的；迷人的

② 本句为主从复合句。句中包含两个由 and 连接的动词不定式结构作目的状语；在目的状语 2 中还嵌套了一个 that 引导的宾语从句，作 ensure 的宾语；宾语从句中，and 连接两个并列的谓语结构，主语均为 it。

By lunchtime, the researchers had reeled in the Exoprobe to download its first 12 hours of
时间状语　　　主语　　　谓语　　　宾语　　　目的状语 1
measurements and, more importantly, to ensure that it was still in one piece and hadn't
　　　　　　　状语　　　　　　目的状语 2　　　宾语从句
been bitten by any inquisitive sharks.

Text 12　Fossil Fuel Divestment Campaign's Victory in Australia Will Be a Moral One
澳大利亚矿物燃料撤资活动的道德胜利

Global climate divestment campaigns led by 350.org and Bill McKibben will have a larger moral impact than financial one.

Journalist and climate activist Bill McKibben is in Australia in June on his epic Do The Math tour, which aims to highlight the danger of fossil fuel company oil and coal reserves and encourage divestment.

①The tour was kick-started by McKibben's *Rolling Stone* article, "Global Warming's Terrifying New Math", which argued that in order to stay below the 2℃ warming limit, the global economy has a budget of less than 565 gigatons of carbon dioxide. Unfortunately, fossil fuel companies have reserves of carbon from oil, coal and gas of almost 3,000 gigatons—far exceeding the climate's safe limit if it were to all be burned.

This "math" has been known for some years before McKibben's article. The Potsdam Institute wrote about humanity's carbon budget back in 2009, noting that even if we stayed

比尔·麦吉本和 350.org 发起的全球气候撤资活动的道德意义远胜于金融意义。

比尔·麦吉本是一名记者，也是一名气候活动家。6 月，他在澳大利亚开始了名为"做道算术题"的历史性巡回演讲，旨在揭露化石燃料公司的石油和煤炭储备风险，并鼓励撤资。

①麦吉本先是在《滚石》杂志上发表了题为《全球变暖骇人的新数学题》的文章，为本次的巡回演讲造势。文章中称，为了使气温上升控制在 2℃ 的上限内，全球经济预算中二氧化碳的排放量应少于 5 650 亿吨。然而，不幸的是，矿物燃料公司从石油、煤炭和天然气中获得的碳的储备量接近 3 万亿吨——如果全部消耗，碳排放将会远超气候变化的安全界限。

麦吉本发表文章之前，人们对这道"数学题"已经熟知多年。德国波茨坦研究所在 2009 年的一篇报告中指出，即使人类的碳排放量保持在碳预算之内，

---

divestment *n.* 撤资　　　　　　　　　　gigaton *n.* 十亿吨

264

within budget, we still had a 25% chance of going over 2 degrees warming. Alarmingly, the Potsdam report said global emissions must start falling by 2015 and that reductions must exceed even the most ambitious public targets tabled by governments so far.

Nevertheless, although McKibben didn't invent the "math", he certainly deserves credit for catapulting it back into the spotlight.

Tied to the tour is the 350.org sponsored carbon divestment campaign, targeting mainly students on campuses around the USA (and now Australia) to pressure their university administrations to dump investments in fossil fuel companies. The message of the campaign is that these students can no longer tolerate "business as usual."

The campaign has started to spread to churches, local councils, and in Australia, work is under way for activists to start campaigning to superannuation funds.

And in the USA it has been remarkably successful. More than 300 American colleges have active Go Fossil Free campaigns.

Universities like Harvard or MIT have multi-billion dollar endowment funds. While individual college funds may represent just a small drop in the ocean of international financial markets, the Go Fossil Free campaigns are trying to tap into something deeper with their divestment campaigns.

Divestment campaigns historically have never been about economic pressure. The effectiveness of the South African apartheid divestment campaigns were due to the moral pressure they placed on governments and businesses. They made toleration of apartheid in the USA, Britain and other countries (including Australia) impossible. University campuses were

气温上升超过2℃的可能性仍然有25%。令人担忧的是，波茨坦研究所的这份报告中还提到，全球的碳排放量必须从2015年起开始回落，并且减少的数量必须高于迄今为止任何一个政府提出的最有野心的公共目标。

虽然这道"数学题"并不是麦吉本的首创，但他再次让该话题成为焦点，可谓功不可没。

本次巡回演讲联合了由350.org赞助的碳撤资活动。该活动主要针对全美国（现在还有澳大利亚）的在校大学生，通过他们对学校管理部门施压，敦促学校从化石燃料公司撤资。活动传达的讯息就是，学生们不再容忍"一切照旧"。

这场活动开始蔓延到教堂和各地市政厅。而且在澳大利亚，活动家们正在针对养老保险基金开展活动。

该活动在美国已经相当成功。超过300所美国高校积极组织"解放矿物燃料"的活动。

哈佛大学、麻省理工学院等多所大学拥有几十亿美元的捐助基金。然而，一所大学的基金在全球金融市场上也只是沧海一粟。"解放矿物燃料"的活动试图通过撤资活动来解决深层次的问题。

撤资活动历来与经济压力无关。南非种族隔离制的撤资运动之所以有效，是因为他们向政府和企业施加了道德压力。通过这场运动，种族隔离制度在美国、英国和其他国家（包括澳大利亚）变得不可容忍。大学校园向来是许多活动的根据地，参与者不光有学生，还有学者以及大学行政基金的托管人。

---

catapult vt. 扔，掷　　superannuation n. 养老金　　apartheid n. 种族隔离

the hubs of much of the campaign activities, engaging not just students but academics and the trustees of university administered funds.

The divestment by the University of California Berkeley's divestment of $3 billion in 1986 was later credited by Nelson Mandela as a catalyst for the collapse of the apartheid government.

Unfortunately, there's every indication that the big fossil fuel companies targeted by McKibben—like Exxon, BP, Chevron and BHP Billiton—are less concerned than Apartheid South Africa was in global public opinion. For example, BP has managed to bounce back from the Gulf of Mexico oil spill.

It's likely they also have more economic and political clout. The big fossil fuel companies are some of the most profitable companies in history. BHP Billiton for example made a modest $10 billion profit in 2012, and Exxon made over $42 billion.

Given these numbers, it is unlikely that even the $32 billion Harvard endowment would make much of an impact, even if the entire fund was invested in fossil fuel companies. ② In Australia, only the University of Melbourne has over a billion dollars in their endowment, and even if all the Australian universities combined divested, the business practices of BHP and Chevron are unlikely to change.

I think the real impact of the divestment campaigns must come from their moral authority. Universities (and hopefully superannuation funds) that do divest are taking a moral stand. That stand must be accompanied by efforts throughout the university to highlight the risks posed by dangerous climate change.

Universities train the business leaders of the future. In fact, the graduate schools are often training the business leaders of today! Most business

---

hub n. 中心　　　trustee n. 托管人　　　catalyst n. 催化剂　　　bounce back 迅速恢复活力

schools include compulsory courses in ethics, but the carbon budget math needs to be embedded into accounting, finance and economics classes from the undergraduate to graduate level.

Lecturers teaching actuaries about risk should be explaining the effects of runaway global warming and the ecological crisis that will occur if we cross over 2 degrees in warming. Engineering and project management students should look at sustainable energy and ecologically sound product supply chains.

And commerce students need to come to grips with the fact that as we get closer to reaching or exceeding our carbon budget, those fossil fuel reserves may become unburnable, leaving investors stranded.

With more and more reports warning of the dire risks if we do not change course, the Go Fossil Free campaign has its work cut out to ensure we don't cross the limit in 2015.

Last year, I had the opportunity to see McKibben and Naomi Klein at the Boston leg of the Do The Math tour and found it excellent and informative.

(*The Guardian*, 2013.5)

伦理必修课，但无论是本科还是研究生阶段，碳预算数学都必须纳入会计、金融和经济学课程中。

风险精算讲师应向学生解读全球变暖进程加快所带来的影响，以及气温上升超过2℃时会发生的生态危机。工程管理或项目管理专业的学生应关注可持续能源及生态无害产品供应链的建设。

商务专业的学生应认识到这样一个事实：当我们逐渐接近或超过碳预算时，矿物燃料储备可能会无法启用，使得投资者陷入困境。

越来越多的报道都警告称如果我们还不改变路线，那么将面临可怕的风险，所以"解放矿物燃料"的活动将会停止，以确保2015年我们不会突破这一限制。

去年，在"做道算术题"巡回演讲的波士顿站，我有幸见到了麦吉本和娜欧蜜·克莱恩，并发现这是一场精彩且意义深远的演讲。

长难句解析

① 本句为主从复合句。句中 Global Warming's Terrifying New Math 为 McKibben's *Rolling Stone* article 的同位语；which 引导的非限制性定语从句修饰 Global Warming's Terrifying New Math，该从句中嵌套了一个 that 引导的宾语从句，作 argued 的宾语。

The tour was kick-started by McKibben's *Rolling Stone* article, "Global Warming's
 主语   谓语   状语   同位语
Terrifying New Math", which argued that in order to stay below the 2℃ warming limit, the
                     非限制性定语从句   宾语从句
global economy has a budget of less than 565 gigatons of carbon dioxide.

② 本句为并列复合句。and 前句子的主干结构为 the University of Melbourne has over a billion dollars；and 后句子的主干结构为 practices are unlikely to change，该句中还包含一个 even if 引导的让步状语从句。

---

embed *vt.* 植入　　　　　　　　　　unburnable *adj.* 不被消耗的

In Australia, only the University of Melbourne has over a billion dollars in their endowment,
地点状语　　　　　　主语1　　　　　　谓语　　　　宾语　　　　状语
and even if all the Australian universities combined divested, the business practices of BHP
　　　　让步状语从句　　　　　　　　　　　　　　　主语2
and Chevron are unlikely to change.
　　　　　系动词　　表语

Text 13

Australia Needs U.S.-Style Green Card Deal for Climate-Threatened Pacific Islanders
为了受气候威胁的太平洋岛民，澳大利亚需要美国式绿卡

Migration Council Australia says working migration could help Pacific economies, counter poverty and reduce the need for aid.

Australia should introduce a "post-disaster humanitarian visa" for Pacific islanders displaced by natural disasters and climate change, a new report from the Migration Council Australia has recommended.

And to boost historically low rates of migration from the Pacific, Australia should consider instituting a green card-style lottery for Pacific islanders to live and work in Australia, and boost seasonal worker numbers to industries such as horticulture.

Migration from Pacific countries to Australia has been consistently low for decades—representing less than 0.5% of all visas granted to Australia—but the Migration Council, an independent migration policy body, argues that the movement of people from the Pacific could benefit source countries and Australia.

Pacific countries, geographically disparate, sparsely populated and, in many cases, economically fragile, are forecast to be at the forefront of the

澳洲移民委员会表示，工作移民能够助推太平洋各经济体，扶助贫困并减少援助需求。

澳洲移民委员会的最新报告指出，澳大利亚应该引入"灾后人道主义签证"，专门为因自然灾害和气候变化而流离失所的太平洋岛民开放。

澳大利亚应考虑对在澳生活和工作的太平洋岛民实行绿卡抽签政策，以此来刺激长久以来较为低迷的太平洋岛屿移民率，同时也能够增加某些产业（如园艺业）中季节性工人的数量。

从太平洋岛国移民到澳大利亚的人数在过去几十年内一直保持低位——不到澳大利亚签证颁发中的0.5%，但是，澳洲移民委员会，这家独立的移民政策机构，认为接纳来自太平洋岛国的居民能够给太平洋岛国和澳大利亚带来双赢。

太平洋岛国的地理位置分散，人口稀少，而且往往经济疲软，它们最易遭受气候变化的影响。那些低地

---

institute *vt.* 创立　　　horticulture *n.* 园艺　　　disparate *adj.* 不同的　　　sparsely *adv.* 稀疏地

impacts of climate change, with low-lying atoll nations particularly vulnerable to rising sea levels and worsening natural disasters.

Research suggests that by 2050, between 665,000 and 1.7 million people will be displaced by climate change across the Pacific.

"For a handful of countries—Kiribati foremost amongst them—climate change will pose an existential threat," the council's paper said. "At some stage in the 21st century Australia, as the major regional power, will be required to play a leading role in managing climate-induced migration."

After disasters, bringing people to Australia would save lives and enable displaced people to earn money to more quickly re-establish themselves back at home.

"It is much easier to provide access to basic food, water and shelter in Australia than it is in isolated, post-disaster countries with little responsive capacity," the report said.

Working migration to Australia could help boost Pacific island economies, counter poverty through remittances, and reduce the need for aid.

Money earned by migrants working in Australia and sent home as remittances flowed directly to families and communities to support small businesses, pay school fees, or help build houses.

"Migration and aid are complements, not substitutes," Henry Sherrell, acting chief executive of the migration council told *The Guardian*.

"More migration opportunities for Pacific citizens to Australia create a triple win, for the migrants themselves, for Pacific countries and for Australia. Pacific citizens can earn four to ten times more income in Australia than their home countries. ①This drives remittances which help underpin economic development while allowing (Australian) labour shortages to be addressed in industries like horticulture."

---

vulnerable to 易受……的侵害
responsive capacity 反应能力
climate-induced *adj.* 气候引起的
remittance *n.* 汇款

The U.S. diversity visa "green card" lottery, implemented in 1995, offers 50,000 visas a year, and is designed to attract migrants from countries with low migration rates to America.

New Zealand runs two similar lotteries for Pacific countries, one for Samoan citizens and the other for a number of Pacific nations. The report suggests Australia could run a similar lottery.

Thirty one countries have signed bilateral working holiday treaties allowing young people to work in Australia, but only one is in the Pacific: Papua New Guinea. Since the PNG working holiday treaty was signed in 2011, no visas have been approved from that country.

Australia has a seasonal worker program for Pacific islanders, which began with a pilot scheme in 2008—2009 granting 56 visas.

It has grown strongly each year, to about 2,800 in 2014—2015, but is still dwarfed by New Zealand's program, which is more than 7,000.

The migration council argues this program should be expanded, with a focus on workers returning on second, third and subsequent visas.

②A study by Abares (the Australian bureau of agricultural and resource economics and sciences) found seasonal workers from the Pacific were more efficient and productive than backpackers on working holiday visas, and those working consecutive seasons were the most productive.

Speaking in Niue last month, the minister for international development and the Pacific, Steve Ciobo, told the secretariat of the Pacific Community that Australia would look to increase labour mobility across the region to support economic growth, including introducing two-year low-skilled work visas for Pacific micro-states, and uncapping the seasonal workers program.

美国的绿卡抽签制于1995年启动,每年发放大约5万张签证,旨在从低移民率国家吸引移民到美国。

新西兰针对太平洋岛国有两个类似于美国绿卡抽签的政策,一个针对萨摩亚群岛居民,另一个针对一些太平洋国家。报告建议,澳大利亚也可以效仿类似的绿卡抽签方式。

全球已有31个国家和澳大利亚签订了双边工作假期协议,允许本国年轻人来澳大利亚工作,但其中只有一个是太平洋岛国,即巴布亚新几内亚。自从澳巴两国2011年签订协议以来,一个签证都还没被批准过。

澳大利亚有一个专门面向太平洋岛民的季节性工作项目,试点开始于2008—2009年,共发放56张签证。

该项目发展快速,2014—2015年,签证发放数量就达到约2 800张。尽管如此,该项目和新西兰的项目相比,依旧是相形见绌,新西兰发放签证数量高达7 000多张。

澳洲移民委员会认为,应进一步扩展该项目,重点应放在二次、三次和后续签证回澳的工人身上。

②澳大利亚农业、资源经济与科学局(Abares)的研究发现,与持工作假期签证的"背包客"员工相比,来自太平洋岛国的季节性员工效率更高,产量更高。而那些连续季节性工作的员工最高效。

上个月在纽埃岛的演讲中,国际发展和太平洋事务部部长史蒂夫·斯欧伯告诉太平洋共同体的秘书长,澳大利亚会努力提高太平洋区域内的劳动力流动性,以支持该区域的经济发展,包括引进面向太平洋小国的两年制低技术工作签证,并扩展季节性工作项目。

---

dwarf vt. 使相形见绌　　　　　　uncap vt. 打开

He said 5,000 Pacific islanders were expected to participate in the seasonal work program in the coming year, a near-doubling from 2014—2015.

"The benefits of labour mobility are obvious: training and upskilling for workers, and linking people who need jobs with employers who haven't been able to source employees locally. But what is less obvious—and perhaps the most positive result of the program—is the generation of remittances, as workers send money back home."

"The average seasonal work program worker remits about \$5,000 over a six-month placement, money that is spent on housing, education, healthcare and household consumption. In some Pacific island countries remittances are greater than foreign direct investment, per-capita income, or aid flows."

On Monday Ciobo launched the Pacific humanitarian challenge, "an opportunity for businesses, organisations and individuals to come up with new ideas around how we prepare for, and respond to, natural disasters in the Pacific."

(*The Guardian*, 2015.12)

斯欧伯表示,接下来的一年内,预计有5 000名太平洋岛民将来到澳大利亚参与季节性工作项目,这差不多是2014—2015年人数的1倍。

"劳动力流动的优势显而易见:对员工意味着培训和技能的提升,并为找工作的人和在当地招不到人的雇主牵线搭桥。不那么显而易见的,但可能是项目中最大的好处是,员工把钱寄回家,产生了汇款。"

"每个季节性员工在六个月的工作期内,平均汇款5 000澳元,这笔汇款被用于住房、教育、医疗以及家庭开支等方面。在一些太平洋岛国,这些汇款甚至超过了国外直接投资、人均收入或国外援助。"

周一,斯欧伯启动了太平洋人道主义挑战项目,他表示:"这对企业、组织和个人是一个机会,关于我们应该如何准备并应对太平洋地区的自然灾害,大家可以集思广益。"

长难句解析

① 本句为主从复合句。主句的主干结构为 This drives remittances。句中 which 引导的定语从句修饰先行词 remittances;while 引导时间状语从句,该从句的主语与主句主语一致,因此省略。

> This drives remittances which help underpin economic development while allowing
> 主语　谓语　宾语　　　　　　　　定语从句　　　　　　　　时间状语从句
> (Australian) labour shortages to be addressed in industries like horticulture.

② 本句为主从复合句。句中括号里的内容 the Australian bureau of agricultural and resource economics and sciences 为 Abares 的同位语;and 连接的宾语从句1和宾语从句2 为并列结构,共同作谓语 found 的宾语。

> A study by Abares (the Australian bureau of agricultural and resource economics and sciences)
> 主语　　后置定语　　　　　　　　　同位语
> found seasonal workers from the Pacific were more efficient and productive than backpackers
> 谓语　　　　　　　　　宾语从句1
> on working holiday visas, and those working consecutive seasons were the most productive.
> 　　　　　　　　　　　　　　　宾语从句2

Text 14

Great Barrier Reef Is Becoming a "Theme Park" with Underwater Hotels and Attractions as Its Beauty Fades, Tour Operator Warns

旅游运营商警告：随着大堡礁美丽的褪色，水下酒店和旅游景点使其成了一个"主题公园"

① A tour operator has warned that Australia's Great Barrier Reef (GBR) is becoming a "theme park" as the natural wonder is increasingly opened up to development in an attempt to lure tourists.

In recent times, several attractions have been built in the GBR, including underwater statues—some of which measure up to 20 feet high—*ABC News* reported. Meanwhile, a hotel constructed on a pontoon near an island in the southern portion of the reef, which features underwater suites, is set to open in November.

"In the past, it was simply the beauty of the reef, the diverse corals and amount of fish life, and things like sharks and manta rays and whales," Tony Fontes, a dive operator in the Whitsunday Islands—which lie off Australia's northeast coast—told *ABC*.

"The tourism industry, desperate to maintain tourist numbers, is looking beyond the natural beauty of the reef because it's not quite what it was," he said. "It's just the past couple of years we're seeing the idea of a theme park coming in… statues and five-star hotels," he said.

Fontes said that the Great Barrier Reef Marine Park Authority (GBRMPA)—the government agency responsible for the care and protection of much of the reef—has drifted away from its original focus, allowing more underwater attractions.

② John Day, a former director of the GBRMPA, said that the change in direction at the organization could be attributed to a perceived need to boost tourism

---

pontoon *n.* 浮桥；平底船
look beyond 往更远处看，展望未来
manta ray 蝠鲼鱼
perceived *adj.* 察觉的；发觉的

after two severe mass bleaching events in 2016 and 2017, as well as several cyclones, caused significant damage to the reef.

In the past, the Great Barrier Reef relied very heavily on its own natural attributes to draw visitors, but unfortunately with the recent bleaching events and cyclones, some of these areas aren't looking quite as spectacular as they used to. So if we can keep tourists coming with some underwater art, as long as it's done under appropriate conditions and in a sustainable way it can enhance the tourism experience, while hopefully these areas recover and come back to what they were.

Coral reefs around the world are facing significant threats because of the impact of human activities. These threats include pollution, resource over-exploitation and unsustainable fishery practices, as well as trends linked to climate change, including ocean warming, reduced levels of oxygen in seawater and ocean acidification.

Researchers say that the two recent mass bleaching events were caused by significant spikes in water temperatures. As the world warms, so does the average temperatures of the planet's oceans, lakes and rivers, making these kinds of events more likely. While corals have a remarkable ability to recover from damaging events, research is showing that this capacity is being eroded in the face of climate change and its related impacts.

Coral reefs are incredibly important to the ocean's ecosystem. While they cover less than 1 percent of the Earth's surface, they are home to around 25 percent of known marine life and host the highest biodiversity of any ecosystem globally. Furthermore, coral reefs provide a significant benefit to the world economy, as well as several essential "natural" services.

---

bleaching *n.* 漂白法；漂白
spectacular *adj.* 壮观的
exploitation *n.* 开发；开采
spike *n.* 增加

cyclone *n.* 飓风
sustainable *adj.* 不破坏生态平衡的
acidification *n.* 酸化
erode *vt.* (逐渐地)丧失

"It has been estimated that 500 million people directly rely on coral reefs for food, resources and livelihoods, and they have an estimated economic impact of $375 billion a year," Emma Camp, from the University of Technology Sydney in Australia, told *Newsweek*. "Important ecosystem services of coral reefs include, but are not limited to: acting as natural barriers providing coastal protection, supporting fisheries, habitat for many marine species, important source of pharmaceutical compounds, cultural significance and value, part of nutrient cycling in the marine environment, and important for tourism," she said.

(*Newsweek*, 2019.9)

"据估计,有5亿人直接依靠珊瑚礁获取食物、资源和生计,且珊瑚礁每年所做的经济贡献为3 750亿美元,"澳大利亚悉尼科技大学的艾玛·坎普告诉《新闻周刊》,"珊瑚礁的重要生态系统服务包括但不限于:作为沿海保护的天然屏障;支持渔业;为许多海洋物种提供栖息地;是药类化合物的重要来源;具有文化意义和价值;构成海洋环境中养分循环的一部分;同时对旅游业起到重要作用。"

长难句解析

① 本句为主从复合句。主句的主干为 A tour operator has warned that…。that 引导的是宾语从句;as 引导原因状语从句;介词短语 in an attempt to…作目的状语。

A tour operator / has warned / that Australia's Great Barrier Reef (GBR) is becoming a "theme park" / as the natural wonder is increasingly opened up to development / in an attempt to lure tourists.
主语 / 谓语 / 宾语从句 / 原因状语从句 / 目的状语

② 本句为主从复合句。主句的主干为 John Day said that…。that 引导宾语从句;after 引导时间状语从句。

John Day, / a former director of the GBRMPA, / said / that the change in direction at the organization could be attributed to a perceived need to boost tourism / after two severe mass bleaching events in 2016 and 2017, as well as several cyclones, caused significant damage to the reef.
主语 / 同位语 / 谓语 / 宾语从句 / 时间状语从句

---

pharmaceutical *adj.* 制药的

Text 15

How Natural Resources Can Save Africa
自然资源如何能拯救非洲

It's become the go-to cliché of modern economics. Natural resources are a "curse." ① When a nation is over-reliant on one or two commodities like oil or precious minerals, corrupt government ministers and their dodgy associates hoard profits and taxes instead of properly allocating them to schools and hospitals. Happy the country that lives on nothing but its wits; cursed be the one that thinks it can get rich by planting or digging or drilling for wealth.

Such is the collective wisdom. So we must ask the collectively wise, how did the U.S. avoid the curse? And what might that tell us about other countries' chances of doing the same? When European settlers arrived in North America, they found a continent groaning with abundance—soil in which anything would grow, stands of timber marching to the horizon. Under the land were vast reserves of gold and silver, coal and oil. Over time, Americans learned how to harvest this natural endowment—not just to build a modern society but also to feed and supply the world.

The story, of course, wasn't always a happy one. The extraction of oil, coal and minerals brought, and still brings, a cost to the environment. Still, the bounty didn't and doesn't belong only to the barons. And that, unlike finding oil in your backyard, has nothing to do with luck. Americans put in place laws regulating how those resources get extracted and how good fortune gets shared.

This summer the world has a chance to work that miracle a second time—and without the worst parts of the American story. As they gather at the G-8 summit at Camp David this month and again

这已经成为现代经济的一个套路。自然资源是一个"诅咒"。①当一个国家过度依赖于一两种像石油或珍贵矿物质这样的商品时，腐败的政府官员和狡猾的同僚们就会牟取利益，而不是把它们恰当地分配给学校和医院。不靠天吃饭，只能靠头脑的国家开心了。而以为靠种植、挖掘或开采可以致富的国家却必受诅咒。

这就是集体的智慧，所以，我们必须问问那些发挥集体智慧的人，美国是如何避免这个诅咒的呢？但这又能告诉我们其他国家这么做的可能性有多大呢？当欧洲定居者到达北美的时候，他们发现了一个富饶的大陆——土壤肥沃，万物丰饶，成片的木林延伸至地平线。土地下面是大量的金、银、煤炭和石油。随着时间的推移，美国人学会了如何收获这些自然的馈赠——不只是建设现代社会，还能够哺育和供给这个世界。

诚然，这并不总是一个圆满的故事。石油、煤和矿物质的开采已经并且仍然在让环境付出巨大的代价。而且，开采的补贴并不只归少数寡头所有，过去不是，现在亦然。这和你在自家后院发现石油不一样，这与运气无关。针对这些资源如何开采和这些财富如何分配的问题，美国人制定了相关法律。

这个夏天，世界有机会再次创造奇迹——而且会避开美国经历中最糟糕的部分。本月，全球领导人齐聚戴维营参加八国峰会，六月份又将在

---

dodgy *adj.* 狡猾的　　　hoard *vt.* 贮藏　　　drill for 开采　　　groan with 布满了……
timber *n.* 木材　　　　extraction *n.* 抽取　　baron *n.* 巨头

in June at the G-20 in Mexico, international leaders focused on the euro and Iran should make time to ensure that a new resource boom benefits the many, not the few.

This new boom won't be in the U.S. It will be in developing regions like Africa. In many ways, Africa is to this century what North America was to the 19th. It has 60% of the world's undeveloped arable land and vast reserves of coal, oil and minerals, together with enormous renewable-energy resources.

Sub-Saharan Africa is also home to 400 million of the world's poorest people. These resources should be theirs. Get the development of them right and the forthcoming financial resources—invested well—can transform the lives of countless numbers of people.

Food and agriculture are the place to start. At Camp David, the G-8, led by President Obama, will work on an ambitious plan for global food security, centered on commitments made and costed by 30 nations in the developing world. By partnering with such leadership, there is a very real chance of lifting 50 million people out of extreme poverty over the coming decade and sparing 15 million children the cruelty of severe malnourishment.

This isn't about the G-8's committing massive new aid increases. It's about continuing present investment and making it smarter. Beyond food, Africa's vast oil and mineral reserves can be a pipeline to investments in health, education and roads. Mineral extraction is an expensive enterprise, and those who invest in it deserve to make a profit. But they should pay what they owe to governments. Transparency is the vaccine to prevent the biggest disease of them all—corruption, which any African will tell you is killing more kids than HIV/AIDS and malaria combined.

②That's why in 2010 the U.S. Congress passed groundbreaking legislation that requires every

---

arable *adj.* 可开垦的 spare *vt.* 免去 malnourishment *n.* 营养不良
malaria *n.* 疟疾 groundbreaking *adj.* 开创性的

extractive company listed on a U.S. stock exchange to publish any payments they make to overseas governments, project by project. That information lets Africans hold their leaders to account for the way revenue is spent.

Even oil companies will benefit: they're less likely to be criticized by those whose resources they are harvesting. But while the Securities and Exchange Commission crafts rules based on this legislation (amid lobbying by those who think it doesn't work for them), the European Union, considering its own new law, contemplates something worse. World leaders can break the logjam by backing tough rules on the transparency of payments.

In hard times, we hear a lot about "resource management." Resource mismanagement—whether food insecurity or corruption in oil and mineral development—is something the G-8 can reverse, and it can do it not by spending new money but by acting in partnership with the developing world.

If I've learned anything in more than 25 years of making noise about this stuff, it's that partnership trumps paternalism. This summer let's hope the G-8 and G-20 listen more intently to the people we hope to serve and bring the boom without the bust.

(*Time*, 2012.5)

票交易市场上的开采公司按项目公布其支付给外国政府的任何款项,这是十分具有开创性的。这一信息使非洲人民能让本国的领导人解释国家财政收入的支出情况。

甚至石油公司都会受益:他们不太可能会受到那些被收购资源的人的批评。尽管美国证券交易委员会的法规就是在这项法案上建立起来的(在那些认为该法案于自己无利的人游说期间),但是欧盟在考虑其新法律的同时,也在考虑更坏的情况。全世界的领导人可以通过在款项的透明度问题上引入严格的措施来打破这一僵局。

在困难时期,我们听说了许多关于"资源管理"的事情。资源管理不善——食物的不安全或石油及矿物质开采的腐败——都是八国峰会能够解决的,他们不用通过新的投资就能完成,但是,他们要与发展中国家合作。

我从事这类工作(为资源发声)已经超过25年,如果说我在其中学到些什么的话,那就是,伙伴关系胜过家长作风。这个夏天,让我们期盼,八国峰会或者二十国峰会能够专注地听听我们想要服务的人们的意见,为他们带去繁荣,而非萧条。

长难句解析

① 本句为主从复合句。主句的主干结构为 ministers and associates hoard profits and taxes。句中包含 when 引导的时间状语从句。

> When a nation is over-reliant on one or two commodities like oil or precious minerals,
> 时间状语从句
> corrupt government ministers and their dodgy associates hoard profits and taxes
> 　　　　　　　主语　　　　　　　　　　　　　　　　谓语　　宾语
> instead of properly allocating them to schools and hospitals.
> 　　　　　　状语

② 本句为主从复合句。句中 why 引导的表语从句作 is 的表语; that 引导的定语从句 1 修饰 legislation; 省略了关系词的定语从句 2 they make to... 修饰先行词 payments。

logjam *n.* 僵局　　　　　　　　paternalism *n.* 家长式作风

That's why in 2010 the U.S. Congress passed groundbreaking legislation that requires every extractive company listed on a U.S. stock exchange to publish any payments they make to overseas governments, project by project.

Text 16 Let the Sun Shine 让阳光闪耀

Forty-five minutes west of Las Vegas, dejected sinners may encounter a sight to lift their sunken hearts: a sea of 347,000 mirrors, reflecting the rays of the desert sun on to boilers mounted on three 460-foot towers. The Ivanpah solar-thermal plant, which opened in mid-February, is the largest of its kind in the world. Fully ramped up, it will deliver around 377 megawatts (MW) of power to 140,000 homes in southern California. Its backers compare it to the nearby Hoover Dam; an astronaut claims to have spotted it from the international space station. It is a striking sight, even if the heat from its heliostats has roasted dozens of unfortunate birds alive.

Solar power in America is growing rapidly, albeit from a small base. Last year it represented 29% of new electricity capacity, behind only natural gas at 46%. Solar output has more than doubled during Barack Obama's time in office; GTM, a research firm, reckons it will grow another 26% in 2014. The Department of Energy wants solar to provide 27% of America's electricity by 2050, up from less than 1% today.

Though dazzling, Ivanpah and large plants like it will not generate much of this growth. The federal loan guarantees that allowed their

从拉斯维加斯向西行45分钟,心情沮丧的罪人也许会因为一幅景象而心情愉悦起来:一大片由34.7万面镜子构成的镜海,将沙漠中的太阳光反射至位于3座高460英尺的塔上的锅炉上。于二月中旬开始运行的伊万帕太阳能光热电站是目前世界上最大的同类太阳能发电站。开足马力,该电厂最多可一次产生377兆瓦电量,足以供应南加州14万户家庭。该电站的投资者将其比作附近美国最高的水坝——胡佛水坝,甚至一位宇航员称在国际空间站上都能看到它。一眼望去,它是令人震撼的,尽管其定日镜上的高热量把一些不幸的鸟儿给烤死了。

美国的太阳能产业起初规模较小,但发展十分迅猛。去年,太阳能发电占新电量的29%,仅次于占比46%的天然气。奥巴马执政期间,太阳能发电量翻了不止一番。据研究公司GTM测算,太阳能发电在2014年会再度增长26%,美国能源部计划到2050年,太阳能要提供全美电量的27%,而如今只有不到1%。

尽管目前看上去形势一片大好,但伊万帕及类似的大型太阳能电站并不会有如此高的增长。联邦政府为助推其发

---

dejected *adj.* 沮丧的
heliostat *n.* 定日镜;日光反射装置

solar-thermal *adj.* 热力太阳能的
dazzling *adj.* 耀眼的

creation have expired. More important are photo voltaic solar cells, a rival technology that converts sunlight directly to electricity. Their cost has fallen so quickly that in many places retail electricity customers are saving money by placing panels on top of their houses or business; 200,000 have done so in the past two years. And there is a lot of room to grow. "There's no market saturation in any state; not even close," says Lyndon Rive of Solar-City, a solar-installation firm. Even David Crane, the boss of NRG, co-owner of Ivanpah, says that photo voltaic installations are the future.

Last year sun-soaked California accounted for over half of America's new photo voltaic installations. That, say solar fans, shows that the sector can thrive even after it loses its subsidies. (The $2.2 billion California Solar Initiative, which gave cash to homes or firms that went solar, has largely expired.) Solar is also blossoming in unexpected places like Massachusetts and North Carolina.

A bigger test will come in 2017, when the federal government's solar-investment tax credit drops from 30% to 10% (unless Mr. Obama can convince Congress otherwise). Still, says Shayle Kann at GTM, this will be no "death knell"; it will simply eliminate some marginal projects. And by then there may be a revival of Ivanpah style solar-thermal plants, as energy-storage technologies improve and utility firms look to them to provide steady power throughout the day.

Yet even if solar power is a boon to consumers, it threatens some utilities. Energy has traditionally been generated centrally, distributed over power lines and sold to consumers. Distributed solar power—generated from rooftop panels—undermines that model. The Edison Electric Institute (EEI), a trade group, warns that distributed generation could do to energy companies what the internet did to newspapers.

---

expire *vi.* 期满

knell *n.* 丧钟声

photo voltaic solar cells 光伏太阳能电池

boon *n.* 恩惠

Bet your bottom dollar

Regulations are adapting to this shift: all but seven states have adopted net-metering policies, which credit solar-enabled homes and businesses for the excess energy they feed back into the grid. At least 22 states allow consumers to buy the electricity produced by solar panels that a third party installs on their homes. This lets people take advantage of solar's savings without having to pay the hefty up-front installation costs. In 2013, third-party-owned systems accounted for most solar installations in California, Arizona, Colorado and Massachusetts.

Some utilities grumble that customers who benefit from net metering escape the costs of maintaining the grid they depend on. ①Last year Arizona Public Service, the state's biggest electric firm, urged regulators to slash the savings that new solar customers would derive from net metering. After a fierce campaign their call was rejected, though the regulator approved a small solar surcharge. Georgia Power also proposed a fat tariff; it too was defeated.

Julia Hamm of the Solar Electric Power Association identifies three ways regulators could help utilities cope with these changes. First, they could demand monthly infrastructure fees from solar users. Second, they could list every component of value separately rather than wrap the cost of infrastructure maintenance, for instance, into usage charges. Third, they could split energy used and consumed into separate transactions, meaning that a solar customer sells all his energy to a utility before buying what he needs.

②Yet those last two proposals leave unanswered the question of what rate utilities should pay customers for their power—or more broadly, what the price of solar, with all externalities factored in, ought to be. And more battles loom; California's regulator must make an important

---

net-metering *adj.* 净计量电价的   hefty *adj.* 异常大的   up-front *adj.* 预先的
grumble *vt.* 抱怨   surcharge *n.* 额外费用   wrap *vt.* 包;覆盖

decision on net metering this month. Further ahead the growth of distributed solar will pose other threats to the utilities' traditional business model. "Net metering is just the pointy edge of the wedge," says Adam Browning of Vote Solar, an advocacy group.

Still, while user-generated solar power makes utilities skittish, many have rushed to embrace it on the supply side. In 2013 they installed roughly 4,100MW of solar capacity, up from 2,390MW in 2012. Renewable portfolio standards, which in 30 states force utilities to generate a certain share of their electricity from clean sources, are part of the reason. But so is hard economics: low installation and labour costs, clean power delivery at peak midday hours and a hedge against fuel-price volatility.

Many of these gains have already been banked. ③ Photo voltaic modules have become slightly dearer lately; costs will rise further if the Commerce Department heeds protectionist calls by some domestic manufacturers and expands tariffs on imports from China. Yet solar firms are not short of ideas to cut costs elsewhere: third-party financing, for example, or securitising pools of solar leases to reduce financing costs. For makers and users of solar power, the future looks bright.

(*The Economist*, 2014.10)

就净计量电价做出一项重要的决定。太阳能产业布局的进一步扩张将对公共事业公司的传统商业模式造成其他方面的威胁。"净计量电价政策行走在危险的边缘。"来自游说团体 Vote Solar 的亚当·布朗宁说道。

尽管用户可自行产生太阳能导致诸多公共事业公司坐立难安，但也有很多公共事业公司敏锐地顺时应势，在供应链上寻找商机。2013 年，他们安装的太阳能发电板所发的电量由 2012 年的 2 390 兆瓦上升到将近 4 100 兆瓦。30 个州的可再生能源配额制要求公共事业公司发电量中的一部分必须要来自清洁能源，这也是部分原因。但硬经济也是如此，因为这些公司既要压缩安装和人力成本，又要在中午用电高峰时保障清洁电力的供应，同时还需要兼顾燃料价格浮动的对冲。

太阳能产业的不少优惠可能已经走到尾声。③ 近来，光伏组件的价格小幅上涨，如果商务部应允了国内部分制造商的保护主义呼吁，并且对来自中国的进口光伏产品加大关税的话，只怕成本会进一步上涨。然而，太阳能公司也不会坐以待毙，他们会通过其他方式来削减成本，比如，第三方融资，或通过太阳能租赁证券化来降低融资成本。对于太阳能制造商和用户来说，前景依旧是一片光明。

长难句解析

① 本句为主从复合句。主句的主干结构为 Arizona Public Service urged regulators。句中 the state's biggest electric firm 作 Arizona Public Service 的同位语；that 引导的定语从句修饰先行词 savings。

Last year	Arizona Public Service,	the state's biggest electric firm,	urged	regulators
时间状语	主语	同位语	谓语	宾语

to slash the savings that new solar customers would derive from net metering.
宾语补足语 — 定语从句

---

advocacy group 游说团体　　　　securitise *vt.* 使……证券化　　　　lease *n.* 租赁

② 本句为主从复合句。主句的主干结构为 two proposals leave unanswered the question。其中 unanswered 作宾语 the question 的补足语，因为宾语后面的定语太长，为了保持句子平衡，故将 unanswered 提前。介宾结构 of...为 the question 的后置定语，两个 what 引导的宾语从句作介词 of 的宾语，主干结构是 what rate utilities should pay customers or what the price ought to be。

Yet those last two proposals leave unanswered the question of what rate utilities should
　　　主语　　　　　　　谓语　宾语补足语　宾语　　后置定语　　　宾语从句1
pay customers for their power—or more broadly, what the price of solar, with all externalities
　　　　　　　　　　　　　　状语　　　　宾语从句2　　　　　　插入语
factored in, ought to be.
　　　　　宾语从句2

③ 本句为并列复合句，由分号隔开。分号前的单句为主系表结构；分号后的单句为主谓结构，其中包含一个 if 引导的条件状语从句，该从句中包含两个并列的谓语，由 and 连接，主语均为 the Commerce Department。

Photo voltaic modules have become slightly dearer lately; costs will rise further
　　　主语1　　　　　　系动词　　　　　表语　　状语1 主语2 谓语　状语2
if the Commerce Department heeds protectionist calls by some domestic manufacturers and
　　　　　　　　　　　　　　　条件状语从句
expands tariffs on imports from China.

第六部分 医疗健康类

SECTION SIX

Text 1

Low-Fiber Diets Cause Waves of Extinction in the Gut
低纤维饮食习惯引起肠道微生物一波接一波的灭绝

In the decades after World War II, a one-eyed Irish missionary-surgeon named Denis Burkitt moved to Uganda, where he noted that the villagers there ate far more fiber than Westerners did. This didn't just bulk up their stools, Burkitt reasoned; it also explained their low rates of heart disease, colon cancer, and other chronic illnesses. "America is a constipated nation," he once said. "If you pass small stools, you have big hospitals."

"Burkitt really nailed it," says Justin Sonnenburg, a microbiologist at Stanford University. Sure, some of the man's claims were far-fetched, but he was right about the value of fiber and the consequences of avoiding it. And Sonnenburg thinks he knows why: Fiber doesn't just feed us—it also feeds the trillions of microbes in our guts.

Fiber is a broad term that includes many kinds of plant carbohydrates that we cannot digest. Our microbes can, though, and they break fiber into chemicals that nourish our cells and reduce inflammation. But no single microbe can tackle every kind of fiber. They specialize, just as every antelope in the African savannah munches on its own favored type of grass or shoot. ①This means that a fiber-rich diet can nourish a wide variety of gut microbes and, conversely, that a low-fiber diet can only sustain a narrower community.

---

fiber *n.* 纤维
colon cancer 结肠癌
gut *n.* 肠道

bulk up 增加；胀大
constipated *adj.* 患便秘症的
inflammation *n.* 发炎

stool *n.* 粪便
far-fetched *adj.* 牵强的

Sonnenburg, his wife Erica, and the graduate student Samuel Smits confirmed this idea in a recent experiment. The researchers started with mice that had been raised in sterile bubbles and then loaded with identical collections of gut microbes. They then fed these mice a high-fiber diet, before randomly switching half of them to low-fiber chow for seven weeks.

Predictably, the fall in fiber caused upheavals in the rodents' guts. In the low-fiber group, the numbers of 60 percent of the local microbe species fell dramatically, and some remained low even after the mice returned to high-fiber meals. Those seven low-fiber weeks left lingering scars on the animals' microbiomes.

These scars can cascade through generations. Mice regularly eat each others' poop, and pups often pick up their parents' microbes in this way. ② Indeed, when Sonnenburg and Smits bred the mice from their first experiment, they saw that low-fiber parents gave birth to pups with narrower microbiomes, which lacked species present in the progeny of high-fiberparents. And if these bacteria-impoverished pups also ate low-fiber food, they lost even more microbes, especially those from the fiber-busting bacteroidales group. As four generations ticked by, the rodents' guts became progressively less diverse, as more and more species blinked out.

It also became increasingly hard to reverse these changes. If the fourth-generation mice switched to high-fiber meals, some of the missing microbes rebounded, but most did not. In other words, these species weren't just lying in wait in small numbers, waiting for the chance to bloom again; they had genuinely vanished. The only way of restoring these missing microbes was through a fecal transplant —

---

sterile bubbles 无菌泡,此处引申为"无菌环境"之意　　　chow n. 食物
rodent n. 啮齿动物　　　microbiome n. 微生物组　　　poop n. 粪便
pup n. 幼小动物　　　bacteroidales n. 拟杆菌目
fecal transplant 粪便移植,全称 fecal microbiota transplantation (FMT),是一种通过重建肠道菌群来治疗疾病的方法

loading them with the entire gut microbiomes of rodents that had always eaten a high-fiber diet.

These changes parallel those that have taken place over the course of human history. Many studies have now shown that the gut microbiomes of western city-dwellers are less diverse than those of rural villagers and hunter-gatherers, who eat more plants and thus more fiber. ③ The Stanford researchers' experiment hints (but doesn't confirm) that this low diversity could be a lasting legacy of industrialization, in which successive generations of low-fiber meals have led to the loss of old bacterial companions. "The data we present also hint that further deterioration of the Western microbiota is possible," the team writes.

"Given the infancy of the microbiome field, I think it is difficult to determine what specific impacts the loss of microbiota diversity has on the host," says Kelly Swanson, a nutritional-science professor at the University of Illinois at Urbana-Champaign. "But I think this paper provides even more evidence for including an adequate amount of dietary fiber in the diet." For context, dietary guidelines recommend that women and men should respectively eat around 25 and 38 grams of fiber per day, but American adults eat just 15 daily grams on average.

This could be problematic for two reasons. First, without fiber, starving microbes often turn their attention to similar molecules, including those in the mucus layer that covers the gut. If they erode this layer sufficiently, they might be able to enter the lining of the gut itself, triggering immune reactions that lead to chronic inflammation .

Second, there's evidence that a diverse microbiome can better resist invasive species like Salmonella or Clostridium difficile , while low diversity is a common feature of obesity, inflammatory bowel disease, and other conditions.

---

hint vt. 暗示
mucus n. 黏液
invasive adj. 侵入的
deterioration n. 恶化
erode vt. 损害；腐蚀
difficile adj. 难对付的
infancy n. 初期
chronic inflammation 慢性炎症

Still, no one has shown that a less-diverse microbiome is the cause of the health problems associated with low fiber intake. This means that it's premature to talk about supplementing our microbiomes with those from communities that eat more fiber. Sonnenburg's team writes, "It is possible that rewilding the modern microbiota with extinct species may be necessary to restore evolutionarily important functionality to our gut." Sure, but first, they'd need to show if the microbial losses in their experiments matter, and to what degree.

After all, the diversity of the human microbiome has been falling long before industrialization. Even the rich gut communities of hunter-gatherers are a pale reflection of those of chimps and gorillas, whose diets are even richer in plants. The point is that animals tend to end up with the microbiomes they need; as our needs and habits change, so does our pool of partners.

Sonnenburg's concern is that these changes play out over millennia, and hosts and microbes have time to acclimate to their new relationships. By contrast, our modern diets and lifestyles are changing our microbiomes very quickly, leaving us with communities that we haven't adjusted to. "Our human genome is constantly trying to keep up with this moving target of a microbial community," he says. "If there are times when changes are exceptionally rapid, it might be problematic for host health."

(*The Atlantic*, 2016.1)

然而，没有证据显示，较低的微生物群多样性是某些健康问题的诱因，而这些健康问题与低纤维摄入量有关。这意味着，用摄入纤维量较高的群体的微生物群来补充我们肠道中的微生物群，这样的提议还为时尚早。松嫩堡的团队写道："也许有必要用已经消失的微生物菌种来野化现代的微生物，从而在我们的肠道中修复进化意义上具有重要功能的微生物。"当然，最重要的是，他们需要在实验中证明，丧失的微生物是否会产生影响，以及这一影响的程度。

毕竟，早在工业化之前，人类肠道内微生物群的多样性已经处于下降之中。虽然狩猎采集者的肠道内拥有丰富的微生物群，但还是比黑猩猩和大猩猩的肠道微生物群少多了，它们的膳食中甚至包含更丰富的植物种类。关键问题是，所有动物最后拥有的微生物群往往是它们所必需的；而随着人类需求和习惯的改变，我们也将如此。

松嫩堡担心，这些改变将花费上千年的时间，宿主和微生物也需要时间来适应他们的新关系。相比之下，现代饮食和生活方式正在快速改变着人类体内的微生物群，我们还并未建立起对体内微生物群的适应性。"人类的基因组正在不停地试图追赶不断变化的微生物群目标，"他说，"如果菌群变化异常迅速的话，宿主就可能产生健康问题。"

长难句解析

① 本句为主从复合句。主句的主干结构为 This means that... and that...；宾语是由 and 连接的两个 that 从句；副词 conversely 作状语。

This means	that a fiber-rich diet can nourish a wide variety of gut microbes	and, conversely,
主语 谓语	宾语从句1	状语
that a low-fiber diet can only sustain a narrower community.		
宾语从句2		

---

gorilla *n.* 大猩猩　　　　　　　　　　genome *n.* 基因组

② 本句为主从复合句。主句的主干结构为 they saw that...；宾语是一个 that 引导的从句；which 引导的非限制性定语从句修饰 pups。

Indeed, when Sonnenburg and Smits bred the mice from their first experiment, they saw that low-fiber parents gave birth to pups with narrower microbiomes, which lacked species present in the progeny of high-fiber parents.
- 状语：Indeed
- 时间状语从句：when Sonnenburg and Smits bred the mice from their first experiment
- 主语：they；谓语：saw
- 宾语从句：that low-fiber parents gave birth to pups with narrower microbiomes
- 非限制性定语从句：which lacked species present in the progeny of high-fiber parents

③ 本句为主从复合句。主句的主干结构为 The experiment hints (but doesn't confirm) that...；宾语是 that 引导的从句；in which 引导的非限制性定语从句修饰 industrialization。

The Stanford researchers' experiment hints (but doesn't confirm) that this low diversity could be a lasting legacy of industrialization, in which successive generations of low-fiber meals have led to the loss of old bacterial companions.
- 主语：The Stanford researchers' experiment
- 谓语：hints (but doesn't confirm)
- 宾语从句：that this low diversity could be a lasting legacy of industrialization
- 非限制性定语从句：in which successive generations of low-fiber meals have led to the loss of old bacterial companions

Text 2 For Toilets, Money Matters
对于厕所来说，钱比较重要

When nature calls, about 1 billion people in the developing world still head to an open field, the bushes, or a body of water to defecate. The practice has contributed to high rates of diarrheal diseases, especially in India, where more than half of people don't use latrines. Prime Minister Narendra Modi, who took power last May, has pledged to build 111 million toilets as part of the Clean India mission, a sanitation campaign. One goal is to end open defecation by October 2019.

But exactly how to get there is surprisingly controversial. Some nongovernmental organizations and government officials in developing countries have long pushed for education campaigns—teaching

在发展中国家，大约有 10 亿人仍在田地、丛林甚至水塘边解决内急。这种习惯导致了腹泻的高发病率，尤其是在印度，一半以上的人不使用厕所。去年 5 月上台的总理纳伦德拉·莫迪承诺修建 1.11 亿个厕所，作为"清洁印度"这一卫生运动的一部分。其中一大目标就是在 2019 年 10 月之前终结露天排泄行为。

但是如何达到这个目标存在着很大的争议。一些发展中国家的非政府机构和政府官员一直推行教育宣传活动——来告诉人们使用厕所

---

defecate vi. 排便　　diarrheal adj. 腹泻的　　latrine n. 厕所　　sanitation n. 公共卫生

people about the health benefits of using toilets. ①Others advocate subsidizing latrine costs for the poor, but some economists argue that financial aid for cheap toilets could backfire by discouraging those who don't receive it from buying latrines on their own for a higher price.

Now, one of the largest controlled experiments to examine sanitation strategies, conducted in India's neighbor Bangladesh and published online this week in *Science*, comes down strongly in favor of cash. After comparing three policies in more than 100 villages, the authors found that the key to getting people to build latrines is to subsidize the cost. They also found that funding poor villagers to install latrines can encourage their unsubsidized neighbors to follow suit in a beneficial spillover effect.

"Given the enormous emphasis Prime Minister Modi has placed on eliminating open defecation in India, these results should be of great interest to the Indian government. It tells us that cutting the price of quality toilets is the single most powerful instrument in getting people to stop defecating outside," says economist Abhijit Banerjee of the Massachusetts Institute of Technology in Cambridge, who was not involved in the study. ②Others caution, however, that building toilets doesn't always mean people will use them or be healthier, or that findings in Bangladesh will be relevant to culturally different India.

The experiment, funded by the Bill & Melinda Gates Foundation in Seattle, Washington, took place in the Tanore, a poor, rural district in northwest Bangladesh. Although open defecation rates are only 3% overall in Bangladesh, in Tanore, about one-third of adults still follow the practice or use unhygienic latrines, such as "hanging" latrines that empty into waterways. Yale University economists Mushfiq Mobarak and James Levinsohn and Raymond Guiteras of the University of Maryland, College Park, chose 107 villages with 18,254 poor households. Some villages received education on the

---

install *vt.* 安装　　　spillover effect 溢出效应　　　unhygienic *adj.* 不卫生的

importance of sanitation, and some received only information on buying and installing a latrine. In a third program, 25% to 75% of villagers received vouchers through a lottery. Each voucher was good for about 50% off the $29 to $58 cost of an installed pour flush latrine—a design that carries feces to a sealed pit.

The vouchers made all the difference, the researchers found 13 months later. Education alone or information on how to acquire a latrine did not significantly increase the portion of people who owned or had access to a hygienic latrine. But education plus vouchers resulted in significant change—for example, a rise in hygienic latrine ownership from 22% in the control group to 45% in villages where half the households received vouchers and education. The study also found a reduction of 14% in open defecation in these same villages.

The big surprise was that even people who didn't receive a voucher were more inclined to buy a latrine at full price if their neighbors received vouchers. This effect was stronger when a higher proportion of households received vouchers. People were also more likely to use their vouchers in neighborhoods where more households received vouchers. For policymakers, the message is clear, Mobarak says: "If you are going to use subsidies, it makes sense to allocate them in a coordinated manner so that many people in a community all get subsidies jointly."

③Varad Pande, an economist with the Dalberg consulting firm in Mumbai, India, who has advised the Indian government and the World Bank about sanitation policies, says the results "resonate with our experience on the ground. ... Both (subsidies and education) need to happen in a well-orchestrated sequence." To Sumeet Patil, an epidemiologist and economist with the Network for Engineering and Economics Research and Management in Mumbai, the result should settle the debate over toilet subsidies.

allocate *vt.* 分配

But others say an encouraging result in Bangladesh may not say much about India, where the hygiene problem is much bigger. ④A survey released last year by the Research Institute for Compassionate Economics (RICE) in New Delhi found that many Indians who have access to a hygienic latrine still prefer open defecation, particularly Hindus, who were not represented in the Bangladesh study. The reasons may involve Hindu caste system beliefs that allowing feces to accumulate in a latrine is impure and that only an "untouchable" can remove them, says RICE.

Executive Director Dean Spears adds: "I would just say we should be very careful about generalizing to Hindu rural north India."

(*Science*, 2015.4)

但是其他人认为孟加拉国的喜人结果可能并不适用于印度,因为印度存在更为严重的卫生问题。④新德里的慈悲经济研究所去年公布的调查结果表明,许多印度人即便有卫生的厕所可供使用,他们仍会选择随地排便,尤其是印度教徒,而这类人群在孟加拉国的调研中并不存在。慈悲经济研究所解释道,或许因为印度教的种姓制度持有一种信仰,他们认为把排泄物堆积在厕所是肮脏的,只有"贱民"才会去移除它们。

执行官迪恩·斯皮尔斯补充到,"我只是想说,将政策普及到印度教徒聚居的印度北部农村地区时,我们应该尤为小心谨慎。"

长难句解析

① 本句为并列复合句。but 前句子的主干结构为 Others advocate subsidizing…;but 后句子的主干结构为 some economists argue that…,其中,that 从句作 argue 的宾语,其主干结构是 financial aid could backfire;by 引导的方式状语中含有一个 who 引导的定语从句,来修饰先行词 those。

Others	advocate	subsidizing latrine costs for the poor,	but	some economists	argue
主语1	谓语1	宾语1		主语2	谓语2

that financial aid for cheap toilets could backfire by discouraging those who don't receive it
　　宾语2(宾语从句)　　　　　　　　　方式状语　　　　　　定语从句
from buying latrines on their own for a higher price.

② 本句为主从复合句。主句的主干结构为 Others caution that…or that…;转折副词 however 作状语;caution 后有两个 that 引导的宾语从句,由逗号和 or 连接而成;caution 的第一个宾语从句的主干结构为 building toilets doesn't mean…,后面是一个省略了 that 的宾语从句;caution 的第二个宾语从句的主干结构为 findings will be relevant to India。

Others	caution,	however,	that building toilets doesn't always mean	people will use them
主语	谓语	状语	宾语从句1	宾语从句2

or be healthier, or that findings in Bangladesh will be relevant to culturally different India.
　　　　　　　　　　　　　　　　　宾语从句3

③ 本句为主从复合句。主句的主干结构为 Varad Pande says…;says 之后的宾语从句前省略了 that;同位语解释说明主语的身份;who 引导的定语从句同样修饰主语,其中包含两个并列宾语。

---

hygiene n. 卫生　　　　　　　　　　generalize vi. 普及

Varad Pande, an economist with the Dalberg consulting firm in Mumbai, India, who has advised the Indian government and the World Bank about sanitation policies, says the results "resonate with our experience on the ground."

（主语 / 同位语 / 非限制性定语从句 / 谓语 / 宾语从句）

④ 本句为主从复合句。主句的主干结构为 A survey found that…；主语后面的定语是一个"动词过去分词+方式状语+地点状语"构成的结构；宾语从句的主干结构为 many Indians prefer defecation，其中 who 引导的定语从句修饰 Indians；particularly Hindus 起补充说明的作用，后面有 who 引导的定语从句修饰 Hindus。

A survey released last year by the Research Institute for Compassionate Economics (RICE) in New Delhi found that many Indians who have access to a hygienic latrine still prefer open defecation, particularly Hindus, who were not represented in the Bangladesh study.

（主语 / 后置定语 / 谓语 / 宾语从句 / 定语从句1 / 宾语从句 / 补语 / 定语从句2）

Text 3　Warning to New Yorkers: There's a Lot of Salt in That
给纽约人敲响警钟：这些食物里盐过多

New Yorkers picking up a quick meal could begin to see a black triangle with a white salt shaker pictured next to some menu items. ① A new rule from the New York City Department of Health and Mental Hygiene goes into effect Tuesday, requiring establishments that are part of chains with 15 or more locations nationally to mark dishes that contain 2,300 milligrams (about a teaspoon) or more of sodium.

"With the high sodium warning label, New Yorkers will have easily accessible information that can affect their health," Health Commissioner Dr. Mary Bassett said in September, after the Board of

纽约人一拿起快餐就可以看到某些菜单项旁边有一个黑色三角形和白色盐瓶的图片。①纽约市卫生与心理健康局的一项新规定将于周二生效，要求全国范围内拥有15个及以上的连锁店的商业机构需要在钠含量2 300 毫克（约一茶匙）或更高的食品上予以标明。

卫生局一致通过了钠警示标签后，卫生专员玛丽·巴塞特博士9月如是说道，"有了高钠警告标签，纽约人将更易于获取那些会影响健康的

---

chain n. 连锁店　　　　milligram n. 毫克　　　　sodium n. 钠

Health unanimously adopted the resolution on sodium warning labels. The board had published its intention to make the change in June and held a public hearing the following month.

"We're talking about a leading cause of death here," Bassett added at a news conference Monday held at an Applebee's restaurant in Time Square.

A sign with the following statement needs to be visibly posted in addition to the icons appearing next to specific items: "Warning: This icon indicates that the sodium (salt) content of this item is higher than the total daily recommended limit (2,300 mg). High sodium intake can increase blood pressure and risk of heart disease and stroke." Violators of the new rule stand to incur a $200 fine, though the city will reportedly not begin to issue fines until March.

In its notice about the amendment, the Department of Health and Mental Hygiene cited cardiovascular disease as the leading cause of death in New York City—responsible for 17,000 deaths in 2013—and hypertension (high blood pressure) as a major risk factor for heart disease and stroke, as the required warning states.

②Though that 2,300 mg cutoff comes from the maximum recommended daily sodium intake, the "Dietary Guidelines for Americans 2010" says that a lot of people should consume even less, or a daily limit of 1,500 mg (the guidelines cite groups including people 51 years old and up, African Americans and those with hypertension, diabetes or chronic kidney disease). The American Heart Association reduced its own recommended limit from 2,300 mg to 1,500 mg in 2010.

Still, Americans tend to eat more than the recommended daily limit regularly—around 3,400 mg of sodium per day, according to the Centers for Disease Control and Prevention. For New Yorkers,

---

信息。"该部门曾公开声明打算在6月时实施该计划,并于接下来的一个月举行公开听证会。

巴塞特在上周一的新闻发布会上补充说,"我们正在谈论死亡的首要原因。"这场发布会在时代广场的阿普勒比餐厅举行。

除了特定项目旁边显示的图标外,还需明显地张贴具有以下语句的标志:"警告:此图标表示,该项目的钠(盐)含量大于每日推荐总量限定值(2 300毫克)。高钠摄入会增加高血压、心脏疾病和中风的风险。"尽管据报道,在纽约,直到3月份才会开始开罚单,但到时一旦违反新规则,将会被处以200美元罚款。

在其关于修正案的公告中,健康与心理卫生署援引了心脑血管疾病作为纽约市民死亡的首要原因——2013年,有1.7万人死于心脑血管疾病——高血压(血压高)也是引起心脏疾病和中风的主要危险因素,正如所需的警告所述。

②虽然推荐每日钠的最大摄入量为2 300毫克,"2010年美国膳食指南"显示,一大部分人应该消耗更少,或最多1 500毫克(该准则包括年龄在51岁及以上的人群、非裔美国人和那些有高血压、糖尿病或慢性肾脏疾病的人群)。美国心脏协会在2010年降低原先建议的上限,从2 300毫克降至1 500毫克。

尽管如此,根据美国疾病控制和预防中心的调查显示,美国人每日的钠摄入量往往比推荐的量要多——每日约有3 400毫克的钠摄入量。纽

---

unanimously adv. 无异议地　　hearing n. 听证会　　recommended limit 推荐标准
stroke n. 中风　　　　　　　hypertension n. 高血压　dietary guideline 膳食指南
kidney n. 肾脏

the number is slightly lower—the health department cites a study that found the city's residents consumed an average of 3,239 mg daily in 2010—but that still means that more than 80 percent of participants went over their recommended limit.

③ The Health Department also pointed to a study that found a 23 percent increase in the average sodium content of items from eight leading fast-food chains between 1997 and 2010, and another that found that a third of the sodium Americans consume is from food in restaurants.

How much sodium is in some fast food favorites?

At Chipotle, a burrito with chicken, white rice, black beans, fresh tomato salsa, cheese and guacamole runs 2,380 mg. Add a side of chips and fresh tomato salsa, and the count goes up to a total of 3,300 mg.

A McDonald's hamburger has 490 mg of sodium, but upgrade to a double quarter pounder with cheese and that's 1,310 mg. A bacon clubhouse burger has 1,480 mg. A big breakfast with hotcakes (regular sized biscuit) runs 2,010 mg.

At Applebee's, several menu items exceed the maximum daily recommended sodium intake, including the chicken quesadilla (2,800 mg), the cedar grilled lemon chicken (2,480 mg), the American BLT (2,610 mg) and the salsa verde pulled pork nachos (4,890 mg).

According to the Health Department's website, New York is "the first city in the nation to require chain restaurants to post warning labels next to menu items that contain high levels of sodium."

New York City has previously amended its health code to phase out the use of artificial trans fat at food establishments throughout the city and to require restaurants with 15 or more locations to post calorie counts on menu items. An attempt by former mayor Michael Bloomberg to ban sugary drinks in

---

burrito n. 墨西哥卷饼 guacamole n. 鳄梨色拉酱 quesadilla n. 玉米饼
sugary drink 含糖饮料

containers larger than 16 ounces was ultimately rejected by the New York State Court of Appeals.

Not everyone is pleased about the city's latest move. "Every one of these cumbersome new laws makes it tougher and tougher for restaurants to find success," New York State Restaurant Association President Melissa Fleischut said when the amendment was passed.

But Zane Tankel, CEO of Apple Metro, the New York metropolitan area franchisee for Applebee's, took the new rule in stride. "We got in front of it simply because you gotta do it," he said at the news conference Monday.

(*Newsweek*, 2015.12)

但最终被纽约州法院驳回。

不是每个人都对这个城市的最新举措感到欢喜。"这些新法律太烦琐,使得餐馆的经营越来越难成功。"当该修正案获得通过时,纽约州餐馆协会主席梅丽莎·佛雷舒特如是说。

但苹果地铁站餐馆(阿普勒比纽约大都会地区的加盟商)的首席执行官赞恩·坦克尔从容应付新规则。"我们正面它仅仅是因为我们必须这样做。"他在星期一的新闻发布会上说。

长难句解析

① 本句为主从复合句。主句的主干结构为 A rule goes into effect;from 介宾短语作后置定语修饰主语;定语从句1修饰 establishments;定语从句2修饰 dishes。

A new rule from the New York City Department of Health and Mental Hygiene
主语　　　　　　　　　　　　后置定语
goes into effect Tuesday, requiring establishments that are part of chains with
　谓语　宾语　时间状语　伴随状语　　间接宾语　　　　　定语从句1
15 or more locations nationally to mark dishes that contain 2,300 milligrams
　　　　　　　　　　　　　直接宾语　　　　定语从句2
(about a teaspoon) or more of sodium.

② 本句为主从复合句。主句的主干结构为 the "Dietary Guidelines" says that…;that 引导的宾语从句作 says 的宾语;括号中的内容为补语,补充说明主语 the "Dietary Guidelines for Americans 2010" 的背景,其主干为 the guidelines cite groups。

Though that 2,300 mg cutoff comes from the maximum recommended daily sodium
　　　　　　　　让步状语从句
intake, the "Dietary Guidelines for Americans 2010" says that a lot of people should
　　　　　　主语　　　　　　　　　　　谓语　　宾语从句
consume even less, or a daily limit of 1,500 mg (the guidelines cite groups including
　　　　　　　　　　　　　　　　　　　　　　　补语
people 51 years old and up, African Americans and those with hypertension, diabetes
or chronic kidney disease).

③ 本句为主从复合句。主句的主干结构为 The Health Department pointed to a study and another,其中含有两个由 and 连接的并列宾语;定语从句1修饰宾语 a study;定语从句2修饰 another (study),该从句中还嵌套了一个 that 引导的宾语从句作 found 的宾语。

The Health Department also pointed to a study that found a 23 percent increase in the average sodium content of items from eight leading fast-food chains between 1997 and 2010, and another that found that a third of the sodium Americans consume is from food in restaurants.

Text 4

American Red Cross Offering Amazon Gift Card in Exchange for Critically Needed Blood Donations
美国红十字会急需献血，用亚马逊礼品卡作交换

The American Red Cross has issued an emergency call for donations due to a "critical blood shortage" of all blood types. ①The aid organization is even throwing in a $5 Amazon gift card to anyone who donates blood in the next 30 days.

There have been about 56,000 fewer donations made in the last two months than is needed, severely affecting the Red Cross blood supply, the Red Cross said in a statement. Blood shortages tend to occur during the summer, particularly near Independence Day.

② "It's crucial that people donate now to meet the needs of patients every day and to be prepared for emergencies that require significant volumes of donated blood," Red Cross Blood Services communications director Nick Gehrig said. "Every day, blood and platelet donors can help save lives, and right now those heroes are needed to give as soon as possible."

The Red Cross noted that summer months are challenging times for blood and platelet donations due to summer activities, vacations and fewer

因所有血型的"严重血荒"，美国红十字会已发布献血紧急号召。①该救助组织甚至还向在未来30天内献血的人赠送价值5美元的亚马逊礼品卡。

过去两个月的献血次数比需求量少5.6万，严重影响了红十字会的血液供应，红十字会在一次声明中说到。"血荒"往往发生在夏季，尤其是接近独立日时。

红十字会血液服务外联主任尼克·格里克说："②现在人们为满足患者每日所需而献血，并为需要大量献血的紧急情况做准备是至关重要的。每天，血液和血小板捐献者都可以帮助拯救生命，而现在这些英雄需要尽快捐献。"

红十字会指出由于各种活动、假期，以及献血活动较少，夏季是血液和血小板捐献的艰难时期。在7月9日

---

throw in 免费赠送
platelet n. [组织] 血小板

meet the need of 满足……的需要

blood drives. In a statement released on July 9, Chris Hrouda, president of Red Cross Blood Services, called on both new and current blood donors to make an appointment to donate.

"Unlike many other lifesaving medical treatments, blood donations cannot be manufactured and stockpiled," Hrouda said. "Red blood cells have a shelf-life of only 42 days and platelets just five days—Each donation, each day makes a difference."

Anyone 17 years or older, who weighs at least 110 pounds and is in generally good health, is eligible to donate blood. There are a few types of blood donations, including whole blood donations, power red donation—a concentrated dose of red cells—platelet donation and AB elite plasma donation. Donations can take a minimum of one hour and as long as three hours.

According to the Red Cross, blood and platelets are needed every two seconds in the United States. These donations are used in patient emergencies, during heart surgery and organ transplants, as well as for patients undergoing treatment for cancer, leukemia or sickle cell disease.

There are several ways to schedule an appointment to donate blood. The Red Cross allows donors to schedule their next donation using the free Blood Donor App, by visiting redcrossblood.org or by calling 1-800-RED CROSS (1-800-733-2767).

Those who donate between July 30 and August 30 will receive a $5 Amazon gift card via email. Donors are encouraged to fill out a RapidPass online health history questionnaire to reduce the time it takes to donate.

(*Newsweek*, 2018.8)

发布的一份声明中，红十字会血液服务部主席克里斯·赫鲁达号召未献过血和献过血的人预约献血。

"与许多其他的救生医疗措施不同，献血所得血液不能被制造和大量储备，"赫鲁达说，"红细胞的保质期只有42天，而血小板只有5天——每一次捐献，每一天都有着不同的含义。"

年龄在17岁及以上、体重至少110磅且身体健康的人都有资格献血。献血有几种类型，包括全血捐献、成分血（浓缩的红细胞）捐献、血小板捐献和AB精英血浆捐献。整个献血过程持续1到3个小时不等。

根据红十字会的说法，在美国，每两秒就有人需要血液和血小板。这些捐赠血液被用于病人急救，如心脏手术和器官移植，以及正在接受癌症、白血病或者镰状细胞病治疗的患者。

预约献血有几种方法。捐赠者可通过访问 redcrossblood.org 或者拨打 1-800-RED CROSS（1-800-733-2767）使用免费的应用程序"献血者"来安排下一次的捐献。

7月30日至8月30日之间的献血者可通过邮件获得价值5美元的亚马逊礼品卡。美国红十字会鼓励捐赠者填写一个RapidPass在线健康历史问卷，以减少献血所需的时间。

---

blood drive 献血活动
eligible *adj.* 合格的
leukemia *n.* 白血病

stockpile *vt.* 大量储备
concentrated *adj.* 浓缩的
sickle cell 镰状细胞

shelf-life *n.* 保质期
plasma *n.* 血浆

长难句解析

① 本句为主从复合句。主句的主干结构为 The aid organization is throwing in a gift card to...。其中 who 引导定语从句修饰 anyone。

The aid organization | is | even throwing in a $5 Amazon gift card | to anyone who donates blood in the next 30 days.
主语　　　系动词　　　表语　　　宾语
定语从句

② 本句为主从复合句。主句的主干结构为 It's crucial that...。It 为形式主语,真正的主语是第一个 that 引导的主语从句;第二个 that 引导定语从句修饰 emergencies。

It's crucial | that people donate now to meet the needs of patients every day
形式主语+系动词+表语　　　真正的主语
and to be prepared for emergencies that require significant volumes of donated blood.
定语从句

Text 5

The Booster in Your Future: The Pandemic Will Challenge All to Behave Differently
未来的"加强剂":疫情逼迫所有人采取不同行动

WAIT, A BOOSTER? The chief executive of Pfizer, Albert Bourla, says those who have received its two-shot coronavirus vaccine are "likely" to need "a third dose, somewhere between 6 and 12 months and then from there, there will be an annual revaccination," depending on the science.

This should not be a cause for dismay. Rather, it is a window into the future—the battle against coronavirus will go on for years, and require agility and different behaviors. Getting that first shot has been hard, but the vaccination campaign has

等一下,注射"加强剂"?辉瑞公司首席执行官阿尔伯特·博拉说,根据科学研究,那些已接种两针新冠病毒疫苗的人,大约在半年到一年之间,"可能"需要"第三针疫苗接种,从那之后,每年人们都将重新接种新冠疫苗"。

这不应该是我们沮丧的理由。相反,这是一扇通向未来的窗口——对抗冠状病毒的战"疫"将持续数年,需要灵活性和行为多样性。第一次接种冠状病毒疫苗已很困难,但总的

---

shot n. 注射
revaccination n. 再次接种
agility n. 敏捷;灵活;机敏

coronavirus n. 冠状病毒
dismay n. 诧异;灰心

on balance been an extraordinary accomplishment, with two highly effective messenger RNA vaccines developed, manufactured and administered in record time. The vaccines train the body's immune system to be ready to attack the virus.

How long that immunity will last is not yet known, but a booster is a good backup should it wane. Even more significantly, a booster might be tweaked to improve efficacy against the evolving variants. The coronavirus is somewhere between measles, which the immune system can recognize over decades, and influenza, which requires a new shot every year—and it is probably closer to influenza in that sense. Hopefully, the manufacturers will be ready with tens of millions of booster doses, while at the same time managing to produce enough for the rest of the world to be immunized.

But Dr. Bourla's announcement underscores that the course of the pandemic is still uncertain. It will not just stop one day. The coronavirus will demand that our lifestyles adapt. People will have to continue to wear face masks in closed, tight public settings. More work must be done to engineer better ventilation. Political leaders must accept the need to ramp up public health surveillance against viral threats, an area where the United States remains woefully unprepared. ① Another worthy goal is to make viral testing as simple as taking a temperature, so that people can test themselves, or get tested before doing things such as going to a concert or getting on a plane.

---

on balance 全面考虑之后;总的来说
immunity n. 免疫;免疫力
wane vi. 衰落;衰败
variant n. 变种;变体;变形
influenza n. 流行性感冒;流感
underscore vt. 强调;突出;强化
ventilation n. 通风;通风设备
woefully adv. 悲伤地;不幸地

extraordinary adj. 非凡的;卓越的
backup n. 后援;增援
tweak vt. 稍稍调整(机器、系统等)
measles n. 麻疹
announcement n. 布告;声明;通告
engineer vt. 设计制造
ramp up 加强,加大

Such tests could serve the same function as metal detectors do in stadiums and airports. Vaccine passports of some kind may become popular, as proof that you are safe to be around others. We need some humility, too. If not enough people are vaccinated, if vulnerable people congregate and transmit, if they ignore restrictions and mitigation, the pandemic will rage on. ② Today, 50.4 percent of the population of the United States aged 18 and over has received at least one vaccine dose—leaving about half the population still vulnerable—and daily new infections are exceeding 70,000, with some states seeing a surge even as vaccines roll out.

At the current torrid pace of vaccination, the United States should reach the 70 percent threshold for herd immunity before long, but the very concept of herd immunity is fragile and elusive, and the barrier could be eroded by new variants that are more contagious and lethal. No miracle will stop the pandemic, only a well-grounded realism, and tools that work, including masks, vaccines—and boosters.

(*The Washington Post*, 2021.4)

这种核酸检测的功效就如同体育馆和机场的金属探测器。某种"疫苗护照"可能会变得流行，证明你对他人不会造成安全威胁。我们也需要谦逊一些。如果没有足够的人接种疫苗，如果体质弱的人群聚集并传播病毒，如果他们忽视了限制、减轻病毒传播，疫情将迅速蔓延。②现在，美国18岁及以上的群体中有50.4%的人至少接种了第一针疫苗，所以大约有一半群体仍处于易受感染状态。每天新增感染人数仍超过7万人，一些州即使已经推出疫苗，其感染病例仍在飞涨。

目前疫苗接种正进行得如火如荼，不久之后，美国将达到群体免疫的门槛，即70%的人中用有免疫能力，但是群体免疫的概念本就脆弱，难以达到，而且这个屏障可能会被传染性更强、更致命的变异病毒腐蚀。没有奇迹可以阻止疫情，只能充分基于现实和使用一些有用的工具，比如口罩、疫苗以及"加强剂"。

长难句解析

①本句为主从复合句。该句的主干是 Another worthy goal is to make…，为主系表结构；不定式短语 to make viral testing as simple as taking a temperature 作表语，表语中的 as…as taking a temperature 为比较状语；so that 引导目的状语从句，从句主干是 people can test themselves, or get tested, before doing things 为时间状语，such as…为后置定语修饰 things。

Another worthy goal is to make viral testing as simple as taking a temperature, so that
　　主语　　　　　　　　　系表结构
people can test themselves, or get tested before doing things such as going to a concert or
　　　　目的状语从句　　　　　　　　时间状语　　　　　　　　　后置定语
getting on a plane.

---

humility n. 谦逊；谦虚
transmit vt. 传播；传染
rage vi. 迅速蔓延；快速扩散
herd immunity 群体免疫
elusive adj. 难以解释的；难以达到的
well-grounded adj. 有充分依据的

congregate vi. 群集；聚集；集合
mitigation n. 减轻，缓解
torrid adj. 狂热的；火热的
before long (时间)不久之后，在短时间内
lethal adj. 致命的；可致死的

②本句为 and 连接的并列句。两个并列句都为主谓宾结构；of the United States aged 18 and over 为后置定语修饰 population，破折号之间的 leaving about half the population still vulnerable 为现在分词短语作结果状语；with some states seeing…为 with 引导的独立主格结构作伴随状语。

Today, 50.4 percent of the population of the United States aged 18 and over has received at least one vaccine dose—leaving about half the population still vulnerable—and daily new infections are exceeding 70,000, with some states seeing a surge even as vaccines roll out.

主语1 ↑ 后置定语 谓语1
宾语1 结果状语
主语2 谓语2 宾语2 伴随状语

Text 6 Better Health, Not Just Better Health Care
更健康，而不只是更好的医疗服务

Health care spending is a hot topic these days. Americans are worried about the cost of health care to their families and companies, and to local, state and federal government. ①They are divided over whether the Affordable Care Act will make the situation worse or better, and how reforms that are supposed to bring greater efficiency will affect their care.

But what does all this anxiety about health care spending have to do with health? Alas, not much.

Americans spend a lot on health care, but we are not a healthy nation. We are currently devoting nearly 18 percent of total spending to health care. Other countries with modern healthcare systems such as France, Germany, Sweden and Canada spend around 12 percent, while their populations score better than ours on many standard measures of health. Some wonder if modeling our health care system on theirs—adopting a single payer system, for example—would make us healthier. But even if such changes were politically feasible, they would not make us much healthier, although they might make care less costly.

The impediments to good health in the United States have little to do with how much we spend for

医疗保健支出问题是近期的一个热门话题。美国人担心医疗保健费用会对他们的家庭和公司，以及地方、州和联邦政府造成影响。①至于《平价医疗法案》将使情况恶化还是好转，以及预期能带来更高效率的医疗改革将如何影响他们的医疗，他们各持己见。

但是，这种对医疗保健支出的担心与健康有什么关系呢？唉，它们之间的关系不大。

美国人在医疗保健上开销很大，但我们不是一个健康的国家。目前，我们将支出总额的近18%用于医疗保健。其他一些拥有现代医疗保健体系的国家，如法国、德国、瑞典和加拿大，在这方面的开销大约为12%，而在许多健康标准指数上，他们人口的得分比我们的要高。一些人想，如果我们模仿他们的医疗保健体系——例如，采用单一付款人系统——是不是能使我们更健康。但是，即便这些改变在政治上可行，它们也不会使我们更健康，尽管它们可能会降低医疗成本。

在美国，健康状况不佳几乎与我们在医疗保健方面的开销及其组

health care or how we organize it. ② Americans' poor health is primarily the result of unhealthful food, too little exercise, drug and alcohol abuse, violence, poverty and too many people living in distressed neighborhoods where children suffer permanent damage to their health and healthy choices are nearly impossible to make. Countries with healthier populations than ours deliver and pay for health care in diverse ways. We could benefit from emulating some of these approaches. But they are also healthier because they are leaner, exercise more, murder each other less often, have more nurturing child care and are less tolerant of poverty.

I am not saying we can forget about health care spending. Our system is extremely expensive and almost certainly will get more so as the population ages and medical science invents increasingly effective, but usually more expensive, ways of treating disease. If we can find ways of producing higher quality care for less money, the benefits can be enormous. Not only will patients be better off, but the savings can be devoted to improving education or low-income housing, or other investments that might actually lead to better health.

Our high health care costs have multiple causes. Compared to other countries with modern health systems, for example, we rely more heavily on highly paid specialists and less on primary care physicians and other less well-compensated caregivers, such as physician assistants and nurse practitioners. Our stunningly complex and fragmented system of paying for and delivering care generates high administrative costs. It also leads to waste, duplication, uncoordinated care and costly medical errors. A much-quoted study by the Institute of Medicine estimated that as much as a third of health care spending did not contribute to better health. The trouble is that one person's waste and duplication is another person's income, which makes change politically hazardous.

---

primarily *adv.* 根本上
fragmented *adj.* 分散的
alcohol abuse 酗酒
duplication *n.* 复制
stunningly *adv.* 令人震惊地
hazardous *adj.* 冒险的

③The realization that we could have higher quality health care for lower cost—or at least less rapidly increasing cost—has prompted an explosion of reform initiatives in both the public and private sectors, mostly focused on improving incentives by correcting two perceived defects on the way we pay for health care. One defect is the predominant fee-for-service system, under which doctors, hospitals and other providers receive payments based on the volume of services they produce but not for keeping their patients from getting sick. The Affordable Care Act not only expanded health care coverage to millions of people, but also provided funds to test new methods of payment intended to reward value produced, rather than volume. Private payers are trying similar experiments.

The other defect is that markets do not work well in health care. Consumers have little information about cost or quality of care and few ways of making informed choices among providers or health plans. Big hospital systems and insurers have consolidated their market power, and, especially, in rural areas, consumers may have few alternatives. Hence, reformers have been trying to develop and publicize measures of performance or quality of care and offer consumers choices in an organized way. The Affordable Care Act's exchanges and Part D, the prescription drug benefit of Medicare, are both attempts to present consumers with more comprehensible choices. The hope is that they will choose the best deal for the money and providers will respond by improving care and cutting unnecessary costs.

If these reforms focus caregivers' attention on how to prevent illness and reduce costly hospitalizations, they will not only lead to better care for less money but actually improve patients' health. These reforms are just getting started, and there is no guarantee all will succeed, but some are likely to work and may already be helping reduce

---

fee-for-service system 有偿服务体系   consolidate vt. 加强   hospitalization n. 住院治疗

costs. Health care spending, which was growing substantially faster than other spending for decades, has slowed markedly in the last few years. The recession and slow income growth bear significant responsibility, but payment and market reforms may also be a contributing factor. However, upward pressure on health spending will likely accelerate as the economy recovers, the baby boomers hit the high health spending years, and medical innovation continues. So complacency is not in order.

Accelerating health care reform is critical. It may well reduce waste and increase the focus on prevention and high quality care. But will we be appreciably healthier? Probably not, unless individuals, families and communities begin dealing with the multiple impediments to health in our daily lives and change their behavior accordingly. The standard tools of health care policy—passing laws and writing regulations that affect health care delivery and financing—won't automatically produce better health, although some will help. We won't have a healthier America, until individuals and communities realize that being healthy is up to us.

(*U.S. News & World Report*, 2014.9)

长难句解析

① 本句为主从复合句。主句的主干结构为 They are divided over whether...and how...; 其中包含两个并列的宾语从句作 over 的宾语; 第二个宾语从句中嵌套了一个 that 引导的定语从句修饰 reforms。

> They are divided over whether the Affordable Care Act will make the situation worse or
> 主语   谓语   宾语从句1
> better, and how reforms that are supposed to bring greater efficiency will affect their care.
>   宾语从句2   定语从句   宾语从句2

② 本句为主从复合句。主句的主干结构为 American's poor health is the result of...; of 介宾短语作后置定语修饰 result; where 引导的定语从句修饰 neighborhoods, 其主干结构是 children suffer permanent damage and healthy choices are impossible to make。

---

baby boomer (尤指第二次世界大战后) 生育高峰期出生的人

complacency *n.* 满足　　　　　　　　　　appreciably *adv.* 明显地

> Americans' poor health is primarily the result of unhealthful food, too little exercise, drug
> 　　主语　　　　　系动词　状语　　表语　　　　　　　后置定语1
> and alcohol abuse, violence, poverty and too many people living in distressed neighborhoods
> 　　　　　　　　　　　　　　　　　　　　　　　　　　　　后置定语2
> where children suffer permanent damage to their health and healthy choices are nearly
> 　定语从句
> impossible to make.

③ 本句为主从复合句。主句的主干结构为 The realization has prompted an explosion…；that 引导的同位语从句作 The realization 的同位语；of reform initiatives 作后置定语修饰 an explosion；mostly focused on improving incentives… 作后置定语修饰 reform initiatives；we pay for health care 是省略了关系词的定语从句，修饰 on the way。

> The realization that we could have higher quality health care for lower cost—or at least less
> 　主语　　　　　　　　　　同位语从句　　　　　　　　　　　　　　　　　插入语
> rapidly increasing cost—has prompted an explosion of reform initiatives in both the public
> 　　　　　　　　　　　谓语　　　　　宾语　　　　后置定语1　　　　　状语
> and private sectors, mostly focused on improving incentives by correcting two perceived
> 　　　　　　　　　　　　　　　　　后置定语2
> defects on the way we pay for health care.
> 　　　　　　　　　　　定语从句

Text 7　Wireless Health Care
移动卫生保健

Bill Gates seems to relish being the skunk at the garden party. The former boss of Microsoft, now a global-health philanthropist, was invited to address a big "m-health" conference in Washington, DC, this week. Some 2,400 proponents of delivering

比尔·盖茨似乎很享受成为游园会上的臭鼬。这位现为全球医疗慈善家的微软前总裁，于本周受邀在华盛顿特区举行的一个"移动保健"会议上发表演讲。约有 2 400 名来自

---

relish vt. 喜爱　　philanthropist n. 慈善家
m-health 移动医疗，就是通过使用移动通信技术——例如 PDA、移动电话和卫星通信来提供医疗服务和信息，具体到移动互联网领域，则以基于安卓和 iOS 等移动终端系统的医疗健康类 App 应用为主
proponent n. 支持者

health services over wireless telecoms, from the private and public sectors, gathered to celebrate the dozens of pilot projects under way around the world.

Mr. Gates, however, warned the participants not to celebrate too soon. ①Just because an m-health pilot scheme appears to work in some remote locale, he insisted, don't "fool yourself" into thinking it really works unless it can be replicated at scale. Rafael Anta of the Inter-American Development Bank was even more cautious: "We know little about impact and nothing about business models."

Happily, evidence of m-health's usefulness is at last starting to trickle in. ②A study this week in the *Lancet*, a medical journal, shows that something as simple as sending text messages to remind Kenyan patients to take their HIV drugs properly improved adherence to the therapy by 12%. WellDoc, an American firm, found in a recent trial that an m-health scheme that relies on behavioural psychology to give diabetics advice on managing their ailment has more effect than putting them on the leading diabetes drug.

Another reason to think that m-health has a promising future is the flurry of business interest in it. One push comes from the rise of cloud computing (providing data storage and processing over the internet), which Peter Neupert of Microsoft argues will be "transformative" for wireless health. UltraLinq, an American start-up, uses the cloud to offer medical imaging on the software-as-a-service model. AT&T, a telecoms giant that already collects revenues of $4 billion a year from health care, has just created a division devoted to pursuing wireless health-care business using cloud computing.

---

wireless telecoms 无线电子通信设备　　trickle in 陆续出现　　adherence to 遵守
flurry n. 飓风

A second shove will come from American policy, which will dispense more than $30 billion in subsidies over the next few years to encourage doctors and hospitals to adopt electronic medical records. This coming digitisation of America's disgracefully paper-based health system will, argues Todd Park of the Department of Health, inevitably boost m-health.

A further impetus is likely to be provided by ideas bubbling up from developing countries. Victoria Hausman of Dalberg, a development consultancy, has surveyed dozens of m-health business models in Haiti, India and Kenya in work for the World Bank. She predicts that mobile banking, which has already taken off in Kenya, will be a great enabler of m-health. Firms are coming up with ways for patients to pay doctors, receive subsidy vouchers and so on, using their phones.

Substituting technology for labour (such as the absent doctor at the government clinic) is another trend. Healthpoint Services, a start-up, is establishing for-profit centres in rural Punjab, in India, that provide health services, as well as clean water. Its health workers roam with backpacks carrying diagnostic equipment; a mobile phone captures and interprets the data, which can then be used for paid telemedicine consultations. This week Procter & Gamble, an American consumer-products giant, announced a commercial partnership with Healthpoint.

No doubt a dose of scepticism is warranted about m-health. But given the growing evidence of its usefulness and the new business models from emerging markets, there is reason for hope too. As Mr. Gates pointed out this week, "Middle-income countries are where most innovation in health care is going to come from."

(*The Economist*, 2010.11)

---

digitisation *n.* 数字化　　impetus *n.* 推动力　　voucher *n.* 凭证
emerging market 新兴市场

长难句解析

① 本句为主从复合句。主句为祈使句,主干结构为 don't fool yourself into...。it really works 为省略了 that 的宾语从句,作 think 的宾语。

Just because an m-health pilot scheme appears to work in some remote locale, he insisted,
　　　　　　　　　　原因状语从句　　　　　　　　　　　　　　　　插入语
don't "fool yourself" into thinking it really works unless it can be replicated at scale.
　谓语　　　宾语　　　　　　　　宾语从句　　　　　条件状语从句

② 本句为主从复合句,主句的主干结构为 A study shows that...。句中 a medical journal 为 Lancet 的同位语;that 引导的宾语从句作 shows 的宾语,该宾语从句的主干为 something improved adherence,其中 as simple as sending text messages to remind Kenyan patients to take their HIV drugs properly 作主语 something 的后置定语。

A study this week in the *Lancet*, a medical journal, shows that something as simple as
　　　主语　　　　　　　　　　　　同位语　　　　　　　谓语　宾语从句　　　后置定语
sending text messages to remind Kenyan patients to take their HIV drugs properly
improved adherence to the therapy by 12%.
　　　　　　宾语从句

Text 8　A New York State of Mind
纽约人的心境

"Hell is a city much like London," opined Percy Bysshe Shelley in 1819. Modern academics agree. Last year Dutch researchers showed that city dwellers have a 21% higher risk of developing anxiety disorders than do their calmer rural countrymen, and a 39% higher risk of developing mood disorders. But exactly how the inner workings of the urban and rural minds cause this difference has remained obscure—until now. A study just published in *Nature* by Andreas Meyer-Lindenberg of the University of Heidelberg and his colleagues has used a scanning technique called functional magnetic-resonance imaging (FMRI) to examine the brains of city dwellers and country

珀西·比希·雪莱曾在 1819 年说过:"地狱就是像伦敦这样的城市。"现代学者们对此看法一致。去年,荷兰研究员们表示,与在安宁乡村里生活的居民相比,伦敦城市居民得焦虑症的风险高出 21%,患心理障碍的风险则高出 39%。但是,直到现在,人们对城乡居民各自的思想活动是如何导致不同患病风险的原因仍尚未可知。最近,德国海登堡大学的安德鲁斯·迈耶·林登伯格和他的同事们在《自然》上发表了相关论文,他们借助功能性磁共振成像的扫描技术来检测城市居民和乡村居民在压力环境下的大脑

---

opine *vt.* 认为　　　　　city dwellers 城市居民　　　　　scanning *adj.* 扫描的

bumpkins when they are under stress.

In Dr. Meyer-Lindenberg's first experiment, participants lying with their heads in a scanner took maths tests that they were doomed to fail (the researchers had designed success rates to be just 25%-40%). ①To make the experience still more humiliating, the team provided negative feedback through headphones, all the while checking participants for indications of stress, such as high blood pressure.

The urbanites' general mental health did not differ from that of their provincial counterparts. However, their brains dealt with the stress imposed by the experimenters in different ways. These differences were noticeable in two regions: the amygdalas and the anterior cingulate cortex (ACC). The amygdalas are a pair of structures, one in each cerebral hemisphere, that are found deep inside the brain and are responsible for assessing threats and generating the emotion of fear. The ACC is part of the cerebral cortex (again, found in both hemispheres) that regulates the amygdalas.

People living in the countryside had the lowest levels of activity in their amygdalas. Those living in towns had higher levels. City dwellers had the highest. Not that surprising, to those of a Shelleyesque disposition. In the case of the ACC, however, what mattered was not where someone was living now, but where he or she was brought up. The more urban a person's childhood, the more active his ACC, regardless of where he was dwelling at the time of the experiment.

The amygdalas thus seem to respond to the here-and-now whereas the ACC is programmed early on, and does not react in the same, flexible way as the amygdalas. ②Second-to-second changes in its activity might, though, be expected to be correlated with changes in the amygdalas, because of its role in

---

bumpkins *n.* 乡巴佬　　　　scanner *n.* 扫描器　　　　amygdalas *n.* 杏仁核
anterior cingulate cortex (ACC) 前扣带皮层　　　cortex *n.* 皮层

regulating them. FMRI allows such correlations to be measured.

In the cases of those brought up in the countryside, regardless of where they now live, the correlations were as expected. For those brought up in cities, however, these correlations broke down. The regulatory mechanism of the native urbanite, in other words, seems to be out of kilter. Further evidence, then, for Shelley's point of view. Moreover, it is also known that the ACC-amygdala link is often out of kilter in schizophrenia, and that schizophrenia is more common among city dwellers than country folk. Dr. Meyer-Lindenberg is careful not to claim that his results show the cause of this connection. But they might.

Dr. Meyer-Lindenberg and his team conducted several subsequent experiments to check their findings. They asked participants to complete more maths tests—and also tests in which they mentally rotated an object—while investigators chided them about their performance. The results matched those of the first test. They also studied another group of volunteers, who were given stress-free tasks to complete. These experiments showed no activity in either the amygdalas or the ACC, suggesting that the earlier results were indeed the result of social stress rather than mental exertion.

As is usually the case in studies of this sort, the sample size was small (and therefore not as robust as might be desirable) and the result showed an association, rather than a definite, causal relationship. That association is, nevertheless, interesting. Living in cities brings many benefits, but Dr. Meyer-Lindenberg's work suggests that Shelley and his fellow Romantics had at least half a point.

(*The Economist*, 2011.6)

---

regulatory mechanism 调节机制
robust *adj.* 坚定的, 强健的
schizophrenia *n.* 精神分裂症
association *n.* 联想
chide *vt.* 责备

长难句解析

① 本句为主从复合句。主句的主干结构为 the team provided feedback。句首不定式短语作目的状语；all the while 后跟分词短语作时间状语。

To make the experience still more humiliating, the team provided negative feedback
　　　　目的状语　　　　　　　　　　　　　　主语　　　谓语　　　　宾语
through headphones, all the while checking participants for indications of stress,
　方式状语　　　　　　　　　　　　时间状语
such as high blood pressure.
　　后置定语

② 本句为简单句。句子主干结构为 changes might be expected to be correlated with…；because of 引出原因状语。

Second-to-second changes in its activity might, though, be expected to be correlated with
　　定语　　　　　主语　　　后置定语1　　　　谓语　　　　　　　宾语
changes in the amygdalas, because of its role in regulating them.
　　　后置定语2　　　　　　　　原因状语

Text 9　Special Report: Stretching the Safety Net
特殊报告：延长安全网

In some rich countries it remains a distant hope, but in Mexico free universal health care became more or less a reality this year. Having insurance used to be contingent on having a salaried job, which left about half of Mexico's population with only the most basic care. But since 2004 a programme called Seguro Popular (Popular Insurance) has been gradually rolled out all over the country to provide better services to those without employment-linked insurance. The overwhelming majority of Mexicans are now covered—"a remarkable feat", according to the *Lancet*, a British medical journal.

在一些富裕国家，这一希望的实现还遥遥无期，而在墨西哥，免费的全民医保大概在今年实现。过去，有一份带薪的工作才能得到医保，因此墨西哥约一半的人口都只能享受最基本的医疗服务。然而，从2004年起，墨西哥在全国逐步展开全民医保项目，为没有职工医保的人提供更好的医疗服务。如今，墨西哥绝大多数人都能享受医保。英国医学期刊《柳叶刀》称其"成绩非凡"。

---

contingent *adj.* 可能发生的
Popular Insurance 大众医疗保险，指的是通过用人单位和个人缴费，建立医疗保险基金，参保人员患病就诊发生医疗费用后，由医疗保险经办机构给予一定的经济补偿

To cover the uninsured, the government has increased its spending on health from 5% of GDP at the turn of the century to nearly 6.5%, which is still lower than in most of the rich world. More than 200 new hospitals and 2,000 clinics have been built and thousands more renovated. The ratio of doctors to patients is up by more than half.

Mexicans' health has perked up dramatically in some areas. Since 2008, when Seguro Popular began providing a vaccine against rotavirus, a common cause of diarrhoea, deaths from the illness have fallen by 60%. When the programme started to pay for treatment of acute leukaemia in children, the survival rate improved from three in ten to seven in ten. Nearly a third of women with breast cancer used to abandon treatment because they could not afford it. Since 2008, when treatment became free, the drop-out rate has come down almost to zero.

Insurance has saved many people from another affliction: poverty. When the poorer half of the population had to pay for medicines or procedures not covered by state hospitals, millions of families were bankrupted by illness. ①Julio Frenk, a former health secretary who oversaw the beginning of Seguro Popular and is now dean of Harvard's School of Public Health, recalls meeting a family in which the mother had needed a Caesarean section and the baby had spent a couple of weeks in intensive care. The child survived, but the medical bill cost his father his animals and tools and meant that his brother had to be taken out of school. "People liquidated their productive assets and their poverty was transmitted to the next generation," says Mr. Frenk. Until the late 1990s nearly 7% of families were dragged below the poverty line each year by medical emergencies. By 2010 the figure had fallen to less than 3%.

---

perk up 振作起来　　　vaccine n. 疫苗　　　rotavirus n. 轮状病毒
diarrhoea n. 腹泻　　　leukaemia n. 白血病　　　liquidate vt. 清算

Seguro Popular is still a work in progress. Quality is patchy and people in remote regions have to trek a long way to see a doctor. Mr. Frenk estimates that about 5% of the population are still not covered. Some conditions are not yet being paid for. There is a shortage of specialist doctors, and some rural clinics are manned by students.

There are also big regional disparities. Nine out of ten pesos going on Seguro Popular are spent by state governments, and the results are mixed. "We need to work on accountability," acknowledges Salomón Chertorivski, the health secretary. When some states inexplicably paid far more than the market value for certain drugs, the federal government set maximum prices for medicines. There have been reports of bent doctors tricking people into paying for their supposedly free care. The government has introduced a system of certification for clinics. But in rural areas it is still hit-and-miss—one reason why Mexico's infant-mortality rate remains stubbornly high.

Success in treating communicable diseases has brought new problems. The biggest killer now is diabetes, brought on by sugary diets and sedentary lifestyles. Mexicans are among the world's fattest people: 70% are overweight, more than in the United States. A third of women are obese, double the OECD average. On a per-head basis, Mexico has the world's highest consumption of Coca-Cola. In rural areas seven out of ten children have a fizzy drink with their breakfast, according to Consumer Power, a civil organisation. ② Public sports facilities are scarce, which may help to explain why Mexico came only 39th in this year's Olympics, level with Georgia, which has only a small fraction of its population. Health care may be expanding rapidly, but so are waistlines.

(*The Economist*, 2012.11)

---

patchy *adj.* 参差不齐的 trek *vt.* 艰苦跋涉 disparity *n.* 不一致
inexplicably *adv.* 难以理解地 hit-and-miss *adj.* 时好时坏的
infant-mortality *n.* 婴儿死亡率 stubbornly *adv.* 顽固地
OECD *abbr.* 经济合作与发展组织(Organization for Economic Co-operation and Development)
fizzy drink 碳酸饮料

长难句解析

① 本句为主从复合句。主句的主干结构为 Julio Frenk recalls meeting a family；a former health secretary 作主语 Julio Frenk 的同位语；who 引导的定语从句 1 修饰先行词 health secretary；in which 引导的定语从句 2 修饰 a family。

Julio Frenk, a former health secretary who oversaw the beginning of Seguro Popular and is
  主语   同位语   定语从句1
now dean of Harvard's School of Public Health, recalls meeting a family in which the
                                              谓语   宾语
mother had needed a Caesarean section and the baby had spent a couple of weeks in
                        定语从句2
intensive care.

② 本句为主从复合句。主句的主干结构为 Public sports facilities are scarce；非限制性定语从句 1 修饰前边的整个句子，其中嵌套了 why 引导的从句作 explain 的宾语；level with Georgia 作状语，补充说明动词 came only 39th；非限制性定语从句 2 修饰先行词 Georgia。

Public sports facilities are scarce, which may help to explain why Mexico came only 39th in
  主语   系动词 表语   非限制性定语从句1   宾语从句
this year's Olympics, level with Georgia, which has only a small fraction of its population.
                       状语   非限制性定语从句2

Text 10　The Nobel Prize: Good Eggs
诺贝尔奖：有用的卵子

This year's Nobel physiology prize goes to Sir John Gurdon and Shinya Yamanaka for a crucial discovery in stem-cell science—how to make what are known as pluripotent stem cells from ordinary body cells. What the citation does not say is that this work also allows clones to be made from adult animals, potentially including people.

A stem cell is one that can differentiate into daughter cells specialised for particular functions, and all the cells in a body are thus derived from stem cells. That includes the stem cells themselves, which

约翰·格登爵士和山中伸弥博士因在干细胞生物科学领域中获得的重大发现——如何将普通体细胞诱导回多功能干细胞，获得了本年度的诺贝尔生理学奖。但并未提及的是，这项成果也使克隆成体动物成为可能，也包括克隆人类。

干细胞可以分化成具有特定功能的子细胞，而体内所有的细胞都是由干细胞分化而来的，包括干细胞自己，它是由胚胎中的"ur"干细胞分化

---

stem-cell *n.* 干细胞　　　pluripotent *adj.* 多功能的　　　citation *n.* 引证

derive from "ur" stem cells found in embryos. These embryonic stem cells are the pluripotent cells, meaning they can turn into many (sometimes all) other sorts of cell.

Pluripotent embryonic stem cells are of great value to researchers but, if the embryos they came from were human, their use is controversial. ①Also, if such cells are ever to play a useful role in medicine (perhaps for repairing damaged tissue), they will need to be available in bulk—and ideally in a form whose DNA matches that of the recipient. Sir John and Dr. Yamanaka have both conducted work that should help make this possible.

Sir John's prizewinning study, published half a century ago, in 1962, when he was at Oxford University, was to transplant the nuclei of cells from adults of a frog called Xenopus laevis into enucleated eggs of that species. The eggs in question then developed into healthy adults.

This showed that DNA is not altered during embryonic development, at least in Xenopus. (That was subsequently shown to be true in other species, too.) It thus suggested it might be possible to get an entire adult cell to perform a similar trick, without involving an egg at all.

That was what Dr. Yamanaka did. He and his colleagues at Kyoto University managed to activate four crucial genes in adult mouse cells. These genes each encode a protein of a type known as a transcription factor, which controls the expression of DNA. Together, they trick the cell in question into thinking it is part of an embryo.

In the first experiment, conducted in 2005, Dr. Yamanaka did not get complete mice, but he did turn the adult cells into pluripotent stem cells. ②Subsequent work by his group and others then produced embryos which, if transplanted into the womb of a female mouse, will go all the way to

而来的。这些胚胎干细胞是多功能细胞，也就是说，它们可以分化成许多其他类型（有时是所有类型）的细胞。

对研究人员来说，多功能胚胎干细胞的研究价值很高，但是，如果是对人体胚胎干细胞的研究，则颇具争议。①如果说，这种细胞将会在医学中做出贡献（也许是修复受损的组织），那么，我们将需要获得大量的这种细胞——理想状态下，干细胞的DNA与受体的相匹配。约翰·格登爵士和山中伸弥博士所做的工作都是为了实现这种可能性。

约翰爵士的诺贝尔获奖研究发表于50年前的1962年，当时，他在牛津大学，要把一种称为非洲爪蟾的成蛙体内的细胞核移植到该物种的去核卵子中。这种卵子将会发育成健康的成体。

研究表明，在胚胎发育的过程中，DNA并未发生改变，至少在非洲爪蟾体内是这样的。（随后在其他物种中的实验也证明这一结论是正确的。）因而，这项研究表明，根本不需要卵子，只需要一个完整的动物成体细胞，就能进行相似的演变。

这正是山中伸弥博士所做的研究。他和他在京都大学的同事共同尝试从成年小鼠的细胞中激活四种重要的基因，这些基因分别编码一种蛋白质，这些蛋白质是转录因子，控制DNA的表达。这四种基因令上述细胞认为自己是胚胎的一部分。

在2005年进行的首次实验中，山中伸弥博士并没有得到发育完整的小鼠，但是他却将成熟的体细胞转变成多功能干细胞。②他的团队和其他人在后续工作中生成了胚胎，而且如果被移植到雌性小鼠的子宫中，这些胚胎最后

---

embryo *n.* 胚胎　　　nuclei *n.* 细胞核　　　enucleated *adj.* 去核的

adulthood. Finally, in 2007, Dr. Yamanaka managed to switch on the same four genes in adult human cells, and thus generated pluripotent human stem cells.

In principle, that opens the door to human cloning, though no one (as far as is known) has tried this in practice—and in most countries such an experiment would be illegal. ③It also opens the door, though, to bespoke tissue repair as it would allow cells of whatever type were desired to be grown from, say, a few skin cells and then transplanted back into the donor without risking an adverse reaction from his immune system.

How well that would work in practice remains to be seen. But if it works well then Sir John and Dr. Yamanaka may turn out to have been the pioneers of a whole, new field: Regenerative Medicine.

(*The Economist*, 2012.10)

长难句解析

① 本句为主从复合句。主句的主干结构为 they will need to be available；句中 in bulk 和 in a form 为 and 连接的两个并列状语；whose 引导的定语从句修饰先行词 form。

> Also, if such cells are ever to play a useful role in medicine (perhaps for repairing damaged
> 　　　　　条件状语从句　　　　　　　　　　　　　　　　补语
> tissue), they will need to be available in bulk—and ideally in a form whose DNA
> 　　　　主语　谓语　　宾语　　状语1　　　　　　　状语2　　　　　定语从句
> matches that of the recipient.

② 本句为主从复合句。主句的主干结构为 Subsequent work produced embryos；句中 by his group and others 作后置定语修饰 work；which 引导的定语从句修饰先行词 embryos，其中还包含由 if 引导的条件状语从句，其中省略了主语和系动词。

> Subsequent work by his group and others then produced embryos which, if transplanted
> 　　主语　　　　　　后置定语　　　　　　　　　谓语　　　宾语　　定语从句
> into the womb of a female mouse, will go all the way to adulthood.
> 　　　条件状语从句　　　　　　　　　　　　定语从句

---

switch on 接通　　　　bespoke *adj.* 定制的　　　　immune system 免疫系统
regenerative *adj.* 再生的

③ 本句为主从复合句。主句的主干结构为 It opens the door；句中 as 引导的原因状语从句的主干为 it would allow cells to be grown from a few skin cells and then transplanted back…，其中 of 介宾短语修饰 cells, of 后是由 whatever 引导的宾语从句。

It also opens the door, though, to bespoke tissue repair as it would allow cells of
主语1 状语 谓语1 宾语1　　　　目的状语　　原因状语从句 主语2 谓语2 宾语2
whatever type were desired to be grown from, say, a few skin cells and then transplanted back
　　　　　　　　　　　宾语2 补足语1 插入语 宾语2 补足语1　　　宾语2 补足语2
into the donor without risking an adverse reaction from his immune system.
　　　　　　　　　　状语

Text 11　To Improve Health Care, Governments Need to Use the Right Data
改善医疗，政府应采用合理数据

Deciding where to seek treatment might seem simple for a German diagnosed with prostate cancer. The five-year survival rate hardly varies from one clinic to the next: all bunch around the national average of 94%. Health-care providers in Germany, and elsewhere, have usually been judged only by broad outcomes such as mortality.

But to patients, good health means more than life or death. ①Thanks to a study in 2011 by Germany's biggest insurer, a sufferer now knows that the national average rate of severe erectile dysfunction a year after removal of a cancerous prostate gland is 76% but at the best clinic, just 17%. For incontinence, the average is 43%; the best, 9%. But such information is the exception in Germany and elsewhere, not the rule.

What matters to patients should also matter to policymakers. Side-effects such as erectile dysfunction and incontinence are not only unpleasant, but expensive to treat. And measuring outcomes is the first step to choosing the best

对于一个被确诊为前列腺癌的德国人来说，选择到哪个诊所就医看起来比较简单。五年来，该病症的存活率在所有诊所都很接近：都在全国94%的平均水平上下浮动。德国与其他国家对卫生保健提供机构的评价通常是以较为宽泛的治疗结果为依据的，比如死亡率。

但对于患者来说，良好的健康状况并不能仅靠生与死来界定。①得益于德国最大的保险公司于2011年所做的调查，前列腺癌患者如今了解到，癌变前列腺切除术后一年严重性功能障碍的全国平均发病率为76%，而在最好的医疗机构这一数据仅为17%。小便失禁的全国平均发病率为43%，而最好医疗机构仅为9%。但该数据并非定律，只是德国和其他国家的特殊情况。

患者关注的重点也应该是决策者关注的重点。对于患者来说，诸如性功能障碍和小便失禁的术后不良反应不只是遭受痛苦，治疗费用也较为昂贵。患者以最低的价格选择最佳治疗方法和卫生

---

prostate n. 前列腺　　insurer n. 保险公司　　erectile dysfunction 勃起功能障碍
gland n. 腺　　　　　incontinence n. 失禁

treatments and providers at the lowest prices. But few places do this well, says Michael Porter of Harvard Business School.

Doctors and administrators have long argued that tracking patients after treatment would be too difficult and costly, and unfair to providers lumbered with particularly unhealthy patients. But better sharing of medical records and a switch to holding them electronically mean that such arguments are now moot. Risk-adjustment tools cut the chances that providers are judged on the quality of their patients, not their care.

In theory, national health-care systems should find measuring outcomes easier. Britain's National Health Service (NHS) compiles masses of data. But it stores most data by region or clinic, and rarely tracks individual patients as they progress through treatment. Sweden's quality registries do better. They analyse long-term outcome for patients with similar conditions, or who have undergone the same treatment, letting medics compare the long-term performance of procedures and implants. Sweden now has the world's lowest failure rate for artificial hips.

Elsewhere, individual hospitals are blazing a trail. Germany's Martini-Klinik uses records going back a decade to fine-tune its treatment for prostate problems. The Cleveland Clinic, a nonprofit outfit specialising in cardiac surgery, publishes a wide range of outcome statistics; it now has America's lowest mortality rate for cardiac patients. And though American politicians inch at the phrase cost-effectiveness, some of the country's private health firms have become statistical whizzes. ②Kaiser Permanente, which operates in nine states and Washington, DC, pools the medical records for all its centres and, according to McKinsey, a consultancy, has

---

(be) lumbered with 充满了
blaze vt. 迸发

moot adj. 未决的
whizz n. 专家

artificial hips 人工髋关节

improved care and saved $1 billion as a result.

Such approaches are easiest in fields such as prostate care and cardiac surgery, where measures for quality-of-life are clear. But some clinics have started to track less obvious variables too, such as how soon after surgery patients get back to work. This is new ground for doctors, who have long focused on clinical outcomes such as infection and re-admission rates. But by thinking about what matters to patients, providers can improve care and lower costs at the same time.

(*The Economist*, 2014.2)

麦肯锡咨询公司的调查结果表明,凯萨医疗机构的医疗条件得到了改善并因此节省了多达10亿美元的资金。

以上方法在前列腺疾病治疗和心脏外科手术等生存质量评估参数明晰的领域最易实施。但有些诊所也开始对其他不甚明显的变数进行数据追踪,比如患者术后多久能恢复正常工作生活。这对于长期关注临床结果,如感染率和再入院率的医生来说,是一个全新的领域。但考虑到患者关注的重点,卫生保健提供机构可以在改善医疗条件的同时降低医疗费用。

长难句解析

① 本句为主从复合句。主句的主干结构为 a sufferer knows that…;宾语从句部分由 but 连接的两个分句构成,but 后的句子中省略了主语 the average rate of… gland 和 is。

> Thanks to a study in 2011 by Germany's biggest insurer, a sufferer now knows that the
> 　　　　　原因状语　　　　　　　　　　　　　　　　　主语　状语　谓语
> national average rate of severe erectile dysfunction a year after removal of a cancerous
> 　　　　　　　　　　　　　　　宾语从句1
> prostate gland is 76% but at the best clinic, just 17%.
> 　　　　　　　　　　　宾语从句2

② 本句为主从复合句。主句的主干结构为 Kaiser Permanente pools the medical records and has improved care and saved…;which 引导的非限制性定语从句修饰先行词 Kaiser Permanente。

> Kaiser Permanente, which operates in nine states and Washington, DC, pools the medical
> 　主语1　　　　　　　　非限制性定语从句　　　　　　　　　　　谓语1　宾语1
> records for all its centres and, according to McKinsey, a consultancy, has improved care
> 　　　　　　　　　　　　状语1　　　　　　　　同位语　　　　谓语2　宾语2
> and　saved　$1 billion　as a result.
> 　谓语3　宾语3　　　状语2

---

re-admission *n.* 再次住院

Text 12

Threat to Mental Health Programme That Aims to Get Patients Back to Work

Cuts come as 70% of working age adults with a mental health condition in England are unemployed.

A programme at South London and the Maudsley NHS foundation trust (Slam), which provides tailored careers advice and coaching to patients, is threatened by budget cuts.

① Slam's individual career management (ICM) programme, which occupational psychologist Claire Price says is the only one of its type in the UK, goes beyond simply getting someone into a job. It assesses the needs of individual clients and tailors its services accordingly, which could mean help with a CV or interview skills, or long-term one-to-one support.

Care and support services minister Norman Lamb said: "This was a locally-led decision, but I understand that Slam have adapted their service to ensure patients do not lose out." Price, however, believes the trust has tried hard to "keep hold of the service" and points out that all mental health trusts are struggling to provide services due to lack of available funding.

"It's just been absolutely awful," she complains. Fair enough if the need had decreased, but the need is increasing. More and more people are going off sick from work with stress-related illness. More and more people are unemployed and experiencing mental health problems because of that.

---

tailored *adj.* 定制的

lose out （在竞争中）失败

Lamb's commitment to helping more people with mental health problems gain and sustain employment is set against a dismal background in which about 70% of working-age adults in England with a mental health condition are unemployed.

②Last year, Department for Work and Pensions figures showed the Work Programme found jobs for only 5.3% of people with disabilities, including mental illness, claiming employment support allowance, against an expected 16.5%.

In response to *the Guardian* Healthcare questions about the need for better employment services, Lamb says that, on 20 January 2014, his department published a study into how the employment prospects for people with mental health problems, such as anxiety and depression, can be improved. The document sets out 25 priorities for change, including making sure that health and employment services work more closely together.

However, Price insists that, within the government's various strategies, she has yet to see any evidence that an individual approach to careers guidance is being proposed.

③Typically, mental health trusts with sufficient funds for careers guidance opt for individual placement support (IPS), a U.S. model that consists of an employment adviser based within a community mental health team who gets patients into paid employment, but without addressing their education, training or career development needs.

Price says: "IPS is successful for patients who are very motivated to find a job and are willing to do any sort of work. And that is great, because some patients have been out of work for so long, 25 years or more. But I think it's only helping a small percentage of patients."

Based on feedback from people mandated to the Work Programme, she believes that, although the programme is intended to provide tailored support, that is not what people experience: "In practice,

兰姆致力于帮助越来越多的心理疾病患者获得工作和维持就业,尽管现实环境不容乐观,在英格兰适龄工作人群中,有70%的人因为心理健康问题而失业。

②去年,英国劳务和退休金部的数据显示,这一工作方案只为5.3%的有缺陷人士(包括心理疾病患者)找到工作并申请到就业支援津贴,离原本预期的16.5%还相差甚远。

针对《卫报》医疗板块提出的有关优化就业服务的问题,兰姆表示,在2014年1月20日,护理和支持服务部发布了一份报告专门研究了该如何改善心理疾病(包括焦虑和抑郁)患者的就业前景。该报告列举了25个亟待改进的方面,包括确保医疗和就业服务合作更加密切。

然而,普赖斯坚持认为,在政府的诸多战略决策中,她依旧没有看到有任何提出个性化就业指导倡议的迹象。

③通常来说,资金充裕的心理健康信托机构会选择个人就业支持(IPS),这是一种美国模式,它包括一名基于社区心理健康团队的就业指导师,他可以帮助病人找到带薪的就业岗位,但不解决病患的教育、培训或职业发展需求等问题。

普赖斯表示:"IPS对于那些十分想找到工作,并且愿意接受任何工作的患者来说,确实是十分有效。这非常好,因为有些患者已经失业很久了,长达25年甚至更久。但我认为,IPS只是帮助到了很少的一部分患者。"

从工作方案的反馈情况来看,她认为,尽管该项目旨在提供个性化的支持,但患者的真实体验并非如此,"事实上,患者并没有得到个性化的

---

dismal *adj.* 凄惨的

they don't get individual support; they get shoved into a room with 50 other people."

For some people, however, being in work damages their mental health and at Slam the ICM model is used to help patients who experience bullying, lack of career progression or discrimination at work. "We can also liaise with the employer to help the client sustain their role, or move to another company if that's the best option for them," says Slam careers coach Catherine Di Lella.

Between 2006—08 the ICM service grew in response to the needs of patients, but funding cuts have resulted in its team of 20 being cut back to nine. Seven career coaches in secondary care worked with people with severe mental illness, but only two remain to cover that demand.

A major hurdle for the Slam team is that, despite positive feedback from clients, the model lacks clinical evidence. In 2011, however, Slam and King's College London launched a joint randomised controlled trial to address this.

The main focus of the trial, which is due to be assessed later this year, is an economic evaluation: costing the time spent with each client, plus the savings on benefits and a reduction in the use of NHS services because people are in work.

Mental health is the single biggest cause of disability in the UK, bigger than cancer or cardiovascular disease. But when it comes to investing in employment support, Di Lella believes the government is looking to make short-term savings by favouring cheaper, generic, target-focused services. In her experience, people with mental health conditions are unlikely to remain in work without an exploration of the type of jobs that suit their personality and motivation.

---

get shoved 被推
cardiovascular *adj.* 心血管的
liaise with 与……联络
generic *adj.* 通用的
randomised *adj.* 随机的

Everyone is capable of work, she argues: "No matter how low that person feels, or how anxious, there is a way back in. It might be a longer journey, but with the right support it's definitely possible."	每个人都有能力工作,她声称:"无论这个人的自我评价有多低、无论此人有多焦虑,他总有路可走,也许路程会比一般人更长一些,但只要给予适当的支持,总会抵达彼岸。"

(*The Guardian*, 2014.2)

长难句解析

① 本句为主从复合句。主句的主干结构为 Slam's individual career management (ICM) programme goes beyond simply getting…;which 引导的非限制性定语从句修饰主语。

> Slam's individual career management (ICM) programme, which occupational psychologist Claire Price says is the only one of its type in the UK, goes beyond simply getting someone into a job.
>
> 主语 / 非限制性定语从句 / 谓语 / 宾语

② 本句为主从复合句。主句的主干结构为 figures showed…;showed 后为省略了 that 的宾语从句;claiming… allowance 作伴随状语。

> Last year, Department for Work and Pensions figures showed the Work Programme found jobs for only 5.3% of people with disabilities, including mental illness, claiming employment support allowance, against an expected 16.5%.
>
> 时间状语 / 主语 / 谓语 / 宾语从句 / 后置定语 / 伴随状语 / 比较状语

③ 本句为主从复合句。主句的主干结构为 mental health trusts opt for individual placement support (IPS);a U.S. model 为 individual placement support (IPS) 的同位语;that 引导的定语从句 1 修饰 a U.S. model;who 引导的定语从句 2 修饰 an employment adviser。

> Typically, mental health trusts with sufficient funds for careers guidance opt for individual placement support (IPS), a U.S. model that consists of an employment adviser based within a community mental health team who gets patients into paid employment, but without addressing their education, training or career development needs.
>
> 状语 / 主语 / 后置定语 1 / 谓语 / 宾语 / 同位语 / 定语从句 1 / 后置定语 2 / 定语从句 2

Text 13 5G Is Coming: How Worried Should We Be About the Health Risks?
5G 即将到来：我们应该对健康风险有多担心？

Judging from the enthusiastic reception of 5G technology by governments and industry, we are on the verge of a technological revolution. Initially introduced to help wireless networks cope with ever-increasing data traffic on their networks, 5G will (its proponents claim) lead to game-changing innovations such as remote surgery, control of driverless vehicles and much more.

①5G, eventually slated to replace present-day 3G and 4G cellular telephone networks, promises to speed up the rate of data transfer by 100 times or more, greatly reduce latency and allow cellular networks to manage far more wireless-connected devices than presently possible.

5G, however, has become intensely controversial in many locations, with citizens' groups, and a few scientists, expressing concerns about the possible health effects of radio-frequency (RF) energy transmitted by 5G base stations. The possibility of harms from environmental exposures to radio-frequency signals has been a long-standing concern of many citizens, leading to public opposition to wireless base stations, broadcasting facilities, cell phones and other commonplace technologies.

Beginning in the 1960s many studies have examined possible biological and health effects of RF exposure, and several thousand papers on the topic now exist. Initially, these studies were motivated by occupational health concerns for workers exposed on the job to high levels of RF energy from industrial heating and other equipment. More recently many

从政府和工业对5G技术的热烈欢迎来看，我们正处于技术革命的边缘。5G技术问世之初是为了帮助无线网络应对其网络上不断增加的数据流量，它（其支持者声称）将带来颠覆性的创新，如远程手术、控制无人驾驶车辆等。

①5G最终将取代目前的3G和4G移动电话网络，它有望将数据传输速率提高100倍或更多，大大减少延迟的时间，并允许移动网络管理比目前更多的无线连接设备。

然而，5G在许多地方引起了极大的争议，公民团体和一些科学家担心5G基站传输的射频（RF）能量可能会对健康产生影响。暴露于射频信号环境中的潜在的危害是许多公民长期关注的问题，这导致公众反对建立无线基站，反对广播设施、手机和其他常用的技术。

从20世纪60年代开始，许多研究已经检测了射频暴露对生物和健康可能造成的影响，现在有数千篇关于该主题的论文。最初，这些研究是出于（对一些工人的）职业健康的考虑，因为这些工人在工作中受到来自工业供暖和其他设备

---

on the verge of 濒临于
proponent n. 支持者
latency n. 延迟时间
long-standing adj. 长期存在的

data traffic 数据流量
cellular telephone 移动电话
radio-frequency n. 射频

studies have been undertaken to examine potential health risks from environmental exposures from communications systems. There has recently been an upsurge of research using millimeter waves, although none at the precise frequencies to be used by 5G systems.

Millimeter waves are absorbed within about 0.5 mm of the skin surface, unlike RF energy at lower frequencies that can penetrate deeper into tissue. Its obvious potential hazards—thermal damage to skin or cornea of the eye—have been examined by numerous studies including many sponsored by the U.S. Air Force beginning in the mid-1990s and also studies on ocular effects of millimeter waves by a group at Kanazawa Medical University in Japan. ② One of these studies was a long-term cancer promotion study on mice, involving periodic exposures to intense pulses of millimeter waves, that found no effects of exposure; the study has unclear relevance to communications signals however.

Most countries around the world have adopted RF exposure limits that are roughly similar to present FCC limits. FCC and similar limits are designed to avoidestablished hazards of RF energy that result from excessive heating of tissue. A few countries and cities have adopted lower limits on precautionary grounds.

These are, in part, a political accommodation to concerned citizens, and in part a hedge against the possibility that low level or nonthermal hazards might be demonstrated in the future. Russia and some of its former Warsaw Pact allies also have much lower exposure limits, an inheritance from the old Soviet Union.

This confusion has been present for many years, but there has been little change in the assessments by health agencies. In its 2018 review, the Swedish Radiation Safety Authority concluded that despite the lack of established mechanism[s] for affecting health with weak radio wave exposure there is however need for more research covering the novel frequency domains, used for 5G. In August 2019,

---

upsurge n. 高涨；高潮　　penetrate vi. 渗透；穿透　　thermal adj. 热的；热量的
cornea n. 眼角膜　　precautionary adj. 预防的

FCC Chairman Ajit Pai announced that the commission proposes to maintain its current RF exposure safety standards, quoting a statement from the Director of the U.S. Food and Drug Administration Center for Devices and Radiological Health that the available scientific evidence to date does not support adverse health effects in humans due to exposures at or under the current limits.

To fully investigate potential hazards of 5G is an open-ended program without a clear stopping point. With cellular communications systems there is a potentially unlimited number of exposure parameters to be explored. Moreover, 5G refers to a set of specifications for operation of a cellular network, not to any particular source or frequency of exposure. Many initial rollouts of 5G networks, in fact, transmit frequencies at power levels that are similar to those of present cellular networks.

(*Scientific American*, 2019.9)

其当前的射频暴露安全标准,并引用了美国食品和药物管理局设备与放射健康管理中心主任的声明:迄今为止,由于射频暴露与当前限制水平相当或低于当前限制水平,所以可利用的科学证据尚不能表明其对人类健康造成了不利影响。

充分调查5G的潜在危害是一个没有明确终点的开放式计划。使用移动通信系统,就有无限的暴露参数有待探索。而且,5G是指用于移动网络操作的一组规范,而不是指任何特定的来源或暴露频率。实际上,许多最初推出的5G网络以类似于当前移动网络的功率水平传输频率。

长难句解析

① 本句为简单句,句子较长。句子的主干为 5G promises to…。to speed up…、greatly reduce…和 allow… 为并列的三个不定式结构,作句子的宾语。

> 5G, eventually slated to replace present-day 3G and 4G cellular telephone networks, promises to speed up the rate of data transfer by 100 times or more, greatly reduce latency and allow cellular networks to manage far more wireless-connected devices than presently possible.
> 主语 / 定语 / 谓语 / 宾语1 / 宾语2 / 宾语3

② 本句是由分号连接的分句构成。involving 介词短语作定语;that 引导的定语从句修饰上面提到的研究。

> One of these studies was a long-term cancer promotion study on mice, involving periodic exposures to intense pulses of millimeter waves, that found no effects of exposure; the study has unclear relevance to communications signals however.
> 主语1 / 系动词 / 表语 / 定语 / 定语从句 / 主语2 / 谓宾

open-ended *adj.* 开放式的;无预期结论的

rollout *n.* 首次展示

Text 14 Computer Test Could Spot Children at Risk of Developing Depression
电脑能检测出有患抑郁症风险的儿童

A simple computer test that has the potential to spot children who are at risk of developing depression or anxiety disorders has been created by British psychiatrists.

The 20-minute test could be used to screen children in the first two years of secondary school, alerting doctors to those most likely to succumb to the debilitating illnesses, researchers say.

The Cambridge University team believes that screening 11- and 12-year-olds could help prevent scores of cases of depression and anxiety, or catch them early on, when treatments can be more successful.

A preliminary study found that children who performed poorly on the test were between two and eight times more likely to be depressed a year later than those who scored well. "The more errors made, the greater the risk," said Ian Goodyer, professor of child and adolescent psychiatry, who led the research.

The test, described in the journal *PLoS One*, exposes difficulties that some people have in processing emotional information, which are associated with a susceptibility to mental illness. The team has since embarked on a follow-up study to assess how useful the test could be.

"We do not know how good a predictor this test is, but this study provides sufficient validity to test it in the field," said Goodyer.

Depression and anxiety are an enormous burden on public health. In a given year, one in four people in Britain will have a mental health problem, with the majority diagnosed with depression or anxiety.

英国精神病学家研发出了一种简单的电脑测试，可能用于分辨那些有患抑郁症或焦虑症风险的儿童。

研究人员说，这个20分钟的测试可以对初中一二年级的孩子进行检查，提醒医生哪些学生最有可能患上衰竭性疾病。

剑桥大学团队相信，对11~12岁的孩子进行检查，可以有效地预防大量抑郁和焦虑症案例的发生，或尽早发现病情，对其进行早期治疗，增加治愈率。

初步研究发现，一年后，那些在测试中得分低的孩子比那些得分高的孩子患抑郁症的可能性要高2~8倍。伊恩·古迪说："错误越多，风险越大。"伊恩·古迪是儿童和青少年精神病学的教授，也是这项研究的带头人。

在《科学公共图书馆·综合》杂志上，该项测试揭露出部分人群在处理情感信息上的困难，而这种困难与对精神疾病的敏感性有关。团队已经开始了后续研究，来评估测试的有效性。

古迪说："我们不知道这个测试的预测有多准，但是，这项研究通过在领域内的验证证明了它的有效性。"

抑郁和焦虑是巨大的公共健康负担。在某一年，四分之一的英国人有心理健康问题，这些问题大多数被诊断为抑郁或焦虑。根据国王基金

---

succumb to 屈服于……　　psychiatry n. 精神病学　　susceptibility n. 敏感性
embark vi. 从事　　　　　validity n. 有效性

According to the King's Fund, depression cost England £7.5bn in treatment, services and lost employment in 2007 alone.

"Effective, early treatment may prevent the course of depression from becoming chronic and relapsing," said Barbara Sahakian, professor of clinical neuropsychology, and senior member of the team. "This will be of great benefit to the individual's wellbeing, and the ability to function at school, work and home." Three quarters of lifetime cases of mental illness emerge before the age of 24.

For the study, the researchers drew on 238 boys and girls aged 15 to 18, from schools in Cambridge and Suffolk. Each had a genetic test to determine the forms of a certain gene they had inherited from their parents. The gene, called 5-HTTLPR, helps regulate the brain chemical, serotonin, and comes in short and long versions.

People who inherit two short versions of the gene (one from each parent) seem more sensitive to the world around them, while those who inherit two long versions appear less sensitive to their environment. Those born with one of each lie somewhere in between.

①The form of the gene is important because previous studies show that people with two short variants are more likely to become depressed when their lives hit rough patches, though they also seem to flourish more in a supportive environment.

Through interviews with the pupils' carers, most often their mothers, the researchers next assessed the children's early home lives, and noted who among them witnessed intermittent arguments for more than six months, and verbal, emotional or physical violence between their parents, before the age of six.

The computer test gauged each child's ability to process emotional information. In one test, the

---

relapse vi. 复发　　　　clinical neuropsychology 临床神经心理学
serotonin n. 5-羟色胺　　intermittent adj. 断断续续的　　　gauge vt. 判定

children were asked to make quick decisions on whether the emotional content of words, such as "joyful" and "failure" was positive, negative or neutral.

②The results showed that children with two short versions of the gene, who grew up with fighting parents and frequent household arguments, scored worse on the tests than the other children, and were more likely to succumb to depression within the next year. In the study, 18.5% of children had two short forms of the gene, and 36% of these had coped with a hard family life in early childhood.

While it is too costly and impractical to give genetic tests to all children, and take detailed histories of their home lives, poor performance on the test might serve as a "biomarker" for young people who are most at risk of succumbing to depression or anxiety disorders, the scientists say.

If the test proves effective at spotting vulnerable children, they could be helped with therapies that break their tendency to focus on the negative aspects of the world around them, or through family sessions that aim to resolve the damaging conflicts that arise in the home.

"The way we perceive and respond to emotions affects our resilience and whether we succumb to depression and other maladaptive ways of thinking. Using the biomarker identified in this study, it is possible to develop a screening programme to identify those at greatest risk," said Prof. Sahakian.

(*The Guardian*, 2012.11)

长难句解析

① 本句为主从复合句。主句的主干结构为 The form of the gene is important; because 引导的原因状语从句中嵌套了一个 that 引导的宾语从句,该宾语从句中还嵌套了一个 when 引导的时间状语从句和一个 though 引导的让步状语从句。

---

maladaptive *adj.* 适应不良的

The form of the gene is important because previous studies show that people with two short variants are more likely to become depressed when their lives hit rough patches, though they also seem to flourish more in a supportive environment.

② 本句为主从复合句。主句的主干结构为 The results showed that…; that 引导的从句作 showed 的宾语，其中 and 连接两个并列谓语，主语均为 children，该从句的主干为 children scored worse and were likely to succumb to…; who 引导的非限制性定语从句修饰 children。

The results showed that children with two short versions of the gene, who grew up with fighting parents and frequent household arguments, scored worse on the tests than the other children, and were more likely to succumb to depression within the next year.

Text 15　Scheme Sees Police Work with Mental Health Staff to Manage Crisis Call-Outs
分类方案见证警察与心理健康从业人员协作应对出警危机

The triage car is staffed by an officer and a nurse who can assess the person and steer them to appropriate care and support services.

A man in his 50s has been drinking heavily in his Loughborough flat all morning and is now threatening to kill himself. He's tearful as he describes his loneliness and mother's death a few years ago. He repeatedly tells the police officers to go away. But as PC Alex Crisp explains: "Police officers have to stay with him, there's a duty of care. The police have to do something, you're accountable ultimately."

分类车辆上有一名警察和一名护士，他们可以评估和引导病人，使病人得到正确的照顾和帮助。

一个 50 多岁的男人一整个上午一直在他拉夫伯勒的公寓里酗酒，现在以自杀作为威胁。他泪流满面地描述了他的孤独和几年前他母亲的去世。他再三要求警察走开，但是正如警察亚历克斯·克莱斯普解释的那样："警察必须留下来陪他，因为我们有照顾他的义务。警察必须做点什么，因为你最终是负责的那个人。"

triage car 分类车　　　　　　　　　　　steer them to 引导他们

It's a dilemma for the police. While officers have to do something, their options are limited. They only receive basic mental health training. Staying with the man until he sobers up consumes valuable police time, but walking away could end in tragedy.

However thanks to an initiative introduced in January, officers are working closely with mental health staff to resolve situations like this. The triage car is a partnership between Leicestershire police, Leicestershire Partnership NHS trust and Leicester probation service. The car is staffed by a police officer and a mental health practitioner and they attend calls where people are experiencing a mental health crisis. The nurse can assess the person, offer advice, and steer them to the appropriate care and support services. For example, they can contact the person's existing care team or refer them to a home treatment service.

"We've got more options," says PC Crisp, a Leicestershire triage car officer. "I've got an expert sitting next to me who can access pathways I can't. As a police officer I've no access to any of that at all. I can't refer into any of those services."

The crew can access previous police and health service records about the individual to make more informed decisions.

"We can look at people's history, their risk history, their diagnostic history, reports about how well they engage. You can start to make a risk assessment from that," explains Dave Spencer, a mental health practitioner with Leicestershire Partnership NHS trust.

The practitioner can assess more accurately than the police whether someone poses a risk to themselves or others.

For example, the man in Loughborough had made several threats to kill himself previously and had never acted on them, and it didn't appear that

---

dilemma n. 困境　　　　sober up（使）清醒　　　　diagnostic history 诊断史

he intended to now. After he refused all offers of support, the team eventually took the decision to leave after an hour and a half.

"We get called out a lot to people threatening suicide," says Emma McCann, a mental health practitioner, involved in the triage scheme. "There's also public order stuff, where people are suffering from mania."

Other incidents have involved people with dementia not recognising their partner and thinking they have been kidnapped. The team carry out two to three mental health assessments a shift on average and provide advice over the phone to colleagues across Leicester, Leicestershire and Rutland. They give advice over the phone for around five cases a shift.

The aim of the triage car is to reduce the number of people being detained by police under section 136 of the Mental Health Act. When a person is detained, for their own protection, they are taken to a "place of safety", which can be a police station or a hospital. If someone is experiencing a mental health crisis, police officers will generally err on the side of caution and use section 136, explains PC Crisp. However section 136 is a "blunt instrument": "You're arresting people for being mentally ill for the purpose of an assessment."

Earlier this year, a report by Her Majesty's Inspectorates of Constabulary and Prisons, the Care Quality Commission and the Healthcare Inspectorate Wales, said too many mentally ill people were being held in police cells. ①A police station is not always an appropriate place for someone suffering a mental health crisis, explains Matthew Wakely, Leicestershire Partnership NHS trust criminal justice and liaison service team manager. "You need somewhere calmer. They'll be staying in a cell which isn't a therapeutic environment. People can feel criminalised. All guidance says people in these situations should be treated as patients."

---

mania *n.* 狂躁   therapeutic environment 治疗环境

Detaining people under section 136 can also be a lengthy and expensive process for the police. ② The person might be detained for up for 72 hours while waiting to receive a mental health act assessment—which determines whether they should be in hospital—carried out by a doctor and an approved mental health professional.

Chief Inspector Pete Jackson from Leicestershire police says there has been a significant reduction of people being detained under section 136. "40% less people get detained by police under the act than prior to the triage car. If they do need to be detained we know why we are doing it and the process is quicker."

Leicestershire isn't the first place in the UK with a triage scheme. Cheshire Constabulary also has one, however the model used is slightly different, says PC Crisp. ③ In Leicestershire the police officer and mental health practitioner sit side by side at the station, each with their own computer, "for data protection purposes", and attend incidents together. In June care minister Norman Lamb announced four areas to pilot new triage schemes, in North Yorkshire, Devon and Cornwall, Sussex and Derbyshire and the Department of Health mentioned Leicestershire as an example of best practice.

It isn't that support for mental health problems isn't there, it's just that the police is the first port of call for many people, says McCann. "Interestingly, with all that is out there, people will go to the police."

(*The Guardian*, 2013.11)

长难句解析

① 本句为主从复合句。宾语从句 A police station… crisis 提前作间接引语，主句为完全倒装结构，还原顺序后主干结构为 Matthew Wakely explains…; Leicestershire Partnership… manager 为 Matthew Wakely 的同位语。

A police station is not always an appropriate place for someone suffering a mental health crisis, explains Matthew Wakely, Leicestershire Partnership NHS trust criminal justice and liaison service team manager.

prior to 在……之前

② 本句为主从复合句。主句的主干结构为 The person might be detained; while 引导的时间状语从句中省略了 the person 和系动词; which 引导的定语从句修饰先行词 assessment, 该从句中嵌套了一个 whether 引导的宾语从句作 determines 的宾语; carried out by a doctor and an approved mental health professional 作后置定语修饰 assessment。

```
The person might be detained for up for 72 hours  while waiting to receive a mental health
   主语          谓语          状语              时间状语从句
act assessment—which determines whether they should be in hospital—carried out by a doctor
                  定语从句           宾语从句                       后置定语
and an approved mental health professional.
```

③ 本句为并列复合句。主句的主干结构为 the police officer and mental health practitioner sit and attend incidents; 句中 each 作 the police officer and mental health practitioner 的同位语; 独立主格结构 each with their own computer (名词+介词) 作状语。

```
In Leicestershire  the police officer and mental health practitioner   sit   side by side
   地点状语1                    主语                                谓语1  方式状语1
at the station, each with their own computer, "for data protection purposes", and
   地点状语2      状语(独立主格结构)                  目的状语
attend incidents together.
谓语2   宾语    方式状语2
```

Text 16 Swaddling Babies Can Cause Them Hip Problems, Doctors Warn
医生警告:用襁褓包裹婴儿会导致其髋关节出现问题

Practice of wrapping babies tightly in blankets or sheets is popular, but studies have shown it can lead to dislocation or abnormal development of the hip.

Babies should be wrapped in a "sympathetic and loose manner", says Dr. Alastair Sutcliffe, Insitute of Child Health, UCL.

① The practice of swaddling babies, which has become fashionable as a way to calm them, risks causing them hip problems as they grow, doctors warn.

用毯子或床单把婴儿紧紧地裹起来的做法很受欢迎,但研究表明,这会导致髋关节脱臼或发育不正常。

伦敦大学儿童健康研究所的阿拉斯泰尔·萨克利夫博士说,父母应该考虑婴儿的感受,把他们包裹得松一点儿。

① 用襁褓包裹婴儿这种方式,因为能使婴儿平静,所以很受欢迎,但医生警告说,这会增加他们成长过程中髋关节出现问题的风险。

---

dislocation n. 脱臼   abnormal development 发育不正常   be wrapped in 被……包裹

Parents have been turning to the old-fashioned practice in order to settle their babies and help them sleep better. ② Swaddling, which involves wrapping the baby in sheets or blankets with their legs out straight and arms pinned so that they cannot move, has been shown to induce sleep and soothe excessive crying and colic.

But, say doctors who specialise in orthopaedics, evidence shows that the practice increases the risk of developmental hip abnormalities. Professor Nicholas Clarke of Southampton University hospital writes in the journal *Archives of Disease in Childhood* that one in five babies are born with a hip abnormality, perhaps because of a breech birth or family history. Although these can resolve unaided, swaddling can delay it.

Swaddling has become more popular, says Clarke. Nine out of 10 infants in north America are now swaddled in the first six months of life. Sales of swaddling clothes increased in the UK by 61% between 2010 and 2011.

But studies have shown that babies who do not have their legs free to bend and kick can suffer dislocation or abnormal development of the hip.

"A high incidence of hip dislocation was reported in Navajo Indians who strapped their infants to a board," Clarke writes. "In Japan, an educational programme initially aimed at grandmothers was commissioned to prevent traditional swaddling." The programme cut the incidence of hip dislocation from between 1.1% and 3.5% to just 0.2%.

Clarke says that parents should be advised on "safe swaddling" if their babies are at risk of hip development problems. "In order to allow for healthy hip development, legs should be able to bend up and out at the hips. This position allows for natural development of the hip joints. The babies' legs should not be tightly wrapped in extension and

---

colic *n.* 腹绞痛
abnormality *n.* 畸形
breech birth 臀位分娩,即婴儿的脚及臀部先出来的生产方式
unaided *adj.* 未受协助的
strap *vt.* 用带子系
incidence *n.* 发生率
hip joint 髋关节

pressed together."

Commercial products for swaddling babies should have a loose pouch or sack for the legs and feet, allowing plenty of room for movement, he says.

Other experts agreed with him. "There is indeed evidence that swaddling can affect the normal development of infants' hips," said Andreas Roposch, consultant orthopaedic surgeon at Great Ormond Street hospital.

Dr. Alastair Sutcliffe, reader in general paediatrics at the Institute of Child Health, University College London, said swaddling had been known to be associated with an increased risk of congenital dislocation of the hip (CDH) for many years.

③The archetypal example is in traditions where a baby is carried with their legs splayed around a mother's waist such as in Nigeria, where there is a virtually unseen rate of CDH, whereas in a country where swaddling is employed, such as far-eastern countries, there is a much higher rate of CDH.

"I would advise that if a baby needs to be wrapped up to get off to sleep that parents do this in a sympathetic and loose manner, not tight, especially around the babies' hips."

(*The Guardian*, 2013.9)

克拉克还说,襁褓商品上应该有一个宽松的育儿袋或布袋来让婴儿放脚和腿,使其能有足够的活动空间。

其他专家也同意他的说法。大奥蒙德街医院负责咨询工作的骨外科医生安德烈亚斯说:"确实有证据表明,用襁褓包裹婴儿会影响其髋关节的正常发育。"

伦敦大学儿童健康研究所普通儿科讲师阿拉斯泰尔博士说,大家很多年前就已经知道,用襁褓包裹婴儿会导致先天性髋关节脱臼的风险增加。

③传统的典型例子是,一个婴儿被母亲抱着,腿张开盘在母亲腰上,就如在尼日利亚,在那里,先天性髋关节脱臼的发生率几乎为零;而在用襁褓包裹婴儿的国家,譬如远东国家,先天性髋关节脱臼的发生率就很高。

"我建议,如果一个婴儿需要被包裹着才能入睡,那么,父母要考虑婴儿的感受,包得松一点儿,不要裹得太紧,尤其是婴儿的胯部。"

长难句解析

① 本句为主从复合句。句首为宾语从句,作 warn 的宾语;正常语序下,句子的主干结构为 doctors warn the practice risks causing problems;which 引导的非限制性定语从句修饰 practice;句中还包含一个 as 引导的时间状语从句。

The practice of swaddling babies, which has become fashionable as a way to calm them,
宾语从句   非限制性定语从句
risks causing them hip problems as they grow, doctors warn.
宾语从句   时间状语从句 主语   谓语

② 本句为主从复合句。主句的主干结构为 Swaddling has been shown;which 引导的非限制性定语从句修饰先行词 Swaddling,该从句中嵌套了一个 so that 引导的目的状语从句。

pouch *n.* 育儿袋   orthopaedic surgeon 骨外科医生   congenital *adj.* 先天的

Swaddling, which involves wrapping the baby in sheets or blankets with their legs out
　主语　　　　　　　非限制性定语从句　　　　　独立主格结构
straight and arms pinned so that they cannot move, has been shown to induce sleep and
　　　　　　　　　目的状语从句　　　　　　谓语　　　　　宾语
soothe excessive crying and colic.

③ 本句为并列复合句,由 whereas 连接,前后两句表对比。句子的主干结构为 The archetypal example is in traditions where…, whereas in a country where…, there is a rate of CDH。where 引导的定语从句 1 修饰 traditions;where 引导的定语从句 2 修饰 Nigeria;where 引导的定语从句 3 修饰 country;句中的 such as 用于举例说明。

The archetypal example is in traditions where a baby is carried with their legs
　主语　　　系动词　表语　　　　　　定语从句 1
splayed around a mother's waist such as in Nigeria, where there is a virtually unseen rate of
　　　　　　　　　　　　　后置定语 1　　　　　　　　　定语从句 2
CDH, whereas in a country where swaddling is employed, such as far-eastern countries,
　　　　地点状语　　　　定语从句 3　　　　　　后置定语 2
there is a much higher rate of CDH.
　　there be 句型

Text 17 Creation: The Origin of Life; The Future of Life
创造:生命之源;生命未来

This modern account of synthetic biology describes a breakthrough that could rival the Industrial Revolution for impact.

This is a brave and unusual book. Brave in its title and subtitles; unusual in its central conceit. It is two books in one, linked as the twin pillars of creation, natural and manmade—which calls for some delicate juggling of content. It is brave in this content, too: Rutherford is dealing with big questions, and he does not shy away from difficult and at times unfashionable material—from cell theory and entropy to the mechanics of DNA replication. And yet his writing is accessible and clear throughout.

这部解释合成生物学的现代作品描述了一个在影响方面可与工业革命匹敌的突破。

这是一本勇敢且不寻常的书。勇敢体现在它的标题和小标题中,不寻常体现在它的中心构想上。它由两本相互关联的书合二为一。这两本书分别阐述了创造的两大支柱,即自然创造和人工创造,这就要求作者对内容进行雕琢推敲。在内容上,它也很勇敢:卢瑟福正在处理重大问题,他从不回避那些晦涩的、有时显得过时的材料——从细胞理论到熵再到 DNA 复制机制。而且,他的作品通俗易懂,思路清晰。

---

impact n. 影响　　　　pillar n. 柱子　　　　entropy n.【热】熵(热力学函数)
DNA replication DNA 复制

This book follows a distinguished tradition of works by scientists and journalists from the journal *Nature* (notably Philip Ball and Oliver Morton), who have written some of the most eloquent and genuinely thoughtful books on science over the past decade. Rutherford belongs in that category: his book displays all the storytelling savvy one would expect from a professional communicator, and while TV and radio documentaries, newspaper articles and blogs are very different in tone from a book, this is carefully crafted over 200 pages.

The *Nature* tradition is a compulsion to explain science seriously and clearly, in a societal context, without too many distracting frills. ①It is an earnestness to inform—almost a mission—which evokes shades of JBS Haldane, who wrote brilliantly for the *Daily Worker* back in the 1930s, motivated by a Marxist ideal to educate the working man. That old-fashioned determination runs curiously through this very modern account of synthetic biology.

Some of the writing here is finely wrought, with virtuoso passages bringing to life the mundanity of a paper cut, or explaining why zircon crystals used in cheap jewellery give a window into the deepest recesses of time. There are also some workmanlike passages written in the third person, which can come as a relief; too much virtuosity is hard to bear. There are a few trivial errors scattered through the text, but you will not find a better, more balanced or up-to-date take on either the origin of life or synthetic biology.

Disappointingly, beyond DNA itself (very much the heroine of this tale) these two pillars of creation have little in common. The origin of life, in my mind, relates to the dynamics of disequilibrium that gave rise to the first cells. One might think that such principles would underpin

---

eloquent *adj.* 有说服力的
mundanity *n.* 尘俗
disequilibrium *n.* 不平衡

frill *n.* 不实际的虚饰
zircon *n.* 锆石

virtuoso *adj.* 技艺精湛的
workmanlike *adj.* 类似手工艺人的

synthetic biology too, but as yet this nascent field has restrained itself to wizardry with DNA, with a brash and breathtaking ingenuity but little interest in evolution. That is not Rutherford's fault; but he is still perhaps a little too much the cheerleader. Remarks such as "Synthia's genome was designed with failsafe devices" would make most evolutionary biologists twitch uncontrollably. While he is right to condemn the (often politically motivated) misrepresentation of risks, biologists have little ability to predict the future. Like the dismal science of economics, we are often only wise after the event. Leslie Orgel famously quipped that "evolution is cleverer than you are." If Rutherford's portrayal of a generation of engineering whiz-kids with a wilful ignorance of biology is fair, there will be some red faces and fortunes lost; but the downside is unlikely to be much worse.

In fact, our virtuosity with genes is modelled closely on what nature herself does all the time. We are not creating unnatural monsters, merely shuffling the gene pack in the same way as nature. And like nature, we are often blind to the potential outcomes. That does not mean they will be bad; and in any case they should be considered in relation to the tragic diseases they are intended to cure, like cancer or malaria. But I wonder if synthetic biology would gain more sympathy in the public mind if the protagonists conveyed a little less hubris. We know less than we think.

None of that is to denigrate this book. ②It is essential reading for anyone interested in the coming revolution, which could indeed rival the Industrial Revolution or the internet, and like them will play out over decades. Rutherford is an insider and knows the people he is writing about. He is also a geneticist, and understands his subject inside out. He is well informed, breezy and conversational in tone, and full of fascinating anecdotes, often in sparkling

---

nascent *adj.* 新生的   misrepresentation *n.* 误传   protagonist *n.* （戏剧）主角
hubris *n.* 傲慢   breezy *adj.* 轻松愉快的

footnotes. Towards the end he writes: "There is a youthful optimism, a remix culture of boundless creativity that believes these new technologies will help rectify the problems we face and, at least in some quarters, an unprecedented willingness to push that agenda." There is also an unprecedented willingness to oppose the agenda, despite its enormous promise, in part through a very human fear of the unknown. We really do need to be informed, and this is the place to start.

(*The Guardian*, 2013.4)

人如沐春风，而且，在精彩的脚注中，有很多吸引人的趣闻轶事。接近尾声时，他写道："有一种年轻的乐观主义思潮，它是一种具有无限创造力的混合文化，这种文化相信，这些新技术将帮助我们纠正面临的问题。至少在某些角落，人们前所未有地愿意推进这一议程。"还有些人，一定程度上出于对未知的恐惧，空前地反对这一议程，尽管其有着巨大的潜力。我们真的需要把握动态，这里就是开始的地方。

长难句解析

① 本句为主从复合句。It 为形式主语，真正主语为后边的不定式结构 to inform；which 引导的定语从句 1 修饰先行词 an earnestness，该从句中嵌套了一个 who 引导的非限制性定语从句，修饰 JBS Haldane；过去分词短语 motivated...作伴随状语，与其逻辑主语 JBS Haldane 为被动关系。

It is an earnestness to inform—almost a mission—which evokes shades of JBS Haldane, who wrote brilliantly for the *Daily Worker* back in the 1930s, motivated by a Marxist ideal to educate the working man.

② 本句为主从复合句。句中 essential 修饰 reading；interested in the coming revolution 作后置定语修饰 anyone；which 引导的非限制性定语从句修饰 revolution，其中包含 and 连接的两个并列谓语，主语均为 which。

It is essential reading for anyone interested in the coming revolution, which could indeed rival the Industrial Revolution or the internet, and like them will play out over decades.

---

rectify *vt.* 改正

Text 18　The Guardian View on Genetics: Diversity Is Destiny
《卫报》对于遗传学的看法：多样性是注定的

The argument that some behaviour is "in our genes" is distrusted by the left. Too often it is used to whitewash terrible injustices. Yet it cannot be entirely dismissed. Certain patterns of behaviour and thought, such as the faculty of language acquisition, are very clearly a part of our genetic inheritance as a species. The instinct for justice itself appears to arise spontaneously in small children. ①The escape from the idea that genes determine our fate is not to pretend that they have no influence, but to come to understand that they can have many different, often conflicting influences, even within the same people and certainly within populations. This is true both of their effects on behaviour and on bodies.

Biology is a science that deals with variations. There is no one perfect type of a species. Diversity, in this sense, is not just something to aim at but something necessary for a population to flourish. The idea that natural selection works only on mutations is a deeply misleading oversimplification. It is much more likely to alter the proportions of an already existing mixture of genes. What is more, game theory shows that the balance of advantage will shift as a result of the shift in a gene's frequency. ②With very few exceptions, such as the change that Noam Chomsky postulates makes possible the complexity of human syntax, few mutations are going to be so overwhelmingly advantageous that they drive out all other variants. More often, if any one variation becomes dominant, there will be an advantage for its opposite. "Normal" is thus a shifting, fuzzy category.

左派不相信某些行为"是由基因决定的"这种说法。它经常被用来美化可怕的不正当行为。但不能完全否定这一说法。某些行为和思维模式，比如语言习得能力，很明显是人类作为一个物种的遗传继承的一部分。正义的本能在小孩子身上似乎是自发产生的。①摆脱基因决定人类的命运这一说法不是假装基因没有影响力，而是要明白基因可以有很多不同的、往往相互冲突的影响，这些影响甚至发生在同一个人的身上，当然也会发生在特定人群中。它们对行为和身体的影响也是如此。

生物是一门解决变异问题的科学。不存在完美的物种类型。从这个意义上讲，多样性不仅仅是一个目标，而是某一族群走向繁荣所必需的。自然选择仅适用于突变的想法是一种极具误导性的过度简化想法。它更有可能改变已经存在的基因混合的比例。而且，博弈论表明，由于基因频率的变化，优势平衡将发生变化。②除了极少数例外，例如诺姆·乔姆斯基的（句法结构）理论使得人类句法的复杂性成为可能，很少有突变会变得极其有优势，以至于可以驱逐所有其他变体。更常见的是，如果任何一种变异成为主导，那么其对立面就会有优势。因此，"正常"是一个变化的、模糊的类别。

---

whitewash vt. 美化，粉饰　　acquisition n. 习得，获得　　inheritance n. 生物遗传性
postulate n. 基本原理，公理　　syntax n. 句法　　drive out 驱赶
fuzzy adj. 模糊不清的

This is especially true of the genes which can influence human behaviour and emotional predispositions . Not only is the chain of causation from gene expression to behaviour unimaginably complex, it is also profoundly affected by outside circumstances. Identical twins, who share the same DNA, are not identical people, because they cannot entirely share the same life and experiences.

What science can do, under these circumstances, is to look for correlations between DNA sequences and observable behaviour. The correlations can, at best, give pointers towards where causes might be found. The latest effort has been to see if there is a genetic cause for homosexuality and the result is clear. There isn't.

Using a data set of nearly half a million people, of whom 27,000 reported same sex contact, researchers found—in their own words—"In aggregate , all tested genetic variants... do not allow meaningful prediction of an individual's sexual behaviour". There are five loci which appear to have a measurable, though far from decisive, influence on sexual preference . Some are also involved with the sense of smell, and one is associated with male pattern baldness .

This leads to perhaps the most interesting feature of the research: it not only shows that there is no clear genetic cause for same sex attraction, but that the attraction itself does not form a coherent whole. Some of the genetic variations weakly associated with same sex behaviour are different in men and women. In place of the old idea that there might be a single cause for a single pattern of behaviour, there is now an understanding of multiple causes for varying patterns of behaviour. In place of a single scale of sexual attraction as posited by Kinsey, in which desire for the same sex and opposite sex are linked so that more

---

predisposition *n.* 倾向
aggregate *n.* 总计,总数
sexual preference 性取向
posit *vt.* 假定;断定

pointer *n.* 提示,线索
locus *n.* 基因座(复数为 loci)
baldness *n.* 光秃;枯燥

of one means less of the other, the researchers suggest that these are independent variables. Diversity is good in itself and humans are more—much more—than the sum of their genes.

(*The Guardian*, 2019.8)

更小,而研究人员认为这些是独立的变量,这一观点取代了金赛的假设。多样性本身就是好的,人类比他们基因的总和多得多。

长难句解析

① 本句为主从复合句,主句的主干为 The escape is not to pretend that...but to come to understand...。第一个 that 引导的是同位语从句,而不是定语从句,引导词 that 在同位语从句中不充当语法成分;第二个和第三个 that 引导的都是宾语从句;even within the...作状语。

The escape	from the idea	that genes determine our fate	is	not to pretend	that they
主语	后置定语	同位语从句	系动词	表语1	宾语从句1

have no influence, but to come to understand that they can have many different, often
　　　　　　　　　表语2　　　　　　　　　　　宾语从句2
conflicting influences, even within the same people and certainly within populations.
　　　　　　　　　　　　　　　　　状语

② 本句为主从复合句。句首的 with 介词短语作主句的状语;such as...为插入语;第一个 that 引导的是同位语从句。主句的主干部分为主系表结构,包含 so...that(如此……以至于……)结构,that 引导的是结果状语从句。

With very few exceptions,	such as the change	that Noam Chomsky postulates
状语	插入语	同位语从句

makes possible the complexity of human syntax, few mutations are going to be
　　　　　　　　　　　　　　　　　　　　　　　主语　　　　系动词
so overwhelmingly advantageous that they drive out all other variants.
　　　　表语　　　　　　　　　　　结果状语从句